G000081193

Essays in Bristol & Gloucestershire History

Study in point of Chronometric History

Elizabeth Ralph

President of the Society in the centenary year 1976 and Secretary from 1948.

Photograph by G. Kelsey

Essays in
Bristol and Gloucestershire
History

---

*The Centenary Volume of the Bristol and Gloucestershire
Archaeological Society*

Edited by

Patrick McGrath and John Cannon

1976

© Bristol and Gloucestershire Archaeological Society

ISBN: 0 900197 10 2

BRISTOL AND GLOUCESTERSHIRE
ARCHAEOLOGICAL SOCIETY

Printed for the Society by Western Printing Services Ltd,
Bristol

Contents

		page
	Editorial Preface	vii
	Centenary Committee	xi
	List of Contributors	xiii
	List of Illustrations	xvii
	Abbreviations	xix
I	The Society 1876–1976 *by* ELIZABETH RALPH	1
II	The Archaeology of Megaliths: an historical note *by* GLYN DANIEL	50
III	Roman Sculpture in Gloucestershire *by* J. M. C. TOYNBEE	62
IV	Bristol under the Normans *by* DAVID DOUGLAS	101
V	The Origins of St. Augustine's, Bristol *by* J. C. DICKINSON	109
VI	The Perpendicular style in the Cotswolds *by* DAVID VEREY	127
VII	Projects for Gentlemen, Jobs for the Poor: Mutual Aid in the Vale of Tewkesbury, 1600–1630 *by* JOAN THIRSK	147
VIII	The Gloucestershire Spas: an eighteenth-century parallel *by* BRYAN LITTLE	170
IX	A Refuge from Revolution: the American Loyalists' residence in Bristol *by* PETER MARSHALL	200
X	Brunel in Bristol *by* R. A. BUCHANAN	217
XI	The economic development of Bristol in the nineteenth-century: an enigma? *by* B. W. E. ALFORD	252
	Index	284

Editorial Preface

A HUNDREDTH anniversary is no small event, and the members of the Bristol and Gloucestershire Archaeological Society were determined that it should not pass unrecorded. When the B & G was founded, Benjamin Disraeli was prime minister and news of the Bulgarian atrocities was fetching Mr. Gladstone out of the first of his many retirements. The world was adjusting to the most recent shift in the balance of power, which had brought a united Germany, under Bismarck, to European predominance. The great Empires of the world were still in the making and decolonisation must have seemed the most remote of possibilities.

For one hundred years, the peaceful work of the B & G has been carried on, sometimes in the most trying of circumstances. All societies of this kind run on the unpaid labour and goodwill of countless individuals, secretaries, guides, treasurers, committee men, organisers of every description. The activities of some of these members are traced in the opening article by Elizabeth Ralph, President of the Society in its centenary year, who was elected to that honour as a tribute to her outstanding contribution for more than thirty years. The work of the others is recorded in the past numbers of the *Transactions*, but we desired in addition to commemorate and recognise it in this preface.

It would be sentimental to imply that all meetings of the Society have been conducted with sweetness and harmony. Some of the founder members, in particular, were formidable characters and Council meetings sometimes saw a clash of heavyweights. In the first few months of the Society's existence, the subject of the library—then a mere handful of volumes—provoked a formal written protest that Council's proposals might "involve the Society in litigation or provoke a schism or both." The danger of over-enthusiasm in a guide is recorded in a cautionary tale from 1879, when the Society visited Birdlip. The Rev. Mr. Brown developed at such length his view that certain earthworks must have been a British village that the rest of the programme had to be curtailed. "It was considered," the minutes commented tartly, "that Mr. Brown was mistaken in his theory." Miss Ralph notes "lamentable incidents" at meetings of Council as late as the 1940s, though she draws a veil of discretion over what took place. Even today, "strange fits of passion" are not totally unknown.

What chance has the Society of surviving to see 2076? This centenary year is a difficult one, with postal, printing and administrative costs rocketing and the financial basis of many local history societies in jeopardy. The Editor of today's *Transactions*, faced with a bill of over £3,000, may read with envy of the £100 paid for the first volume. But here Miss Ralph's essay can not only guide us, but offer hope. It is clear that the Society, in its first hundred years, rarely had an easy time, but faced crisis after crisis. There are repeated references to rising costs and to the difficulty of finding good committee members to replace those who had gone. It would be strange if a Society that has survived two world wars should succumb to the perils of inflation.

But if the Society does survive to witness its second centenary, we may be sure that the changes will be considerable. The differences between 1876 and 1976 are clearly revealed in Miss Ralph's narrative. The Society has become less exclusive and more modest than in those former days of sumptuous repasts, champagne entertainments and elegant luncheons, when "morning dress" was expected at meetings, and carriages were ordered for 9.30 p.m. To read Miss Ralph's pages is to peer into a by-gone age of leisure and affluence. There were hazards, of course. In 1880 Sir William Guise and three other members were stranded when their horse, on a steep hill, decided he had done enough for the day. It is hard to say whether in 2076 visits will be made by the Society's private helicopter or whether the exhaustion of natural resources will have restored the horse to its former importance.

In 1976 the routine work of the Society is carried on increasingly by members professionally interested in history and archaeology—archivists, museum curators, librarians and lecturers—who have taken over, to a great extent, the role performed in the nineteenth century by the clergy and gentry. Another change has been the growing part taken by women members. The Society was well over fifty years old before the first lady member of Council was elected—and though a female had addressed the Society as early as 1894, it was on the becoming subject of costume in the middle ages.

One can hardly doubt that in 2076 the need for our Society will be as great as ever. There will assuredly still be buildings left to protect and preserve. Indeed, with the development of technological and urban civilisation, the need to identify with one's own countryside and one's own past seems to grow more urgent.

A camel has been described as a horse designed by a committee. We are not sure how to describe this book. Its general plan and appearance have been shaped with the advice of the members of the Centenary Committee, whose names are printed on page xi, and whose assistance we acknowledge with gratitude and pleasure. The volume is not intended to offer any coherent or systematic survey of Bristol and Gloucestershire history, but to catch something of the many-sided interests of members of the Society. We issued invitations to scholars working in the history of the area to write on subjects of their own choice. There is, we hope, something for everybody, from Roman sculpture to industrial archaeology and from chamber tombs to perpendicular architecture.

PATRICK MCGRATH
JOHN CANNON

Centenary Committee

The members of the Centenary Committee, which was responsible for advising on the preparation of this volume, were as follows:

Miss D. Bailey
The Rev. Canon J. E.
    Gethyn-Jones
The late Rev. Canon
    D. A. R. Keen
Robert Knapp
David Large
H. G. M. Leighton
Bryan Little

Mrs. Frances Neale
Miss Elizabeth Ralph
G. T. St. J. Sanders
Brian Smith
The Very Rev. A. G. G.
    Thurlow, Dean of
    Gloucester
David Verey
Miss Mary Williams

We should also like to acknowledge the assistance received from Mr. Gordon Kelsey of the Arts Faculty Photographic Unit of the University of Bristol; from Mrs. P. Martin, who designed the dust-jacket, and from Mrs. P. Roberts and Mrs. S. Harrison, who helped to prepare the manuscript for printing. The index has been prepared by Mr. and Mrs. John Farrell, whose assistance we gratefully acknowledge.

List of Contributors

ALFORD, Bernard William Ernest. Member of the Society since 1966; B.Sc.Econ., Ph.D., London; educated London School of Economics; Assistant Lecturer, L.S.E., 1961–62; Lecturer, University of Bristol 1962–73; Senior Lecturer 1973; author of *A History of the Carpenters' Company* (1968); *Depression and Recovery? British Economic Growth, 1918–1939* (1972); *W. D. & H. O. Wills and the development of the UK Tobacco Industry, 1786–1965* (1973).

BUCHANAN, Robert Angus. Member of the Society since 1964; M.A., Ph.D., Cambridge; educated St. Catharine's College, Cambridge; Senior Lecturer in the History of Technology, University of Bath since 1965; publications include *Industrial Archaeology of the Bristol region* (1969); *Industrial Archaeology in Britain* (1972).

CANNON, John Ashton. Chairman of Council of the Society, 1968–71; M.A., Cambridge; Ph.D., Bristol; educated Peterhouse, Cambridge; Lecturer and Reader, University of Bristol 1961–75; Professor of Modern History, University of Newcastle upon Tyne 1976; author of *The Fox–North Coalition* (1970) and *Parliamentary Reform, 1640–1832* (1973).

DANIEL, Glyn Edmund. President of the Society, 1962; M.A., Ph.D., Litt.D., F.S.A.; educated University College, Cardiff and St. John's College, Cambridge; Fellow of St. John's since 1938; Lecturer 1948–74; Disney Professor of Archaeology, Cambridge since 1974; publications include *A Hundred Years of Archaeology* (1950); *The Megalith Builders of Western Europe* (1958); *The First Civilisations* (1968).

DICKINSON, John Compton. M.A., B. Litt., Oxford, F.S.A., F.R.Hist.S.; educated Keble College, Oxford; Lincoln Theological College; ordained priest 1949; Fellow of Emmanuel

College (1947–50) and Pembroke College, Cambridge (1950-60); Lecturer in Theology, University of Birmingham, 1960–62; Senior Lecturer, 1962–73; Hon. Canon of Peterborough, 1970–73; publications include *The origins of the Austin Canons* (1950) and *Monastic life in medieval England* (1961).

DOUGLAS, David Charles. President of the Society, 1956; M.A., Oxford; Hon.D.Litt., Wales; Hon.D.Litt. Exeter; Docteur *hc*, Caen; F.B.A.; F.R.Hist.S.; educated Keble College, Oxford; Professor of History, University College of South West 1934–39; Professor of Medieval History, University of Leeds 1939–45; Professor of History, University of Bristol 1945–63; Emeritus Professor, Bristol since 1963; publications include *The Norman Conquest* (1926), *English Scholars* (1939) and *William the Conqueror* (1964).

LITTLE, Bryan Desmond Greenway. Vice-President of the Society since 1972; M.A., Cambridge; educated Jesus College, Cambridge; writer and lecturer on local history and architecture; publications include *Cheltenham* (1952); *The life and work of James Gibbs* (1953); *The city and county of Bristol* (1954); *Catholic Churches since 1623* (1966) and *Sir Christopher Wren* (1975).

MCGRATH, Patrick Vincent. President of the Society, 1968; M.A., London; F.R.Hist.S.; educated Queen Mary College, London; Lecturer, University of Bristol 1946–57; Senior Lecturer 1957–63; Reader 1963; author of *Records relating to the Society of Merchant Venturers of Bristol in the seventeenth century* (1952); *Papists and Puritans under Elizabeth I* (1967) and *The Merchant Venturers of Bristol* (1975).

MARSHALL, Peter Donald. M.A. Oxford; Ph.D. Yale; educated Balliol College, Oxford; Lecturer in American History, University of Bristol 1953–66; Professor of History, McGill University 1966–72; Professor of American History, University of Manchester 1972; publications include *The Anti-Slave Trade Movement in Bristol* (1968) and *Bristol and the abolition of slavery: the politics of Emancipation* (1975).

RALPH, Elizabeth. President of the Society for the centenary year 1976; Hon. life member of the Society; Hon. general secretary of the Society since 1948; Hon. M.A., University of Bristol 1953; F.S.A.; Chairman of Society of Archivists

1957; archivist of the City of Bristol, 1937–71; publications include *Guide to the parish records of the city of Bristol and the county of Gloucester* (with I. E. Gray, 1963); *The Church Book of St. Ewen's, Bristol* (with Betty Masters, 1967) and *A History of Bristol and Gloucestershire* (with Brian Smith, 1972).

THIRSK, Joan. B.A., Ph.D., London; M.A., Oxford; F.B.A.; educated Westfield College, London; Reader in Economic History, University of Oxford and Fellow of St. Hilda's College, Oxford since 1965; Ford Lecturer in English History at Oxford, 1975; publications include *English Peasant farming* (1957); *Tudor Enclosures* (1959); *Agrarian History of England and Wales*, vol. iv (ed.) and *Seventeenth-century economic documents* (1972).

TOYNBEE, Jocelyn Mary Catherine. M.A., Cambridge; D.Phil. Oxford; Hon.D.Litt. Newcastle; Hon.D.Litt. Liverpool; F.B.A.; educated Newnham College, Cambridge; Fellow of Newnham College 1927–62; Professor of Classical Archaeology, University of Cambridge 1951–62; Laurence Professor Emerita since 1962; Hon. Fellow of Newnham College since 1962; publications include *The Hadrianic School* (1934); *Art in Roman Britain* (1962) and *Animals in Roman Life and Art* (1973).

VEREY, David Cecil Wynter. President of the Society, 1972; M.A. Cambridge, A.R.I.B.A., F.S.A.; educated Trinity College, Cambridge; Senior Investigator, Historic Buildings, Ministry of Housing and Local Government 1946–65; publications include *Shell Guides* to six counties in England and Wales; *The buildings of England: Gloucestershire* (1970); *Cotswold Churches* (1976).

List of Illustrations

Frontispiece

1 Elizabeth Ralph

(*Between pages* 44–45)

2   Sir William Vernon Guise, Bt.
3   Canon William Bazeley
4   Roland Austin
5   John E. Pritchard
6   Mrs. Elsie Clifford
7   Dr. Joan Evans
8   Belas Knap long barrow
9   Dry-stone plugging in Rodmarton long barrow
10 Stone relief of Genii Cucullati
11 Stone statuette of Mother-goddess
12 Bronze statuette of Mars
13 Stone relief of Minerva

(*Between pages* 140–141)

14 Altar from Dorn
15 Altar from Dorn
16 Northleach parish church
17 The west door of Fairford parish church
18 Grotesque human head from Chedworth parish church
19 Gargoyle at Chedworth
20 Detail from Cirencester parish church
21 Fanvaulting at Cirencester
22 Parapets at Fairford parish church
23 Nave arcade in Northleach parish church

List of Illustrations

(*Between pages* 188–189)

24 Dowry Square, Hotwells
25 Commemorative medal of George III at Cheltenham
26 The original well at Cheltenham
27 View of the Hotwell on Bristol Delftware dish
28 Map of Clifton and the Hotwell, 1787
29 George III taking Cheltenham waters
30 Clifton Suspension Bridge
31 Dredger designed by Brunel
32 S.S. *Great Britain* returning home
33 Old Temple Meads station

Abbreviations

Cal. S.P.D.	*Calendar of State Papers, Domestic*
DNB.	*The Dictionary of National Biography*
FFBJ.	*Felix Farley's Bristol Journal*
GJ.	*Gloucester Journal*
JRS.	*Journal of Roman Studies*
PLB.	The Private Letter Books of Isambard Kingdom Brunel, deposited in the Library of the University of Bristol
PRO.	*Public Record Office*
RIB.	R. G. Collingwood and R. P. Wright, *The Roman Inscriptions of Britain*, vol. i (1964)
TBGAS.	*Transactions of the Bristol and Gloucestershire Archaeological Society*
VCH. Glos.	*The Victoria County History of Gloucestershire*

I

The Society 1876–1976

By Elizabeth Ralph

THE Bristol and Gloucestershire Archaeological Society came
into being in 1876, a quarter of a century after similar societies
had been established in many other counties, but at a time when
there had been a change in emphasis in archaeological interests,
which was reflected in the form the Society took and which has
influenced its subsequent activities.

The initial Victorian interest in antiquarianism was stimulated by the Gothic Revival in ecclesiastical architecture and a
realisation that ancient and curious objects could be found to
illustrate the past history of the British Isles as well as the classical culture of the Mediterranean.

By the 1870s there was a new awareness of the contribution
archaeological research could make to our knowledge of the
surroundings in which we live. Sir John Evans, whose daughter
was later to be a distinguished editor of our *Transactions*, was
involved in constructing the framework of prehistory. During
the same period General Pitt-Rivers, later in 1892 our President,
was establishing the techniques of scientific excavation. In the
field of conservation, the Society for the Preservation of Ancient
Buildings was set up in 1877, and in 1888 carried out a model
exercise in church restoration on the thirteenth-century building
at Inglesham, close by Lechlade. The intention was "not to
pretend to put (a building) back into a state at which it may be
supposed to have been at any given time, but to preserve, so far
as is practicable, the record of what had been its state during all
the period of its history".

This type of outlook was reflected by the decision to invite
Dr. John Beddoe, Fellow of the Royal Society and a distinguished anthropologist, to be chairman of the first committee
set up to consider the formation of the Society, and by the

Bishop of Gloucester and Bristol's comment at the inaugural meeting that the Society was not intended as a medium for "junketings and picnics".

The Bristol and Gloucestershire Archaeological Society, through the agencies it has been instrumental in establishing and through the efforts of individual members, has often shown itself in advance of accepted opinion in the past hundred years. It was responsible for the preservation of Arlington Row at Bibury, the Theatre Royal in Bristol and the Dutch House in Wine Street, Bristol, the latter sadly destroyed in the air raids of 1940. Its attitude on these occasions was regarded as either odd or obstructionist, but today there would be a public outcry if buildings of this kind were threatened with demolition. These are some examples of its work in a particular field; less spectacular, but not less important, have been the other activities described in the following pages.

When the British Archaeological Association visited Bristol in 1874, John Taylor, the City Librarian of Bristol, wrote a paper calling attention to the architectural and historical treasures of the area. This paper was publicly displayed in the City Library for the signatures of those who were interested. John Taylor's appeal and no doubt the learned dissertations and pleasant excursions enjoyed during the visit of the Association acted as a stimulus to local antiquaries to investigate more fully the many archaeological and historic sites with which Bristol and Gloucestershire abound.

Some thirty years before, a county archaeological society had been formed under the Presidency of Sir William Vernon Guise. It met with little support or encouragement and after four years the Society was dissolved and its archaeological interest absorbed in the Cotteswold Naturalists Field Club, which had been established in 1846.

The fresh stimulus resulted in the setting up of a committee in Bristol under the chairmanship of Dr. John Beddoe to consider the formation of a Society. Mr. Palmer Hallett of Claverton, Bath acted as honorary secretary. In appointing a Fellow of the Royal Society as chairman, the members of the committee guaranteed that the work of this proposed society would be on a scientific basis and "that the new society meant neither dilettantism nor picnics nor any combination of the two". The committee expressed the view that such an association for the investigation of the antiquities of the county on the model of those already established in the neighbouring counties of Somerset (1849) and Wiltshire (1854) would supply a real and long-felt need.

The first step was to appoint a provisional committee under the chairmanship of the Earl of Ducie, the Lord-Lieutenant of the county. Under the patronage of the Duke of Beaufort, the Lord Bishop of Gloucester and Bristol, Lord Dynevor, Lord Fitzhardinge, Lord Redesdale and Lord Sherborne, it issued a circular throughout the county, as a result of which over 400 people expressed their desire to become members. After some preliminary discussions, the committee called a public inaugural meeting on the 21 April 1876 in the Bristol City Museum, at which the committee reported on what it had already achieved. The Earl of Ducie presided over the meeting at which 67 persons were present, among whom were Sir John Davis, Sir William V. Guise, Sir Brook Kay, Sir John Maclean, the Bishop of Gloucester and Bristol, the Bishop of Clifton, eighteen clergy, two Members of Parliament, the Mayor of Gloucester, seven doctors, seven women and a number of gentlemen from Bristol and Gloucestershire.

In opening the proceedings the chairman said that "the meeting had been called to see if they could collect the scattered fragments of archaeology which existed in the county and give them some sort of cohesion in the shape of an Archaeological Association". He pointed out "among the landed proprietors, among the local clergy and among the residents of such towns as Clifton and Cheltenham there must be many people who were fit to be members of such an association. From the labouring man who dug up an early tobacco pipe with the remark 'may it be as old as Moses' to the philologist who detected traces of a by-gone race in the radical elements of a language— all could contribute something, and if welded together might be of service to the Association."

Sir William Guise, who was to become the first President and who also served as President of Council for the first ten years, spoke of the literary treasures of Gloucestershire, complaining that the county archives though extensive were un-indexed and inadequately housed. The Bishop of Gloucester and Bristol proposed that a Bristol and Gloucestershire Archaeological Society be established, and Sir William Guise seconded the proposal. There followed good-humoured comments as to the relative position of the names "Gloucestershire" and "Bristol" in the title of the new society. Sir John Dorrington of Lypiatt Park, later President, said "Bristol supplied a compact body of literary men, living within easy range of one another, having daily opportunities of meeting, libraries at hand, and all things necessary for the organisation of a society, whilst Gloucestershire brought to the society a scattered body of allies, ready to avail themselves of the organisation which Bristol created, and to supply the materials on which the society would work."

The provisional committee then reported that it had enrolled over 400 members and was able to say that the finances were sound. It had considered the question of organisation and had prepared a code of rules, based on those of other archaeological societies, both county and metropolitan. Whereupon the Hon. and Rt. Reverend Bishop of Clifton proposed that the Society's establishment be based on these rules and that they be referred to the Council when appointed. When considering the classes of membership, the committee was in favour of having a number of patrons who should be confined to members of the House of Lords having property or residence in the area and to members of the House of Commons representing it. This did not meet with complete approval and a nobleman to whom the Society, so it was said, "was more indebted than any other", on being asked to become a patron, replied by denouncing the name as "a relic of evil days". This caused concern and the committee was in great doubt whether to proceed, but having already had several letters of acceptance, found it difficult to change its policy. Consequently the Society was graced with twenty-one patrons.

The affairs of the Society were vested in a Council which met for the first time on 3 May 1876 under the chairmanship of Sir William Guise. This Council had a saving sense of humour and spoke of itself as self-elected, unrestricted and irresponsible, and open to all the temptations to which such bodies are liable. Truly a delightful condition of affairs, and, as Roland Austin said, "almost superior to the ideal committee of one".

The thirteen members present were the Mayor of Bristol,

J. R. Bramble, J. F. Nicholls, John Reynolds, John Taylor, Robert Lang (Hon. Treasurer), William Adlam, the Reverend Prebendary Scarth, the Reverend J. T. Ellacombe, the Reverend R. C. Nightingale, the Reverend Dr. F. W. Gotch, Dr. John Beddoe and Palmer Hallett. A Finance Committee was appointed, and the first banking account opened at Miles Bank, Bristol. At first the Council met every month and then irregularly until it decided to meet four times a year, which it has done ever since. Dr. Beddoe and J. R. Bramble with the secretary and treasurer formulated the first rules which remained substantially the same until 1918. The objects of the Society were set down as follows:

> To collect and classify original and existing information on the antiquities of this district and to thus accumulate materials for an improved county history
> To establish a library and museum for the preservation and study of these and other objects of antiquarian value
> To promote by meetings, publications, etc. such an interest throughout the district in the monuments of its past history as shall tend to counteract their present liability to inconsiderate and needless destruction.

It is clear that from the beginning the Society's main concern, indeed its very reason for existence, was the preservation of sites and buildings of archaeological and historic interest at a time when there was no legislation for their protection. Neither the Office of Works nor Local Authorities had power or means to enable them to preserve any monument.

With these objects in mind the Council began its work. For the efficient running of the Society, the county was divided into nine districts, each district having a Vice-President and a local secretary. The constitution provided for the election of a President, Vice-Presidents, officers and a Council of thirty. Honorary members could be elected, the first being Professor George Rolleston, a distinguished professor of Anatomy and Physiology, who had taken a deep interest in the foundation of the Society and had done much to ensure the success of its first meeting. Field meetings were arranged in Bristol and Gloucester. These were organised by local committees set up in the areas to be visited. While the Council was happy to leave the arrangements to a local committee, it always exercised the right to revise the programme. In 1876 a publishing committee consisting of J. D. T. Niblett, W. C. Lucy, John Bellows, F. S. Waller, the Mayor of Gloucester, S. H. Gael and C. S. Taylor made arrangements for the printing of the first volume of *Transactions*. Although the membership was only 513, it was agreed to print 750 copies. It was not until 1887 that the Society undertook its first excavation, but it is interesting to record that during the first year, the Council set up a committee to prevent the destruction of the tower of St. Werburgh's church, Bristol. A number of members, no doubt encouraged by the President's remarks on the preservation of the county's treasures, were keen to establish libraries and museums both in Bristol and Gloucester. Requests were made for books and archaeological objects. Through the efforts of Sir John Maclean, arrangements were made for the Society to exchange its publications with other learned bodies. In October 1876 the Council advised "that museums belonging to the society should be established in Bristol and Gloucester". Both cities offered accommodation, and it was agreed to accept. A small committee consisting of Sir William Guise, Dr. J. W. Caldicott, the secretary and treasurer was appointed to carry out the resolution. There had been controversy in Council about where the books and objects should be housed and some criticism of the composition of the committee. Five Bristol members, Dr. John Beddoe, Francis Fox, Thomas Kerslake, John Latimer and Edward Strickland, all influential men in the Society, wrote a letter of protest, questioning the Council's power to appoint so unrepresentative a committee. They stated that "Bristol was the headquarters of the society and the organ of intercourse and correspondence with other societies." In no uncertain way they expressed their disapproval: "we, being some of the original promoters of the foundation of the society therefore protest against this act of Council . . . in stifling the voice of a minority; also against the appointment of any place otherwise than within Bristol the birthplace of the society and by much the most important and considerable place within the society's district . . . believing that a persistence in such purpose may possibly involve the society in litigation or provoke a schism or both". Eventually another committee was appointed and its proposals accepted by Council. This meant that donors of books and objects were to have the option of naming the place of deposit, that books and objects having special connection with Bristol or Gloucester were to be allotted appropriately, and the rest to be ballotted for. As time passed, the Society's library in Gloucester became the main library, for it was here that the publications of other learned societies were housed, while only books relating to Bristol were added to the library in Bristol. The setting up of museums was not thought sensible or profitable and the archaeological finds were deposited in the city museums of Bristol and Gloucester.

From the very outset the Society had many expert members, and it is therefore no wonder that, started as it was under such excellent auspices, it became influential. For ten years Sir William Guise was President of Council with Palmer Hallett as honorary secretary until he was joined by the Reverend William Bazeley as joint secretary, and later general secretary, from 1879 to 1907. In 1882 Palmer Hallett retired and suggested that one of the honorary secretaries should be resident in Bristol. The Reverend Dr. J. W. Caldicott, headmaster of the Bristol Grammar School, was appointed. Three years later Dr. Caldicott left Bristol and William Bazeley carried on alone until Canon C. S. Taylor became joint secretary in 1893. The Society owed much of its vigour and vitality to the guidance and energy of William Bazeley. In 1892 it recognised his work as honorary secretary for thirteen years by presenting him with a handsomely embossed two-handled silver bowl dated 1756 and a purse of gold. He continued as secretary until he became President in 1908. It was not so easy to get a treasurer willing and able to serve for any length of time. Between 1876 and 1909 there were no less than seven, each pleading that the duties occupied too much time. This is hard to understand when the total income in 1880 was £157 14s. and the expenditure much the same. It may be that the treasurers found the attitude of the editor intolerable. At one time Sir John Maclean refused to print the accounts in the form in which they were submitted. The treasurer declined to alter them, whereupon Sir John advocated the appointment of a chartered accountant to get them into proper order. The following year, the Council accepted the accounts, ordering them to be printed in the *Transactions*, but again the editor protested against the form and failed to print them. The Council then instructed that the treasurer's accounts for 1890, 1891 and 1892 be printed on a single sheet and inserted in volume xvii, thus relieving the editor from all responsibility in the matter.

Sir William Guise, Sir John Maclean as editor, and William Bazeley ran the affairs of the Society, making most of the decisions, thereby dispensing with committees. In 1888 the auditors suggested to Council that the Finance Committee should be revived, that it should report regularly, that it should examine all bills before presentation to Council and should estimate the expenditure for each year. In 1890, the Council made a short-sighted decision to dispose of the surplus stock of the *Transactions* and in a rather dramatic way ordered that the volumes should be destroyed in the presence of Sir Brook Kay and Sir Francis Hyett.

The work of the Society, as indeed of similar organisations in other counties, was carried out without reference to any central body until 1888. In that year a union of archaeological societies in England with the Society of Antiquaries of London as a nucleus was proposed, with a view to the better organisation of archaeological research and the preservation of ancient monuments. Our Society was represented at the first Congress of Archaeological Societies, held at Burlington House. Because the records of British archaeology were scattered among the Transactions of so many societies, the Congress published a yearly index of titles of papers contributed to every archaeological society and other bodies publishing archaeological material in the United Kingdom. These annual indexes were issued with the *Transactions*.

When in 1896 the Society celebrated its twenty-first anniversary, it could number among its Presidents such names as Sir William Vernon Guise, Earl Bathurst, Thomas Gambier Parry, Sir John Dorrington, Sir John Maclean, Sir Brook Kay, Sir Henry Barkly, Lord Sherborne, General A. H. L. F. Pitt-Rivers, Lord Fitzhardinge and other able and learned men. The Council took this opportunity of inviting the Presidents to present their portraits to the society. Sir William Guise gave a portrait of his father and Miss Maclean of her father. The portraits were hung in the Society's library and ten years later the secretary reported that many other portraits had been received from past Presidents. The custom appears to have ceased sometime before 1914. Unfortunately it has not been possible to trace the whereabouts of these portraits.

By 1898 a number of the Presidents had died including Sir William Vernon Guise who had directed the affairs of the Society with extraordinary enthusiasm, and Sir John Maclean whose greatest contribution to the Society was as editor of the *Transactions* but who, one suspects, exercised considerable influence on general policy. Although not a President, mention must be made of one of the distinguished Vice-Presidents, the Rt. Reverend William Hugh Clifford, Bishop of Clifton who died in 1893. He was the first President of the Clifton Antiquarian Club and a Vice-President of the Somerset Archaeological and Natural History Society. He took a great interest in our society, attending most meetings and frequently acting as guide on archaeological excursions.

The retirement of Canon Bazeley as honorary secretary in 1907 brought to a close the first phase in the Society's history. In paying tribute to his service, it was recorded that "by his skilful management, general ability and unfailing courtesy the whole activity of the society centred around him, with the result that the researches into the history and antiquities of the county have never waned". Although it was reported at a successful summer meeting at that time "that practically a new generation of archaeologists had taken the place of that which composed the society at its inauguration", Canon Taylor referred to the period as a "testing time" for the Society and observed that "the pioneers and leaders had passed away and that the men to take their places were not forthcoming". With the retirement of Canon Bazeley, a new secretary was found in Michael Lloyd-Baker who it was said "was a country gentleman with considerable leisure and reputed to possess organising ability". Four years later he resigned because of pressure of county work and also because he felt that he could not maintain Canon Bazeley's standards. He was the nephew of Colonel A. B. Lloyd-Baker, a most devoted member of the Society, who at the age of 94 still takes an active interest.

The outbreak of the First World War meant the curtailment of most of the Society's activities. The Council managed to meet once or twice a year and to hold its annual business meeting. In

1917 the President of Council, the general secretary, Arnold Eardley Hurry, and the treasurer, James A. Smith all retired.

With the appointment of Sir Francis Hyett, the title of President of Council was changed to Chairman and the tenure of office limited to three years. Roland Austin, who was the Society's librarian and local secretary for Gloucester, became honorary general secretary and asked if he might be responsible for collecting the subscriptions and keeping the accounts of the Society. Council agreed that he should collect the subscriptions, but appointed F. Hannam Clark as treasurer. So successful was Austin that all arrears of subscriptions, which amounted to £70, were recovered and the year closed without a single subscription owing.

In 1918 John E. Pritchard was elected President and in his presidential address took the opportunity for reviewing the work of the Society since its inception. Having been an active member since 1888, he was able to speak from personal knowledge of the Society's achievements. From 1901 until 1910 he had been secretary for Bristol and during the first year was responsible for the election of 55 new members. When he resigned, he was presented with a piece of plate to the value of £100, for it was said "that no one was more loyal or worked so constantly for the Society's interest and advancement". His care for the antiquities of Bristol can best be judged by the long series of "Bristol Archaeological Notes" printed in the *Transactions*. He kept an eagle eye on every excavation which took place in Bristol, and it may be said that whenever or wherever a hole was dug, Pritchard was a vigilant observer and, equally important, a careful recorder. He showed great vigour and pertinacity in opposing the threatened demolition of buildings of historic interest. In 1919, the Lord Mayor in welcoming the Society to Bristol spoke of the efforts of John E. Pritchard in saving from destruction such important buildings as the Dutch House, the old Board Room of St. Peter's Hospital, the Registrar's house adjoining the Cathedral and the Red Lodge. Pritchard was fully aware that the Society could not rest on its laurels and was ever-ready to give fresh stimulus. The effects of the war were such that a re-organisation of the Society's affairs was necessary, and the first major amendment of the rules was made. The districts were changed to the parliamentary divisions of the county, the duties of the officers were more clearly defined, and conditions of membership set out in greater detail. The annual subscription was not increased, probably because of the decline in numbers during the war. However, Pritchard with his unflagging energy secured 93 new members in one year, many of whom were his own friends. To enable the Society to carry out excavations, he launched an appeal to establish an Excavation Fund. Within a year, £137 was contributed and an Excavation committee, of which he became both chairman and treasurer, was set up. It is therefore not surprising that he was asked to serve as Chairman of Council for a fourth year. It must be remembered that at this time Roland Austin was honorary general secretary and soon to become editor. They made an admirable combination and together revitalised the work of the Society.

When the Society celebrated its fiftieth anniversary, the membership, at 743, was as high as it had ever been. At a meeting on the 21 April 1926, Roland Austin gave a brief survey of the Society's achievements and closed with these words: "May we not expect that a similar report will be made on the 21st April 1976, though I fear that not many of those in this room will be able to hear it." Of those present in 1926, the following are still members—the Reverend E. P. Baker, Mrs. E. M. Clifford, Mr. I. V. Hall, Mr. C. Roy Hudleston and Colonel A. B. Lloyd-Baker. The 1926 meeting also included three people who were elected to membership in 1876: Walter Derham, Major H. M. Herapath and E. C. Sewell. Letters of greetings were read from four other members unable to attend: Canon J. T. Harding, Dr. J. E. Shaw, Colonel T. H. Yabbicomb and Mr. Ernest Hartland.

The year 1927 must have been a momentous one in the life of the Society for in September Roland Austin wrote to the Chairman of Council stating that he wished to be relieved of his many offices. Since 1917 he had been honorary general secretary, combining it with many of the duties of the treasurer; he had also been editor for five years. In addition he was the Society's librarian and had recently been responsible for organising the meetings. Major H. Stratton Davis was appointed secretary and continued so until 1935. He will be remembered for his work in connection with the Archaeological Trust and as an able guide on many excursions. Wilfrid Leighton, who at the time was secretary for Bristol, became honorary treasurer. He was a capable and experienced treasurer and in 1933 became chairman of the Archaeological Trust, managing its financial affairs. As there was no suitable candidate forthcoming for the office of editor, Roland Austin agreed to continue.

The Society made history in 1929 by electing Miss Ida Roper the first woman member of Council. She was a recognised authority on the monumental effigies of the county. In 1931 her series of notes on the effigies of Bristol and Gloucestershire originally published in the *Transactions* was re-printed in a limited edition, handsomely bound. It is worthy of note that Mrs. E. M. Bagnall-Oakley, who also devoted her attention to the study of effigies, costume and embroidery was the first woman to address the Society and to write for the *Transactions* as early as 1894. In 1930 Mrs. E. M. Clifford was elected to the Council. She was to become one of the most important influences in the life and activities of the Society during the next thirty years.

The outbreak of hostilities in 1939 affected the work of the Society. The Council met and agreed that for the duration of the war, the affairs of the Society should be delegated to the officers, who were empowered to make such decisions as were necessary. Roland Austin who had been elected President was asked to continue in office for the period. Owing to the grave position of national affairs in the summer of 1940 the usual annual business meeting was, for the first time in the Society's history, not held. It was, however, agreed to continue publishing the *Transactions* as far as circumstances permitted. If the decision of Council to leave the affairs of the Society in the hands of the officers had been adhered to, the Society might have been spared the unhappy years of 1940–48. During this time the meetings of Council often resulted in lamentable incidents and much discord was caused by some members wishing to go against the will of the majority.

The years immediately after the war were difficult ones. The membership had fallen to 465 and subscriptions were not sufficient to meet the Society's commitments. The continued rise in expenditure and the cost of printing the *Transactions,* which was more than twice what it had been a decade before, caused much concern. The Excavation Fund, having made contributions to the work being done at Whittington Roman villa and to the Bristol Exploration committee, was exhausted. Mrs. Clifford launched an appeal to replenish the Fund and received an encouraging response. There were also problems of administration as well as finance. When Wilfrid Leighton retired as treasurer, the Council found it difficult to fill the office. There were now fewer people with leisure time to spare and in the five years that followed there were three treasurers, until the Hon. W. R. S. Bathurst, who had been auditing the accounts, was persuaded to take charge. For twenty years he kept a careful watch on the Society's investments and finances, until his untimely death in a motor car accident in 1970. His task was made the more easy by the generous benefactions of Dr. Joan Evans in 1954, which provided the Society with an investment income which was of great assistance in financing the *Transactions*, supporting excavations and in preserving ancient buildings. In 1970 Mr. H. G. M. Leighton accepted the invitation to become treasurer, thereby continuing the connection begun by his father in 1918.

In 1948 Miss Elizabeth Ralph, who had been secretary for Bristol since 1943, became honorary general secretary. Two years later, Dr. Joan Evans accepted the editorship of the *Transactions*.

Since the 1950s the standing committees of Council have played an increasingly big part in the administration of the Society's activities. Alderman Hannam Clark of Gloucester was chairman of the Library committee for ten years until 1960 when Colonel A. B. Lloyd-Baker took over, followed by Mr. G. T. St. J. Sanders. For seventeen years Mrs. Clifford was chairman of the Excavations and Buildings committee, and when she retired in 1961 Major H. Stratton Davis carried on for four years, after which Mr. David Verey accepted the office. His chairmanship was particularly valuable at a time when much of the work of the committee was concerned with the conservation of buildings and sites. During the past year Dr. John Cannon has taken over the duties. In 1964 Wilfrid Leighton, who had been chairman of the Finance & General Purposes committee for sixteen years, retired and Mr. Patrick McGrath became chairman. As in 1876 the work of the Society today is carried out by its Council and officers, who endeavour to fulfil the objects of the Society which have remained basically the same. Although it can no longer finance excavations, the Society continues to publish a comprehensive series of archaeological reports, subsidising them heavily. It has succeeded, in cooperation with public authorities, in preserving many historic sites and buildings.

For the sake of clarity and because the main objects of the Bristol and Gloucestershire Archaeological Society have continued unchanged for one hundred years, it seems best to treat each aspect of its work under a separate heading.

TRANSACTIONS

One of the objects of the Society has always been to publish papers on the records and history of Gloucestershire in general and the cities of Bristol and Gloucester in particular. Even a cursory glance at the volumes of *Transactions* will show that this purpose has, generally speaking, been carried out very fully, for there is hardly a subject concerning the county which has not received attention.

Though the Society has been established for one hundred years, the actual number of volumes does not coincide. The usual practice has been to publish one volume for each year, but circumstances made it necessary for the *Transactions* of 1895–96, 1896–97 and 1918–19 to be issued in three single volumes. In the case of the first two, this was done so that the *Church Plate of Gloucestershire* and the first accumulative index could be issued in lieu of the annual volume. During the Second World War, a special volume, *Rolls of the Gloucestershire Sessions of the Peace, 1361–1398* by E. G. Kimball was issued as volume lxii of the *Transactions*. An accumulative index came out in 1941 instead of a volume, and the *Transactions* for 1946–48 appeared as a single volume.

During the one hundred years, nine editors have served the Society, which must always deem itself fortunate that men and women of distinction have occupied the office. The first two volumes were prepared by an editorial committee, of which Sir John Maclean was a member and no doubt took the most active part. Of the first volume, 750 copies were printed at a cost of £100, John Bellows of Gloucester, an influential member of the Society, being the printer. When the second volume was

ready, tenders were received from printers in Bristol, Cheltenham, Exeter and Gloucester and it was that of Jefferies of
Bristol which was accepted. This firm printed volumes ii to xvi.
In 1883 a disastrous fire at Jefferies destroyed a large part of the
back numbers of the *Transactions*. Fortunately twenty-five sets
had been deposited at Bristol Museum, but it was necessary to
reprint 250 copies of volume v, part 2 and the whole issue of
volume vi.

In 1878 Sir John Maclean was invited to become editor and
was responsible for fourteen volumes until 1894. The standard
of editing achieved under his experienced guidance did much
to enhance the Society's prestige. Sir John's particular interest
was in historical documents, and during his period of editorship
he contributed no less than fifty papers on a variety of subjects,
including histories of manors, chantry certificates, inventories of
church goods and Feet of Fines. He was able to draw on
knowledgeable and enthusiastic members such as Dr. G.
Rolleston, Dr. John Beddoe, John Bellows, John Taylor and
John Latimer (the latter two being particularly concerned with
the history of Bristol), Sir Henry Barkly, A. S. Ellis, G. T. Clark
an authority on military architecture, the Reverend David
Royce, Mrs. Bagnall-Oakley who was the first to work on the
effigies of the county, and Canon W. Bazeley whose first paper
appeared in volume ii of the *Transactions* and the last in volume
xlvi. When Sir John retired, the Society recognised its debt to
him by presenting him with a silver inkstand. The next editor
was the Reverend (later Canon) C. S. Taylor, then vicar of St.
Thomas, Bristol, but in 1896, he moved to Banwell and in
consequence felt he should resign. Because of his great service
to the Society since its inception, he was presented with Dugdale's *Monasticon Anglicanum*, a very fine copy from the Ashburnham Library, purchased for £31 10s. Happily in 1899 he
was able to resume the office. During the short break, C. Trice
Martin of Clifton College undertook the supervision of volumes
xx and xxi. The high standard set by Sir John Maclean was
continued by Canon Taylor who contributed to nearly every
volume. For volumes xv to xl he wrote twenty-three papers,
some of considerable length. Sir John Maclean's resignation
coincided with the termination of Jefferies as printers. Tenders
were sought and that of Osborne of Gloucester was accepted but

only for one year. Canon Taylor asked for a Bristol printer to be considered and Messrs. Arrowsmith were appointed, agreeing to print at £3 5s. for sixteen pages.

In looking through these early pages, one cannot help being impressed by the industry of some contributors. When the first volumes of *Transactions* were issued, practically nothing had been published relating to the history of Gloucestershire for nearly seventy years. Such histories as Atkyns, Rudder, Fosbroke and Rudge had all been published during the eighteenth or early nineteenth centuries. Although there never seems to have been a dearth of contributions, at one time (1900) the editor wrote "the present state of the *Transactions* cannot be considered satisfactory. The volumes are in arrears and there is a lack of suitable material." He was referring to the publication of extracts from the Feet of Fines, which he considered more suitable for a Record Series than for the *Transactions*. He was disquieted by the fact that archaeological discoveries were not recorded. Severely rebuking those involved, he complained that "Things are found and lightly examined or not examined by any competent authority at all, and are forgotten. Excavations are made and no proper record is prepared." So depressed was he that he called for a revival of interest in the Society's work and pointed to the need for new members to take over the burdens that others had carried.

In 1914 Canon Taylor resigned and Dr. G. H. West filled the office for one year after which Dr. E. Sidney Hartland, a distinguished student of folklore and anthropology, became editor. His wide learning and experience as a writer brought great advantage to the Society's *Transactions* during the next seven years. These were difficult years with the rising cost of printing.

By 1920 the *Transactions* were costing as much as £240. Arrowsmith's of Bristol who had been the printers since 1894, at a time when the cost had been fixed at £125, including an honorarium to the editor, asked for a 45 per cent increase, submitting figures showing that even that advance was lower than that asked on other contracts in hand. Reluctantly, the Council sought competitive estimates and that of Titus Wilson of Kendal at £300 was accepted, with the decision to print one annual volume instead of the two parts. It had been customary to issue the first part in February and the second in July of each year. However, what the volumes lacked in size they gained in quality. For at this time such men as Sir Francis Hyett contributed bibliographies of Gloucestershire sources; W. St. Clair Baddeley wrote on Romano-British history, Francis Were on heraldry, while his index to Bigland's *History of Gloucestershire* was a monumental task. In Bristol John E. Pritchard, year by year contributed his "Archaeological Notes" which were detailed accounts of what he observed as he walked round the city. Alfred Fryer published the results of his exhaustive survey of Gloucestershire fonts.

In 1923, owing to ill health, Hartland resigned and Roland Austin agreed to be editor. At that time he was already the Society's librarian and honorary secretary, combining with this most of the work of honorary treasurer. For twenty years he was editor, until he resigned in 1949 with the publication of volume lxvii of the *Transactions*. During this period twenty-four volumes were issued under his scholarly care. Failure on the part of Wilson to produce the volumes on time caused Roland Austin to give the work back to Bellows of Gloucester, who printed the Society's *Transactions* until 1966 when the firm was taken over by Norman Bros of Cheltenham, who were in turn taken over by Greenaways who continued to print until 1973. Three accumulative indexes were done by Austin himself and are masterpieces of the art of indexing.[1] Few societies can be better equipped in this respect than our own. Roland Austin's services to the Society were acknowledged when he was made an Honorary member. The Council also decided that volume lxviii should be dedicated to him as some recognition of his services.

The high standard of editorship set by Roland Austin made it difficult to find a successor. However, the Society was fortunate in securing the services of Dr. Joan Evans. In 1956 she invited Captain H. S. Gracie to assist with the editing of volume lxxv and when in 1959 Dr. Evans was elected President of the Society of Antiquaries of London, she relinquished the office and Captain Gracie was appointed editor. He continued until 1973 when ill health forced him to resign. Mr. Brian Smith, County Archivist for Gloucestershire, then took over.

[1] The Society has continued to publish an accumulative index every ten years.

OTHER PUBLICATIONS

In addition to the *Transactions* a number of extra works have been published since 1883 when the first volume of the Berkeley Manuscripts was issued. In 1881 the Society approached Lord Fitzhardinge for permission to see certain records at Berkeley Castle with a view to publication. Sir William Guise, Sir John Maclean and John Taylor, City Librarian of Bristol, were allowed to inspect the manuscripts of John Smyth, steward at Berkeley Castle in the seventeenth century, together with the Register of the Abbey of St. Augustine, Bristol. It was suggested that the *Lives of the Berkeleys* should be printed first and that Smyth's *Hundred of Berkeley* should follow. The books were to be privately printed for the members of the Society. To these proposals Lord Fitzhardinge agreed and an editorial committee with Sir John Maclean as editor was set up. Ambitious plans for publication were made which unfortunately were not realised. Three hundred copies were to be printed on hand-made paper and bound in vellum at a cost of £1 per volume to each subscribing member. The cost of printing the first volume was £300 and as only £153 was subscribed, it was with some disappointment that the Council was forced to abandon its original plans and effect some saving by binding the volumes in stiff paper covers at a cost of 9d. a copy. It was possible to publish the second volume in 1884 and in the following year, the third volume was issued. By then the total amount subscribed was £780 while the expenditure had been £911.

When, therefore, Sir John Maclean proposed that the cartulary of St. Augustine's Abbey, Bristol should be transcribed and published, the Council was reluctant to take on further financial commitments. This valuable historical document has not yet been published and is available only to a limited number of students at the discretion of the Trustees. In 1892, Council closed the Berkeley Manuscript Fund and transferred the debt to the general fund, offering the remaining copies to members at the original subscription price of £3 for the three volumes.

It is not surprising that when in 1887 Lord Sherborne asked the Society to consider publishing the Winchcombe Cartulary in his possession, the Council hesitated to agree and appointed a committee to issue a circular letter inviting subscriptions. The response was not good enough to meet the estimated cost of printing and the Council was compelled to decline. The Reverend David Royce had already transcribed and edited the cartulary and he took upon himself the whole responsibility of printing the manuscript, opening a subscription list to the general public. On his death, his widow offered the stock of unsold copies of *Landboc, sive Registrum Monasterii de Winchcumba*, nominally worth £199, for £100. The Council purchased the volumes "knowing that they were not likely to prove profitable to the Society and were calculated to give more trouble to the secretary and librarian, but felt obliged to consider favourably the offer on account of the magnificent gift to the society of Mr. Royce's archaeological library".

In 1889 *An Analysis of the Domesday of Gloucestershire* by C. S. Taylor, then vicar of St. Thomas, Bristol was published.

A proposal that the Society should cooperate with the British Record Society for the publication of early county records, as similar bodies elsewhere were doing, was rejected by the Council which thought it desirable to preserve its independence. A further suggestion to take on the work of the British Record Society as far as it related to Gloucestershire was also rejected. In the end it was agreed that for ten guineas a year the British Record Society would supply 500 copies of six sheets of records which would be issued with the *Transactions*. The first of these was the *Calendar of Bristol Wills, 1572–1792 and wills in the Great Orphan Books, 1378–1694*, edited by E. A. Fry and issued in volume xx, part one. This was a continuation of the work of T. P. Wadley, who in 1886 had published in three instalments in the *Transactions*, "Notes or Abstracts of the wills contained in the Great Orphan Book." After the Bristol wills were completed, the early *Inquisitiones Post Mortem* were printed. These continued to be issued until 1914 when the British Record Society decided that no further publications would be made.

After many years of work, *The Church Plate of Gloucestershire*, edited by J. T. Evans, was published in 1905 and sent to all members who had paid subscriptions for the years 1894–97. At a cost of £130, 500 copies were printed. In 1913, *A descriptive Catalogue of the printed maps of Gloucestershire, 1577–1911*, edited by T. Chubb, was issued in lieu of the *Transactions*, volume xxxv, part two.

The Bibliographer's Manual of Gloucestershire Literature, compiled by F. A. Hyett and William Bazeley, was issued to members in the years 1895–97 and was completed in 1916 by the publication of the *Bibliographical Supplement*. It takes its place as one of the best of our county bibliographies. Not content with this, Sir Francis Hyett, with the help of Roland Austin, Librarian of Gloucester, began to compile a bibliography of printed matter relating to men and women connected with the county and Bristol. This has never been published but is preserved in the Gloucester City Library. It is now more than three quarters of a century since *The Bibliographer's Manual* was completed, and since then a considerable collection of printed material relating to Gloucestershire and Bristol has been published. The Society might well consider printing a further supplement if someone will undertake the task.

It was not until 1932 that another additional publication appeared. This was *Bristol Church Plate*, by Canon R. T. Cole. Canon Cole generously contributed more than two thirds of the printing costs. The survey did not cover all the Bristol churches and when in 1964, S. A. Jeavons offered to prepare a catalogue of all the church plate in Bristol, the Society readily agreed to publish it. A year later S. A. Jeavons died and Mr. John Cooper agreed to complete the task. It is still in progress.

In 1935 the *Saxon Charters of Gloucestershire* by G. B. Grundy was issued to members. During the war years, the *Rolls of the Gloucestershire Sessions of the Peace, 1361–1398*, edited by E. G. Kimball, was issued as volume lxii of the *Transactions*.

The enthusiasm of W. L. King and Mr. Irvine Gray enabled the Society in 1961 to publish *A Gloucestershire and Bristol Atlas*, being a selection of maps and plans from the sixteenth century, including Isaac Taylor's large-scale map of the county. This volume was sold to members and the general public. In future, it is likely that all publications other than the *Transactions* will be undertaken by the Records Section.

ROBINSON BEQUEST COMMITTEE AND RECORDS SECTION

Through the generosity of Alfred Bruce Robinson, the Society received a legacy of £5,000 for the publication of parish records. He had been a member of the Society for about five years when he died in 1943, but it was not until after the death of his widow in 1947 that the first instalment of the bequest was received.

In order to carry out the terms of the legacy, the Society appointed a committee, known as the Robinson Bequest committee, under the chairmanship of Mr. (now Sir) Anthony Wagner. In 1951 the committee was reconstituted as the Records Section with Dr. Margaret Sharp as chairman. Wilfrid Leighton, who drafted the new constitution and guided the committee through the difficult period of establishing a publishing policy, became the first general editor and supervised the publication of the first volume *Bristol Marriage Licence Bonds, 1637–1700*. Since 1953 Mr. Patrick McGrath has been general editor and has seen nine publications through the press. As a result of Mr. Robinson's generous gift, the Society has been able to publish three volumes of marriage licences and allegations, two volumes of parish registers, one volume of medieval churchwardens' accounts, one volume of settlement papers and a guide to parish records in Bristol and Gloucestershire, all records in which Alfred Bruce Robinson was keenly interested. In addition, volumes dealing with records other than parish records have been published. The first of these was *Local Government in Gloucestershire, 1775–1800*, by Esther Moir. This was followed by F. D. Price's edition of *The Commission for Ecclesiastical Causes within the Dioceses of Bristol and Gloucester, 1574*. By 1972 most of the legacy had been spent and the Council decided to continue these publications by means of direct grants from the Society's general funds and in 1973 the Records Section became a standing committee of Council. As Gloucestershire, unlike Bristol, has no record-publishing society this provision meets a great need.

EXCAVATIONS

The pattern of Gloucestershire field archaeology had already largely emerged many years before the founding of the Bristol and Gloucestershire Archaeological Society in 1876, by the discovery and publication of numerous chambered long barrows, now known to be neolithic, and Roman villas. A long barrow at Avening had been explored in 1809, and Hetty Pegler's Tump was open in 1821 and again in 1854; others explored included Nympsfield (1862) and Rodmarton (1863). From the late seventeenth century onwards the discovery of several Roman villas and other buildings had been published, including Daglingworth (1690), Woodchester (1793), Witcombe (1818), Wadfield (1863), and Chedworth (1866). Chambered long barrows and Roman villas remain the antiquities for which the county is chiefly distinguished and known far beyond its borders. In addition, *Archaeologia*, vol. 19 (1821) included an able account of Cotswold hill-forts by T. J. Lloyd-Baker, great-grandfather of one of our oldest members, Lt. Colonel A. B. Lloyd-Baker.

Soon after the Society was formed, the celebrated grave-group of the Early Iron Age was discovered on Birdlip Hill in 1879 and presented to the Gloucester Museum through the good offices of John Bellows.

The first excavation undertaken by the Society was the exploration of the Roman villa at Tockington Park in 1887. As the Society had no funds a special appeal was made and £42 subscribed. The work began under the guidance of Sir John Maclean and a full report with coloured illustrations of the pavement was published in the *Transactions*.[1]

In 1899, the secretary, the Reverend (later Canon) William Bazeley wrote to the owner and tenant of Hayles Abbey asking for permission to carry out excavations on the site with a view to making a plan of its buildings and of saving the remaining cloister arches from collapse. This fine Cistercian abbey founded in the mid-thirteenth century had suffered three major fires, and after the dissolution the abbey was used as a quarry for almost three hundred years. Mrs. Dent of Sudeley Castle had constantly asked that something might be done to arrest the destruction but the opportunity was lacking until the Society decided to take action. William Bazeley with W. St. Clair Baddeley carried out the work, the Society making a generous contribution towards the cost. The excavations excited public interest and in that year 800 visitors came to the abbey. The following year, the Economic Life Assurance Society, the owners of the site, spent £50 in renovating an ancient barn to be used as a museum, while the Society met the cost of furnishing it. The ruins of the abbey and the contents of the museum were then vested in Trustees. Harold Brakspear, architect of Malmesbury Abbey, made a careful ground plan and published it with

[1] *TBGAS*, xii. 159–169; xiii. 196–202.

a report on the architecture in the *Transactions*.[1] Thirty years later, Sir James K. Fowler became Custodian of Hayles and with the experience gained as warden of Beaulieu Abbey, the mother house of Hayles, restored the site to decent order and built a more substantial museum to house the relics. In 1945 further excavations were carried out which revealed almost the whole plan of the abbey.[2] In 1948 the site was given to the National Trust and later the Trust vested the property in the Ministry of Works, now the Department of the Environment, which has recently re-furnished the museum.

In 1903 W. St. Clair Baddeley excavated the Roman villa at Ifold, Painswick, which had been discovered in 1868.[3] His report is an account of each day's work with photographs and plan. The finds were few but included an important R.P.G. stamped tile which was later described and published by F. J. Haverfield.[4]

It was reported to the Society in 1906 that the Roman villa at Witcombe was in danger. This villa had been accidentally discovered in 1818 and excavated by Samuel Lysons.[5] The site was on the estate of W. F. Hicks Beach who had taken steps to protect the tesselated floor, but it was now in need of further care. The Society issued an appeal which raised £180 and erected wooden buildings over the pavements. Within five years more damage was done by visitors walking over the floors and thereby loosening the tesserae and so it was decided that three floors should be taken up and relaid, but apparently this was not done, although a public appeal was made in 1912. Seven years later the villa was taken over by H.M. Office of Works and the balance of the fund which had been collected in 1912–13 was handed over. In 1938 Mrs. E. M. Clifford was asked by the Office of Works to re-excavate prior to consolidation of the fabric and the work continued until the outbreak of war in 1939. As soon as it was possible, a report on the excavation was published.[6] Since then the Ministry of Works has devoted several weeks each year to further excavations which we hope will continue until the whole has been examined and conservation undertaken.

[1] *TBGAS*, xxii, 257–71; xxiv, 126–35.   [2] *TBGAS*, lxv, 187–98.
[3] *TBGAS*, xxvii, 156–71.   [4] *TBGAS*, lii, 229.   [5] *Archaeologia*, xix, 178–83.
[6] *TBGAS*, lxxiii, 5–69.

In 1910–11 the Society through the President, Canon
Bazeley, superintended the excavation of Hucclecote villa where
the finds included a dozen or so bronze coins dating from A.D.
360 to A.D. 390 and tiles with inscriptions several of which were
unknown. The finds were placed in Gloucester Museum and
Canon Bazeley sent a note to *The Times*.[1] In 1933, C. de Lisle
Wells invited Mrs. Clifford to re-examine the site, which proved
to be of greater interest than was at first thought.[2]

The only work of excavation in which the Society participated in the following year took place at Sea Mills Farm on the
Kingsweston estate, Bristol, where trial trenches were dug with
a view to locating the whereabouts of a Roman site believed to
exist in the neighbourhood. The trial digging produced only
some twenty-five coins and one or two bronze ornaments. Ten
years later when the site was to be developed as a housing
estate, Professor E. K. Tratman carried out further excavations
which confirmed that Sea Mills was a Roman station. Again in
1934, 1937 and 1938 further excavations took place under the
guidance of Dr. D. P. Dobson. When in 1945 it was known that
the only land yet undisturbed was to be built upon, Mr. G. C.
Boon excavated the site.[3]

During the war years of 1914–18 the activities of the Society
had ceased and when peace came, the difficulty of obtaining
labour at a reasonable cost prevented the Society from undertaking any active work. However, in 1920 John E. Pritchard
proposed that an Excavation Fund be set up with an Excavation Committee, of which he became first chairman. When
therefore in 1922, the discovery of a Roman pavement in
Victoria Road, Cirencester was reported to the Society, the
Council was able to make a grant towards the excavation which
was supervised by W. St. Clair Baddeley. At the same time a
length of walling in the workhouse grounds at Cirencester was
excavated by him but the results were inconclusive.[4] Although
it was generally believed that the earthworks surrounding the
town were remains of defences of the Roman period, it was not
until 1952 when Miss D. M. Rennie excavated the site on behalf
of the Ministry of Works that it was established that the

---

[1] *The Times*, 22 Feb. 1911.   [2] *TBGAS*, lv, 323–76.
[3] *TBGAS*, xlv, 192–201; lix, 302–23; lxi, 202–23; lxvi, 258–95.
[4] *TBGAS*, xliv, 100–20.

construction was A.D. 175–200.[1] The result of this excavation raised the question of the probable site of the Dobunni tribe in this area. Mrs. Clifford, therefore, undertook the excavation of a site at Bagendon which proved to be their headquarters. The full report of this excavation was published in 1961 as *Bagendon: a Belgic Oppidum* by E. M. Clifford.

Because of the importance of Cirencester, the Roman city of *Corinium*, and the developments which were taking place there, the Society of Antiquaries in 1958 sponsored the formation of a Cirencester Excavations committee to direct emergency excavations in advance of building operations. Professor (Sir) Ian Richmond became the first chairman, Captain H. S. Gracie its honorary secretary and work began under the direction of Miss K. M. Richardson. Since the formation of the committee the Society has been pleased to make contributions each year.

The Roman villa at Chedworth discovered in 1864 has been of much interest to the Society. Indeed the Society may claim to have saved it by the initiative which it took in 1923 through W. St. Clair Baddeley in raising the subscription necessary to acquire the property and placing it in the care of the National Trust.

In 1924 the Society financed excavations at Chapel Haye, Churchdown undertaken by R. W. Murray and J. W. Barnard, then secretary of the Society's Excavation committee. Chapel Haye is a field of about six acres in which in 1904 St. Andrew's church was built. A great number of skeletons were found which, in the opinion of Sir Arthur Keith, were fourteenth century in date.[2]

In conjunction with the Cotteswold Field Club, the Society in 1925 undertook major excavations on Leckhampton Hill camp and the nearby round barrow, agreeing to meet the cost of labour from its Excavation Fund. The work was done with great care by W. H. Knowles, J. W. Gray, A. E. Paine and E. J. Burrow who published reports in the *Transactions*.[3] Recently further excavations on Leckhampton Hill have been undertaken as part of a programme of research excavation on the hill forts of the Cotswold scarp in the Cheltenham region. An

---

[1] *Antiquaries Journal*, XXXVII, 206–15.
[2] *TBGAS*, lv, 277–84.   [3] *TBGAS*, lviii, 81–112.

interim report on the first stage by Sara T. Champion has been published in the *Transactions*.[1]

For many years the farm buildings at the east end of Deerhurst church, and on the former chancel or sanctuary site were a matter of concern to the Society which always thought it desirable that the site should be cleared and the area excavated to find the plan of the apse and contiguous buildings. In 1926 W. H. Knowles, with the approval of the Society of Antiquaries and our own Society, obtained the consent of the Trustees of the Croome Estates and under his supervision, with the necessary funds raised by the Society, work began. The results gave great satisfaction and a full report was printed in the *Transactions*.[2] This report, like all those by W. H. Knowles, is an example of acute observation and experience, and was the more valuable for the exact drawings and plans included. In 1971 Mr. Philip Rahtz began further excavations on this site.

Belas Knap long barrow, which is now in the care of the Department of the Environment, is visited by a great number of people each year, being one of the finest and most complete examples in this country. It was opened between 1863 and 1865 when a series of chambers containing human remains was found, but unfortunately the excavation was inadequately supervised and the barrow was left in an unsatisfactory condition. The Society, anxious about the state of this important monument, approached the owner Colonel Fairfax Rhodes, who agreed to convey the site to the then Office of Works. This was done in 1928. There had been investigations by various people before a lengthy excavation was carried out by Sir James Berry for the Office of Works in 1929 and 1930. The Society raised the necessary money by public appeal, and Sir James uncovered a laterally chambered barrow with three (possibly four) chambers and a horned entrance with dry stone walling.[3] Later the Office of Works restored the barrow to its present form by using the evidence which the examination had produced.

In 1930 the Society published the results of many years' work by Mrs. Clifford at Barnwood. In passing it should be noted that her comprehensive report was acclaimed as a model of how such investigations should be recorded in that Mrs. Clifford had

[1] *TBGAS*, xc, 5–21.   [2] *TBGAS*, xlix, 221–58.
[3] *TBGAS*, li, 273–304; lii, 123–50.

enlisted the help of the foremost authorities on its various sections. Today this is normal practice.[1]

The Presidency of W. H. Knowles (1930), a noted architect of Newcastle upon Tyne who had taken an active part in excavations on sites along the Roman Wall, and had retired to Gloucestershire, introduced a remarkable stimulus, for in his Presidential address he urged the Society to undertake excavations on a sensible scale at a site of major importance such as Gloucester or Cirencester. This led to the formation of the Roman Gloucester committee which included Sir Mortimer Wheeler and R. G. Collingwood. From that date until the outbreak of the Second World War, interim reports on this work, compiled largely by W. H. Knowles were published in the *Transactions*. His second suggestion, that systematic excavation of some barrows be undertaken, was in fact carried out, as far as long barrows are concerned, by Mrs. Clifford at Notgrove, Nympsfield and Rodmarton; and during 1939–1945 this work was continued by W. F. Grimes at Bibury and Hampnett.

The observant eye of Miss Helen Donovan (Mrs. O'Neil) led to the discovery and excavation of a Saxon weaver's hut at Bourton-on-the-Water, which was published by G. C. Dunning with assistance from Miss Donovan.[2]

The problem of Spoonley Wood and Wadfield Roman villas has been with the Society since 1889. It was hoped that the Archaeological Trust might have taken care of it but while the committee was of the opinion that the preservation of these remains was of the highest importance, the cost of clearing the site and the difficulty of access made it impossible for the Trust with its limited funds to take over the property, even if it had been found legally possible. Sir Charles Peers, the Chief Inspector of the Office of Works, visited the sites and also decided that it would be impossible for them to take action. By 1944 the site and protective buildings were in a deplorable state and so the Society agreed to give £150 towards the cost of immediate repairs for which Thomas Overbury was in charge. Appeals were made for more money and the Pilgrim Trust gave £100, but by 1952 it was felt that further work would be misplaced and so the £100 was returned to the Trust, the members of the Society cutting down the ivy and other growth and covering the

[1] *TBGAS*, lii, 201–54.   [2] *TBGAS*, lviii.

pavements. While carrying out this work it was found that two of the pavements had previously been extensively restored.

In 1933 the Council noted with concern that the practice of carrying out excavations on important sites by enthusiastic but often inexperienced archaeologists was increasing. This enthusiasm for archaeological research was in many ways a most satisfactory sign, but it was pointed out that in some cases irreparable damage could be done by excavators who neglected the work of survey and record. The Council drew the attention of members to the fact that the Society was recognised by H.M. Office of Works as the proper authority for dealing with archaeological matters in the county and stressed that among its members were archaeologists of experience and national repute who were willing to advise and assist in properly authorised work. At this time and indeed during the 1920s and 1930s most of the excavations were carried out by members of the Society who met their own expenses, the Society only being able to offer comparatively small grants unless special appeals were made. The Society did of course meet the costs of publishing the reports of the excavations in the *Transactions*. The activities of most of the other county archaeological societies followed a similar pattern between the two wars.

In 1934, the Society visited Notgrove long barrow when Mrs. Clifford drew attention to the neglected state of this important monument which was unfenced and being trampled on by people and cattle. Sir Alan Anderson offered to protect it by enclosing it with stout railings. Later Mrs. Clifford excavated the barrow which proved to be a much larger monument than the existing plan revealed. At the west end a stone-built "rotunda" with a burial cist in the centre was discovered. The finds were presented to Cheltenham Museum, to join those presented by Witts in 1881, from his excavation there.[1]

In 1936, Mrs. Clifford excavated the earthworks at Minchinhampton, Amberley and Rodborough as a result of which she deduced that they constituted a formidable scheme of defence and were built in the Early Iron Age.[2] The following year she excavated Nympsfield long barrow and showed that the monument had a single cruciform plan and not double as formerly

---

[1] *Archaeologia*, lxxxvi, 119–61.   [2] *TBGAS*, lix, 287–307.

believed.[1] In the same year (1937) an excavation was begun on the medieval moated manor at Prestbury by Miss H. Donovan and Major J. G. N. Clift, and was carried out at intervals until the work was suspended by the outbreak of war in 1939. Excavations were resumed in 1951 at the invitation of the Ministry of Works.[2]

Rodmarton long barrow had been excavated by Samuel Lysons in 1868 and the skeletons which were then found were given to the Museum of Human Anatomy at Cambridge while the other finds were acquired by the British Museum. In 1939 this site was re-excavated by Mrs. Clifford and Professor Glyn Daniel, with important results.[3]

It was at this time that W. H. Knowles resigned as chairman of the Excavations committee and Mrs. E. M. Clifford who had been involved in a number of excavations in the county became chairman. The outbreak of war in 1939 meant of course an end to excavation work.

By 1943, an extensive amount of air-raid damage had been done in many parts of the country and it became clear that when reconstruction took place at the end of hostilities, archaeologists would be faced with problems of great magnitude and complexity. At the same time opportunities would arise for obtaining historical evidence from the excavation of bombed sites. With this in mind, the Society of Antiquaries convened a meeting of representatives of nearly all the archaeological societies as well as those of institutions and universities to consider the formation of a Council for British Archaeology. Such a Council would speak with authority both to the general public and to the government. In 1944 the Council for British Archaeology was founded as the central element for the planning of post-war archaeology in Great Britain. The Society, which had been a member of the Congress of Archaeological Societies, automatically supported the newly-established Council which assumed the functions of the Congress. Wishing to secure the fullest representation of archaeological interests throughout the country, regional groups were formed, each group being represented on the Council. Within five years the status of the

---

[1] *Proceedings of the Prehistoric Society*, N.S.4, 188–213.

[2] *TBGAS*, lxxv, 5–34.

[3] *Proceedings of the Prehistoric Society*, N.S.6, 133–65.

Council as the body representing British archaeological opinion received official recognition in the form of a grant-in-aid from the government. The grants provide for subsidising archaeological publications by constituent bodies and this Society has received several generous contributions.

After the war, the task of providing adequate funds to cover the cost of excavations was beyond the scope of most county societies. It was soon realised that money would have to be raised by public appeal if the desired excavations were to be carried out on the bombed sites in the heart of the ancient city of Bristol. The Lord Mayor thereupon launched an appeal and as a result the Ancient Bristol Exploration Fund was established which provided money for excavations to be carried out on the castle site and on sections of the town walls. Mr. Kenneth Marshall who directed the work of the last season prepared the report which was published in the *Transactions*.[1]

Although the Society was no longer able to sponsor excavations, several of its members carried them out at their own expense with perhaps a small grant from the Society. What remained of the Ivy Lodge round barrow at Kings Stanley was excavated by Mrs. Clifford in 1948. Some twenty years earlier it had been largely destroyed by the removal of stones to repair adjacent walls; it was here that the Woodchester beaker was found. Other finds included a coin of Constans A.D. 337–50, a bronze brooch which Sir Cyril Fox judged to be about A.D. 50–75 and skeletons which Sir Arthur Keith said belonged to the Romano-British period. The excavation revealed that while the cairn was built by the beaker folk, it was later used for Romano-British burials.[2]

In the same year (1948) extensive excavations were begun by Mrs. H. O'Neil on Whittington Court Roman villa through the kindness of Mrs. Evans Lawrence. It proved to be of three periods ranging from late 1st or early 2nd century to the 5th century demonstrating that life in Roman houses in this area continued until then.[3]

Most of the excavations both in Bristol and Gloucestershire were now being organised by the Ministry of Works or by Local Authorities. Members of the Society superintended or took part in many of these. Such excavations as that at Rodborough

[1] *TBGAS*, lxx, 5–50.   [2] *TBGAS*, lxix, 59–77.   [3] *TBGAS*, lxxi, 13–87.

Common by Miss D. M. Rennie,[1] Prestbury Moat by Mrs. O'Nell[2] and various excavations in Bristol are but a few examples.[3] The watchfulness of Mr. R. W. Knight, a member of the Society, led to the discovery near Tormarton in July 1968 of the skeletons of two young men who had been killed by being attacked, one from behind, by warriors armed with socketed spears of a type used between 1000 and 950 B.C. The skeletons and bronze spearheads were presented by the landowners, the Duke of Beaufort and Mr. B. B. Blake to Bristol City Museum. This find is here mentioned because only one other comparable find is known from the United Kingdom (Dorchester-on-Thames).[4]

In 1969 the construction of the M5 motorway provided an opportunity for archaeological investigation, and to this important work under the supervision of Mr. P. J. Fowler, the Society was able to make a generous grant, subsequently printing the reports in the *Transactions*.[5]

In 1973 a Committee for Rescue Archaeology in Avon, Gloucestershire and Somerset (CRAAGS) was set up to manage with the Inspectorate of Ancient Monuments in the Department of the Environment the large grants of money made by the Government for 'rescue archaeology' in the three counties. The Society is one of the bodies represented on the committee. In the same year the Avon Archaeological Council was established to promote the archaeological interests of the newly-constituted County of Avon. As the new county included within its boundaries the City of Bristol and the southern part of Gloucestershire, the Society became a constituent part of this Council.

PRESERVATION OF SITES AND BUILDINGS

From its very beginning the Society has been concerned with the preservation of important and historic sites and buildings in Gloucestershire and Bristol. In the early days when there was no legislation or statutory powers, the Council of the Society found itself often as the sole objector. Through the collective efforts of interested and informed members it was successful in getting

---

[1] *TBGAS*, lxxviii, 24–43.   [2] *TBGAS*, lxxv, 5–34.
[3] *TBGAS*, lxxix, 221–86.   [4] *TBGAS*, xci, 14–17.
[5] *TBGAS*, xc, 22–63; xcii, 21–81; xciii, 101–130.

sites protected and buildings saved from destruction. It would be rash to suggest that the Society accomplished all that it hoped for.

In 1882 strong protests were made to the Dean and Chapter of Bristol concerning the proposed destruction of the Minster House in College Green, but without success. On the other hand, John E. Pritchard was able to save the Registrar's House near the Cathedral. The Society was also successful in 1889 in preventing the conversion of the old church plate of Dursley into what was called "suitable vessels". When the tower of Westbury College, Bristol was threatened with destruction in 1893, the Society with the support of the Society of Antiquaries of London alerted the public to the fate of this building and through the liberality and public spiritedness of Arthur Shipley of Westbury-on-Trym, it was purchased and vested in Trustees for the use of the parish. The tower was in a bad state of repair and when a public appeal was launched for the necessary funds, the Society made a worthy contribution.

Between the years 1888 and 1909 the camps of Durdham Down and Stokeleigh in Leigh Woods on the other side of the river Avon were in danger. Through the generosity of Captain G. D. Wills, a member of the Society, the Stokeleigh camp and part of Leigh Woods was made over to the National Trust while another part was vested in the Leigh Woods Trust, on which the Society is represented. The woods are now held in trust for the enjoyment of the public and recently proposals have been made for the area to become the Avon Gorge National Nature Reserve.

In 1912 when H.M. Commissioners of Works approached county councils to furnish lists of monuments in danger of decay, the Bristol and Gloucestershire Archaeological Society gladly accepted the invitation to prepare lists of ancient monuments worthy of permanent protection in Gloucestershire. Although the lists were submitted, little came of them and such buildings as Llanthony priory, St. Oswald's priory and others continued to lack proper protection because of inadequate funds. After years of agitation by the Society, the City of Gloucester bought the ruins of St. Oswald's priory and the land adjacent and now the latter has been scheduled. It is also about to complete the purchase of Llanthony priory.

Before the establishment of Diocesan Advisory committees, the Bishop or the Chancellor of the diocese sought the opinion of the Society on many matters relating to churches. In 1917 the Chancellor asked advice on the removal of the two pulpits in Berkeley church and in 1919 on the removal of the Hicks family monuments in Chipping Campden church. In 1921 the Society urged the Bishop of Bristol to set up an Advisory committee, expressing the hope that the Society might be represented. Members have served on both the Gloucester and Bristol Diocesan Advisory committees and at present two members, Mr. David Verey and Mr. H. G. M. Leighton, are the respective chairmen. These committees meet generally on a monthly basis to consider proposals contained in petitions for faculties and archdeacon's certificates and to assist parishes which apply voluntarily for advice. When in 1926 the Bishop of Bristol set up a committee to enquire into the future of the city churches, he invited the Society to nominate two members to serve and J. J. Simpson and A. C. Powell were appointed.

In 1920 the Society urged the Town Trustees to resist any proposal to remove the Market Hall at Dursley which is such a distinctive feature of the town. Representations were made to the owners of the New Inn, Gloucester that in carrying out the necessary repairs proper regard be given for the preservation of the character of its elevation. But again without legislation the Society depended entirely on the goodwill of the owners.

As a result of the Town Planning Act of 1919, urban authorities of 20,000 or more population were required to prepare planning schemes, and in 1925 the Bristol and District Joint Planning committee asked that a member of the Society should serve on the committee. Five years later when the Cheltenham Borough Council was preparing its Town Planning scheme, it paid particular regard to the Society's request that important archaeological sites should be preserved, and W. H. Knowles and D. W. Herdman prepared lists of scheduled buildings. It was not however until the Town and Country Planning Act of 1932 that provision was made for the preservation of buildings. The Society appointed a committee to consider and advise on any matters which might arise under the provisions of this Act. The listing of buildings was tackled in a methodical way, the local secretaries seeking the help of members in their districts.

By 1939 most of the county and Bristol had been done. The lists for Bristol which had been prepared under the guidance of J. Ralph Edwards were to prove most valuable in 1940 after the heavy raids on the city when a number of the listed buildings were destroyed.

The Town and County Planning Act of 1947 made the first real attempt not only to list buildings of architectural and historic interest but to grade them. The Society was asked to assist in the compilation of such lists. Aware of the magnitude of the task, a joint committee with the Council for the Preservation of Rural England and the Gloucestershire Panel of Architects was set up and with the help of experienced members such as Mr. David Verey, Mr. H. F. Trew and Mr. Thomas Overbury and others such lists were prepared. By the end of 1952 more than half the local authorities in the country had lists of scheduled buildings and Gloucestershire was well covered. In 1956 the Ministry of Housing and Local Government agreed to send to the Council for British Archaeology notices in respect of proposed demolition of listed buildings, and these notices were then to be passed on to the county society. This has made the task easier, for it has ensured that the Society has been informed of all cases. Hundreds of applications have been dealt with by the Excavations and Buildings committee. In 1971 there was an alarming growth in threats to listed buildings and Gloucestershire came third in the country with 49 per cent more applications than in 1970. The next year the county dropped to fifth position. The Society has frequently found itself at variance with those responsible and has not hesitated to voice its criticism. At Public Enquiries it is regularly represented and without the expert knowledge and keenness of a few of its members, little could be accomplished.

Throughout the county in rural and urban areas alike, many cottages and small houses still survive. Although not of great architectural merit, they are of importance as representing the domestic architecture of the area. A majority of the threats arise from proposed re-development of property and road improvements. This is particularly so in some of our market towns, such as Dursley, Stroud and Wotton-under-Edge.

It is now possible to look back upon twenty-five years of planning legislation designed to protect buildings of historical and architectural interest. Societies such as ours engaged in conservation tend to complain about the weakness which still exists but it must be acknowledged that there has been real progress since the first Town and Country Planning Act. There are in the county buildings which are not protected by this Act, such as St. Oswald's priory, Blackfriars in Gloucester, and Odda's Chapel, Deerhurst. It was with great satisfaction that the Society learned in 1963 that the Ministry of Public Building and Works had taken into guardianship the remains of Blackfriars and Odda's Chapel.

One of the most interesting projects which the Society undertook was the complete restoration of Stoke Orchard church with the uncovering of its wall paintings. In 1949 Sir Arthur Clapham visited the church with Mrs. Clifford and was greatly impressed by its beauty and interest; he agreed to be one of the signatories to a public appeal made by Mrs. Clifford for funds to repair the buildings and uncover the wall paintings. The appeal was successful so that the fabric was repaired under the supervision of H. Stratton Davis without cost to the fund and the paintings uncovered by Mr. Clive Rouse. The National Coal Board which occupies Stoke Orchard Court gave valuable help in photographing the paintings. Without the assistance of the Society the task would have been impossible for a village of less than 400 people.

It can be said that in every case of preservation or reparation, members have taken an important part, and in some cases have been solely responsible for the success attained, which has often been secured largely owing to the feeling that the influence of the Society has been behind those members.

ARCHAEOLOGICAL TRUST

In 1928 the Royal Society of Arts suggested Arlington Row, Bibury which had been acquired by them should be cared for by the Bristol and Gloucestershire Archaeological Society. Thereupon the Council considered the proposal and decided to form a Trust, inviting members of the Society to subscribe and become members. With the aid of funds raised jointly by the two societies, the Trust cared for this group of picturesque houses for twenty-one years. Its success was due almost entirely to the efforts of its two chairmen J. J. Simpson and Wilfrid

Leighton. The Trust was also fortunate in having two architects H. Stratton Davis and H. F. Trew as its honorary secretaries.

When the Trust was established, it was hoped that other property and objects of archaeological and architectural interest would come under its control—a hope that remained unfulfilled. Sites such as the Roman villas at Spoonley Wood and Wadfield were offered to the Trust but could not be accepted owing to lack of funds.

By 1946 it became apparent that the Trust had not the money to keep Arlington Row in good repair and that within a few years it would be faced with considerable expenditure in providing amenities such as electric lighting and improved water and drainage facilities. It was felt that the management of the property would be better in the hands of some body such as the National Trust. After protracted negotiations, Arlington Row was conveyed to the National Trust in 1949. This course was made possible by the generous grant of £1,000 by the Pilgrim Trust, with the promise of further assistance when the cottages needed to be modernised. It was however largely through the efforts of Wilfrid Leighton, chairman of the Archaeological Trust at the time, that £3,000 was raised which enabled the National Trust to accept Arlington Row, the future of which is now so satisfactorily assured.

GLOUCESTER ROMAN RESEARCH COMMITTEE

In 1930 W. H. Knowles in his Presidential address summarised what was known of Roman Gloucester and urged a re-awakening of interest in the subject and the organisation of active research. The Council of the Society appointed a committee of persons representing the civic life of Gloucester and its scientific societies, and including persons of prominence interested in the history of Gloucester. Its function was to study the antiquities of Gloucester associated with the Romano-British period and to secure their preservation; to prepare a complete survey of the Roman site, and, as opportunity permitted to investigate its remains by excavation. An executive committee was appointed under the chairmanship of W. St. Clair Baddeley with Mr. L. E. W. O. Fullbrook-Leggatt as honorary secretary.[1]

[1] *TBGAS*, liii, 267–84.

Excavations began in the school grounds of the Crypt school and later, on the Barbican, Bon Marché and Upper Quay Street sites. W. H. Knowles supervised this work and his excellent and careful reports are published in the *Transactions*.[1]

During the Second World War all activities were suspended. In 1946 the Council proposed that the Gloucester Roman Research committee be resuscitated in view of the opportunities likely to occur for making investigations on sites of buildings scheduled for demolition. Mr. Fullbrook-Leggatt was elected chairman. And so with the City Museum, the committee helped to sponsor several important excavations on the sites of Nos. 1–5 King's Square, Friars Orchard and the King's school garden, all of which were done under the supervision of Mrs. H. E. O'Neil.

In 1967 the Gloucester Roman Research committee ceased to exist as such, being reconstituted as the Gloucester and District Archaeological Research Group.

THE LIBRARY

One of the original aims of the Society was to form libraries both at Bristol and Gloucester, the donors of books having the right to choose the place of deposit. During the first year the Society established friendly and co-operative relations with other county archaeological societies which resulted in the exchange of publications. In order to help the Society in its efforts to establish a library, the Royal Archaeological Institute presented a complete set of the *Archaeological Journal*; the Society of Antiquaries gave the current series of its *Proceedings* from the year 1859; and the Royal Historical and Archaeological Association of Ireland with equal liberality gave the fourth series of its *Journal* whilst the Monmouth and Caerleon Antiquaries Association donated a copy of the *Roman Antiquities of Lydney Park, Gloucestershire*. There is little doubt that these acquisitions were obtained through the enthusiasm and influence of Sir John Maclean. Many members also gave books. The first

---

[1] *TBGAS*, lvi, 65–81; lix, 37–38; lx, 166–168. One find, a limestone head of a man, dated first century A.D. has received national notice. The Roman head has Celtic elements and the sculpture is evidently a local product. (Mortimer Wheeler *Roman Art and Architecture*, p. 218).

list of books was printed in the *Transactions* of 1880 and thereafter a list appeared each year.

By 1886 it became apparent that the dividing of the Society's
books between Bristol and Gloucester caused great inconvenience and it was decided that there should be one library
and that it should be housed in Gloucester Museum. The
number of books added to the library so increased that the
accommodation became inadequate, and in 1895 the Society's
books were moved from the Gloucester Museum to John
Bellows' house in Eastgate, Gloucester, where the Society
shared a large room as a library with the Cotteswold Field Club.
Rules were drawn up for the use of the library and the secretary
was responsible for the care of it. The books were to be kept
under lock and key, the secretary was to prepare a catalogue, a
copy of which was sent to every member. The library was open
once a week for the purpose of issuing books. At that time £25
was spent annually, £10 being paid to the Librarian, £10 spent
on binding and the purchase of new books and £5 to the
Gloucester Museum.

In 1902 the library was greatly enhanced when Mrs. Royce
presented her late husband's archaeological books to be kept as
the Royce Memorial Collection. This important collection still
forms the basis of the Society's library. Canon David Royce of
Stow on the Wold was a noted scholar and his collection of
books and manuscripts is witness to this. Because his interests
were wide, the books cover general antiquities, architecture,
campanology, ecclesiology, ethnology, folklore, genealogy and
heraldry.

Due to the efforts of John E. Pritchard a library was formed
in Bristol and was housed in the Society's Bristol Room at the
Literary and Philosophic Club in Berkeley Square, Bristol. It
was here that the Bristol members of the Society met for lectures
and *conversaziones*. The first list of books was printed in the
Transactions. When in 1921 the Society held meetings at the
Red Lodge, Bristol, its Bristol library was transferred there.
Twelve years later the library was moved to the City Museum.

Once again the accommodation at Eastgate, Gloucester
became inadequate and the Society was hard pressed to find
suitable premises. Prolonged discussions with the City authorities for rooms within the Public Library continued for about

three years. In 1913 arrangements were made for the Society's library to be housed in a room in the Public Library under the supervision of the library staff. This meant that the library would be accessible daily from 9 a.m. to 9 p.m. These excellent arrangements were due to the influence and assistance of Roland Austin, then City Librarian. He became the Society's first librarian and the Society owes him a great debt. After his appointment a library committee was established to manage and supervise the library and an annual grant was made from the Society's funds to buy new books. He was responsible for the first catalogue of what then numbered 3,000 books which were valued at £1,000. It is interesting to note in passing that the cost of moving that stock of books by Roland Austin's assistants was 12s. 9d. For nearly forty years Roland Austin was the Society's librarian, during which time he built up a fine library. On his resignation, P. W. Bennett took over and in 1956 was succeeded by Mr. A. J. I. Parrott. On his retirement Mr. V. A. Woodman was appointed. When the library was moved to St. Michael's Rectory, opposite the City Library, in 1957, the stock of books was 5,728.[1] The Society is indebted to successive City Librarians of Gloucester who in turn have looked after the library. Both the Society and the city of Gloucester have derived mutual benefit from this arrangement.

MEETINGS

From the very beginning, visits to places of interest in Bristol and Gloucestershire played a big part in the activities of the Society. This is not surprising for Gloucestershire is one of the loveliest counties in England, full of beautiful villages, interesting market towns, noble churches and fine manor houses, all set in gentle landscape. Also the county can boast of having more than its share of historical monuments.

At first a summer meeting of three or four days' duration was held. This was followed by two winter meetings, one at Bristol and the other at Cheltenham or Gloucester. When the winter

---

[1] They are in a pleasant room which serves the purpose of a reading room for members of the Society. There are a considerable number of books on Bristol and Gloucestershire. Added to these are many books giving background material for the study of local history and a wide selection of county histories.

meeting of 1881 was held at Cheltenham, the extreme inclemency of the weather made it impossible for many members to attend because the roads and railways were impassable from drifted snow. The following winter meeting was not held until April 1883 and thereafter became known as the spring meeting. The one-day autumn meeting was not introduced until as late as 1937. In the early days some of the districts, particularly the West Gloucestershire district of the Society, were very active and arranged one or two meetings each year.

In 1903 evening meetings began in Bristol and Gloucester and in 1905 extended to Cheltenham and Tewkesbury. At all these meetings papers were read on archaeological and historical subjects and were often accompanied by exhibitions of local antiquities or of special collections made by individual members. A local committee was appointed to make the necessary arrangements but later one person, the Meetings secretary, became responsible.

The first summer meetings was held in Gloucester on the 23 August 1876 when Sir William Vernon Guise of Elmore Court presided and 100 members were present. At the business meeting, Robert Lang, the Treasurer, who held office for one year, reported that the newly-formed Society was financially sound with a balance of £672, despite the heavy expenses incurred in its inauguration. In his Presidential address, Sir William Vernon Guise spoke of the labours of such men as Stukeley, Dugdale and Lysons in preserving so much of the past. He said that "it was only within the last 40 years or so that archaeology—the scientific study of antiquities had been pursued in a systematic manner by large bodies of enquirers associated for a common purpose".

At the close of the business meeting, John Bellows, the head of a distinguished firm of printers in Gloucester, guided the party round the city, tracing the Roman wall. Afterwards the members visited the Cathedral under the guidance of J. D. T. Nibblett and F. W. Waller. In the evening the first of the Society's dinners took place at the Bell Hotel at a cost of 4 shillings excluding wines. After dinner three papers were read. On the next day, the members left the hotel in brakes to visit Deerhurst and Tewkesbury where the Mayor gave a sumptuous luncheon in the grounds near the Abbey. That evening eight papers were read! One of the attractive features was the temporary museum where members displayed a large variety of interesting exhibits. On the third day, members went by a special train to Berkeley, where Lord Fitzhardinge invited them to inspect the castle; and after visiting the church, one hundred members had lunch at the Berkeley Arms Hotel. This was the first of many delightful summer meetings at which the annual business meeting was held. In 1953 the annual meeting was divorced from the summer meeting and held alternately in Bristol and Gloucester, usually on a Saturday in March. The change of date allowed more members to attend and hear the Presidential address.

In 1877 the summer meeting was held in Cirencester when the Rt. Hon. the Earl Bathurst was President. This was a sad occasion for Lord Bathurst died during his year of office. It is worthy of note that he gave his Presidential address at the age of 87.

When the Society met in Bristol in 1878 "upwards of 100 people assembled at the Queen's Hotel, Clifton at 10 o'clock. Some delay occurred in starting, in consequence of the fine morning having tempted a larger number to join in the excursion than was expected, and hence additional carriage accommodation had to be provided; but, through the exertions of Mr. John Reynolds, the conductor of the excursion, this was soon obtained, and at about half past ten the whistle gave the signal to start, and a somewhat long train of four-horse brakes and wagonettes and private carriages passed through Whiteladies Road and across Durdham Down to Westbury-on-Trym."

Cheltenham was visited in 1879 and on that occasion the auditors drew attention to a debit balance of £57 "arising in a great measure to the heavy expenses incurred there" and asking that "greater vigilance should be exercised to curtail expenditure at the annual meetings". One of the places visited was Birdlip where the party had luncheon at the Black Horse Hotel (now a private house). It was here that the Cotteswold Field Club had been formed in 1846. The Reverend Mr. Brown gave a long dissertation on the Roman campaigns of the district, after which he conducted the party to the site which he believed to have been a British village close by. It was, however, "considered that Mr. Brown was mistaken in his theory". The time occupied in this investigation rendered it necessary to abandon the intended visit to the church and castle of Brimpsfield.

The following year an invitation was received to meet in Stroud for which occasion it had been arranged to uncover the Woodchester pavement, for the first time for many years. To meet the additional costs, the local committee suggested that the general public be admitted to the *conversazione* in the evening on payment of five shillings for gentlemen and three shillings and sixpence for ladies. It proved a popular meeting with at least 200 persons present. The President (John Dorrington) gave a diversified address on the Stroud area describing life in the hills from prehistoric times to the present day. At the close of the annual meeting, the party at once proceeded to the carriages which were drawn up in front of the Subscription Rooms and here the first mishap occurred. The carriages were engaged to convey a certain number of persons but while the meeting was taking place, a great many additional tickets were issued to persons who had given no notice to the secretaries, consequently no provision had been made for their accommodation. These, and some persons who had no tickets, took possession of the carriages and so when it was time to start there were about twenty members and ladies left in the street. Another brake was soon provided and with the addition of a fly sufficient accommodation was found. Then the second mishap took place. As they began to climb the hill to call at Bownham Park "the fly drawn by a single horse and containing Sir William Guise, Mrs. Elwes and another lady and gentleman got as far as Butter Row when the horse refused to go any further and after repeated attempts the driver said 'he could not get him to go on, and he must leave the party in the road and return home'." This he did and the ladies and gentlemen sat down at the road side where they were found three-quarters of an hour afterwards by Mr. Halliwell, who hearing of their misfortune at once drove to their assistance. These detailed accounts of the excursions are printed in the *Transactions*.

On the visit to Tintern and St. Briavels, the writer reported "The weather was perfect, showing beautiful examples of sunlight and shadow. The shadows of the flying clouds chased each other over the broad expanse, whilst the whole river in some places appeared to be black as ink and in others glistened like a silver mirror." Today, high printing costs have removed from the reports such poetic descriptions of the scenery.

Members often received gracious hospitality when visiting country houses. At the Chepstow meeting 1881, the Society was entertained by Mr. and Mrs. Marling at Sedbury Park when "the tables were abundantly supplied, not only with tea and its concomitants but with wine and the choicest fruits of the season for those who preferred refreshments of that nature".

Travelling around the countryside in horse-drawn brakes restricted the limits of their daily wanderings to what now seems a very small area. The journeys were made in a leisurely manner, often stopping to breathe the horses, giving an opportunity for enjoying the beauty of the countryside. Sometimes journeys were made by train and the railway companies were particularly accommodating. In 1885 the Midland Railway Company was asked to stop the express from Gloucester at Ashchurch. When visiting Newnham, the Severn and Wye and Severn Bridge Railway Company conveyed the members by a special train through the Forest of Dean to Lydbrook Junction and from there to Kerne Bridge and Symonds Yat where an excellent lunch "was most ably served by host Davis." After lunch, the party rowed down the Wye. In 1886 members visited Deerhurst leaving Gloucester on the "Berkeley Castle" steamboat and making their way up river to Deerhurst Pier.

When General A. H. L. F. Pitt-Rivers was President, the Society held its annual meeting jointly with the Wiltshire Natural History and Archaeological Society at Cirencester. The summer meeting of 1894 was held at Ledbury, the second time in three years. They met in the ancient Town Hall and conducted their business amidst the cries of the market hucksters underneath. The President Michael Biddulph received the members at the Lodge where "the gardens were prettily illuminated and an excellent selection of music was played".

In 1898 the Society visited London for a week and the attendance was greater than at any other meeting. For a county society to pay an organised visit to London was a great achievement. But under the Presidency of Sir John Dorrington and a committee of distinguished men, the visit was bound to be a success. The Middle Temple was visited under the guidance of

Judge Baylis, Sir John Stuart Knill talked about the Guildhall, Lord Dicton showed members round the Tower of London, whilst Sir Christopher Turner described the city churches.

The summer meeting at Tewkesbury in 1902 was claimed to be the most pleasant and instructive gathering ever held under the auspices of the Society. Practically a new generation of archaeologists had taken the place of that which composed the Society at its inauguration. Because of the big attendance it was suggested that membership of the Society be limited to 500, but this proposal was rejected and a steady increase in membership continued. The popularity of the meetings was due no doubt to efficient organisation and good leadership. For every meeting a programme with archaeological notes was issued. These notes for many years were prepared by Canon Bazeley and usually occupied thirty pages. Lodging arrangements were always made: a single room with attendance was 2s. 6d. and a double-bedded room, 4s. Luncheon was served at 2s. 6d. and table d'hôte breakfast was available at 2s. The cost of the annual dinner in 1905 was still 4s. exclusive of wine. Such men as Canon Bazeley and W. St. Clair Baddeley acted as guides. With many experts in the field, discussions at these meetings were lively. It has been said that on the rare occasions that these two men agreed, one could be sure of reaching eternal truth. Many amusing incidents are recorded. On one occasion when visiting a parish church to see some newly-discovered medieval frescoes they were aghast to find that the sexton, having been directed to see that everything was bright and clean, "had been smitten with the unhappy inspiration of white washing over the frescoes because they made the wall look so dirty and patchy".

When in 1911, some members asked to be allowed to travel in motor cars because the coaching and railway facilities were not convenient, the Council reluctantly abrogated the rule, asking that due care should be taken to avoid inconvenience to those members travelling in horse brakes. It was not until 1914 that the motor charabanc first appeared to take members round the Warwickshire countryside in the last summer before the war. From 1914 to 1918 only the one-day annual meeting was held, but after the war, a two-day summer meeting took place in Bristol in July 1919.

The summer meeting of 1920 was at Malvern when Earl

Sir William Vernon Guise, Bt.

Founder President of the Society.

By courtesy of Lady Guise of Elmore Court   *Photograph by G. Kelsey*

Canon William Bazeley

President of the Society in 1908 and Secretary from 1879 to 1907.

Roland Austin

President of the Society from 1939 to 1944 and Editor from 1923 to 1948.

By courtesy of Gloucester City Librarian

John E. Pritchard
President of the Society in 1918.

By courtesy of Mr. C. Pritchard

Mrs. Elsie Clifford
First woman President of the Society in 1949.

Dr. Joan Evans
President of the Society in 1961 and Editor from 1950 to 1959.

Aerial photograph of Belas Knap long barrow.

Dry-stone plugging in Rodmarton long barrow.

Corinium Museum: Stone relief of Genii Cucullati.

By courtesy of Corinium Museum   *Photograph by Annette Thornton*

Corinium Museum: Stone statuette of Mother-Goddess. (*Scale cms.*)

By courtesy of Corinium Museum   *Photograph by C. Shuttleworth*

Private Collection: Bronze statuette of Mars from Wycomb.

Photograph by Royal Commission on Historical Monuments (England)

Gloucester City Museum (on loan): Stone relief of Minerva from Lower Slaughter.

By courtesy of Society of Antiquaries of London

Beauchamp as President invited the members to Madresfield Court, where they were entertained to tea and shown a specially-arranged exhibition of silver, deeds and books. In the same year arrangements were made for a meeting at Chepstow and Tintern, but owing to the impossibility of obtaining motors and accommodation for lunch and tea, the meeting was abandoned. The difficulties caused by the railway strike made it necessary to cancel the spring meeting in 1921. The summer meeting was held jointly with the Royal Archaeological Institute in Gloucester. This was the first meeting planned by Roland Austin and was acclaimed a great success. When, however, Austin became editor in 1923, J. J. Simpson agreed to relieve him of the work and organised his first meeting at Tetbury and Malmesbury.

In 1923 the meeting which was to have been at Chipping Campden was at the last moment postponed owing to an epidemic of smallpox which had prevailed in Gloucester for some months and because of "natural apprehension felt by the residents of Campden at visitors from the infected area coming in their midst".

To celebrate the fiftieth anniversary of the formation of the Society, the spring meeting was held in Gloucester on 21 April 1926. By this time Roland Austin was again Meetings secretary and when in 1928 he asked Major H. Stratton Davis to take on the office of honorary general secretary, Stratton Davis would only do so if the two offices were separated. Therefore Thomas Overbury, an architect with an intimate knowledge of Gloucestershire and the surrounding counties, consented to become Meetings secretary provided that he had sole responsibility and control for the arrangement and conduct of the spring and summer meetings. He arranged a number of excellent visits, often acting as guide. The meetings became increasingly popular and were attended by unusually large numbers of members. Thomas Overbury was helped by W. H. Knowles and G. McNeil Rushforth, who shared the work of preparing programmes. This exceptional "triumvirate" came to an end first by the resignation of Thomas Overbury in 1934 and then by the death of G. McNeil Rushforth in 1938 when the Society lost one of its most distinguished members, a man who rendered services of no ordinary kind. Gordon McNeil Rushforth became a member in 1920 and immediately interested himself in the planning of the meetings of the Society, taking an active part in the preparation of the itineraries. For him an archaeological meeting was no mere picnic or excursion: it was a serious task, including much preparation and research. In his wide knowledge of a number of subjects, especially ecclesiastical glass, its provenance, history and heraldry, he was excelled by no one. He knew the great churches of France and could always draw upon them for comparison. Rushforth had a most attractive manner and all who knew him valued the association. He contributed important papers to the *Transactions* on the glass of Gloucester Cathedral, Tewkesbury Abbey and the Lord Mayor's Chapel, Bristol. His writing is characterised by exact information, perfect finish and lucid style.

When Thomas Overbury resigned as Meetings secretary, the office was vacant for two years, until E. W. Lovegrove took over. Although not a young man, he carried out this arduous task with great enthusiasm. In 1937 he arranged an autumn meeting which became a regular part of the annual programme. In 1938 the Society visited Northampton. Not since 1898, the year of the famous meeting in London, had the Society ventured so far. He continued until the outbreak of war in 1939 when the autumn and spring field meetings were abandoned. It had been planned to arrange a summer meeting in 1940 to prevent the Society from becoming moribund, but even this, intended "as a mere shadow of the usual full programme", had to be cancelled in view of the possibility of invasion. All routine work was delegated to the officers for the duration of the war and only annual general meetings held.

After the war, Colonel Barwick Browne, a retired Indian Army officer with experience in organising meetings, was appointed. His efficient organisation was appreciated by members. He arranged many splendid meetings taking the Society to Banbury, Lichfield and Salisbury. The summer meeting at Lichfield was a memorable occasion. For the first time the Society had elected a woman President, Mrs. E. M. Clifford, and E. W. Lovegrove who was nearly 80 years of age acted as guide, describing the churches of Tamworth, Repton, Barton-under-Needwood and Lichfield Cathedral with great vigour. The following year, when Lady Apsley was President, she invited the Society to hold its annual meeting at Cirencester Park when she read her Presidential address and entertained the members to a fork supper.

By 1955 Colonel Browne felt that he must resign and George M. Robins took over the onerous duties. With the help of his wife for seven years he organised some of the happiest and most successful meetings. It was during his time that the Society began to stay in university halls of residence rather than in hotels. On his retirement in 1962, Mr. Paul Page was appointed. His first meeting, which was centred on Withington, made history, when seven houses were visited in one day. For the first time, the Society visited the Gower coast under the guidance of the President, Dr. Glyn Daniel. At the summer meeting in Oxford the following year, the Society was fortunate in enlisting the aid of its President the Very Reverend Douglas Harrison, then Dean of Bristol and Professor Ian Richmond, two Oxford men. They not only acted as guides but gave delightful informal talks in the evenings after dinner. For the most part, the Society depended on a few of its members to act as guides at the various meetings. One such distinguished member was W. I. Croome, who for several years was guide on visits to the churches in Gloucestershire. When he died in 1967 the then Dean of Gloucester the Very Reverend Seriol Evans said of him: "It was his love of the church and of all beautiful things expressed in the work of men's hands, combined with an eagerness to impart to others from the stores of his own experience that was the source of his inspiration." We shall not esaily forget the tall and dynamic figure that stood beneath many a Gloucestershire chancel arch to address the Society.

When Mr. Page resigned in 1968 the first woman Meetings secretary was appointed. Miss G. R. Wright held the office for only two years before her tragic death in a motor car accident. Miss Dulcie Bailey, who for ten years had helped with the administration of field meetings, took over the whole task.

After the war when field meetings began again, the Council dropped the practice of including in the *Transactions* the descriptive notes which formed a valuable record of the Society's excursions and lectures, and were enjoyed by those members unable to attend the meetings. However, in 1964 the Council somewhat reluctantly agreed that reports of the meetings should be printed. These have proved most useful as a record of many delightful excursions. It has not been possible to describe all the meetings and indeed detailed accounts of the visits made during the past twenty years would be out of place, for many members will remember them with much pleasure.

To supplement the field meetings there were evening lectures. On the 22 December 1903 the first evening meeting was held in Gloucester. Francis F. Fox, who was President of Council, presided and read a paper on Roods and Rood Screens, illustrated by means of the magic lantern and lime light. H. Medland followed with a talk on the various buildings which had stood on the site of the Wilts. and Dorset Bank at the Cross in Gloucester. Members subscribed five shillings for each meeting and received two tickets for reserved seats. Carriages were to be ordered for 9.30 p.m. Then followed a series of winter lectures. Later the subscription varied and by 1914 the general public could purchase tickets at one shilling for each lecture. For ten years H. T. Bruton of Gloucester, a partner in the firm of Bruton and Knowles, organised these successful meetings which attracted large audiences. In 1913 Roland Austin took over and so began his long and distinguished service to the Society.

At about the same time, similar evening lectures were arranged in Bristol. Begun by John Latimer, they were continued by John E. Pritchard until 1910, when Lewis Upton Way carried on until 1914. No meetings were held during the war years, either in Gloucester or Bristol, but when they were resumed in Bristol on the 17 November 1919, Wilfrid Leighton became secretary for Bristol. From 1920 the meetings were in the Red Lodge at Bristol. The tickets which were issued stated that Morning Dress would be worn and that coffee would be served from 8 to 8.10 p.m. In 1924 Sir Charles Oman while President gave one of the evening lectures in Bristol and on that occasion a dinner was held in the Red Lodge in his honour. The charming menu card still survives and is signed by those present. They dined on Clear Turtle Soup, Tranches of Salmon, Vol au Vent of Sweetbreads, Roast Golden Plover, Benedictine Jelly with Apricot Cream, Foie Gras on Toast, and Dessert.

Evening lectures continued to be held in Bristol and Gloucester until about 1936 when attendances at these meetings declined so much so that Mr. C. Roy Hudleston, who was then secretary for Bristol, was reluctant to continue them. From 1937 to 1944 no evening meetings were arranged. In 1943 Miss Elizabeth Ralph was appointed secretary for Bristol and she arranged both winter lectures and evening field meetings which have continued with great success through the efforts of successive secretaries for Bristol. It was not so easy to organise these meetings in Gloucester. From time to time Mrs. E. M. Clifford arranged a lecture either in Gloucester or Cheltenham, but it was not until Mr. Robins agreed to take over that much success was achieved. However, it became increasingly difficult to get support for evening lectures in Gloucester and after 1958 only afternoon or evening excursions in the summer have been held.

Of necessity this is no more than a brief account of the activities of the Society during the past one hundred years, but it is fitting that such a record should be compiled. The contribution which the Society has made during this period to historical knowledge, the development of archaeology and the preservation of buildings in Bristol and Gloucestershire is an important one and has been due to the energy and enthusiasm of its members. Today the membership at over 800 is higher than it has ever been. The Bristol and Gloucestershire Archaeological Society can look forward with confidence to another century of useful work.

II

The Archaeology of Megaliths: an historical note

By Glyn Daniel

In his presidential address to the first meeting of the Bristol and Gloucestershire Archaeological Society, Sir William Guise said, "It is only within the last forty years or so that archaeology—the scientific study of antiquities—has been pursued in a systematic manner by large bodies of enquirers associated for a common purpose." To a certain extent he was right in ascribing the beginnings of archaeology in Britain to the eighteen-thirties. But on the continent of Europe it had begun earlier, and when Christian Jurgensen Thomsen opened the Danish National Museum to the public in 1819, it was organised in an archaeological way. There were three divisions of the prehistoric material then on display, and these were arranged according to a supposed Age of Stone, Age of Bronze and Age of Iron.[1]

At first this division was based on a theory of the technical development of man's tools: it was a museum ordering based on a technological model of the past, but quite soon this model was proved to be correct by excavations in the barrows and peat bogs of Denmark, and in the prehistoric villages along the edges of the Swiss lakes. In 1865, a decade before Sir William Guise spoke, Sir John Lubbock in his *Prehistoric Times* proposed to divide the Age of Stone into the Palaeolithic and Neolithic—neo-Greek words which he coined—and later the Mesolithic was established between them. By the end of the century the prehistoric past was revealed as belonging to five stages viz., Palaeolithic, Mesolithic, Neolithic, Bronze Age and Iron Age, and this was the framework of man's past, within which archaeologists worked, until the Carbon 14 revolution provided them with a completely independent dating system which

[1] G. E. Daniel, *The Three Ages* (Cambridge, 1943); *A Hundred Years of Archaeology* (1950); *The Origins and Growth of Archaeology* (1967).

enabled them to look historically rather than archaeologically at the past.

There could be no archaeology of megaliths until this technological three- (or five-) age model was accepted, and until the excavation of megaliths was carefully done and interpreted in terms of this model. Those who, like myself, write about the history of archaeology make a distinction between antiquary and archaeologist; the antiquary guessed at the past of early man or interpreted it by reference to literary sources, the archaeologist uses the material remains themselves as the key to the past. There were, of course, endless antiquarian speculations about megaliths but these were in terms of literary sources like the Bible and classical writers. Many of the folk names for megaliths such as Samson's Bratful are derived from biblical sources, and the attribution of monuments to giants is an indication of the belief that there were once giants in the land. One of the great fascinations of what Caesar and others wrote about the pre-Roman inhabitants of Gaul and Britain was their account of that curious sect of wise men, teachers and priests referred to as Druids, and it is not surprising therefore that early antiquaries in Britain and France attributed megaliths to the Druids.

John Aubrey, in his *Essay towards the Description of the North Division of Wiltshire* written between 1659 and 1670, says of the Ancient Britons, "Their priests were Druids some of their temples I pretend to have restored, as Avbury, Stonehenge etc as also British sepulchres." He was the first person to bring Avebury and Stonehenge out of guesswork into the context of prehistory. "The celebrated antiquity of Stonehenge" he wrote, "as also that stupendous but unheeded antiquity at Avbury, I affirme to have been temples, and built by the Britons."

The Reverend Henry Rowlands, whose dates were 1655 to 1723, and who was vicar of Llanidan on the island of Anglesey, wrote a book, published in Dublin in 1723, entitled *Mona Antiqua Restaurata: an Archaeological Discourse on the Antiquities, Natural and Historical, of the Isles of Anglesey, the Ancient Seat of the British Druids*. In this work he attributed all the Anglesey, and indeed all the Welsh, megalithic monuments, usually referred to as cromlechs, to the Druids. And so did William Stukeley, that brilliant eighteenth-century antiquary: yet we must remember that though he was besotted with Druidomania he was an accurate field archaeologist and made observations of a basic archaeological character which were of very great importance. It was by a careful assessment of his plans and drawings that the Cunningtons were able to rediscover the Sanctuary on Overton Hill.[1]

Well before the nineteenth century, strictly archaeological observations had been made about megaliths. Edward Lhwyd, Keeper of the Ashmolean Museum in Oxford, and one of the great polymaths of the end of the seventeenth century, was in Ireland in 1699 when the great prehistoric tomb of New Grange was discovered in a hitherto unknown huge mound. He described the finding of this great megalithic tomb, noting the carved stone at the entrance and the carvings on the walls and roofing stones of the tomb. He also noted that a Roman coin had been found at the top of the barrow and commented, with great percipience, "A gold coin of the Emperor Valentinian, being found near the top of this mount, might bespeak it Roman; but that the rude carving at the entry and in the cave seems to denote it a barbarous monument. So, the coin proving it ancienter than any Invasion of the Ostmans or Danes, and the carving and rude sculpture, barbarous; it should follow, that it was some place of sacrifice or burial of the ancient Irish."[2]

There had been excavations in megalithic monuments long before archaeology became a formal discipline in the nineteenth century. In 1588 the *langdysser* or "long-dolmen" known as the Langben Rises Høj, north of Roskilde, in Denmark, was excavated. Although the results of the excavations were meagre —some urns and other unexciting finds—the excavation was deliberately conducted to find out the name and nature of the monument. The archaeologists who excavated this site had hoped to find the remains of the giant-warriors described in folk-ballads, but were disappointed.[3]

In 1685 a megalithic tomb was discovered and excavated at Cocherel near Dreux in the valley of the Eure in northern

[1] S. Piggott, *William Stukeley: an Eighteenth Century Antiquary* (Oxford, 1950), pp. 48-9.

[2] E. Lhwyd to Dr. Tancred Robinson, *Philosophical Transactions of the Royal Society* (1712), xxvii, 503-4.

[3] O. Klindt-Jensen, *The History of Scandinavian Archaeology* (1975).

France. The tomb was obviously a good example of what we should now call the Paris Basin type of *allée couverte* or gallery grave. The records relating to this excavation are among the earliest systematic accounts of a megalithic tomb, or for that matter any, excavation, in western Europe. They describe a tomb six feet high, roofed with megalithic slabs, one of which was thirteen to fourteen feet in length. There was clear evidence of cremation and inhumation in the tomb and this puzzled the excavators who decided the remains were those of a battle between the ancient Gauls and the barbarians from outside Gaul. The Abbé of Cocherel gave it as his view that the people buried in the megalithic tomb were Huns who had arrived in France under Attila. Dom Bernard de Montfaucon described the Cocherel find in his *L'Antiquité expliquée et representée en figures* published in Paris in 1791. He too commented on the existence of cremated and inhumed remains in the same tomb, and decided that the burnt bodies were Gauls, while the un-burnt bodies belonged to "some barbarous Nation, that knew not yet the Use either of Iron or of any metal". Incidentally this is one of the very earliest clear statements of the idea of a stone age in the early past of man. Montfaucon compared the Cocherel tomb with similar tombs in northern Europe of whose existence he had learned through the work of Olaus Magnus, Archbishop of Uppsala, whose *De gentibus septentrionalibus*, published in 1555, attributes these monuments not to giants or fairies, but to ancient historical peoples—the Goths and the Suevi. Montfaucon himself was most anxious to disabuse people of the idea that the Cocherel tomb had contained giants. "The bodies were of the common stature" he wrote "whatever some may have affirmed to the contrary."[1]

The proper archaeological study of megaliths began in the early nineteenth century, when archaeology itself began. Indeed the word megalith which comes from two Greek words *megas*, great and *lithos*, stone was, according to the Oxford English Dictionary, first used in 1839 in the title of a book by A. Herbert called *Cyclops Christianus, or an Argument to disprove the supposed Antiquity of Stonehenge and other Megalithic Erections*. In 1865, when Sir John Lubbock wrote his best-selling book *Prehistoric Times*, he referred to Stonehenge as "the most exciting of our megalithic

[1] G. E. Daniel, *The Prehistoric Chamber Tombs of France* (1960).

monuments" and in 1872 when Fergusson published his *Rude Stone Monuments in all Countries: their Age and Uses*, he referred to the thousands of our countrymen who annually went to see the French megaliths at Carnac.

James Fergusson's book was not the first general treatment of megaliths: the Baron Bonstetten's *Essai sur les Dolmens* was published in Geneva in 1865. In the early twentieth century two very important works appeared: Oscar Montelius's *Der Orient und Europa*, and T. Eric Peet's *Rough Stone Monuments and their Builders* (1912). All these important and pioneer works between 1865 and 1912 suffered from two fundamental defects which have bedevilled the study of megalithic monuments from the nineteenth century until now. First, and perhaps Herbert's *Cyclops Christianus* with its phrase "other megalithic erections" was to blame here, it was assumed that all monuments using the characteristic features of what is referred to as megalithic architecture, namely orthostatic walling and capstones for roofing, were somehow connected wherever in the world they might be found. Out of this misconception developed the idea of a "megalithic race", or at least "a megalithic people". There is no basis for this idea at all, and the error is one only too common in archaeology and ancient history. Because pyramidal buildings occur in Central America and Egypt it is assumed that all pyramids must be connected. This is the error of conceptualisation which occurs too frequently in archaeology. People ask themselves, "Who invented agriculture and where?" Yet it is the questioner who has invented this problem by conceptualising agriculture. The questions he should be asking himself are how and where were barley and wheat cultivated in the most Ancient Near East, rice in China, and maize and the squashes in America. Similarly with megaliths. The question is not, "Who invented megalithic architecture and when and where?" When we realise that orthostatic walling and trabeate roofing were used by many groups of people in all sorts of different places at all sorts of different times, we will no longer pose the wrong questions as nineteenth-century archaeologists did. There is nothing in common between the megaliths of the Cotswolds and those of Algeria or Bulgaria or the Deccan except the use of large stones for walling and roofing. No one ever supposes that wherever dry-stone walling occurs in the world it means that there was a Dry-Stone Walling Race or People. Our understanding of megaliths has suffered because of the largeness of the stones involved.

The second fundamental defect relates not only to megaliths but to all thinking about the prehistoric past of barbarian Europe. From the moment that the Danish and Swedish archaeologists in the early nineteenth century had built up a technological model of the past, they had speculated on the nature of culture change. How did man change from a Stone Age to a Bronze Age man, and what did the introduction of iron-working mean? From the 1830s onwards the words "independent invention" and "diffusion" were bandied around, and very gradually the strength of informed opinion decided that all the innovations in man's culture in barbarian Europe were due to diffusion from what seemed to be the early home of high culture and civilisation, namely the area from Egypt to Mesopotamia called the Fertile Crescent by Breasted and later the Most Ancient East by Gordon Childe. The nature of the diffusion process was always in dispute but there was a great emphasis on invasions—sometimes of large numbers of people, sometimes of small groups. Oscar Montelius took over and developed the earlier views of Thomsen and Worsaae and he began his book *Der Orient und Europa* with these words: "At a time when the people of Europe were, so to speak, without any civilisation whatsoever, the Orient, and particularly the Euphrates region and the Nile valley, were in enjoyment of a flourishing culture. . . . The civilisation which gradually dawned on our continent was for long only a pale reflection of Oriental culture.[1] I well remember Gordon Childe quoting those words with approval in his presidential address to Section H of the British Association for the Advancement of Science at the Cambridge meeting of 1938. Childe's vision of European pre-history and the process of culture change was very much that of Montelius brought up to date.

Professor A. C. Renfrew has recently written a very good analysis of the development of ideas about culture process in prehistoric Europe in his *Before Civilisation: the Radiocarbon Revolution and Prehistoric Europe* (1973) and these ideas are of course fundamental to any discussion of theory about the

[1] O. Montelius, *Der Orient und Europa*, p. 2 (Stockholm, 1899).

archaeology of megaliths. While it is true that Montelius declared himself a firm believer in diffusion, he had not always held these views and at first thought the *dosar, dysser,* or "dolmens" of Scandinavia originated there, that the Passage Graves of Scandinavia developed out of them, and the Long Stone Cist developed out of the Passage Graves. It was his extensive travels in southern Europe and his realisation that Passage Graves were to be found in Spain and Portugal, France and the British Isles that changed his views. He could not any longer bring himself to argue that the megalithic tombs of western and south-western Europe were derived from Denmark and Sweden. His final views were thus stated:

> One does not have to probe deeply into the study of . . . conditions in the north during the stone age . . . to see that the original homeland of the dolmens cannot be sought in north Europe. They could not spread from here to the southern shores of the Mediterranean, to Palestine and to India . . . this would be absurd. So powerful a movement, able to influence the burial customs of so many and widely distributed peoples, simply cannot have originated here, thousands of years before our era. It is indeed remarkable enough that, originating in the Orient, it should already have reached us here at so early a date[1].

Here was a clear and definite statement of megalithic origins, and it coloured the established views of archaeologists until the radiocarbon dating revolution of the 1950s and 1960s. But in what part of the Orient was megalithic architecture supposed to have originated? Déchelette and others were happy to compare tombs like Los Millares in Spain, Ile Longue in Brittany, and New Grange in Ireland with the Mycenean *tholoi.* Elliot Smith plumped, in a definite and assertive way, for ancient Egypt as the home of megalithic architecture. "Practices such as mummification and megalith building", he wrote, "present so many peculiar and distinctive features that no hypothesis of independent evolution can seriously be entertained in explanation of their geographical distribution."[2] He argued that the long

---

[1] *Ibid.,* p. 31.
[2] Sir G. Elliot Smith, *The Migration of Early Culture,* pp. 20–1 (1929).

barrows of the Cotswolds, for example, were copies of Egyptian mastabas, and even designed and published what he thought was likely to be the tomb intermediate between mastaba and long barrow: this he published in his *Human History* (1930) where it is his figure 55 with the caption "a hypothetical tomb, such as might be made for an Egyptian in a foreign land, without crafts-men sufficiently skilled to make a proper mastaba tomb". It was admittedly hypothetical, and no example of such a tomb has ever been found anywhere in the wide ranges of country that lie between Cairo and Cheltenham.

Few people took seriously the Egyptocentric hyperdiffusion-ism of Elliot Smith and Perry. Childe was inclined to do so for a short while but then moved to the definition of the Orient as Crete and the Cyclades. Such an origin had been advocated in 1930 by Peake and Fleure and by Daryll Forde[1] and, after its advocacy and clear statement by Childe in his *The Dawn of European Civilisation* (first edition 1925, last edition 1957) and Christopher Hawkes in his *The Prehistoric Foundations of Europe* (1940) it became the established and orthodox view. Megalithic architecture had come to western and northern Europe from Crete and the Cyclades, brought by traders and settlers who travelled across the Mediterranean and along the western sea-ways from southern Iberia to the Orkneys and Scandinavia.

I was brought up to think about British megaliths in this orthodox way, and so was all my generation. It seemed that the task was to work out the details of this megalithic movement: it seemed to be a twofold affair, the spread of Passage Graves, and the spread of *allées couvertes* (or Gallery Graves as I christened them in 1941), and I argued this in my paper, "The Dual Nature of the Megalithic Colonisation of Prehistoric Europe" in 1941,[2] and again in my *The Megalith Builders of Western Europe* (1958). Of this book Professor Richard Atkinson said that it marked a milestone in the development of megalithic studies: but he did not say that it was the last milestone on a road going in the wrong direction. It was already out of date when pub-lished: as was Beatrice Blance's article on "Early Bronze Age

---

[1] H. J. E. Peake and H. J. Fleure, "Megaliths and Beakers", *Journal of the Royal Anthropological Institute*, ix, 47–71; C. Daryll Forde, "The Early Cultures of Atlantic Europe", *American Anthropologist*, vol. 32, pp. 19–100.

[2] *Proceedings of the Prehistoric Society*, N.S.vii, 1–49.

Colonists in Iberia" (1961).[1] As A. C. Renfrew pointed out so
clearly in his article "Colonialism and Megalithismus" (1967),[2]
the Cretan-Cycladic parallels do not work: and as Warwick
Bray remarked in conversation and in his Ph.D. thesis, the west
Mediterranean origin of the Gallery Graves is equally untenable.
But it was the dating of our European megaliths by C14 that
finally disposed of the Orient orthodoxy that had reigned for
sixty years since Montelius; in the fifties and sixties we have
come to realise that we were, to use the title of Saloman
Reinach's book, in the grip of *Le mirage orientale*.

The general implications for megalithic theory of these new
dates have been clearly set out by Renfrew in his book *Before
Civilisation* (1973) to which reference has already been made. In
the first place there can no longer be any reasonable doubt that
the megalithic temples of Malta are the earliest monumental
structures in the world: some of them, built long before 3500
B.C., antedated the monumental buildings of Egypt and Mesopotamia such as the pyramids, mastabas, and ziggurats. Secondly,
some of the megalithic monuments of Portugal and Brittany go
back also well before 3500 B.C., and some of the Breton monuments well into the fifth millennium B.C.; and here of course we
are using calibrated dates. Even New Grange on calibrated
dates was built before 3000 B.C., and early Passage Grave sites
in Denmark come from the same context. Gone for ever are the
easy parallels between New Grange, Ile Longue and Mycenae:
but where and how did Passage Graves come into existence in
western Europe? There are two possibilities, the first is south
Portugal and south-east Spain, and the second is the coasts of
Brittany. L'Helgouach, in his masterly survey of the Breton
megaliths published ten years ago, still asserts an Iberian
origin for the French and Irish Passage Graves and this is an
arguable position, the more so now that we have many very
early dates for Iberian megaliths, not only from C14 dating, but
confirmed by TL dating.[3] But it is still possible to argue, as I did
in 1967, that the Breton Passage Graves are the earliest in the

---

[1] *Antiquity*, xxxv, 192–202.　　[2] *Ibid.*, xli, 276–88.

[3] J. L'Helgouach, *Les Sépultures Mégalithiques en Armorique* (Rennes, 1965);
E. H. Whittle and J. M. Arnaud; "Thermoluminescent dating of Neolithic
and Chalcolithic pottery from sites in Central Portugal", *Archaeometry*,
xvii, 5–24.

western European series, and the Passage Grave is a funerary monument copying a domestic monument—a circular hut.[1]

In the third place, there can no longer be any reasonable doubt that the long sepulchral mound is a version of the long house. In northern Germany and Denmark, in northern France, and certainly in the British Isles the long mounds with megalithic chambers should be thought of as lithic versions of non-lithic funerary structures which were themselves mortuary versions of long houses. The *dosar, dysser* of Denmark, the *allées couvertes* of northern France, and many of the chambered long barrows in Britain and Scotland and the court cairns in Ireland all stem back to the tradition of a non-lithic funerary mound in northern Europe.[2]

What then of the Cotswold long barrows such as Hetty Pegler's Tump, Notgrove and Nympsfield, which I discussed in their historical and general context in my address to the Bristol and Gloucester Archaeological Society when I was honoured by being President in 1962.[3] The excavations of Professors Atkinson and Piggott at Wayland's Smithy are crucial to our understanding of the origin of the Cotswold long barrows. Here there was a monument, Wayland's Smithy I, which was a communal grave for at least 14 persons with no megalithic structure, and was covered by a small long barrow. At a later date, this monument, presumably the product of people who had come from northern France, the Low Countries and Germany, was enlarged and had inserted into its western end a megalithic tomb with a plan which calls to mind those of south-eastern Brittany. Here we have a probably fusion of the two main traditions of megalithic architecture: the Passage Grave tradition of western Europe and the long grave tradition of northern Europe. There is still a dual nature to the megaliths of Europe, but it is now to be seen as a tradition of what I have elsewhere called "Northmen and Southmen".[4]

But was it a megalithic colonisation? I no longer think so. There were no special megalithic people: megalithic structures are an integral part of our Neolithic societies. They have loomed large in our antiquarian and archaeological thought because they are large and impressive. We must now recognise that our

[1] G. E. Daniel, "Northmen and Southmen", *Antiquity*, xli, 313–17.
[2] *Ibid.*   [3] *TBGAS*, lxxxii, 5–17.   [4] *Antiquity*, xxxix, 126–33; xli, 313–17.

megalithic tombs, just as our megalithic temples in Malta and our great non-funerary monuments, like Stonehenge and Avebury, were the native products of barbarian Europe in the fifth to third millennia B.C. And it is not just that the pendulum has swung back to independent evolution: the well-dated facts leave no universal diffusionist model of thought possible.

We started with the Druids. What has now happened to them? Are they a discredited solution by antiquaries in the sixteenth to eighteenth centuries whose only source was classical writers? The Druids were the holy men of the Celts of Gaul and Britain. Unquestionably the builders of megalithic tombs and temples had holy men as well as engineers, architects, and, so it would now seem, astronomers. Did this tradition of learning and religion, which had lasted for at least two millennia, die out or was it incorporated in a new faith? I am not suggesting that our generation should restore the megaliths to the Druids, but the early faith of the megalith-builders may have survived in a more powerful and important way than we have hitherto thought. This point has been well made by Christopher Hawkes, and deserves the most careful thought when we remember the use made of megalithic monuments in Roman and post-Roman times.[1] It was not for nothing that Wood-Martin called one of his studies of the Irish megaliths *Traces of the Elder Faiths*.

[1] C. F. C. Hawkes, "Prehistory and the Gaulish Peoples", in *France: Government and Society* (1957), ed. J. M. Wallace-Hadrill and John Mc-Manners, pp. 1–18; S. Piggott, *The Druids* (1975, 3rd ed.); G. E. Daniel, *Megaliths in History* (1972).

REFERENCES IN THE TEXT

Atkinson, R. J. C. (1965) "Wayland's Smithy", *Antiquity*, 126–33.
Daniel, G. E. (1941) "The Dual Nature of the Megalithic Colonisation of Prehistoric Europe', *Proc. Preh. Soc.*, 1–40.
(1965) "Wayland's Smithy", *Antiquity*, 126–33.
(1943) *The Three Ages* (Cambridge).
(1950a) *A Hundred Years of Archaeology* (London).
(1950b) *The Prehistoric Chamber Tombs of England and Wales* (Cambridge).
(1958) *The Megalith Builders of Western Europe* (London).
(1960) *The Prehistoric Chamber Tombs of France* (London).
(1963) "The Long Barrows of the Cotswolds", *Trans. Bristol and Gloucestershire Archaeological Society*, 5–17.
(1967a) *The Origins and Growth of Archaeology* (Harmondsworth).
(1967b) "Northmen and Southmen", *Antiquity*, 313–17.
(1972) *Megaliths in History* (London).
Daryll Forde, C. (1930) "The Early Cultures of Atlantic Europe", *American Anthropologist*, 19–100.
Hawkes, C. F. C. (1957) "Prehistory and the Gaulish Peoples" in (ed.) J. M. Wallace-Hadrill and John McManners, *France: Government and Society* (London), 1–18.
L'Helgouach, J. (1965) *Les Sépultures Mégalithiques en Armorique* (Rennes).
Klint-Jensen, O. (1975) *The History of Scandinavian Archaeology* (London).
Lhwyd, E. (1712) Letter to Dr. Tancred Robinson published in *Philosophical Transactions of the Royal Society*, XXVII, 503–4.
Montelius, O. (1899) *Der Orient und Europa* (Stockholm).
Peake, H. J. E. and Fleure, H.J. (1930) "Megaliths and Beakers", *Journal of the Royal Anthropological Institute*, IX, 47–71.
Piggott, S. (1950) *William Stukeley: an Eighteenth Century Antiquary* (Oxford).
(1975) *The Druids* (London: Third Edition, first published 1968).
Renfrew, A.C. (1967) "Colonialism and Megalithismus", *Antiquity*, XLI, 276–88.
(1972) "Malta and the calibrated radiocarbon Chronology", *Antiquity*, XLI, 141–4.
(1973) *Before Civilisation: the radiocarbon revolution in prehistoric Europe* (London).
Smith, Sir G. Elliot (1929) *The Migrations of Early Culture* (London).
(1930) *Human History* (London).
Whittle, E. H., and Arnaud, J. M. (1975) "Thermoluminescent dating of Neolithic and Chalcolithic pottery from sites in Central Portugal", *Archaeometry*, XVII, 5–24.

III

Roman Sculpture in Gloucestershire

By J. M. C. Toynbee

INTRODUCTION

As is very well known, the area that is now Gloucestershire was one of the most highly romanised regions of the British province and among the richest in the surviving works of the artists and craftsmen who were active under Roman rule. The most spectacular of their productions are undoubtedly the splendid polychrome mosaic pavements, figured and geometric, from town and country sites. But equally important and much more numerous are the sculptures that form the subject of this paper. These are worked mainly in the local oolite limestone or in bronze, occasionally in jet or bone, very rarely in foreign marble. The stone and jet sculptures were obviously produced in this country, whether by the hands of native or of immigrant carvers. No less obviously the marbles were imported from abroad; and of the bronzes some could represent the achievements of well-trained continental workers, while others strongly suggest that their inexperienced authors were of Romano-British origin. Here, by treating the material topographically, an attempt is made to present a general, over-all picture of the kinds of sculptures that appeared in the contexts of Roman sites of different types—towns, villas, rural settlements, most of which would seem to have been also cult-centres. There is also a number of isolated pieces whose association with rustic shrines can be only very tentatively postulated.

The present study makes no claim to offer a complete and detailed catalogue of all the Roman sculptures found in Gloucestershire.[1] Many of them have been described or at least

[1] A full-dress catalogue of the Roman sculptures of Gloucestershire by Mrs. Annette Thornton of Girton College, Cambridge is in preparation for the British contribution to the *Corpus Signorum Imperii Romani*.

mentioned, according to the various subjects depicted and the various media employed, in my *Art in Britain under the Romans* (1964); but special emphasis will be laid here on finds made since that book appeared. The great majority of the discoveries, whether long known or of recent date, are votive in character; and it may be said that the outstanding interest of these sculptures, taken as a whole, lies in the light that they throw on the religious life of the county in Roman times.

Apart from a few instances where there is external dating evidence, the Roman sculptures of Gloucestershire provide no sure chronological data. Crude workmanship is no more a certain pointer to late date than good workmanship is necessarily to an early one. Some reasonable suggestions as to period can sometimes be made. But it would be distinctly misleading if one were to try to construct, on stylistic grounds, typological sequences or "schools" for the great mass of this provincial material.

Objects of pottery, such as antifixes, figurines, and pots with relief-work, are not included as works of sculpture in this survey.

TOWNS

A Cirencester (Corinium)

FUNERARY STELAI

The two sculptured gravestones of Roman cavalrymen riding over prostrate foes, found in the Watermoor cemetery area, just outside the southern city wall, both date from the early years of the Roman occupation, when there was a cavalry fort on the site of the future forum of the civil town. But in competence of execution they differ considerably. That of the helmeted Frisian Genialis, who had served in a Thracian squadron, with his ensign of unusual type and the ornamental head-harness of his sprightly horse, is much superior to that of the bare-headed Dannicus from Raurica (Switzerland), who had served in Albanus' troop of the squadron of Indus, with his ill-proportioned figure and clumsily built mount. Both would have been the work of provincial military carvers.[1] The only

[1] F. Haverfield, "Roman Cirencester" *Archaeologia*, xix, figs. 12, 13; J. M. C. Toynbee, *Art in Britain under the Romans* (1964), p. 191 and nn. 1, 3, pl. 47, a (subsequently referred to as Toynbee 1964); *RIB*. pp. 32, 33, nos. 108, 109, pls. 3, 4.

known civilian stele with a portrait of the deceased, also from Watermoor but housed in the Gloucester City Museum, is that of Philus, a Gaul who had migrated to Britain and is shown wearing his cucullus, an ample hooded cloak reaching to the knees. His hair-style, with straight locks combed forward onto the brow in the Trajanic manner, the fact that he is beardless, and the lettering and formula of his inscription all suggest a date not later than *c.* 100–110.[1]

<h3 style="text-align:center">GRAECO-ROMAN DEITIES</h3>

To judge from the number of his surviving representations, *Mercury* was perhaps the most popular of those Graeco-Roman deities at Corinium whose classical guise probably concealed native deities of similar characteristics and functions. A possibly local, crudely worked bronze figurine shows the god standing naked and somewhat grotesquely featured, with huge head-wings, a purse in his extended right hand and in his lowered left hand a hole through which the shaft of a caduceus must once have passed.[2] A now headless and footless stone torso, worked in high relief, which wears a short cloak fastened on the right shoulder and covering the chest, is also likely to be Mercury.[3] Betrayed as native by his consort, Rosmerta, seated beside him is the very ill-proportioned Mercury, with head-wings, cloak, caduceus, and purse on a badly defaced votive relief with gabled top.[4] But Corinium has also produced what is probably the most finely carved and classical relief of Mercury worked in the province, where the god, with flowing cloak, winged petasos, caduceus, and purse, is accompanied only by his cock and ram.[5] As a work of art it is on a par with the head in the round that once topped a statuette, where the orthodox winged petasos and the classical plasticity in the modelling are admirably combined with such Celtic traits as the patterned hair, large, wide-open eyes, and a vigorous bluntness of mien.[6]

---

[1] Toynbee 1964, pp. 197–8 and n. 5 on p. 197, pl. 48, a; J. F. Rhodes, *Catalogue of the Romano-British Sculptures in the Gloucester City Museum* (1964), no. 2, pp. 12, 13, 15; *RIB*, p. 53, no. 110, pl. 4.

[2] B596: 2½ inches high: unpublished.   [3] B1377: unpublished.

[4] B2046: unpublished.   [5] B2050: Toynbee 1964, p. 156, pl. 40, a.

[6] B1376: J. M. C. Toynbee, *Art in Roman Britain* (2nd ed. 1963), pp. 131–2,

Easily the most sophisticated work of Roman sculpture found at Corinium is the bronze statuette of *Cupid*, 16 inches high, which came to light in 1732[1] and is now in the Ashmolean Museum, Oxford. In the back are two slots for the attachment of the now vanished wings. The fingers both of the right hand raised above the head and of the lowered left hand are parted; and in each hand the figure could have held a bronze scroll or branch on which a lamp was poised. It is, in fact, most likely that the Cupid, almost certainly the product of a Mediterranean workshop, served as a table lampstand in a wealthy citizen's private house.[2]

Minerva, probably, like Mercury, a native deity in Graeco-Roman guise, is represented in Corinium by the fragments, two heads and one torso, of three substantial stone statues in the round.[3] Each head wears a crested Corinthian helmet with down-turned peak, one helmet being carved on either side of the bonnet with what appears to be a coiled snake. The torso carries on its chest a Medusa on an aegis: it does not seem to have belonged to either of the heads. The statues of which these fragments formed part would have been wholly classical in type.

The only other Graeco-Roman goddess represented by surviving sculptures in Corinium is *Diana*. A bronze figurine, again completely classical in type, but provincial in execution, shows her as huntress, plucking an arrow from her quiver as she runs.[4] She may also be portrayed in a small, girlish stone head, with thickly waved hair, again of Graeco-Roman character.[5] But there can be little doubt that she appeared on a high relief of which tantalising fragments survive, namely two booted female feet with the fore-paws of a dog beside the right foot, all very competently carved.[6] An Italian marble fragment found at

no. 19, pl. 29 (subsequently referred to as Toynbee 1963); 1964, pp. 70, 71.

[1] Haverfield, *op. cit.* pp. 202–3, pl. 12; Toynbee 1963, pp. 130–1, no. 13, pl. 32; 1964, p. 76.

[2] *Cf.* the two bronze statuettes of youths from Pompeii, which clearly functioned as lamp-stands (lychnouchoi): *La Critica d'Arte* (1939), iv. pl. 10 (where, however, the right arm is not raised, but extended at right-angles to the body). [3] B2032, 958, 957: all unpublished: Toynbee 1964, p. 79.

[4] B595: unpublished: Toynbee 1964, pp. 84–5.

[5] C2213: unpublished: Toynbee 1964, p. 85, n. 3.

[6] C2751: unpublished: Toynbee 1964, p. 161.

Maiden Castle, Dorchester, offers the nearest parallel in
Britain: preserved are a naked female foot beside a tree-trunk
and the forepaws and hind-quarters of a hound.[1] The town has
so far yielded only one other rendering of a Graeco-Roman
deity, a bronze figurine of a *Lar*, suggesting that the worship of
the traditional Roman household gods was known in Gloucestershire. The figure holds the usual drinking-horn and patera and
could have been imported from Gaul or even from Italy.[2]

GRAECO-ROMAN PERSONIFICATIONS

The classical Genius, personifying a locality or group of
people and not infrequently portrayed in the art of Roman
Britain, appears at Corinium in relief on a stone altar with the
dedicatory inscription "G(enio) s(acrum) huius loc(i)". The
figure has the usual attributes—mural crown, cornucopia, and
patera.[3] A crudely carved male figure in relief in a niche, wearing a short tunic and holding in his right hand a patera, might
possibly portray a Genius, although the mural crown and
cornucopia are absent.[4] It is again just possible to recognise as
part of a Genius the lower half of a draped male figure worked
in relief in a deep niche: it was found in 1971 in the centre of the
town.[5] He appears to wear shoes and his garment reaches to
just below the knees, but in the absence of attributes this
interpretation is purely conjectural.

One of the most impressive of surviving Romano-British
sculptures carved in this country in local stone is the head and
portions of the neck, chest, and shoulders of an elderly bearded
personage—certainly outstanding among Corinian works of
art.[6] The slight backward twist of the head away from the chest
towards the spectator's right, together with the thick, tousled
hair and beard, leaves little doubt that this sculpture represents
part of a reclining *River-god*. It is, indeed, a masterpiece of provincial carving—classical in its three-dimensional plasticity,

[1] R. E. M. Wheeler, *Maiden Castle, Dorset* (1943), pl. 31, a.
[2] B594: unpublished: Toynbee 1964, p. 85.
[3] Toynbee 1964, p. 163, pl. 41, a; *RIB*, p. 30, no. 102, pl. 3.
[4] C2749: unpublished: Toynbee 1964, p. 163, n. 4.
[5] 1971/13; *Insula xviii*: unpublished?
[6] B2052: Toynbee 1963, pp. 138–9, no. 31, pl. 36; 1964, pp. 86–7, pl. 19.

Celtic in the effect of rude, untamed strength that it conveys. In striking contrast to this stone is the minute bone figure of a *Water-nymph* shown kneeling naked with her pitcher, surely an imported work.[1] A stone figure of *Fortuna*, unfortunately headless, seated in a high-backed chair was found in 1971 in the bath-suite of a large house on the Beeches site. In her left hand are what may be the remnants of a cornucopia; but the wheel at her right side clinches her identity.[2]

ORIENTAL DEITIES

Two finds indicate the worship of, or at least an interest in, oriental deities in Corinium. One is a tiny bronze head of *Jupiter Dolichenus*, the principal god of northern Syria. He has a curly, bushy beard and thick, curly hair crowned by his characteristic, conical Syrian hat.[3] The other is a small, badly weathered stone head wearing a Phrygian cap and probably featuring *Attis*.[4]

CELTIC DEITIES

Graeco-Roman deities and personifications and, occasionally, oriental divinities had, then their worshippers in Corinium. But the most substantial proportion of the extant religious sculptures found in the town consists, as is only to be expected, of renderings of local Celtic gods and goddesses. Among these may be reckoned a small stone head topped by the stumps of two horns, perhaps *Cernunnos*;[5] a curly-haired beardless male head;[6] the relief of a *Warrior-god*, with spear, sword in sheath with chape, and a round shield, standing in a pedimented niche, probably a native Mars (*cf.* p. 91);[7] a stone plaque carved in relief with a squatting, horned god, with snakes in place of legs, possibly again *Cernunnos*;[8] and the standing male figure cut in

---

[1] Toynbee 1964, p. 366, pl. 83, a.

[2] A. McWhirr, *The 1971 Excavations: a Brief Report*, p. 6, fig. 7; *Antiquaries Journal*, liii. pl. 25, b,

[3] C105: Toynbee 1963, p. 40, no. 34, pl. 38; 1964, p. 96.

[4] Unpublished: said to have been found in Corinium, but the precise find-spot is not recorded.

[5] B1374: unpublished: Toynbee 1964, p. 106 and n. 2.

[6] B2053: unpublished: Toynbee 1964, p. 107.

[7] B996: unpublished: Toynbee 1964, p. 178.

[8] B2034: unpublished: Toynbee 1964, p. 180.

very crude relief on a small altar found near the centre of the town—the offering of a very humble devotee.[1]

While the names and functions of most of the personages whose portraits have just been listed remain uncertain or unknown, two series of votive carvings at Corinium, those representing the *Genii Cucullati* and the *Matres*, provide us with a reasonably clear idea of the nature of their subjects. That the *Genii Cucullati*, shown either singly or, more often, as a triad and characterised by their muffling hooded cloaks, were godlets of fertility and the afterlife is clear from their attributes and the company that they keep. The hoods, which generally shroud their heads, are suggestive of the underworld and of the mystery of death, as on the small votive plaque on which a trio of Genii trot in single file towards the right, while one of them holds a patera for offerings to some divine being superior to them.[2] Another relief shows a single Genius grasping what appears to be an egg, an emblem of immortality, and standing beside a Mother-goddess, who holds in her lap a pile of fruit that she has, perhaps, received from the Genius.[3] On a third relief from the town three Genii, two of whom have swords (indicating victory over death), are grouped with a seated Mother-goddess, to whom the Genii are clearly subordinate and who holds on her lap the gift of a large cake or loaf, all beneath a shell-canopy;[4] and yet another triad, worked partly in relief and partly in the round, is accompanied by what appears to be a veiled and seated Mother.[5] But in a very fragmentary jet group carved in the round, the Genius, whose hood is thrown back from his head, has as his companion a nude male personage, probably another local god.[6] We shall meet these Genii again on other sites in Gloucestershire (*cf.* pp. 86–90). Genii Cucullati are known on the Continent; but their worship in triads would seem to be peculiar to the British province.

[1] 1963: unpublished.

[2] C2750: J. M. C. Toynbee, "Genii Cucullati in Roman Britain" *Collection Latomus*, xxviii, 1957, 461–2, no. 5, pl. 64 fig. 1 (subsequently referred to as Toynbee 1957).   [3] B2048: Toynbee 1957, p. 462, no. 6, pl. 66, fig. 1.

[4] A360; found in 1964: unpublished. Illustration between pp. 44–5.

[5] Found in 1972: A. McWhirr, *Current Excavations*, figs. on pls. 4, 5; *Britannia*, iv. 307, pl. 36, A, B; *Antiquaries Journal*, liii, pl. 24, b.

[6] C744: Toynbee 1957, pp. 462–3, no. 7, pl. 64, figs. 3, 4; 1964, p. 364.

More familiar and apparently more widely worshipped in the northern provinces, both in Britain and abroad, are the *Matres*, goddesses of fertility in this world and the next and represented in votive sculpture either singly or in triads, like the Genii Cucullati. Four carvings at Corinium are dedicated to them. One stone takes the form of a single goddess veiled, amply draped, and seated on a high-backed arm-chair, with three fruits, perhaps apples, in her lap. The piece is sculptured in the round, but at the back it is flat and unworked, as though it were intended to be set against a wall or in a niche.[1] The other three sculptures are reliefs showing triads of the goddesses, one of them particularly notable, as Haverfield long ago observed, for its completely classical, naturalistic treatment.[2] The Mothers are seated in easy, relaxed postures on a curved bench, each with her child beside her; and the children's attitudes are even more spontaneous and varied. On the two remaining reliefs the goddesses are enthroned rigidly side by side in identical, hieratic poses in the Celtic style. On the larger piece two hold each a tray of fruit, the third a tray of loaves;[3] on the smaller relief the central Mother holds a swaddled baby, her companions have fruit.[4]

With the great Corinthian capital, carved on each of its four sides with a human bust sprouting from the acanthus foliage, we return to unknown and unnamed Celtic divinities.[5] The busts in question are those of a woman wearing a sleeveless tunic, with fruit in her hair and an oval tray (?) in her left hand; a Maenad-like woman with a slipped tunic, two clusters of grapes framing her face, and a wand; a nude man with thick, curly hair and beard, holding a double axe and a vine branch; and a fierce, Silenus-like man with snub nose and wild eyes, holding a knotted stick in one hand and a drinking-horn to his lips in the other. Equally unidentified and much cruder, not to say

---

[1] C2759: unpublished. Illustration between pp. 44–5.

[2] C2786: Haverfield, *op. cit.* pp. 183–4, fig. 10; Toynbee 1963, pp. 154–5, no. 72, pl. 76; 1964, pp. 171–2.

[3] C2756: Haverfield, *op. cit.* pp. 181, 183, fig. 8; Toynbee 1963, p. 155, no. 73, pl. 84; 1964, p. 172.

[4] B2047: Haverfield, *op. cit.* 182–3, fig. 9; Toynbee 1964, p. 172, pl. 43, a.

[5] Haverfield, *op. cit.* pp. 191–3, fig. 16, pls. 9, 10; E. von Mercklin, *Antike Figuralkapitelle* (1962), pp. 178–9, no. 431, figs. 834–7; Toynbee 1963, p. 165, no. 95, pls. 97–100; 1964, p. 145.

barbaric, in its execution, is the small bronze female bust which served as a terminal and was once mounted perhaps on a chariot or on a piece of furniture. The highly patterned hair, the huge, bean-shaped eyes, the wedge-shaped nose, and the slit-like mouth all proclaim its native origin; and its nudity suggests that some local goddess, rather than a human woman, is portrayed. It was found in the upper gravel surface, mainly of third-century date, of the courtyard of a Roman house.[1]

GENRE SCULPTURE

Three studies of birds illustrate this class of sculpture at Corinium—a stylised eagle's head topping a socketed bronze vertical terminal from a chariot or article of furniture;[2] a minute, but exquisitely life-like, silver-gilt cockerel;[3] and a fine, naturalistically worked stone eagle with folded wings, found not far from the basilica and possibly once associated with a statue of Jupiter or of an emperor in the god's guise.[4] There are also two bronze knife-handles in the form of a hound in pursuit of a hare—a favourite motif on such objects.[5]

ARCHITECTURAL SCULPTURE

The fragment of a competently carved relief, which contains part of one wing, one arm, part of the torso, and part of the drapery of what may have been a flying Victory, could possibly be the relic of a pedimental composition of the Bath temple type.[6] There is also a portion of a small architectural frieze carrying a stylised floral scroll which contains a human head crowned with flowers that are held in place by taeniae.[7]

MISCELLANEOUS

Found at Corinium in the eighteenth century, but now preserved in the Yorkshire Museum, York, is a bronze steelyard-

---

[1] *Antiquaries Journal*, xlii, 176–7, pl. 23; Toynbee 1964, pp. 103–4, pl. 26, a, b, c.   [2] *Archaeological Journal*, cxv, 71, 74–5, no. 37, fig. 3.

[3] Found in 1967 in *Insula vvi: JRS*, lviii, 198, n. 13f pl 17, fig. 3.

[4] Found in 1972: A. McWhirr, *Current Excavations*, fig. on p. 4; *Britannia*, iv. 307, pl. 36, A; *Antiquaries Journal*, liii, 1973, pl. 25, b; J. Wacher, *The Towns of Roman Britain* (1975), p. 312, pl. 60.

[5] *Archaeologia Cantiana* xxxviii, p. 150.

[6] Unpublished: Toynbee 1964, pp. 138–9, n. 6.

[7] Unpublished: Toynbee 1964, p. 143, n. 1.

weight in the shape of the nude bust of a youth, with hair arranged in crisp, straight locks on the forehead and bunched on either side of the face.[1] The style is wholly classical; but who the youth is we do not know, since no identifying attributes are present. One eye of a lifesize bronze statue has been discovered in the basilica.[2]

The above summary survey should suffice to illustrate the wide variety in content, style, and medium to be found in the sculptures recovered from the site of Corinium; the variety of religious cults that the city's inhabitants practised; and something of the varying levels of its social, cultural, and economic structure.

B. Gloucester (Glevum)

The Roman sculptures found at Gloucester are fewer in number than those which Cirencester has produced and cannot be classified so neatly. But at Gloucester too the series begins with military objects belonging to the early years of Roman rule, when there appears to have been on the site of Kingsholm, now a suburb just to the north of the medieval city, a fort manned by auxiliaries and preceding the foundation of the legionary fortress and of the colonia that succeeded it on the site of Gloucester. A sepulchral stele came to light in 1825 at Wooton, a short distance to the east of Kingsholm, where later in the nineteenth century another tombstone and a series of cinerary pots—all now lost—were also found. The surviving stele commemorates Rufus Sita of the Sixth Thracian Cohort and is a cleanly cut piece of vigorous and naturalistic carving. Its material, moreover, is exceptional for Gloucestershire as being, not the local oolite, but the better-quality and presumably more expensive Bath stone. The sculpting must either have been commissioned from, and executed in, a Roman workshop in the Bath region or, more probably, have been carried out at Kingsholm by an army carver on an imported slab.[3] The naked appearance of the helmeted rider, armed with spear and sword

---

[1] *Archaeologia*, x, 136, pl. 13, fig. 4.   [2] J. Wacher, *op. cit.* p. 298, pl. 56.
[3] Gloucester Museum: Toynbee 1963, pp. 157–8, no. 82, pl. 87; 1964, p. 190 and n. 3; J. F. Rhodes, *Catalogue of the Romano-British Sculptures in the Gloucester City Museum* (1964), no. 1, pp. 6, 11, 12.

and about to slay a prostrate foe, may be accounted for by the loss of the paint in which his clothes and body-armour may once have been rendered.

The existence of a fort, or even of a pre-Gloucester legionary fortress, at Kingsholm has been recently confirmed by the discovery there, in the winter of 1972–73, of a bronze cheek-piece embossed in high relief with the figure of Jupiter, sceptered and seated to the left on a throne with ornamented back and legs: the god wears a cloak folded over his left arm and wrapped across his knees.[1] In view of the elaboration of its figure-work and of the high standard of its execution, the piece would seem to have been designed for one of the decorated helmets that were worn in the Roman cavalry sports (hippika gymnasia) that Arrian describes;[2] but it seems not to have been finished and hence never actually worn. Does this imply the existence of a workshop for making such things at Kingsholm or the importation of an unfinished object from a workshop abroad? Or was it merely the model for a design that could be copied on helmets produced in a British arms factory? The find was associated with a timber building of pre-Flavian date. On armour of this type renderings of Jupiter are very rare. The only other instances known to me are a bust of the god on a bronze breast-plate mount from Manching in Bavaria, which dates from the first half of the third century, and the fragmentary standing figure of him on a similar mount, unpublished, from Carnuntum.[3] Again, seated figures on this class of equipment are virtually unknown elsewhere; and one can only speculate as to what would have appeared on the companion cheek-piece— another Jupiter seated rightwards or an enthroned Juno or Minerva? The hollow-cast bronze leopard with enamel spots and the solid-cast lion's head from Kingsholm could have been chariot fittings belonging to the military phase of the site.[4]

Undoubtedly the most remarkable object in the Gloucester Museum is a male stone head, beardless and 8 inches high, which has hitherto always been classed as a Romano-Celtic

[1] *Britannia*, iv. 309, pl. 34, B.   [2] *Tactica*, ch. 34 ff.

[3] *Aus Bayerns Frühzeit: Friedrich Wagner zum 75. Geburtstag* (1962), p. 190, no. 3, pl. 16 and p. 193, n. 22.

[4] Bristol Museum: F771, 775: unpublished.

work. It was found unstratified in a disturbed deposit of Roman and medieval material in St. Aldate's churchyard, behind the Bon Marché site.[1] It would seem to have been carved by a Celtic sculptor who had learned from the Romans the art of monumental sculpting in stone and to be imitating either Julio-Claudian or Trajanic hair-style, while remaining at the same time completely faithful to native, pre-Roman tradition in all the details of the piece. The locks of hair are richly patterned; the ears are stylised; the nose is wedge-shaped; the narrow face tapers; the mouth is slit-like and almost lipless; and the enormous eyes are bulging and lentoid in shape. These traits carry us back immediately to the bronze heads of Belgic warriors on the Aylesford bucket in the British Museum.[2] We have no means of knowing whether the head was meant to be a human portrait or to represent a god: the aloof, almost wrapt and unearthly expression rather favours the second alternative. A curious feature is the straight, vertical line in which the head and neck terminate behind, rather suggestive of a medieval bracket or corbel; and the head has, in fact, recently been proposed as a Romanesque work.[3] If that were so, we should have here a remarkable example of the survival, or re-emergence, of Celtic facial traits in medieval times. Heads with bean-shaped, bulging eyes, wedge-shaped noses, and sometimes with slit-like mouths and patterned hair do, indeed, occur not infrequently on works of early medieval art, particularly in bronze in Ireland and in stone in France, where the Celtic tradition was strongest. But the Gloucester head's closest affinities would still seem to be with the Aylesford bucket heads and with such undoubtedly Romano-Celtic stone heads as that at Corbridge.[4] I have not as yet seen any English stone medieval parallel. Is it possible that the head is Romano-Celtic and sliced down behind for re-use in a medieval building?

Almost certainly architectural in context was the large stone

---

[1] Gloucester Museum: Toynbee 1963, pp. 125–6, no. 7, pl. 8; 1964, p. 56 and n. 1; Rhodes, *op. cit.* no. 3, pp. 14–16.

[2] J. W. Brailsford, *Later Prehistoric Antiquities of the British Isles* (1953), pl. 21, no. 1.

[3] By David Brown of the Ashmolean Museum, Oxford and Kevin Greene of the University, Newcastle upon Tyne.

[4] Toynbee 1963, p. 146, no. 42, pl. 49; 1964, p. 108.

antefix found in 1860 just north-east of the cathedral.[1] It consists of a palmette forming the background to a head which, despite its furrowed brow and rugged features, would seem to be female in view of the earrings and the hair waved on either side of a central parting. The personage portrayed could be a local goddess, designed to protect the building on which the antefix was mounted. Just possibly the carving represents a somewhat unsuccessful attempt at a tragic mask. The absence of drilling and the plain eyes would seem to indicate a late first, or early second, century date for the piece.

Finds made in the forum area in 1968 may be the relics of a public monument once adorning the colonia. These were a large statue-base, clumsily reconstructed in Roman times, and about thirty fragments of cast bronze from the statue, perhaps equestrian, that it carried.[2]

The religious sculptures found in Glevum are all, as works of art, of a humble character. Three stone reliefs featuring the Celtic Mercury with female companions come from the same (east) side of Northgate Street, which suggests that a shrine dedicated to Mercury stood in that area. Excavations in Northgate Street in 1857 did, in fact, reveal a building with a colonnaded portico, but no religious association can be definitely connected with it.[3] The most competently carved of the trio shows Mercury on the left with head-wings, cloak, purse, caduceus and a cock beside him, and, on the right, a goddess, probably Rosmerta, wearing a long robe and holding a patera and a staff topped by a pelta-shaped ornament: an iron-bound bucket stands on the ground between them. A second, much rougher, relief depicts, from right to left, Mercury with caduceus and purse, possibly with head-wings, a goddess, probably again Rosmerta, who carries what seems to be a reversed caduceus, and Fortuna with rudder and cornucopia. A more recent find is a relief of which the bottom part is lost. The god on the right has Mercury's usual caduceus and purse, but no head-wings, while any attributes that Rosmerta on the left may have held

---

[1] Gloucester Museum: Toynbee 1963, pp. 165–6, no. 96, pl. 103; 1964, pp. 151–2; Rhodes, *op. cit.* no. 6, pp. 19–21.

[2] *JRS*, lix, 225; *Antiquaries Journal*, lii, 57, pls. 12, b; 13, a.

[3] Gloucester Museum: Toynbee 1964, p. 157, pl. 40, b; Rhodes, *op. cit.* nos. 9–11, pp. 22, 24–7.

are no longer distinguishable. Here the rounded forms of the figures stand out boldly from the background.

A small bronze stud, 14 mm. in diameter, in the form of a head with thick hair framing the face, was found in 1966 in a second-century layer at Newmarket Hall. It may represent a native god.[1] The same could be the case with a sheet brass head with a thick, elongated neck, 71 mm. high, discovered in 1969 on the 63–71 Northgate Street site, along with Flavian coins and pottery in a deposit associated with a timber building immediately outside the Roman north gate. Here, however, the face is beardless and no traces of hair are visible. The head, which is partly torn away from the neck, is formed round a pellet of lead, but the neck is hollow and pierced as though for a nail to secure it to the end of a ritual wand or sceptre. The brass alloy resembles gold and the black enamel eyes are of glass.[2] Another miniature work, a partly broken rectangular plaque of jet, 48 mm. high, found in 1966 on the Newmarket Hall site, carries in relief what must again be the portrait of a Celtic deity. Here the whole figure is shown, male, naked, facing the spectator, and squatting on the ground with knees drawn up and legs placed wide apart. His left hand rests against his head, which is crowned either by a tall headdress or a mass of stylised hair. In his right hand he holds a drinking-horn to his lips.[3]

There is, then, more known evidence for the survival of native religious traditions in the romanised colonia of Glevum than there is for the worship there of purely Graeco-Roman deities. Two other votive sculptures from the city are to be related to the devotees of an oriental cult or cults. Certainly connected with the cult of Attis is an altar which takes the unusual form of a pillar round below and square above and topped by a square capital, in which is the focus.[4] On one side of the shaft is the naked figure of Attis, mainly worked in high relief, the shoulders and elbows, which project beyond the contours of the column, being rendered in the round. Attis is preserved from the peak

---

[1] Gloucester Museum A8231: unpublished.

[2] Gloucester Museum 74/1968–146: unpublished: *Antiquaries Journal*, lii, 65.   [3] Gloucester Museum A8353: *JRS*, lvii, pl. 16, fig. 4.

[4] Gloucester Museum A6295: *JRS*, lii, 180–1, pl. 24, fig. 3; Toynbee 1964, p. 167, pl. 42, a; Rhodes *op. cit.* no. 8, pp. 21–3.

of his Phrygian cap, much of which, together with most of his
face, has been battered away, down to the centre of his thighs.
Of the face there survives only the mouth with teeth, or perhaps
the tongue, visible between the lips. In his right hand he holds
to his lips a syrinx, the individual pipes of which must once have
been marked in in paint. Tucked in the crook of his left arm is
a rounded object, just possibly a bagpipe, of which the details
could again have been originally painted.[1]

The second oriental subject is a youthful male bust carved in
the round and preserved from the peak of the Phrygian cap to
just above the waist. It is 15 inches high. The hair is curly, the
battered face broad and chubby; and the dowel hole drilled in
the termination of each shoulder indicates that the now vanished arms were made separately and were extended laterally,
but whether horizontally or bent at the elbows remains unknown.[2] Had the latter been the case, the figure would most
probably have represented Mithras' rock-birth, with a knife
and a torch in his upraised hands and the torso emerging from
a pile of rocks.[3] In the former case, the child would be likely to
be Attis, with cymbals in his outstretched hands; and his type of
Phrygian cap with ear-flaps is much more often found in
renderings of Attis than of Mithras. That there was a shrine of
Attis in Glevum, apparently frequented by fairly humble
devotees, we may surmise from the altar.

Two small sculptures from the Roman city were apparently
quite secular in character. A bronze bucket mount in the shape
of an ox-head, while still in the Celtic tradition, was clearly
much influenced by naturalistic Roman art.[4] In 1966–67 there
came to light on the Newmarket Hall site part of a rectangular
candelabrum foot of Purbeck marble, with a sculptured lion's
paw projecting from one external corner.[5] Representational

[1] F. Collinson, "Syrinx and Bagpipe: a Romano-British Representation?"
Antiquity, xliii, 305–8, pls. 44, 45.

[2] Gloucester Museum A2641: Toynbee 1964, p. 100, pl. 25, a, b; Rhodes,
op. cit. no. 4, pp. 16–18.

[3] *Cf.* M. J. Vermaseren, *Corpus Inscriptionum et Monumentorum Religionis
Mithriacae*, i. no. 353, fig. 100.

[4] Gloucester Museum: *Aspects of Archaeology in Britain and Beyond* (ed.
W. F. Grimes 1951), pp. 194–5, fig. 50, b.

[5] Gloucester Museum: *City of Gloucester Museum and Art Gallery Report
1 April 1966–31 March 1968*, fig. on p. 9.

carving in this material is most unusual, the only other instance
of which I am aware being the life-size torso of an eagle found
in Roman Exeter in 1972.[1]

C. Sea Mills (*Abona or Abonae*)

Sea Mills, situated on the right bank of the Avon, a short
distance from its outflow into the Severn estuary, was probably
the site of a fort during the early stages of the Roman occupation. But of the four Roman sculptures found there none has
definite associations with a military phase. A decidedly provincial looking bronze statuette of Jupiter, 5.8 cm. high and
found in 1966, of which the feet and the sceptre, once held in
the upraised left hand, are lost, shows the god naked and grasping in his right hand a twisted object, probably the central
portion of a thunderbolt. Hair and beard are thick and curly.
Two small incised circles mark the nipples.[2]

In the same year there was discovered a small stone altar,
44 cm. high and carved in somewhat bold relief on all four
sides.[3] On what appears to be the principal side or front there
is a rudely worked human face above the capital, between the
bolsters. The main field on this side is occupied by an eagle
perched to the right on a globe and facing a curved object that
tapers towards its lower end and resembles a cornucopia,
although no fruits are visible emerging from the top. On the
back there are a bull's head in the centre and a knife on the
right, both suggestive of sacrifice; but the connection with them
of the object on the left, which looks like a small herm standing
on a bevelled base, is not immediately obvious; but the object
might be a sacrificial dagger, with hilt and sheath. On the right
side are two more sacrificial items—a jug and a handled patera.
The most enigmatic objects are on the left face. On each side
there is a column surmounted by a heavy, square, and plain
capital and resting on a square base: these might indicate a
shrine. Between them is a three-pronged feature, at first sight
trident-like. But its stem is supported by a low foot and there is

---

[1] Unpublished. Most unlikely to be Roman is an oval ivory plaque found
in fragments in the bed of a stream on the outskirts of Gloucester and
showing in relief a woman holding a wreath and riding in a two-horse
chariot towards the left.

[2] Bristol Museum F4145: unpublished.   [3] Bristol Museum: unpublished.

a curious notch three-quarters of the way up it on the right side. Possibly it is a candelabrum which would have carried a lamp at the top of each of its branches, although no trace of such lamps is visible. Since an eagle occupies the place of honour on the front, we might imagine that the altar was dedicated to the cult of Jupiter or of an emperor.

Both the bronze Jupiter and the altar are likely to date from the time when Abona was a major civilian settlement, a township and a port. And to this phase should most probably be assigned a stele, not properly a piece of sculpture, since it is not carved in relief but has figures crudely and boldly incised on its surface.[1] Within the gabled top of the stone is cut the bust of a girl inside a semicircle, presumably meant to represent a niche. Above the niche is a star and on either side of it a jumping dog and a strutting cock. The inscription reads "Spes/C Senti". "Spes" occurs both as a pagan and as an early Christian name; and the text could be interpreted as "Spes, the wife of Gaius Sentius". Alternatively, it could mean "the hope (i.e. daughter) of Gaius Sentius". The dog and cock could either represent the young woman's pets or be symbols—both in a pagan and in a Christian context—of fidelity and the dawn of new life beyond the grave.

A miniature jet carving, 1.8 cm. wide, a human head worked in the round, was found at Sea Mills in 1891. Its stylised hair and protruding eyes indicate a survival of Celtic tradition far into the Roman period in Britain. Flattened behind, it would have been attached to some object.[2]

VILLAS

It would seem that in the fourth century in Britain the large country houses owned by wealthy members of the landed gentry outrivalled the towns as cultural centres. Such, at any rate, is what their figured mosaic pavements suggest; and it is significant that some of the most classicistic works of sculpture found in Gloucestershire come from three of its villas.

A. *Woodchester*

From this site come two sculptures carved in foreign, probably

[1] Bristol Museum: Toynbee 1964, pp. 202–3, nn. 1–3; *RIB.* pp. 42–3, no. 137   [2] Bristol Museum F1923: unpublished.

Lune (Carrara) marble and obviously imported from abroad. One depicts a goddess wearing a long tunic girded below the breasts and a cloak wrapped round her lower limbs. Head, arms, and any attributes that she may have held are lost; but the bull's head beside her right foot identifies her as Diana/Luna, who is often shown riding in a bull-drawn chariot.[1] The second piece is the torso of Cupid from a replica of the well-known statuary group of Cupid embracing Psyche. Part of Psyche's right breast appears below Cupid's left shoulder, part of her left hand rests on his abdomen, and, at the rear, her right hand appears beneath the stump of his left wing.[2] These marbles need not, of course, have been carved as late as the fourth century, when the Woodchester villa was at its peak. They could have been earlier works acquired by the villa owner. But a fourth century date for them is by no means to be excluded. One of the best surviving replicas of the Cupid and Psyche group, slightly different from the Woodchester replica, comes from the luxurious fourth century House of Cupid and Psyche at Ostia and displays a late technique in the rendering of the hair and drapery.[3] Neither hair nor drapery survive on the Woodchester group. But the harsh cutting of the folds of the tunic of Diana/Luna is suggestive of fairly late workmanship.

B. *Spoonley Wood* (*near Winchcomb*)

At the feet of a skeleton in a grave, in a field near the villa, there came to light an intact marble statuette of Bacchus, also clearly an imported work, although somewhat clumsy, coarse, and ill-proportioned in its carving. The god is naked and wreathed, rests his left hand on a tree-trunk support, on which a vine spray with clusters of grapes is worked in relief, and holds a cup in his right hand above the head of a leopard, which squats on the ground beside him.[4] Whereas the Woodchester Diana/Luna could well have been sculptured in a Mediterranean land, the Bacchus has a provincial look suggestive of a provincial, but continental, workshop. The grave could have

[1] British Museum: Lysons 1797, pls. 38, 39; *Guide to the Antiquities of Roman Britain in the British Museum* (1958), pl. 20, no. 11; Toynbee 1964, p. 84.
[2] British Museum: Lysons 1797, p. 37, figs. 1, 2; Toynbee 1964, p. 76.
[3] R. Calza and M. F. Squarciapino, *Museo Ostiense* (1962), pp. 42–3, no. 17, fig. on p. 144. [4] British Museum: *Guide, etc.* (1958), pl. 20, no. 10.

belonged to the villa owner or to some member of his family, who regarded Bacchus as an other-worldly "saviour" god.

Sophisticated, classicistic imports from abroad are not the only Roman sculptures found on villa sites. Half a mile south of the Spoonley Wood villa, and almost certainly derived from it, there was ploughed up in 1948 the torso of a stone eagle, the head, legs, and tail being lost.[1] The material is local oolite and the modelling, although plastic, is coarse, while the feathers on breast and wings are conventionally indicated by diagonal and criss-cross incised lines. In this last respect the sculpture differs markedly in treatment from the much more naturalistic stone Cirencester and Purbeck marble Exeter eagles (*cf.* pp. 70, 77). Possibly this bird too was originally perched on the hand, or on a globe held in the hand, of a statue of Jupiter or of an emperor.

C. Witcombe (near Gloucester)

Like the villa at Spoonley Wood, that at Witcombe has yielded two Roman sculptures, one classical, the other native in character, but this time both of bronze. The classical piece is the figurine of a long-robed woman holding a wreath, popularly known as "Flora", possibly personifying spring.[2] The other sculpture is a small box-lid, cast in the shape of a long-eared dog with pointed snout, curled in a ball, as though for sleep, but with one round, watchful eye still open.[3] The nose, back, ribs, and powerful hind-paws are vigorously modelled. It is a most attractive example of stylised naturalism from the hand of a Celtic artist.

D. Chedworth

This villa has produced no sculptures of Graeco-Roman type, since the bronze figurine of a priest, holding a dish and now in the site-museum, was not found there. The three reliefs from the site are of oolite stone. The best piece is a gabled votive slab

---

[1] Gloucester Museum A6274: *JRS*, lxix, 127, p. 18, fig. 6; Toynbee 1964, p. 129; Rhodes, *op. cit.* pp. 18, 19.

[2] Witcombe Park: *TBGAS*, lxxiii, 58, p. 10; Toynbee 1964, p. 92.

[3] Witcombe Park: *TBGAS*, lxxiii, 50, pl. 9; Toynbee 1964, p. 334, pl. 79, b.

carrying a niche, in which there stands, facing the spectator, a figure that probably represents a local Hunter-god.[1] The face is unfortunately lost, but the other details are clear enough. The god wears a cloak, a short, girded tunic, and boots. In his right hand he holds up a hare by the hind-legs above the head of a hound that is seated on the ground beside him and looks up expectantly. On the right, emerging from behind the god's legs, are seen the fore-parts of an antlered stag. While it is obviously a work locally carved, the modelling is reasonably good and the animals are life-like. It may have come from the temple found half a mile south-east of the villa and probably in some way associated with it.[2]

Very different, almost barbaric, in fact, in quality are the figures carved on two small altars from the villa site. On one of these the figure has thick hair, is in relief, and stands in a frontal pose, with a hammer in his left hand and in his right a tall staff. He has been described as Sucellus.[3] But the inscription above him reads "[L]en(o) M(arti)" and identifies him as the god worshipped by the Treviri.[4] On his body is a series of holes set quincunx-wise. Two holes mark the eyes. The second altar is even cruder and is merely incised with a frontal figure consisting of a round head with projecting ears, a rectangular body without any rendering of legs and with very rudimentary arms and feet. Again two holes mark the eyes and there is a quincunx of five more holes on the torso. An identification as Mars Olludius has been proposed for it.[5] The last two reliefs were clearly the offerings of very humble devotees attached to the estate; and the fine fourth century ticlinium mosaic pavement with figure scenes of classical content has no surviving parallels in sculpture. On the other hand, the two small figures of which only the feet remain on their bases, one sandalled, the other wearing boots with down-turned flaps, were probably of much

---

[1] Chedworth Museum: Toynbee 1963, p. 156, no. 78, pl. 79; R. Goodburn, *The Roman Villa, Chedworth* (1972), pp. 27, 34, pl. 9.

[2] Goodburn, *op. cit.* p. 34.

[3] Chedworth Museum: E. M. Clifford, "Roman Altars in Gloucestershire", *TBGAS*, lx, 302, fig. 11.

[4] *JRS* xxxix, 114, no. 7; *RIB*, p. 38, no. 126; Goodburn, *op. cit.* p. 27, pl. 10, fig. 1.

[5] Chedworth Museum: Clifford, *op. cit.* pp. 301–2, fig. 9; Goodburn *op. cit.* p. 27, pl. 10, fig. 3.

higher quality than were the three reliefs, to judge from the careful rendering of the details of the footgear.[1]

E. *Compton Grove*

From the villa at Compton Grove, a short distance due north of Chedworth, is reported a piece of sculpture classical in content, namely a bronze figurine of Venus. Nothing can be said of its style and probable place of origin, since its present whereabouts are unknown and it seems to be unpublished.[2]

RURAL SETTLEMENTS AND COUNTRY SHRINES

In the case of some of the sites belonging to this category their nature and extent are more or less fully known. But for the rest, since the sculptures that they have produced are virtually all of a votive character, it is not easy to determine whether they were settlements with habitations or religious centres, each with a temple, or temples, at which the local population, and even pilgrims from a distance, gathered for cultic purposes.

A. *Lydney*

Very well known is the character of the Roman site at Lydney, ensconced within the earthwork defences of an Early Iron Age hill-fort which was occupied during the first century B.C. and the first half of the first century A.D. It is situated on the right bank of the Severn, nine miles north of Chepstow, and over-looks the Gloucester–South Wales road. The Roman settlement, not built, according to the coin evidence, before *c.* A.D. 364, was, of course, the elaborate cult-centre of the Celtic god Nodens, a healing deity, and apparently a place of pilgrimage. It com-prised, beside a temple, a large residential building or guest-house, a substantial bath-suite, and a long building subdivided into small compartments, resembling the abaton at Epidaurus, where the sick spent the night in the hope of being cured during their sleep by a visitation from Asklepios.[3] It is obvious that

---

[1] Chedworth Museum: Goodburn *op. cit.* p. 27. The niche with carved lateral pilasters and a carved shell canopy may have been intended to house a statue: Chedworth Museum: Goodburn, pp. 27, 34, pl. 10, fig. 2.

[2] Location unknown: *TBGAS*, xlvii, 75, n. 7; Goodburn, *op. cit.* p. 11.

[3] R. E. M. and T. V. Wheeler, *Report on the Excavation of the Prehistoric, Roman, and Post-Roman Site in Lydney Park, Gloucestershire* (1932), pp. 22–63.

some works of art found in a shrine of this type could antedate its foundation, being offerings that had for some years or even for some generations been in the families of the pilgrim-devotees who brought them to dedicate to Nodens.

Of the sculptures in the round found at Lydney three are classical in content. A stone statuette about 30 inches high when complete with its now vanished head, could well be earlier than the late fourth century, a period, however, in which Graeco-Roman art traditions still flourished in many areas of the Roman world.[1] Here we have a female figure seated on a low, backless throne, wearing a long-sleeved tunic girded below the breasts and a cloak that passes over the left shoulder and is wrapped round the legs. The left leg is crossed over the right leg —an unusual attitude for seated figures from this province, but found in such early Hellenistic works as Eutychides' famous statue of the Tyche of Antioch-on-the-Orontes.[2] The cornu-copia held in the crook of the Lydney figure's left arm suggests that she may be Abundantia, or possibly Fortuna, although there is no trace of the latter's wheel or globe with rudder (*cf.* p. 67). A bronze figurine of a winged Victory, poised on a globe and $3\frac{3}{4}$ inches high, is clumsily worked and could be either as late as the late fourth century or a provincial product of earlier date: it might once have rested on the hand of a large bronze statue of Jupiter or Minerva or an emperor.[3] The same doubt as to the date of its manufacture attaches to a bronze steelyard-weight in the form of a bearded bust with naked chest, traces of drapery on the shoulders, and an elaborate diadem or headdress—perhaps intended for Jupiter.[4]

Again classical in their content, but definitely late in style and technique, are some small bronze sculptures in relief. The best preserved and most striking of these is what is probably a dia-dem on which is represented the frontal figure of the Sun-god standing in his chariot, wearing a radiate crown, and armed with a whip. He is flanked on either side by a flying Cupid, who grasps a torch, and a Triton, the Triton on the left holding a conch-shell, that on the right, an anchor, in either hand.

---

[1] *Ibid.*, p. 68, no. 4, pl. 24, a, b.
[2] *Cambridge Ancient History: Plates iii* (1930), pp. 124–5.
[3] Wheeler, *op. cit.* p. 91, no. 140, pl. 30, a.
[4] *Ibid.*, p. 91, no. 141, pl. 30, a.

Another fragment, also apparently from a diadem, shows a dancing Cupid holding a basket, with a swag of leaves and fruit to the right of him.[1] Other similar fragments display a reclining Triton with an anchor and shells and the figures of warriors or gladiators in action.[2] These diadems were in all likelihood ritual headgear worn by the priests who served the shrine.

Sculptures of another series from Lydney are all, with one exception, of bronze and were clearly all votive offerings to Nodens in his capacity as healer. There are a bronze human arm and hand in the round and a crude bone plaque shaped to the form of a naked woman with streaming hair and her hands resting on her abdomen, the details being incised. These were perhaps thank-offerings for the cure of a diseased limb and for safety in childbirth.[3] The remaining bronzes all depict dogs, the dog being in the Graeco-Roman world the healing animal *par excellence* and hence an attribute of Nodens. Three of these are in the form of thin plates intended to be fixed to the temple walls, while three are in the round. All are very roughly worked and were obviously the gifts of humble and uncultured folk.[4]

A seventh bronze dog from this site, modelled in the round, is among the most famous and attractive of all the sculptures that this province has yet produced. It is a real masterpiece of Romano-Celtic art.[5] It is 4 inches long and portrays what may be characterised as a greyhound or Irish wolfhound lying on the ground with its powerful fore-paws extended, its hind-paws and tail tucked together beside its body, and its long snout turned back towards its rump as though some person or object had caught its attention. The characteristically canine pose, the strong haunches, the supple back, and the slender, collared neck are as naturalistically treated as in any of the best animal studies in the art of Graeco-Roman times. Meanwhile Celtic stylisation manifests itself in the round eyes, in the elongated nozzle, in the decorative hatching of ears and coat, in the curious whirligigs, perhaps of hair, on the hips and shoulders, and in the generally blunt handling of the forms. This dog could, of

---

[1] *Ibid.*, p. 90, nos. 123, 124, pl. 27.   [2] *Ibid.*, p. 90, nos. 125–7, pl. 28.

[3] *Ibid.*, p. 89, nos. 121, 122, pl. 26.

[4] *Ibid.*, p. 89, nos. 115, 116, 119 (plates), 117, 118, 120 (in the round), pl. 26.

[5] *Ibid.*, pp. 88–9, no. 114, pl. 25; Toynbee 1964, pp. 126–7, pl. 34, b, c.

course, have been cast quite a long time before its dedication in the shrine of Nodens and have served originally as a pure ornament.

The varying social and cultural backgrounds of the pilgrims and visitors whom Nodens attracted are, indeed, vividly reflected in the Roman sculptures found at this centre of his cult.[1]

B. *Wycomb*

The Roman site at Wycomb, near Andoversford, already partly occupied in the Iron Age, was a large settlement, 8 acres in area and almost urban in character. It had a street system with paved roads and buildings of a quite substantial kind, as foundations and building-stones found on the site suggest. One building would appear to have been a temple. Hypocausts are recorded. Most of the coins from the place are of late date; but "samian" pottery was widely distributed throughout the settlement.[2]

The Roman sculptures found at Wycomb, four carved stones and a bronze figurine, are all of a votive character. The stones are crudely worked in relief, probably by local masons, and represent native deities locally worshipped. Two consist of blocks of stone with figure carving on the front of each and on the back and sides patterns in the form of incised diagonal, vertical, and horizontal lines.[3] On the sides of the larger of the two blocks, below the diagonal incisions, are six small squares in two tiers of three, with horizontal ridges above, between, and below them. We have no clue as to the meaning of these patterns, although they might just possibly be intended to represent wicker-work or drapery. They are most unlikely to be purely decorative and could have had some quasi-magical or ritual significance.

On the front of the larger block, $4\frac{1}{4}$ inches high, $2\frac{5}{8}$ inches wide at the base, $1\frac{3}{8}$ inches thick, and rounded at the top, is a

[1] An enamelled bronze bull's head from Lydney, worked in the Celtic style and doubtless once a bucket mount, although dating from within the Roman period in Britain, is much earlier than the Nodens complex: Wheeler, *op. cit.* pp. 75–6, fig. 11, no. 12.

[2] Information kindly supplied by Mr. R. N. Eagles of the Royal Commission on Historical Monuments (England) from the forthcoming volume on the Cotswolds. [3] In private hands: unpublished.

very ill-proportioned male figure who seems to be standing as
he faces the spectator. From his small, round head all traces of
facial features have vanished. The shoulders are abnormally
heavy and square; and the arms and hands are far too large in
relation to the body and legs. The personage appears to wear
an under-tunic, the lower edge of which is visible just above the
knees, and a close-fitting over-tunic or cloak, with three-
quarter-length sleeves. Both hands are extended downwards
with the fingers outspread; and under each hand stands a small,
male, frontal figure, round-headed, short-legged, and generally
squat in appearance. The small figure on the spectator's left is
well preserved in outline, although the whole of the surface has
been worn away. The figure on the spectator's right is, though
recognisable, much more damaged. Both seem to wear the same
costume as the main central figure. We clearly have here a
native god flanked by two minor godlets or by two worshippers.

The smaller block presents from front and back the appearance of a herm, with a small round head, suggestive of a finial,
broad chest, and sloping shoulders, but without a neck or arms.
This stone is $3\frac{1}{2}$ inches high, including the head, $2\frac{3}{4}$ inches wide
at the base, and $1\frac{1}{2}$ inches thick. Again very rudely carved on
the front is a small figure which seems to be long-robed and
female, seated on a chair, of which the sides are visible to right
and left of her. Her arms hang downwards and her hands
appear to rest on the sides of her seat. She may be veiled; but
the surface is so much corroded that no details can be clearly
discerned. She could be a Mother-goddess of some kind.

The two other stones take the form of a panel with curved
top, on the surface of which is cut a shallow niche containing a
trio of figures, although on one stone the lateral figure on the
spectator's right has been smashed away. The two groups are
almost identical and must undoubtedly have come from the
same hand.[1] Their carving is rather better than that of
the figures on the blocks, but still very rough in execution. In the
centre is a hooded figure, a Genius Cucullatus, wearing a knee-
length cloak, while on either side of him stands a hoodless figure
in a short tunic, holding in his hands a large circular object—
whether a bag or basket or a cake or bunch of fruit it is impos-

[1] In private hands: Toynbee 1957, pp. 465–6, nos. 10, 11, pl. 65,
figs. 3, 4.

sible to say. Both of these lateral figures are likely to be the
godlet's worshippers with offerings.

Of the cult of the Genii Cucullati there is, as we have
seen, plenty of evidence at Cirencester (*cf.* p. 68). We shall meet
it again on two other sites in Gloucestershire (*cf.* pp. 88–91),
which was, so far as we at present know, one of the two main
areas of Britain in which it flourished: the other was along the
line of Hadrian's Wall.[1]

The bronze piece from Wycomb, a figure of Mars 3 inches
high, is both classical in character and much superior in
execution to the four carved stones, but all the same con-
spicuously provincial. It was, perhaps, an import from Gaul.[2]
The god stands with his left leg advanced beyond his right
leg and on it most of his weight is supported. He has rugged
features and a thick, curly beard; and his thick hair, which
flows in waves down the back of his neck, is crowned by a
tall, conical helmet without neckguard, cheek-pieces, or crest,
but with a broad brim shading the brow in front. He wears a
plain metal cuirass with a curved, dipping rim across the
abdomen in front and terminating in a row of scallops above a
series of lappets, either of metal or leather. Under the cuirass
is a knee-length linen tunic. The cuirass has shoulder-plates and
on the left upper arm lappets are visible, those on the right arm
being concealed by a fold of the god's cloak. This cloak passes
in thick folds diagonally across the back, with one end caught
round the elbow of the lowered left arm and then hanging down
beside the left flank. The other end crosses the raised right
upper arm in front and then falls down behind it in vertical
folds, one of which forms a zig-zag. The legs are protected by
plain greaves held in place by criss-cross laces at the rear. The
feet are bare, the toes of the left foot being particularly clearly
defined. In his raised right hand Mars would have held a spear;
and his lowered left hand, whose thumb and first finger are
parted, would have grasped the rim of a shield that rested on
the ground beside him. The figurine is as carefully finished
behind as in front. Its workmanship is in general neat and crisp
and the proportions are good. But despite his full martial
panoply this Mars, found on a rural site, as were some other

[1] *Ibid.*, pp. 458–61, nos 1–4, pls. 62, fig. 2; 63, figs. 1–3.
[2] In private hands: unpublished. Illustration between pp. 44-5.

renderings of him in similar guise in Gloucestershire (*cf.* pp. 92–4), was probably worshipped, not principally as the Roman War-god, but as a god of agriculture, vanquisher of sterility in crops and of death and sickness in animals and man.

C. Daglingworth

The village of Daglingworth, about three miles to the north-west of Cirencester, has long been known to have been at least a cult-site in Roman times from the rectangular slab of local oolite, now inserted into the exterior of the north wall of the vestry of the church, which bears the inscription "ma[trib]us et ge[nio l]oci"—a dedication to the Mother-goddesses and to the local Genius.[1] When and precisely where the slab was found is not known. But in 1690 the foundations of a Roman building came to light in a field, formerly known as 'Cave Close", now as "Well Field"; and in 1951 in the same field the plough turned up a carved and inscribed stone 10 inches high and 9 inches wide at its greatest extents. It is a badly weathered votive tablet of oolite, curved at the top and forming a framed niche in which four figures are sculptured in high relief.[2] The scheme of this relief is precisely the same as that of the can-opied scene from Corinium (*cf.* p. 68)—a Mother-goddess, here unfortunately headless, seated on the extreme right and approached from left to right by three Genii Cucullati in a row. But whereas the Corinium goddess is completely frontal, here she is turned three-quarters towards the left to receive from the foremost Genius an offering in the shape of a round cake or bunch of grapes. All three Genii are muffled in thick, hooded cloaks that reach to the knees. The inscription below—"Cudae Lo . . . v"—throws no light upon the picture.

Two years later, and close to the spot on which this panel was found, there appeared the tantalising fragment of another sculpture, the lower left-hand corner of another slab of the same type, $5\frac{1}{2}$ inches wide and $6\frac{1}{2}$ inches high.[3] This sculpture was

---

[1] J. H. C. Toynbee, *Daglingworth in Roman Times* (1959), p. 3; *RIB*, pp. 38, 39, no. 130.

[2] Corinium Museum: Toynbee 1957, pp. 463–4, no. 8, pl. 65, fig. 1; 1959, p. 4, pl. 1; fig. 1; 1964, pl. 44, b; *RIB*, p. 39, no. 129.

[3] Corinium Museum: Toynbee 1957, pp. 464–5, no. 9, pl. 65, fig. 2; 1959, p. 4, fig. 2.

obviously part of a group of figures executed in relief again within a framed niche; and it shows the legs and body of a man standing three-quarters towards the right and wearing an undergarment reaching to the knees. Over this he has a chasuble-like cloak of the same length, which covers the front of the body, passes over the shoulders, and falls down behind the back. One full, elbow-length sleeve of the undergarment is carefully rendered, while the right arm and hand are concealed beneath the front portion of the cloak. The head is lost; but on the right side of the neck is a thick, vertical fold of material, clearly belonging to the lower part of the hood that enveloped the head. We may reasonably guess that two more Genii Cucullati and a Mother-goddess once completed the scene.

D. *Lower Slaughter*

In the Farnworth gravel pit at Lower Slaughter, near Bourton on the Water, there came to light in 1957 evidence of a Romano-British settlement dating, as the coin finds indicate, from the mid-second to the fourth century. There were revealed circular hut floors, ovens, a corn-drying oven, the masonry foundations of a rectangular building, and many potsherds. Five wells were also discovered in the pit, into one of which eight worked stones, six of them sculptured, had been hurled.[1] All the carvings carry the marks of either severe weathering or heavy damage, sometimes of both; and all must belong to the pre-fourth century phase of the settlement, since the well into which they were thrown was close to, and most probably associated with, the rectangular building proved by coins to have been erected in the middle of the fourth century. The weathering suggests that these carvings had been exposed to view for many decades before their burial in the well. On one of the four reliefs presenting human figures the heads seem to have been deliberately scraped off; while the two seated figures, each carved in very high relief, almost in the round, on the face of a block of stone, had been decapitated before being thrown away, since careful searching through the filling of the well for the missing heads proved fruitless.

The evidence does, in fact, strongly support the view that the

[1] Gloucester Museum: *JRS*, xlviii, 49–55, pls. 8, 9; Rhodes, *op. cit.* pp. 30–6, no. 13.

whole collection may have been deposited in the well in the late fourth or early fifth century by Christian iconoclasts who were anxious to get the pagan objects out of sight.

Of the three small altars from the well only one is carved on its principal side and that extremely crudely. On the spectator's right is a frontal and apparently naked male figure, with a triangular face and eyes and mouth rendered by gouged-out holes (*cf.* p. 81). His left arm and hand have vanished, as has his right hand; and beside his shapeless right arm which dangles by his side there is no distinguishable attribute or adjunct. Equally indistinctive is the small quadruped, facing towards the spectator's left, that occupies the left-hand portion of the field. The creature does, however, seem to have large ears and curling horns. If it has these features, it could be a ram and the male figure could conceivably be Mercury.[1]

The two headless, frontally seated figures are equally impossible to identify with any certainty. But both must be deities. One, 8 inches high, who has a bare chest, boots, and drapery swathed round the waist above and reaching to the ankles below, would appear to be male.[2] But there are no attributes to give a clue to its identity. Here the modelling is three-dimensional and plastic; and the same is true of the second seated figure, $8\frac{1}{2}$ inches high, which is probably female, since it wears a long robe reaching to just above the feet. At the figure's sides are traces of objects too much damaged to be safely interpreted. But if one can correctly trace the remnants of an aegis on the chest, she would be Minerva.[3]

The remaining three sculptures from the Lower Slaughter well are all votive panels, two carved in fairly, one in very, low relief. The last, 6 inches high at its greatest extent, where the figures' heads seem to have been deliberately defaced, shows three frontal Genii Cucullati in a row, the lower portions of their hoods being clearly visible. The carving is so flat, two-dimensional and rudimentary, with narrow grooved lines detaching the cloaks from one another and from the background and with no details of the costumes rendered, that one gets the impression that the piece may have been unfinished when

---

[1] *JRS*, xlviii, pl. 8, fig. 3.   [2] *Ibid.*, pl. 9, fig. 3.

[3] *Ibid.*, pl. 9, fig. 2. The interpretation of the object at the figure's left side as a cornucopia is very uncertain.

dedicated.[1] A second votive slab, $11\frac{1}{2}$ inches high, represents the same trio of godlets in their hooded, enveloping cloaks, but this time accompanied by a fourth, non-hooded figure wearing a cape and a short tunic, either another deity or a worshipper. This piece is worked in higher relief than is the first, but is still essentially two-dimensional. All the facial features have been worn away. The slab is topped by a pediment in which is carved a rosette, a symbol of life beyond the grave, flanked by two birds, symbols of the souls of the dead—all tokens that reflect the fertility and healing functions of the Genii.[2]

The third votive panel, presenting yet another trio of frontal male figures and $9\frac{1}{2}$ inches high, is the best preserved of the whole series as to its details, although one head has been broken off. These personages are warriors, each wearing a short tunic girded by a belt and carrying a small circular shield with a central boss, from behind which hangs down what appears to be a sword in a sheath with chape. No helmets crown their thick curly hair, which frames the face and hangs down onto the shoulders.[3] It would seem that we have here a triplicate version of the single Warrior-god with similar dress and attributes, but with the addition of a spear, on the stone from Corinium (*cf.* p. 67), which probably portrays, as do these three, a native form of Mars, The Lower Slaughter panel provides the first proof from Roman Britain that such local Warrior-deities were, like the Matres and the Genii Cucullati, worshipped in triads.

That the settlement on this site was an important religious centre is clearly indicated by the varied character of the sculptures from the well; and to the picture that they give must be added the evidence of a relief found at Lower Slaughter in 1769, and coming almost certainly from the same gravel spread as that in which the well was excavated, and undoubtedly belonging to the same cult-group as the objects found in 1957, but definitely classical in character. This stone shows an orthodox Minerva, competently modelled and standing in a gabled niche with a shell canopy behind her head. She wears a crested helmet, a long girded tunic without any trace of an aegis, and a cloak. In her right hand she holds a spear, while her

---

[1] *Ibid.*, pl. 8, fig. 2. [2] *Ibid.*, pl. 8, fig. 1. [3] *Ibid.*, pl. 9, fig. 1.

left hand rests on the rim of an oval shield.[1] Possibly she once displayed a painted aegis.

E. The Stroud–Nailsworth Area

This region of Gloucestershire has been exceptionally prolific in its yield of religious sculptures in the form of altars and votive tablets carved in relief. Some of the altars, in particular, are so similar to one another in content and style that they would seem to offer evidence for a series of closely related settlements or centres of cult established at various points throughout the area and served by the same closely related carvers' workshops. These altars have been most usefully brought together and published by Mrs. Clifford in our *Transactions*.[2]

King's Stanley, about $3\frac{1}{2}$ miles south-west of Stroud, has produced five small sculptured altars all showing a standing frontal figure and all now in the British Museum.[3] One depicts a somewhat crudely worked Genius wearing a knee-length tunic with elbow-length sleeves, holding a cornucopia in his left hand and a patera above an altar in his right. Another portrays a Warrior-god, unhelmeted, with long, curly hair, wearing a short, belted tunic and equipped with a spear, a round shield with central boss, and a sword in a scabbard with chape. He is, in fact, of the same type as the Corinium and Lower Slaughter native counterparts of Mars (*cf.* pp. 67, 91). The other three altars each carry a more classical type of Mars in that the god is helmeted, while his dress and accoutrements are the same as those of the native figures. An altar in the Gloucester Museum of unrecorded provenance is so similar to those from King's Stanley that it could well have come from the same site and from the same hand or hands.[4]

Another site productive of altars is *Bisley*, about $4\frac{1}{2}$ miles almost due east of Stroud. One altar, rather badly defaced, displays the unusual figure of a mounted Mars riding a clumsily executed horse towards the right. He is helmeted and armed with a round shield and possibly a spear.[5] From Bisley, too,

[1] Gloucester Museum (on loan from the Society of Antiquaries of London): *ibid.*, pp. 54–5, fig. 6. Illustration between pp. 44–5.   [2] Clifford, *op. it.*
[3] *Ibid.*, figs. 1–5.   [4] *Ibid.*, fig. 20; Rhodes, *op. cit.* pp. 21, 23, no. 7.
[5] British Museum: Clifford, *op. cit.* fig. 6.

come four altars said to have been found in a tumulus or barrow, each showing a figure of Mars (in one case badly damaged) standing and facing the spectator. The god has a crested helmet, possibly a cuirass, a short tunic, and a cloak; and he holds a spear in his right hand and grasps with his left the rim of a shield that rests on the ground beside him—another more classical trait. One of the four is the work of a much inferior hand.[1] These altars, once in Lypiatt Park adjacent to the village of Bisley, are now in the Stroud Museum, as are two more carved stones, also once in Lypiatt Park and presumably of the same provenance. One is an altar with a snake coiled round it; the other has on it the busts of a man and woman and could be a funerary piece, not belonging to the votive series.[2] The most pleasing of the Bisley sculptured altars, now in the British Museum, shows Silvanus, or his local Hunter-god counterpart, wearing a conical headdress, a cloak, and a girded tunic. His left hand rests on a gnarled stick and in his right he holds aloft a dead hare above the snout of a long-eared dog that stands on its hind-legs in the attempt to seize the quarry.[3] Possibly also a local Hunter-god is the naked figure on an altar from *Cherington*, $4\frac{1}{2}$ miles east of Nailsworth. He has long hair reaching to the shoulders, wears no cap, and holds a hunting-spear in his left hand. Beneath his now vanished right hand, on the ground, is what appears to be a dog.[4] At *Hazelwood*, about a mile east of Nailsworth, was found yet another Mars altar, where the god wears a crested helmet, a belted tunic, and a cloak and is armed with a spear, a sword in a sheath with chape, and a round shield.[5] The type is the same as that on the three King's Stanley altars (*cf.* p. 92).

At *Custom Scrubs* (or *The Scrubs*), $1\frac{1}{2}$ miles almost due north of Bisley, were found two gabled votive tablets carved in a most distinctive style and clearly by the same hand.[6] One portrays Mars wearing tunic, cloak, boots, and a triple-crested helmet that fits closely, like a hood, round the face and terminates in a scalloped edging at the base of the neck. The eyes and mouth

---

[1] *Ibid.*, figs. 21–4. [2] *Ibid.*, figs. 27, 28. [3] *Ibid.*, fig. 7.
[4] Pavey-Smith Collection Nailsworth: *ibid.* fig. 29.
[5] Stroud Museum: *ibid.*, fig. 30.
[6] Gloucester Museum: Toynbee 1963, p. 152, nos. 63, 66, pls. 65, 66; Rhodes, *op. cit.* pp. 27–30, no. 12.

are mere slits and the nose is wedge-shaped. The god is equipped with a spear, an oval shield that rests on the ground at his left side, and a sword in a sheath with chape hanging from a broad belt. His abdomen is sheathed in a smooth-surfaced, apron-like feature, probably meant to represent metal armour. By his right side is an altar or pedestal surmounted by a double cornucopia —an emblem of fertility and a clear proof of the agrarian functions that were attached to Mars in Gloucestershire. The whole effect is very flat and two-dimensional and sharply grooved, rigidly patterned lines indicate the folds of cloak and tunic. Cut in rough letters in the niche in which Mars stands is an inscription—"Deo Rom[u]lo Gulioepius donavit Iuventinus facit", interesting as equating Mars with Romulus and as preserving one of the very few craftsmen's signatures that survive from Roman Britain.[1] The second panel from the site depicts a Genius, with disproportionately broad chest and shoulders. He wears a tunic and cloak rendered in the same manner as are Mars' garments, holds a patera over an altar and a cornucopia, while his close-fitting hood marks him out from the orthodox Graeco-Roman Genius type.

F. Cinderford (parish of Ruspidge)

In 1970 four male heads, carved in sandstone were noted in the garden of 47 Buckshaft Road, Cinderford, where they had stood as ornaments when that house was occupied by Mr. Arthur Jackson, who died in 1969. Through Dr. Anne Ross who had studied the heads and believes them to be genuine Romano-Celtic work, they were acquired by the Gloucester Museum.[2] Mr. Jackson's niece has informed the museum that she remembers her uncle chipping stones in the garden. Were they ancient, they would presumably portray local deities and attest the one-time presence of a native cult-centre in the area. There is, of course, no positive proof that Mr. Jackson carved these heads. But despite Dr. Ross's verdict I must confess to feeling very dubious about their antiquity. L260 and A2436 in particular strike me as having a distinctly modern look, the other two as being suspiciously grotesque in appearance. They

---

[1] *RIB*, p. 40, no. 132.

[2] L260: 290 mm. high; A24363: 600 mm. high; A26364; 580 mm. high; A24364; 350 mm. high.

are uncomfortably reminiscent of the large number, nearly 200, of such heads that suddenly appeared in 1966/7 and later in gardens and allotments in the Bradford area, many of which are quite certainly not Celtic.[1]

ISOLATED PIECES

Those works of Roman sculpture that have been discovered in isolation at various places in Gloucestershire can be briefly listed, passing from north to south and then westward. Their find-spots and present locations seldom tell us anything of the contexts for which they were made.

A. Lemington (1½ miles north-east of Morton-in-the-Marsh)
Chedworth Museum[2]

The crude figure of a native goddess, labelled with the high-sounding name of "Dea Regina",[3] is cut in low relief in a recessed panel on a block of stone 10½ inches high. She has bushy hair, gouged-out holes and a slit for eyes and mouth and holds objects that cannot now be identified.

B. Dorn (*c.* 1 mile north-west of Morton-in-the-Marsh)

Presumed to be lost, but photographed in 1905.[4] Now known to have been acquired in 1924 by the Royal Ontario Museum, Toronto (Cat. No. 924.74.1).

Carved in relief in a recess on the face of an altar-shaped block of stone, 44 inches high and with a triangular excrescence at the top, in place of a focus, is the frontal figure of a Genius of the orthodox Graeco-Roman type. The face has been smashed away, but the mural crown or modius that usually surmounts the head is clearly visible. He wears a short tunic, a cloak, and boots and holds a cornucopia in his left hand. His lost right hand was extended over an altar at his side and would have grasped a patera. With this sculpture was found another altar-shaped block, again topped by a triangular excrescence and also carved in relief with a Genius, this time veiled and less well preserved. It, too, is now at Toronto (Cat. No. 924.74.2). At

---

[1] *Daily Telegraph* 11 January 1967; *JRS*, xlvii, 179; S. Jackson, *Celtic and other Stone Heads* (1973). [2] Clifford, *op. cit.* fig. 12. [3] *RIB*, p. 37, no. 125.
[4] *TBGAS*, lxxxi, 194–5, pl. 19. Illustrations between pp. 140–1.

Dorn air photographs taken in 1960 did, indeed, reveal a rectangular enclosure with traces of a street-grid, suggestive of a small Roman town.[1] Hence, no doubt, the classical character of the sculpture.

C. *Stow-on-the-Wold*
Ashmolean Museum, Oxford[2]

Carved in a recess on the front of a stone block, $13\frac{3}{4}$ inches high and tapering towards the top, is the frontal figure of Mars, very roughly worked. He seems to wear a crested helmet, but his knee-length tunic shows no details. In his right hand he holds a short spear and his left hand rests on the top of a rectangular shield at his side.

D. *Lechlade*
Ashmolean Museum, Oxford[3]

This upper portion of a stone figure, $8\frac{1}{2}$ inches high, of which everything from the waist downwards has gone, clearly belongs to a Genius, veiled and holding in his left hand a cornucopia. His chest is nude, but he has a cloak draped over his left shoulder. The right fore-arm and hand are lost. Since the back is unworked, the figure must have been intended to stand against a wall or in niche.

E. *Churchdown* (halfway between Cheltenham and Gloucester)
In private hands.[4]

A small, pillar-like block of sandstone, $3\frac{1}{2}$ inches high, has been carved in the shape of a very stylised human head and neck, the latter, which is as wide as the former, being encircled by a broad torque. This attribute suggests a Celtic god, while the treatment of the eyes, nose, and mouth and the elongation of the neck betray native workmanship.

F. *Coaley* (6.4 miles north of Dursley)
On loan to the Gloucester Museum: L163.[5]

This badly battered oolite stone head, about half life-size,

---

[1] *JRS*, li, 132–3, fig. 6, pl. 11, fig. 2.

[2] *Ashmolean Museum Report of the Visitors* (1955), pl. 4, c.

[3] *Oxoniensia*, xiii, 76, pl. 7, a.

[4] Unpublished: found in the garden of War Close, Churchdown, in 1965.

[5] Unpublished.

which was found in the garden of Woodleigh House, may possibly be of Roman date. The face has a somewhat chubby look and the hair is rendered in wavy locks.

G. *Symmondsall* (3½ miles north-east of Wotton-under-Edge)
Property of Dr. and Mrs. Davies, Berkeley House, Wotton-under-Edge).[1]

A small votive tablet with rounded top, said to have been found at Symmondsall, presents in a small recess a row of three very crudely carved frontal figures that appear to be standing, but could be meant to be seated. They have large round heads, rectangular bodies, with very slight indication of the arms, and short legs. They are possibly the Matres.

H. *Newington Bagpath* (6 miles north-east of Wotton-under Edge)
Ashmolean Museum, Oxford[2]

This semicircular stone relief, 15 inches wide and 10 inches high, was formerly built into the wall of a medieval barn at Calcot Farm. It is badly weathered, but a group of four figures can be discerned. On the right is a horseman riding towards the right, wearing a helmet, and holding a small round shield: he recalls the mounted Mars from Bisley (*cf.* p. 92) and may be Mars too. In the centre of the picture is a seated figure holding a sceptre, who appears to be female and could be a Mother-goddess. Behind her in the background stands a round-headed figure, perhaps an attendant or a worshipper. Finally, on the left of the scene, is another standing personage, male and wearing a short tunic. He appears to be pouring a libation with his right hand over an altar and might be the dedicator of the slab, the Julius of the inscription just below the group, which reads "Iulius l[ibens] s[olvit]", "Julius willingly fulfilled his vow". Crude as the carving is, this is an unusually complex and interesting scene of native cult.

I. *Churcham* (3 miles west of Gloucester, west of the Severn)
Inserted above the north door of the village church is a stone

[1] Unpublished.
[2] *TBGAS*, lx, 347–8, pl. 4 opp. p. 345; *Ashmolean Museum Report of the Visitors* (1955), pl. 4, a; *RIB*, p. 41, no. 135.

plaque very roughly carved with the standing figure of a native god.[1] He has a huge head, square body, and tiny legs. His arms are extended laterally and in either hand he holds a trilobate object. On the ground on either side of him is a wheel.

J. Chepstow

Let into the inner face of the south-west wall of the ruined banqueting-hall of Chepstow Castle is a square stone panel containing a trio of frontal and naked male figures.[2] Occupying the left-hand and central portions of the picture and filling the whole height of the slab is the largest figure of the three. He seems to have a round headdress or perhaps a thick mop of hair. In his right hand, which is extended laterally, he holds what appears to be either a flaming torch or a spreading sprig of leaves. Below his right hand is an indeterminate circular object and above his left arm, also extended, and touching the left side of his head is an oblong feature, also indeterminate. In the right-hand portion of the panel are two small figures, one above the other, representing either lesser deities or worshippers of their larger companion, who is undoubtedly a god. The lower personage holds a torch or a sprig in his extended right hand, while the upper one has the fingers of his raised right hand outspread in a gesture of greeting. Here, as on the Newington Bagpath relief (*cf.* p. 97), we have a complex religious scene the significance of which is hidden from us.

K. Horfield Common (near Bristol)
Bristol Museum[3]

In Kellaway Avenue there came to light a bronze figurine of Mercury, a classical and almost certainly imported work. It is 6.4 cm. high and shows the god naked, with wings on his head and at his ankles, and poised on his right foot. In his raised right hand he would have held his now vanished caduceus.

L. Unknown Provenance

A very badly weathered votive stone relief in the Gloucester Museum[4] of unrecorded find-spot shows a female figure wearing a long robe and a veil. In her left hand she holds what might

---

[1] *TBGAS*, xlv, 91–3 with pl.   [2] Unpublished.   [3] F2350: unpublished.
[4] A2740: Rhodes, *op. cit.* pp. 35, 36, no. 14.

be a cornucopia, while her right hand rests on a tree-trunk on the spectator's left. An indeterminate vertical feature emerges from behind her right shoulder. There can be little doubt that she is a goddess of some kind. Another sculpture of unknown provenance said to have been found in Gloucestershire is the bronze figurine of a bull, $1\frac{3}{4}$ inches high and 2 inches long.[1] It is well preserved and naturalistic in style.

SUMMARY

To summarise this survey—no county can outrival Gloucestershire in the great variety, both in subject-matter and in execution, of the Roman sculptures that its soil has yielded. Of the towns Corinium, the *civitas* capital, has produced both the most sophisticated (e.g. the bronze Cupid) and some of the most native (e.g. the Genii Cucullati reliefs) of the sculptured works. The colonia of Gloucester is remarkable for its Celtic head as well as for its series of locally made carvings of Mercury and oriental gods; but what was probably its most classical monument, a large bronze statue, is unfortunately known only from fragments. In both towns funerary stelai attest the military character of their initial history; whereas at Sea Mills it would seem to be the life of the civilian town alone that its sculptures represent. On the whole, it is the countryside that has proved to be the richest numerically in material, providing examples both of classical marbles (the Woodchester and Spoonley Wood villas) and of votive bronzes of varying standards of workmanship, in addition to a great wealth of unsophisticated stone figures and reliefs that illustrate the religious cults of simple folk, spread widely throughout our area. It can, in fact, be concluded that there are few facets of religious worship in Roman Britain that have not been illuminated by the sculptures from this county.

[1] British Museum 1883, 1–6, 1: unpublished,

SELECT BIBLIOGRAPHY

Clifford, E. M. (1939) "Roman Altars in Gloucestershire", *Transactions of the Bristol and Gloucestershire Archaeological Society*, lx, pp. 297–307.

Goodburn, R. (1972) *The Roman Villa, Chedworth.*

Haverfield, F. (1917–18) "Roman Cirencester", *Archaeologia*, lxix (1920) 161–209.

Lysons, S. (1797) *An Account of Roman Antiquities discovered at Woodchester in the County of Gloucester.*

Rhodes, J. F. (1964) *Catalogue of the Romano-British Sculptures in the Gloucester City Museum.*

Toynbee, J. M. C. (1957) "Genii Cucullati in Roman Britain", *Collection Latomus*, xxviii, pp. 456–69.

(1959) *Daglingworth in Roman Times.*

(1963) *Art in Roman Britain* (ed. 2).

(1964) *Art in Britain under the Romans.*

Wheeler, R. E. M., and T. V. (1932) *Report on the Excavation of the Prehistoric, Roman, and Post-Roman Site in Lydney Park, Gloucestershire.*

ADDENDUM

Cirencester (Corinium)

In 1974 there came to light at Phoenix Way a carved stone block, probably once part of the west gate of the Roman city. The sculpture shows the left-hand upper part of a much battered figure of *Mercury*, worked in high relief in a niche. The facial features are smashed away; but there is a thick, curly lock of hair on the left side of the brow, surmounted by a floppy petasos, with one wing surviving. A thick fold of the god's cloak covers his left shoulder: his chest and left upper arm are bare. The figure would appear to have been originally a fine piece of sculpting (*Britannia* vi, 1975, p. 273, pl. 2i, fig. B).

IV

Bristol under the Normans

By David Douglas

STUDIES concerning Bristol in the twelfth century have occupied only a subordinate place in the vast literature which has been devoted to the history of the city. Nonetheless, the growth of Bristol at about that time was of some special significance, and it may be useful to note, however briefly, why this should have been so. Despite all that had taken place in this region at an earlier date it was not until 1051 that Bristol seems to have entered individually and prominently into the national story. In that year according to the Anglo-Saxon Chronicle, Earl Godwine, Earl of Wessex, and his sons, revolted against King Edward the Confessor, and the most famous of those sons, namely Harold the later King who was to die at Hastings, was exiled. Flying westward on that occasion he took ship from Bristol, and in due course reached Ireland where he took refuge among the Norse settlers in Dublin. Twelve years later, having been restored to favour, he was to use Bristol as his base when conducting his great campaign against the Welsh in 1063. Already, it would seem, Bristol was beginning to play its own part in the politics of England. But it was the Norman Conquest which inaugurated for the city, as for England, a new period of wider historical development.

As is well known, the Norman Conquest and the Norman settlement of England were only effected gradually, and it was not until about the beginning of 1068 that Bristol was brought to accept the new order. Then, however, the acceptance of the Norman regime was so complete that when in the summer of 1068 three of the sons of King Harold came over from Ireland to attempt a rebellion against the Normans in England, they were repelled by the citizens of Bristol aided by the thegns of north Somerset. The new Norman king for his part was quick to recognise the importance of the town that was rising to power in the boundaries of Wessex and Mercia. The area of Bristol was still small. But Bristol controlled an important bridgehead. It perhaps possessed a mint, and it was beginning to be surrounded by defensive walls. Its inhabitants were moreover already indulging in trade overseas, particularly with Ireland, and they were evidently in possession of ships.

For these reasons Bristol was now claimed to be part of the King's manor of Barton Regis. William the Conqueror soon handed it over to his wife, Matilda of Flanders. After Matilda's death in 1083 it passed to one of the Norman king's principal lieutenants, Geoffrey bishop of Coutances, one of the chief architects of the Domesday Survey. Bristol was subsequently given to another of the greater Norman magnates—Robert fitz Hamon from Creully near Bayeux who was later to be celebrated as the conqueror of Glamorgan, and as the founder of Tewkesbury Abbey. Evidently Bristol had become a possession to be coveted, and it is not wholly surprising that on the death of Robert fitz Hamon it reverted once more to the royal house passing by marriage into the hands of Robert Earl of Gloucester who was an illegitimate son of King Henry I.

Bristol's close connection with the Anglo-Norman royal house was at once a cause and a result of the town's advance to prosperity. As early as 1125 William of Malmesbury described Bristol as a flourishing port, and commented, with surprise and admiration, on its trade with Ireland and with other countries beyond the seas. Indeed, one of the less reputable features of that trade had already attracted the severe censure of Wulfstan the great Bishop of Worcester who died in 1095. Apparently, it had been the practice of Bristol traders to export British boys and girls overseas as slaves, and it needed the strong intervention of this powerful and saintly prelate to put a stop to this disgusting traffic.

Certainly, the rapid growth of Bristol's commerce made the town of special interest to the monarchy. And this interest was shown not only in the construction of defensive ramparts, but also in the first erection of a royal castle. This castle, placed near the junction of the Frome and the Avon, was intended to provide a means of controlling Bristol and also of defending the town from assaults from elsewhere. It was, in fact, to play a

considerable part in the disturbances which followed the death
of William the Conqueror, and it was described by the Anglo-
Saxon Chronicle as being a fortress of great strength. And
during the same period the burgesses of Bristol for their part
were beginning to display that spirit of aggressive adventure
which was to characterise so much of the later medieval history
of the city. Not only were they carrying out trading, and sometimes piratical, ventures but they were prone to pillage the
surrounding countryside. Bath, for instance, had reason
throughout the twelfth century to complain of their activities.
The same enterprise which was carrying Bristol's trade overseas
was also being shown in the increasing influence that was being
exercised by the city in the political life of England.

Thus, for example, Bristol took a prominent share in the civil
war which, on the death of King Henry I in 1135, started
between Matilda the late King's daughter who was the wife of
Geoffrey Count of Anjou and Stephen of Blois, Henry's
nephew. Throughout Bristol was consistently to sustain the
Angevin cause, and this was to prove in due course to be of
great advantage to the city. King Stephen was himself for a
time a prisoner in Bristol castle, and the eventual succession of
Matilda's son in 1154 as King Henry II of England owed much
to Bristol's support. It is not surprising therefore that one of the
earliest acts of Henry II as King was to give Bristol the first of
its royal charters. The city was in fact approaching the apex of
its political strength. Indeed, after the middle of the twelfth
century it was reckoned by some to rank in wealth and power
third among the cities of England.

The charter of Henry II for Bristol was issued in 1155, and it
was in general terms, being mainly concerned to confirm such
privileges as the city already possessed. What was more significant was the continuing link between Bristol and the ruling
dynasty, and this was confirmed afresh in 1180 when John, then
Count of Mortain and soon to be King John of England,
ratified in detail the privileges which had been accorded to
Bristol by his father. Finally, among these twelfth-century royal
charters must be mentioned that issued by Henry II in 1171
which confirmed the special rights which the burgesses of
Bristol had already acquired in the city of Dublin. The political
link thus established between Bristol and Ireland was to be

sustained and strengthened. And it is surly of high interest that
many of the medieval Irish boroughs, such as Cork, Limerick
and Waterford were in due course given privileges modelled on
those which had earlier been granted to Bristol.

Meanwhile, Bristol itself was steadily growing in size and
prosperity. A feature of its history in the twelfth century was the
development of the various suburbs adjoining the original
nucleus round the bridge. The castle to the east had marked the
beginning of this development, and beyond the castle there
were growing new settlements in the area which is now Old
Market. But the main development of the twelfth century was
towards what was still the independent manor of Bedminster.
Thus was to be formed the distinct suburb of Redcliffe, and
beyond this was the area under the jurisdiction of the Templars,
later to be known as the Temple Fee. All these suburbs had
their own independent life and they often quarrelled with each
other. But while these districts had conflicting interests, they
had also much in common. They were all concerned to develop
the trade of the town of which they formed a part. It
was natural therefore that their unity should soon come
to be formally recognised.

During this earlier period, too, many families were being
founded on wealth derived from Bristol. Among them it is
natural to mention in particular that of Robert Fitz Harding.
He may originally have been a royal official in the city. Certainly, he acquired much property and more power in Bristol.
And just before the accession of Henry II the family of Fitz
Harding began a new period of prosperity when they received
the Berkeley lands which had been forfeited by an adherent of
King Stephen. The whole familiar story is interesting in this
context as illustrating how even in the twelfth century a towns-
man of the prosperous borough of Bristol could thrive to such
effect that he raised his family into the ranks of the feudal
aristocracy. Indeed, the career of Robert Fitz Harding may
perhaps have a further general interest for according to the Song
of Dermot it was through his intervention when a very old man,
that Dermot, the exiled King of Leinster, sought and obtained
the help of King Henry II of England, and thus prepared the
way for the Angevin penetration into Ireland. And throughout the Middle Ages, the house of Berkeley played a vital,

and sometimes a determining, part in the development of Bristol.

The increasing influence of Bristol on the national life of England in the twelfth century had moreover its ecclesiastical as well as its secular connotations. As early as the tenth century Westbury-on-Trym had for a short time been a centre of Benedictine monasticism. But the ecclesiastical development of Bristol itself was to come later. The parishes of St. Werburgh, of All Saints, and of St. Mary Le Port can probably be traced back to the eleventh century or beyond, but it was Robert, Earl of Gloucester, the son of King Henry I, who established the first Benedictine house in Bristol. This was a cell of Tewkesbury Abbey which he established in 1129 on a site just north of the old city across the Frome where is now to be found the church of St. James.

Soon there was to follow another and more spectacular development associated with Robert Fitz Harding. For the culminating event in the career of this remarkable man was his establishment of the notable Augustinian monastery which is now the cathedral of Bristol. The family of Fitz Harding was to continue yet further its ecclesiastical patronage in the city. His wife supplemented her husband's great benefaction by founding a house of Augustinian canonesses near the summit of St. Michael's Hill, and endowed it with lands outside the city in what is now Southmead. But it was Robert Fitz Harding's own foundation of St. Augustine's abbey which was above all significant. For the spread of Augustinian communities was a feature of the religious life of the twelfth century and Bristol was here sharing in that enthusiasm. One of the most influential of the early Augustinian foundations had been that of St. Victor in Paris which had earlier sent several of its canons to England, and it is therefore significant that the first Augustinian abbot in Bristol had probably been at one time a monk at St. Victor in Paris. The connection between Bristol and the house of St. Victor was long to be sustained

In this way, was exemplified what was perhaps the most important feature of the development of Bristol in the twelfth century. Bristol under the Normans came to make an ever increasing contribution to the political, economic and ecclesiastical life of England. But the world of which Bristol after the

Norman Conquest came to form a part was much wider even than England itself.

The point is worth elaborating, especially at the present time. Whether the Norman Conquest was or was not a "good thing" is endlessly and tediously debated, and usually in terms which have little relation to the conditions of the twelfth century. There can, however, be no doubt that the Norman Conquest linked England more closely than ever before, since Roman times to Western Europe. The King of England was also duke of Normandy. He claimed with varying degrees of success to be overlord of Brittany and Maine, and he was certainly a dominant force in northern France. England was thus brought more intimately into the political system of Europe, and in that system twelfth century Bristol was caught up. Its earliest ruler after the conquest was a Flemish princess who had married a Norman duke; its castle was begun by a Norman bishop; and later it was governed by a Norman lord the centre of whose power lay between Caen and Bayeux.

The process reached a new climax when with the active assistance of the city of Bristol the Angevin cause triumphed, and in 1154 Henry II from Anjou inherited and enlarged the great empire which the Normans had created. He was King of England; he was duke of Normandy; he was count of Anjou, of Maine, of Brittany and of Tourraine. And through his wife he was also duke of Aquitaine. Under him in fact Bristol became an integral and a significant part of a great realm which stretched from the Tweed to the Pyrenees, and which indeed comprised more of modern France than was ruled by the French kings of the house of Capet reigning from Paris. And in all this Bristol shared.

Nor was this all. The twelfth century was precisely the period when western Europe as a whole was beginning to attain a new sense of unity and a new access of political strength. Many causes could be suggested for this development which was to be of such importance to the future. There might for instance be cited in this connection the shift in the balance of power from Germany westward across the Rhine and southward across the Alps—a shift of which the Norman conquests of England and Sicily were at once a symptom and a partial cause. Again, economic and demographic forces operating at this time might be adduced to account for the changing social structure of twelfth century Europe. A rapid growth of population is alleged to have occurred during these years, and there were notable improvements in communications. Better roads were being built and more rivers bridged, whilst technical advances were made in the practice of agriculture. The enlarged villages of the west became less isolated, and at the same time the wider development of commerce, which was thus facilitated, fostered the growth of the nascent trading communities in the rising towns such as Bristol.

Indeed some of these early developments have a very modern flavour. Western Europe, as Dr. Southern remarks, emerged in the twelfth century as "a single powerful and aggressive economic system". Thus what might perhaps be called a "common market" extended from Yorkshire through the industrial towns of Flanders to the fairs of Champagne and on to the ports of the Mediterranean. And of this common market Bristol in the twelfth century began to form a part. Bristol shipping thus rapidly became a feature of the life of the borough, and here the connection with Ireland was particularly valuable. Indeed, much of Bristol's growing prosperity at this time depended on the developing Irish trades. But Bristol merchantships were also pushing down the Severn and then southwards to Europe. Cloth was the main export commodity together with hides from the Bristol tanneries. In Gascony, especially, Bristol merchants would sell such goods, or exchange them for the wines which they would import from the region of Bordeaux. Altogether it is a fascinating picture which today offers plenty of opportunities for speculation and comparison.

Perhaps, however, some qualification is needed. Today we are often and very properly reminded that a European community to be truly united must be something more than simply a common market. Similarly, it had been contended that it was not merely—or even chiefly—economic forces which in the twelfth century fostered the unity of the West. Enhanced political significance is now for instance often attributed to the reforming movement in the western Church which was sponsored in particular by the successors of Pope Gregory VII. Undoubtedly, the policy of these men caused profound changes in the pattern of western ecclesiastical life, and brought the

Church into conflict with many secular rulers, as, for instance, Henry I and particularly Henry II, of England.

But perhaps the political results of this movement are not even thus to be circumscribed. Did the ecclesiastical revival of that age help to foster Latin Christendom as a self-conscious and distinct political entity? Did it also contribute at this time to a growing cleavage between Eastern and Western Europe, between Rome and Constantinople, between Byzantine culture and the Latin revival in art and letters which was so soon to take place in the West? In short, was it for ecclesiastical and cultural, as well as for economic reasons that Western Europe now acquired a new sense of its separate identity? These are deep questions which admit no easy answers. But they were certainly of major concern to the men of twelfth-century Bristol. Bristol's vigorous youth as a borough was passed during a critical period in the history of Europe, and a reconsideration of those distant happenings might even trench upon fundamental questions relating to that "European civilisation" of which we hear so much today.

This slight sketch has inevitably been concerned mainly with generalities. But it may have suggested how profitable would be a new and detailed study of the history of Bristol during the century that followed the Norman Conquest.

V

The Origins of St. Augustine's, Bristol

By J. C. Dickinson

THE process by which the abbey of St. Augustine, Bristol came into existence has long been recognised as a complex one. Some of the problems involved have been considered by Mr. Sabin,[1] and other writers have made wary remarks on the subject.[2] The prospect of clearing up at least the main points of what is certainly a singularly tangled problem have recently been greatly improved by the text of the cartulary or *Red Book* of St. Augustine's Bristol now being available to scholars through a microfilm deposited in the Bodleian Library,[3] whilst a recent edition of the Anglo-Norman *Chronicle* of Wigmore Abbey[4] has made more usable a related source inadequately utilised in the past. The catalogue of the Berkeley archives[5] provides one or two useful charters and mentions briefly the Roll of Abbot Newland, which contains notes on the history of the abbey worthy of close attention, despite certain obvious historical howlers.[6] Notes in *The Maire of Bristowe is Kalendar* have little

[1] A. Sabin, "The Foundation of the Abbey at Bristol", *TBGAS*, lxxv, 35–42.

[2] E.g. D. Knowles, C. N. L. Brooke and V. London, *The heads of religious houses in England and Wales, 940–1216* (Cambridge, 1972), p. 155; B. Smalley, "Andrew of St. Victor, Abbot of Wigmore", in *Récherches de théologie ancienne et médiévale*, x, 358–73.

[3] MS. Film Dep. 912; the original is largely of thirteenth-century date. See G. R. C. Davis, *Medieval Cartularies of Great Britain* (1958), no. 77.

[4] Ed. J. C. Dickinson and P. T. Ricketts in *Transactions of the Woolhope Naturalists' Field Club*, xxxix, 413–45.

[5] I. H. Jeayes, *Descriptive Catalogue of the Charters and Muniments . . . of Berkeley Castle* (Bristol, 1892).

[6] The original of Newland's Roll is amongst the Berkeley archives (Catalogue No. 97, p. 290) and was compiled in 5 Henry VII. The portions which concern the establishment of St. Augustine's Abbey were printed by I. H. Jeayes in *TBGAS*, xiv, 119–30 whence the following text is taken:

value.[1] Until the *Red Book* has been edited with the same care for detail that Dr. Ross bestowed on the cartulary of Cirencester Abbey complete appreciation of its contents will not be practicable. It is unfortunate that it contains no early papal privileges or episcopal confirmations to throw light on the very early stages of the process of foundation of the abbey; the fact that the copies of many of its deeds have the list of witnesses omitted is a further disadvantage.

Over the outer door of the noble reconstructed gate-house of the Abbey an inscription of a most unusual type asserts *Rex Henricus Secundus et Dominus Robertus filius Hardingi filii regis Daciae huius monasterii primi fundatores exstiterunt.*[2] What precisely were the parts which these two played in establishing the abbey of St. Augustine? To this question charters in the *Red Book* and elsewhere give us a fairly clear answer, albeit one which is a little hazy chronologically.

A well-known deed of King Stephen refers to Henry, duke of Normandy . . . *qui eiusdem loci fundator est,*[3] but this rather wide statement is to be compared with the somewhat unusual phrase in one of Henry's own charters in which he speaks of the *ecclesiam . . . quam inicio iuventutis mee beneficiis et protectione cepi juvare et fovere causa et amore dei.*[4] This, in effect, implies that King Henry

---

This goode lorde (Robert fitz Harding) fundatour and Chanon of the Monastery of Seint Augustines bi Bristowe began the fundacion of the/same in the yere of our Lord mcxi And bilded the churche And all other howses of offices according to the same bi the space of vi yeres. And so after in the yere of our lord mcxlvi Robertus Bisshope of Worcetr Boniface Bisshope of Excetr Nicholas Bisshope of Landaf And Gregorie Bisshope of Seint Asse dedicate the church of the saide Monastery. And then after Alured Bisshope of Worcetr inducte vj chanons of the Monastery of Wigmore gederid And chosen by Sir Robert fiz Herding our fundatour in to our churche and Monastery aforesaide on the Ester day which was that yere the xj day of Aprile And in the yere of our lord mcxlviij (pp. 125-6).

Richarde the first Abbot of oure Monastery was inducte on Esterday and the xj day of Aprile in the yere of our Lord mcxlviij And the XI yere of the Regne of King Steryn And rewlyd XXXVIIJ yeres And decessid the iiij day of September And is beried the yere of our Lord mc$_{iiij}^{xx}$vj. (p. 126).

[1] R. Ricart, *The Maire of Bristowe is Kalendar*, ed. Lucy Toulmin Smith (Camden Society, N.S. 5, 1872).

[2] W. Barrett, *The History and Antiquities of the City of Bristol* (Bristol, 1789), p. 287.

[3] *Calendar of Charter Rolls*, iii. 377.

[4] W. Dugdale, *Monasticon Anglicanum*, ed. Caley, Bandinell and Ellis (1830), vi (i), 366 = Cartulary f. 17r.

was not responsible for the original initiative that led to the establishment of a monastery at St. Augustine's, but aided the house in its very early stages, when he was a young man. Such is precisely the impression we get from the early charters of Henry, which have survived. The earliest of these, as has recently been suggested, must be associated with his visit to Bristol in 1153.[1] It is fortunately not necessary in this context to investigate in detail the series of benefactions of Henry granted both before and after his accession to the throne, which concern his dealings with Robert fitz Harding and St. Augustine's. They are very complex and suggest that Robert's acquisitions of the Berkeley estates was far from being a straightforward process. All that need here be noted is that from 1153 onwards Henry was a benefactor to the newly-founded monastery, but was not the *fundator* in the technical sense of having the patronage of the house, nor was this right exercised by his successors.

What then was the part played by Robert fitz Harding? That he was the founder, in the sense of having originated the monastery, and its legal patron is quite certain. Although my extensive researches in the bulky manuscripts from the great abbey of St. Victor at Paris (to whose Order St. Augustine's belonged) now in the Bibliothèque Nationale produced very little useful material regarding English Victorine houses in general or Bristol in particular, the superb necrology of the house does contain an obit. of Robert fitz Harding which shows him as the founder of Bristol—*Robertus filius Herdic* [*sic*] *ecclesie sancti augustini de Bristou canonicus et fundator, de cuius beneficio habuimus x marcas argenti.*[2] This alone would be adequate grounds for regarding Robert as the originator of the new monastery, but its testimony is abundantly confirmed by various references in the *Red Book.* In one of Robert's deeds of gift to the canons we find mention of their church which "by the grace of God and by the help of the lord king I have founded" (*per gratiam dei et per auxilium domini mei regis ecclesiam fundavi*).[3] Other charters amply confirm this. One of his sons refers to the church of St. Augustine *quam dominus pater meus ad honorem dei fundavit*[4] and

---

[1] *Regesta Regum Anglo-Normannorum*, ed. H. A. Cronne and R. H. C. Davis (Oxford, 1958), iii, nos. 309 and 310, there described as 'pretended original".
[2] Paris: Bibliothèque Nationale, Ms. Lat. 14673 f. 167r.
[3] Cartulary f. 34r.   [4] *Ibid.*, f. 36r.

one of Earl William of Gloucester mentions "the monastery (*cenobium*) of regular canons which the same Robert set up in the church of the blessed Augustine of Bristol".[1] There is no doubt that in no sense can Henry II claim the title of founder of the monastery at St. Augustine's, whatever Stephen's charter may assert to the contrary, but that this must be reserved to Robert fitz Harding, despite valuable help which he received from Henry in the early stages of establishing the house.

When was the monastery of St. Augustine's founded? Before we attempt to answer this question it is essential to stress that the process of foundation of a religious house in twelfth-century England was much more complex and often much more prolonged than is usually recognised.

Although the traditional approach to this matter demands that we ask what was the date of the foundation of a monastery, the more one studies the process the more obvious it becomes that this is a highly undesirable way of formulating the question. It is undesirable because it fails to realise that there was no single event or stage which could be taken as marking the inception of a religious community, and that the process of foundation did not follow any uniform course or come to completion quickly. For a new monastery to come into existence there were obviously four necessities—provision of a body of religious, provision of a site, the provision of endowment and the erection of a church and domestic buildings. With certain houses of Austin canons such as Nostell and Llanthony we find first a community of hermits acquiring a site but little or no endowment. In the cases of others which were founded by the conversion to monastic purposes of an existing parish or collegiate church, the endowment and the place of worship considerably pre-date the foundation of the religious community, though there would follow the re-construction of the church and addition of permanent monastic buildings, a process which might take a century or more to carry to completion. If we accept the rather controversial assumption of many medieval annalists that the monastery begins when a community arrives on the site, we close our eyes to the fact that in some cases, at least, preparation

---

[1] *Ibid.*, See *Earldom of Gloucester Charters*, ed. R. B. Patterson (Oxford, 1973), no. 12.

for the monastery had begun long before, and to the fact that the accumulation of adequate endowment and construction of conventual buildings might go on for some years afterwards. Though it would, perhaps, be going too far to aver that dates of foundations of monasteries should be regarded as myths (though useful myths), it is certainly true that it is much more fruitful to pose the question "how was the monastery founded?" rather than "when was it founded?", provided that we are clear that the answer to the former question is incomplete without careful attention to the question of chronology. Let us seek then to discover how the abbey of St. Augustine came into existence.

The invaluable deeds of the *Red Book* throw very little light on the first moves made to establish a monastery of St. Augustine. The main proportion of the charters of Robert fitz Harding evidently belonged to the period after his acquisition of the Berkeley estates in 1153–4 and no gift of Henry is earlier than the time of his visit to Bristol in 1153. Unfortunately there is no clear sign of the date of Robert's early donations. The *Red Book*'s copies of the relevant deeds mostly omit the lists of witnesses and very few of the originals remain. This being so we are forced to turn from the humdrum but reliable evidence of the cartulary and contemporary charters to the historical notes in Abbot Newland's Roll and the *Red Book* which are useful but far from infallible.

Along with this material we should study the *Wigmore Chronicle* although this unhappily makes only one direct reference to Bristol and that is both imprecise and curious. This tells us that at one juncture in the quite extraordinarily complex and prolonged process of the foundation of the abbey there came to England, in the month of August, a canon named Richard of Warwick, "who afterwards became abbot of Bristol", to visit his friends: "he came to Shobdon and harvested the corn and put it in stacks and left it in the care of the bailiffs and then went away".[1] This visit apparently took place soon after the death of bishop Robert of Hereford in April 1148, so presumably occurred in the summer which followed it. A more general matter mirrored in the *Wigmore Chronicle* may very well have had important repercussions on the early history of the monastery of St. Augustine. This is the quite extraordinarily

[1] *Wigmore Chronicle*, ed. Dickinson and Ricketts, p. 429.

protracted history of the foundation of Wigmore. Beginning as a very small Victorine community of two canons at Shobdon in or about the year 1140, it was soon transferred to Eye. Sometime later it was moved to the parish church of Wigmore, but was only finally settled some distance away from there at what was to be its permanent site thirty years or so after its commencement, the foundation stone of the conventual church there being laid in 1172 and a dedication taking place in 1179.

What is perhaps more significant than these transmigrations is the evidence of the smallness of the community and the signs of a quite remarkable lack of stability, canons coming and going in a way contrary to normal monastic practice. The Shobdon community began with two French canons from St. Victor, but these were soon replaced by three of their brethren "born and bred in England". One of the brethren was apparently designated as abbot-elect, but he was "often maligned by Sir Hugh de Mortimer and his followers. Like the simple, gentle man he was, he left all that he had in his charge without a guardian, and returned to his abbey". There followed the visit of Richard of Warwick and the election as head of the community of one brother Henry, who seems to have been known as prior, not as abbot. Under him the situation improved and "he received into his community more canons", but following a violent disagreement with Sir Hugh "left all his possessions in the custody of the canons . . . and returned to his abbey of St. Victor whence he had come." After him came from abroad brother Robert of Cherbourg who "took the place of prior because they wanted to have an abbot over them". Soon after, the scholar, Andrew of St. Victor, whom Dr. Smalley has rescued from obscurity, was acquired and made abbot, but "there was a breach between abbot Andrew and his canons, because of which the abbot went away and left them to their own devices" (c. 1149). One Roger was now elected abbot and on his death c. 1161, by which time, at long last, the communal life seems to have got on an even keel, at the persuasion of the canons Andrew returned as abbot from St. Victor "after much thought" about 1162. It is difficult to believe that this very unsettled conventual life at Wigmore which took place at the very time when St. Augustine's was in process of foundation allowed the former house to colonise the Bristol house as early as 1148. We shall see that there are signs that the belief that it did so is unfounded.

Let us now consider the notes in Newland's Roll and the *Red Book* which concern the foundation of St. Augustine's.[1] The following errors of detail in the former are obvious enough: (i) the regnal year of Stephen's reign given here, like others elsewhere in the Roll, is wrong; (ii) the reference to bishop Alfred spells his name slightly incorrectly and makes him bishop by 1148 though he held this office only from 1158 to 1160; (iii) the first abbot Robert had died or resigned in 1176 and was not abbot in 1186 as is here stated; (iv) the dedication of the church by the four bishops mentioned could not have taken place in 1148, as is stated. However, to conclude that the rest of the information given is worthless, would be to commit the sin of throwing out the baby with the bathwater. Examination shows us that in certain important particulars the testimony of the Roll may well be sound.

We are first told that Robert fitz Harding began the foundation of the monastery of St. Augustine in the year 1140 and "bilded the churche And all other howses of offices according to the same bi the space of vi yeres." It is worthy of note that we are told *not* that Robert founded the monastery in this year, but that he "began" its foundation. This sounds like an authentic fact and there is nothing inherently improbable in the date given for this as far as we can tell at present. So we may accept its authenticity, as also the equally plausible statement that the first stage in the foundation here was the erection of the church and what were doubtless intended to be temporary buildings.

The *Red Book* notes proceed to assert that four bishops, whose initials and sees it gives dedicated the monastic church in 1146. The Newland Roll makes a similar statement but rashly expands the initials into names which cannot possibly be reconciled with the date of 1146. Examination makes it quite clear that the *Red Book* details concerning the bishops are based on a deed in the *Red Book* and are quite correct but pertain to a dedication which took place about 1170.[2] It is not clear why the date 1146 was

---

[1] For the texts, see note 6 above 109–10.

[2] The Newland Roll's source for the bishops present at the dedication is almost certainly the deed in the Cartulary (f. 34r) recording a gift to St. Augustine's made by Robert's son Maurice *in dedicatione ecclesie* which records

brought into the picture by the *Red Book* annals, though it is just possible that some other dedication ceremony, perhaps of an unfinished or temporary church took place in this year.

The next annal belongs to 1148 to which year the Newland Roll assigns two events. Firstly it asserts that on Easter Day "and the xj day of Aprile" "Richard the first Abbot of oure Monastery was inducte". The fact that the Roll not only pinpoints the date of Easter exactly but gets it correct is a very remarkable fact which was almost certainly obtained from a liturgical Calendar of the house, whose accuracy hereon must be accepted. The formal induction of the head of a house and his convent into their new church—whether the latter was already dedicated or not—was clearly a historic date to be had in special remembrance; we find the brethren of Merton taking possession on Ascension day "with festive procession"[1] and what was probably a similar ceremony took place at Plympton in September when the bishop "constituted" there canons who had arrived in the previous February.[2] The Newland Roll also assigns to Easter Day something else—"And then after Alured Bisshope of Worcetr inducte vj canons of the Monastery of Wigmore . . . in to our churche and Monastery aforesaide on the Ester day". With this we must compare the third and last of the *Red Book*'s annals "—Alur. Episcopus Wigorn. introduxit primo canonicos in monasterio predicto anno domini millesimo cxlviij." and the invaluable note at the end of a charter of

the presence of "R. bishop of Worcester, B. bishop of Exeter, N. bishop of Llandaff and G., bishop of St. Asaph". In its usual rather wild way the Newland Roll expands these initials incorrectly. An original deed (printed by G. W. Potto Hicks in "The Consecration of St. Augustine's Bristol," *TBGAS*, lv, 257–60) shows that Bishop Bartholemew of Exeter (1161–84) and Bishop Roger of Worcester (1164–79) participated in the dedication of the church, but does not mention the other two, who must be Bishop Nicholas of Llandaff (1148–83) and Bishop Godfrey of St. Asaph (1160–75, suspended 1170). The date of this dedication cannot be fixed precisely. It must have been after Bishop Roger's consecration in 1164 and either at a time when Robert was a canon of the Abbey (which he became at an unknown date) or after his death which is assigned to 5 February 1170–1 (*Complete Peerage*, ii, 125). The ceremony predates the death of Bishop Godfrey in 1175. Thus, 1170 may be taken as the approximate date of the dedication of St. Augustine's.

[1] J. C. Dickinson, *The origins of the Austin canons* . . . (1950), p. 117, n. 2.
[2] *Ibid.*, p. 113 n. 6.

Robert's son Nicholas that the donation of the latter therein recorded was made in the presence of bishop "Alur" "on the day in which the canons entered their new church."[1] These notes concerning Alfred are confusing but certain points about them are clear. Of these the most obvious is the fact that as Alfred was bishop of Worcester only from April 1158 to 1160 he cannot have been officially concerned with anything that happened in 1148. On the other hand he was clearly concerned in some way with the origins of St. Augustine's. What was his contribution?

The answer to this question, hitherto regarded as insoluble, becomes clear once it is appreciated that it is almost certain that the present cathedral of St. Augustine does not stand on the site of the original monastery. The main authority for this is no less a person than William Worcestre who, in his attractive rambling way alludes to "the ancient and original church of the said abbey which is now a newly built church",[2] this being a reference to the church of St. Augustine the Less which he elsewhere describes as "newly built in this year 1480"[3] and as "the parish church close to the abbey of regular canons of St. Augustine, dedicated in honour of St. Augustine".[4] This view that the site of the original monastic community was that later occupied by the church of St. Augustine the Less is fortified by other pieces of evidence. Most important is the indubitably accurate statement in the charter of Nicholas that in the time of Alfred (1158–60) the canons entered their new church.[5] This must imply an induction of the type which had already taken place in 1148. It is highly unlikely that the "new church" of which the canons thus took possession about 1159 was a rebuilt version of the one set up a mere decade earlier, and highly probable that the reference is to a new building in the most obvious sense of the word. Further it is to be noted that, just as we have signs of two churches, and possibly of two dedications,

[1] ea die . . . qua novam suam ecclesiam canonici ingressi sunt f. 34v.

[2] vetus et primam ecclesiam dictae abbathiae quae modo est ecclesia parochialis noviter edificata. *Itin. Symonis Simeonis et Willelmi de Worcestre*, ed. J. Nasmith (Cambridge, 1778), 180.

[3] *Ibid.*, 229. After the convent of St. Augustine's moved to their new church this old building would, of course, be retained in use. From 1234 it was apparently used for parishioners and may have been rebuilt at this time, though the matter is obscure.   [4] Itm Will. de W. ed. Nasmith 247.   [5] Note 1 above.

so there are traces of two convents. Careful reading of the *Wigmore Chronicle* shows nothing to suggest that Richard, the first abbot of Bristol came from this house, but rather that his only connection with Wigmore was an isolated visit to it in 1148 just after he had been installed as head of what was quite a small community at Bristol. Richard was certainly a canon of St. Victor itself,[1] the mother house of Wigmore and one much more likely to be in a position to colonise the new foundation at Bristol than was Wigmore at this time. What was the connection of Wigmore with St. Augustine's? There is no reason to reject the Newland Roll's note that six canons from there were instituted at Bristol by bishop Alfred and it is reasonable to connect their arrival with the entrance into the new church which took place in his very brief episcopate. If we accept the transference of the canons from their original site then there is seen to be a substantial accuracy in the *Red Book*'s note that Alfred "first introduced canons in the aforesaid monastery", a statement which was accurate when applied to the house which the writer knew but nonsensical if applied to the original site whose existence was brief and doubtless quickly forgotten. It was of course this second church which was dedicated by the four bishops in or about 1170.

On this transference two comments may be made. In the first place it is to be noted that in the twelfth century it was a very long way from unknown for a newly-founded monastery to change its original site at an early stage in its history. This was particularly common amongst English Cistercians' houses and found to a lesser extent amongst English houses of Austin canons.[2] Secondly it was certainly very easy for memory of the temporary site to be lost in later days as it was at Bristol. Thus major annalists give the date of the foundation of Merton priory as 1117 but give no hint at the settlement elsewhere which preceded it in 1114 and is only known to us owing to the fortuitous survival of a narrative of the foundation of the house.[3] Thirdly there are clear signs that in the years which immediately pre-

---

[1] He is termed *canonicus noster professus* in the necrology of St. Victor.

[2] E.g. Merton whither brethren moved after having settled elsewhere for two and a half years, Dickinson, *op. cit.* p. 117.

[3] Of the eighteen charters granted to the house by Earl William of Gloucester (Patterson *op. cit.* nos. 11–30) only the first terms the house an

ceded the episcopate of bishop Alfred, St. Augustine's had greatly increased in status the original foundation of Robert apparently having been smallish. But from 1153 the founder's benefactions increased and was reinforced by the favour of King Henry, who in his young days had conceived an affection for the place as one of his charters very unusually goes out of its way to recall— "quam inicio iuventutis mee beneficiis et protectione cepi juvare et fovere, causa et amore Dei"—so that the means for expansion were certainly there. We have no evidence why this expansion entailed moving to a new site but clearly the site of St. Augustine the Less would not be suitable for the conventual buildings of the largish monastery which the house was now becoming. Fourthly it is very likely that this expansion of the community was intimately connected with its abbatial status. Victorine houses were normally abbeys but as the *Wigmore Chronicle* shows us very clearly this position was by no means granted automatically, a reasonable sized convent with the appropriate endowments being usually an essential pre-requisite for acquiring this rank.

The evidence regarding the process of foundation of the abbey of St. Augustine is confused and its interpretation demands more technical treatment than it has often been accorded. But given this and the dismissal of certain obvious chronological howlers a reasonably homogenous picture can be reconstructed.

In or about 1140 Robert fitz Harding decided to establish a monastery on the site which, as we shall see, folk memory associated with St. Augustine of Canterbury and in the following six years erected the requisite church (on the site of the later church of St. Augustine the Less) and domestic buildings. At a juncture which is unknown he sought to people his house with canons of the abbey of St. Victor of Paris, a step which was almost certainly inspired by the foundation of the Victorine house which ultimately settled at Wigmore but was begun at Shobdon in or very near the year 1140. Richard of Warwick, a

abbey. The editor's assignment of this to 1148 is by no means certainly correct; it may be a later re-issue after abbatial rank had been obtained. The two charters of duke Henry are of doubtful authenticity (above, p. 111, n. 1). A note of Leland refers only to *fundatio Monast. S. Augustini Bristol et congregatio fratrum ibidem* taking place on Easter Day 1148 (J. Britton, *History and Antiquities of the Abbey . . . of Bristol* (1830), p. 6.

canon of St. Victor, became the head of the first community at St. Augustine's which, we may suspect, was small and ill-endowed and which was inducted into its new church on Easter Day 1148, the church possibly, though not certainly, having been dedicated in 1146. From 1153 onwards, thanks to Robert and his royal master, the endowments of the house and, one may suspect, its numbers increased. At a date which is uncertain, but may be as early as 1153 the house acquired abbatial status. In the brief episcopate of bishop Alfred almost certainly the convent moved to a new church (or more probably to the eastern part of it) on the site of the later cathedral, the building being dedicated by four bishops about 1170. The convent which Alfred inducted was reinforced by six canons which the founder acquired from the sister Victorine house at Wigmore, now on an even keel after passing through very troubled waters.

There remains for consideration the question of the nature of the site on which the abbey was founded, a matter which is very much more complex and intriguing than is normally the case. The impression given by the cartulary is that the early stages of the house's history were carried through without formal written records thereof being drawn up, as was not unusual at the time. As has already been indicated, there is no hint in the very ample documentation of the *Red Book* that the monastery developed through utilisation of an existing church or chapel, as did so many other houses of the order at this time, nor is there any indication of the founder acquiring a convenient open space on which to construct the monastic buildings, as was even more usual.

As we have noted, the sole detailed reference to the site of the monastery occurs somewhat casually in a charter of Earl William of Gloucester in which he confirms to the "church of St. Augustine of Bristol and the regular canons of the same church . . . the *locus* that is called Bileswicke in which their church was founded."[1] The placename itself means nothing more romantic than "Bill's dairy farm,"[2] but the term *locus* is

---

[1] Patterson *op. cit.* no. 23 = Cartulary f. 15r/v. The *Red Book*'s deeds copied under Bilswick unfortunately are largely concerned with the abbey's relations with St. Mark's Hospital and throw no light on its own origins.

[2] A. H. Smith, *The Placenames of Gloucestershire* (4 vols. 1964–5), iii. 95.

more significant than might appear. Although in the ecclesiastical context of the twelfth century it might mean "a place" in
a vague sense, it very frequently denotes a place with a religious
association. Professor Hamilton Thompson has written of this
"special sense in which the word is applied to religious foundations, corresponding to the English *stow*. *Cf.* such common titles
of monasteries as *Novus Locus*, *Bellus Locus*, or *Locus Sancti
Edwardi* (Shaftesbury and Netley) *Locus Regalis' Rewley*."[1] He
goes on to cite a papal privilege to St. Botolph's, Colchester
terming it a *locus* and the narrative of the foundation of Nostell
priory, where the original site of the community was termed
vetus locus. Examples of such usage could be easily multiplied
and include the site of Chetwode priory, of which it was
observed *vulgariter autem locus ille a laicis heremitagium nuncupatur.*[2]

Although the archaeological evidence regarding the early
history of the site of St. Augustine's has been grossly neglected,
there is one well-known piece of evidence which almost certainly shows its religious use in pre-Conquest times. This is the
remarkable carving of the Harrowing of Hell, which is assigned
by Professor Zernecki to the first half of the eleventh century.[3]
It was found about 1832 during alterations in the chapter house
which included the removal of the four feet of earth laid on the
post-Conquest floor by the cathedral canons in the course of
their adaptation of the building to modern uses in 1713.[4] This
stone was found serving as a coffin lid of one of several other
graves discovered at the time.[5]

In the twelfth century, and for some time after, the chapter
house was a usual place of burial in contemporary monasteries
for people of importance, as the graves at Rievaulx and Byland
yet remind us, and it may very well be that this stone had been
re-used and was not, when re-discovered, covering a pre-
Conquest grave. But there can be not the slightest doubt of its
early date and, it is reasonable to assume that, whether it was

---

[1] A. H. Thompson, *Bolton priory* (Leeds, 1924), p. 13, n. 4.

[2] Dugdale, *op. cit.* VI (1) 499. William of Worcester writes of the
Sanctuarium locum sancti augustini (N.S. 210, p. 105). *Itin* ed. Nasmith 188.

[3] Letter to the writer.   [4] Barrett, *op. cit.* p. 286.

[5] G. Pryce, *Notes on the ecclesiastical and monumental architecture and sculpture
of the middle ages in Bristol* (2nd ed. 1853) p. 12. It is to be hoped that all
available evidence on these finds will soon be collected and studied by
competent authorities.

made at Bristol or not, at least it was brought there long before the time of Robert fitz Harding. It is however just within the bounds of possibility that part of a pre-Conquest cemetery extended below the chapter house; much less likely is it that the stone was one of a number used to level up the ground, as would be necessary when the elaborate monastic buildings of the twelfth century were constructed on the falling ground south of the church.

Tentatively we may associate with this pre-Conquest cemetery the burial of someone believed to be called Jordan and to have been a companion of St. Augustine. Evidence of his cult is late. Leland mentions it[1] and there are also references to it in the late fifteenth century account rolls of the abbey. Argument from this sort of frail evidence is always temerarious but it is by no means impossible that this is another element in the very ancient tradition linking the College Green area with St. Augustine of Canterbury and suggesting the existence there of a very old cemetery.

As we have already seen, there is nothing at all to show that there was a church or chapel in this area in late Anglo-Saxon times, though such a possibility should not be entirely ruled out. However the *Red Book*'s apparent silence on this suggests that if it ever had existed the building itself was no longer in use in Robert's day. Excavation of the site of St. Augustine the Less is most greatly to be desired. At present all that the existing evidence allows us to believe is that there was a pre-Conquest cemetery in the region of the cathedral. Why should this be? For the answer to this question we must seek the aid of place-name evidence.

Here two points are significant. First of all, given the likelihood that the *locus* of St. Augustine's must have been termed *stow* by that huge percentage of the locals who knew no Latin, it is very feasible that the *stow* which constituted the second element in the original form of Bristol's name here implies not "a place where people assembled" but "a place where people gathered for religious purposes". Secondly, though both derivations are theoretically possible, and although the hugely defective literary evidence of pre-Conquest times does not

---

[1] ibique in magna area sacellum in quo sepultus est S. Jordanus, unus ex discipulis Augustini Anglorum apostoli.

allow us to say that beyond all doubt the site we are considering had been called "St. Augustine's" long before Robert fitz Harding's day, all the evidence there is points strongly to this.

Many years ago, when first beginning to study the history of the English Austin canons, I noted as a point to be explained in due course that there were two houses of the order whose heads were very often referred to not by a mere placename, in the usual way, but by a title which featured the dedication of their house. The first of these was St. Oswald's, which was the title frequently given to Nostell priory, which was established on a site linked with the Northumbrian king in local popular memory, and was thus, like St. Bees, Whitby and Monk Wearmouth, one of the sites in Northern England associated with holy people of old and restored to religious life by the foundation of a Norman monastery.

Now the charter evidence suggests very strongly that, similarly, the site on which Robert fitz Harding founded his monastery had a special connotation of this type, and was then termed St. Augustine's. The head of the place is referred to with greatest regularity as "the abbot of St. Augustine's, Bristol," the dedication being added in contexts where for other houses it was not found necessary. Thus in the foundation charter of Keynsham abbey[1] the witnesses include the heads of ten monasteries, of whom nine occur purely with the name of their house (Gloucester, Evesham, Pershore, Ford, Margam, Neath, Worcester, Taunton and Bruton) but the tenth is "Richard abbot of St. Augustine's Bristol" and a similar usage is found in another deed of Earl William.[2] Likewise in a letter to the abbot and general chapter of St. Victor sent by English heads of houses the titles used are Wigmore, St. Augustine's Bristol, and Keynsham.[3] Although the matter is utterly incapable of absolute proof given the total lack of medieval documentation on this sort of point, there seems little doubt that the tradition which is still held in Bristol of a connection between St. Augustine and the site of the abbey was deep-rooted when Robert fitz Harding decided to found his monastery there.

---

[1] Patterson, *op. cit.* no. 99; the source of this may be B.M. Lansdowne MS 447 f. 14r.

[2] Patterson no. 101; it has a total of nine heads of monastic houses.

[3] B.M. Cott. Charters iv 58.

This leads us to ask which of the two major saints called Augustine is the one here commemorated, and whether any reason is known to connect him with Bristol. The first question is happily settled by one of the early charters in the *Red Book* which concerns a gift of lights to the church made to "the Blessed Virgin Mary and blessed Augustine apostle of the English".[1] That St. Augustine of Hippo should have been the one concerned is in the highest degree unlikely since his cult at this time was very unimportant indeed. A further point which may well be significant is that this dedication is almost entirely unknown among the very numerous English houses of Austin canons,[2] so that it is not unreasonable to assume that there may have been some special reason for its presence at Bristol.

Is there any good authority to support the tradition that St. Augustine of Canterbury visited the place ultimately to be known as Bristol? In view of the stupendous shortage of evidence on such matters in early Anglo-Saxon history, it is most surprising to find that the saint visited the region and may well have been at the very place. No writer of the early middle ages surpasses in authority the Venerable Bede, and he, in one of his most famous passages, tells how in 603 St. Augustine met British bishops of the province on the boundary of the Hwicce and the Anglo-Saxons at "a place which is to this day called Augustine's Ac that is Augustine's Oak".[3] Where this meeting took place depends, of course, on the position of the boundaries of the kingdom of the Hwicce in Augustine's time. The latest authoritative study of this semi-insoluble question concludes that in the seventh century the land of the Hwicce may well have comprised "Worcestershire, the southwestern part of Warwickshire and all Gloucestershire except for those parts lying to the west of the river Leadon and West of the Severn below Monsterworth."[4]

Certain geographical comments may here be made. Firstly, although we have no signs of anything like a town at Bristol until long after Augustine's time, the fact that an important

[1] Cartulary f. 33r.
[2] Wellow abbey near Grimsby with the curious joint dedication to St. Augustine and St. Olaf seems to be the only parallel.
[3] See the discussion of this in *Placenames of Gloucestershire*, iv, 33.
[4] *Ibid.*, iv, 31.

bridge was built in late Anglo-Saxon times at Bristol would suggest that there was an old route crossing the river here, which might go back to Augustine's day. Secondly, Aust only ten miles north of Bristol had an ancient crossing leading to Caerwent and Caerleon-on-Usk, and possibly derives its name from this, which may originally have been *Trajectus Augustus* after the *Legio Augusta*.[1] Hence if Augustine had arrived at the spot where St. Augustine's abbey was later to be, he would have found what may still have been a main road heading in the direction of Caerleon—in his day an ancient centre of the British church. Thirdly, it ought not to be taken for granted either that the Oak (wherever it was) still existed in post-Conquest times or that the name which it bore in Bede's day was still extant.

The scantiness of our evidence on the England of St. Augustine's day makes it quite impossible to dogmatise on the veracity of the tradition connecting him with the place which later became Bristol. But very helpful geographical factors and a surprisingly large number of crumbs of other evidence certainly support its authenticity more than might be expected; nor is there anything which contradicts it. It would be perfectly reasonable to hold that the abbey of Robert fitz Harding was built on a site which an authentic tradition of over five centuries connected with the famous visit of St. Augustine to the area.

If this is so, then it demands that, for once, we must quarrel with the English Placename Survey. In the discussion of the origin of the name of Bristol, the writer, after pointing out that "the meanings of *Stow*, 'place' ", best established by its compounds, are "place where folk assembled" and, in an extended and more particularised sense, "religious place". He goes on to add the comment "the former seems the more likely in Bristol".[2] In point of fact, all such evidence as there is suggests the opposite conclusion. The mints of Bristol, all the earliest archaeological evidence, and the Harrowing of Hell carving all belong to the late tenth or early eleventh century, there being nothing to suggest that the place had anything to cause folk to linger there in earlier days.[3] Nor is there any evidence of any

---

[1] *Ibid.*, iii 129 *cf. ibid.*, iv 17 "Aust Passage may in fact mark the site of a Roman crossing to South Wales".   [2] *Ibid.*, iii, 840.

[3] See D. Walker, *Bristol in the early middle ages* (Bristol Hist. Assoc. 1971).

administrative centre nearby. It is difficult to find grounds to support the belief that the *stow* of *Bristow* was originally used because folk lingered there on secular affairs. On the other hand, there is, as we have seen, what is by contemporary standards a number of crumbs of evidence that on the hill outside the little city was a meeting place in the ecclesiastical sense. It is further worthy of note that, as is pointed out in the *English Place-name Elements*[1] the use of "stow" to denote "holy place" or "church" is frequent in the Welsh border counties. It is very probable that if St. Augustine had never existed, Bristol would have been called something else.[2]

[1] (2 vols. 1956) ii, 160.

[2] For help on several points of detail the writer is indebted to Prof. G. Zarnecki, Prof. R. J. Cramp, Mr. P. A. Rahtz, Mrs. F. Neale and Miss Mary Williams. It is hoped that the above essay will help to stimulate long-overdue research into various aspects of the most unusual and most interesting history of St. Augustine's. For the archaeologist excavation of the site of St. Augustine's the Less and the land adjoining the east side of the cloister would be valuable from various angles. The history of the churchyard of St. Augustine's and the nature of the medieval abbey's relations with parishioners ought to be studied and a full-scale chronology of its architecture worked out.

(If the present writer was temerarious enough to join in the attempts to locate the site of St. Augustine's ever-to-be remembered Oak, he would opt for a spot not far from Aust.)

VI

The Perpendicular style in the Cotswolds

By David Verey

ON the Cotswolds, the yields of the wool trade in the fifteenth century entirely remodelled great churches like Cirencester, Chipping Campden, Northleach, Fairford, Winchcombe, Lechlade, Chedworth and Burford, and large numbers of churches, in fact nearly all of them, were given new windows and towers. By 1327 the great Court masons had progressed to a new style of their own. What we see in the south transept in Gloucester Cathedral is the style of St. Stephen's Chapel, Westminster, which had arrived there, so to speak, with the body of the murdered King Edward II.[1] The new king built his father's tomb and gave enough money for the next rebuilding plan at Gloucester to be begun. So the Perpendicular style, England's contribution to Gothic architecture, was launched, and lasted everywhere in England for about two hundred years without very much change, although there were regional developments ending on the Cotswolds in a *crescendo*.

The body of the church was the responsibility of the lay people, and wool merchants were prepared to spend money on it. By contrast, at this date, the clergy were generally mean in their expenditure, and as they were responsible for the chancels, these were not usually altered in Perpendicular times. Wool prices were at their highest level in 1480. Rich wool merchants endowed chantry chapels, later to be abolished, but not always destroyed, at the Reformation. This was the time when the Cotswolds reached their greatest economic success and international fame and importance.

Even a hundred years earlier the account books of Datini, the famous merchant of Prato, near Florence, show how, in 1382, Datini's activities included the purchase of wool in the Cots-

[1] *The Cotswolds—a New Study*, eds. C. and A. Hadfield (1973), p. 238.

wolds. Only two things in Datini's life were important, religion and trade, and on the first page of his ledgers were written the words "In the name of God and of profit."[1] His scarlet biretta was dyed in England, and the finest and most expensive wool which he imported was English, and came mostly from the Cotswolds, referred to in his papers as "Chondisgualdo"—in particular from Northleach (Norleccio) and Burford (Boriforte), and from the abbey lands of Cirencester (Sirisestri).

Here is a typical letter to Datini in Florence from his Italian agent in London in 1403: "You say you have written to Venice to remit us 1,000 ducats with which in the name of God and profit, you wish us to buy Cotswold wool. With God always before us, we will carry out your bidding, which we have well understood. In the next few days our Neri will ride to the Cotswolds and endeavour to purchase a good store for us, and we will tell you when he has come back."

At the beginning of the fifteenth century the Papal tax-collectors who purchased wool from the great abbeys often reserved the amount of the clip they wanted, even before the sheep were shorn. Datini's agent wrote apologising for some wool from Cirencester which had proved unsatisfactory, by saying he had been obliged to buy up the clip before seeing it, "For one must buy in advance from all the abbeys, and especially from this one, which is considered the best." On the other hand, one could wait to buy till the summer fairs, and Datini was told the best time to buy was around St. John's Day (June 24) "for it is then that the Cotswold fairs are held, and that those who want good produce should buy it". Datini also imported unbleached cloth from the Cotswolds.

By English law, all wool exported for the European market was obliged to go first to Calais, where the Staple was fixed— the only exceptions included wool for Italy. The Datini records show that the firms he used shipped their wool the whole way by sea, straight from London or Southampton. One of the wool-merchants' brasses in Northleach refers to Thomas Busshe as a merchant of the Staple of Calais and shows the arms of the city of Calais.

It is difficult to image how sumptuous the churches were just before the Reformation, with so many chantry chapels fitted up

[1] Iris Origo, *The Merchant of Prato* (1957).

by the wool merchants. The Garstang chapel in Cirencester is perhaps a good example of what they were like, and there is also a surviving example at Burford; but where was the Wilcox chapel in Bibury?

In the nave aisles at Bibury there are two piscinas, one on the north and one on the south, and it is probable these are all that are left of two chantry chapels. In 1493 Richard Bagot was Oseney Abbey's tenant at Arlington. In his will—he died in 1528—he wishes to be buried in the Wilcox Chapel in Bibury and gives "to all the lights in the church a quarter of barley, and a cow to maintain a taper of 4 lbs. of wax to be set before the image of Our Blessed Lady in Wilcox Chapel". He also gives to Oseney Abbey "the wages of a priest to sing for my wife's soul and mine for 3 years in Wilcox Chapel".[1] On the suppression of the monastic communities certain particulars of the Bibury estate, held by Oseney Abbey, are of special interest, in that they mention a "tithe of wool and lambs", and the "wages of the abbot's shepherd". This shows that the abbot kept sheep at Bibury till the very end, and the low fourteenth-century barn, later converted into cottages known now as Arlington Row, could well have been his wool-store. Thus we see the continuous benefits church and people derived from the trade in wool.

Before the murder of Edward II, his favourite Despenser's mature Decorated rebuilding of Tewkesbury Abbey represents one of the most lavish surviving expressions of the architectural tastes of the court.[2] In the same way the influence of court architecture can be seen in the humbler churches in Gloucestershire which were patronised by the almost royal de Clare family, such as the Decorated north chapel at Badgeworth and the old church at Charfield (now looked after by the Redundant Churches Fund) with its porch so like work at Usk, a monastic foundation of this family.

The Perpendicular rebuilding of St. Peter's Abbey at Gloucester represents the next stage in courtly architectural development, and must have put Gloucester ahead of Tewkesbury and Winchcombe, where it had previously lagged behind.

[1] F. S. Hockaday Abstracts, *Catalogue of the Gloucestershire Collection*, ed. R. Austin, no. 360.

[2] Richard Morris, "Tewkesbury Abbey, the Despenser Mausoleum," *TBGAS*, xciii, 155.

The funeral of Edward II at Gloucester seems to have been dictated by the Court after slow and careful preparation. The subsequent elaboration of his father's shrine was paid for by Edward III. There is, however, a noticeable time-lag between the Perpendicular remodelling at Gloucester and the spread of the new style to the country churches on the Cotswolds, which may in part be due to the Black Death.

The pestilence reached southern England in 1348 and spread rapidly in the spring of 1349 to the rest of the country. Some villages escaped, only to fall victims to later outbreaks, especially that of 1361. The next century, however, saw a spate of church building and embellishments in a greater determination to earn divine forgiveness, with more chantry chapels and more images and more superstition.[1] The monasteries, which were highly taxed, extorted as much as they could from their estates, so it was left to the laymen to pay for the Perpendicular improvements to the country churches, though monastic influence on architectural style remained paramount.

The most influential mason-architect in the Cotswolds at the turn of the thirteenth to fourteenth century was, according to John Harvey, Walter of Harford, a medieval village near Naunton.[2] He was employed by the Abbot of Winchcombe and finished the "new work". Winchcombe Abbey, of which unfortunately nothing remains whatever, seems to have been more influential than Gloucester at that time; but after the burial of Edward II it was a different matter. William de Ramsay (III) was the King's Chief Mason and responsible for Gloucester Castle, and Harvey supposes that a local man called John de Sponlee may have been Ramsay's collaborator in the Abbey. John de Sponlee came from Spoonley near Winchcombe. He then progressed to Windsor where his great work at the Castle began in 1350, when he was "already master mason". St. George's Chapel was started for Edward IV in 1475. The lierne vaulting of the nave was not finished till 1509. To what extent were the Cotswold parish churches influenced by this monastic and courtly architecture? There were certainly links with St. George's Chapel, as we shall see.

[1] Rowland Parker, *The Common Stream* (1975), p. 100

[2] John Harvey, *English Medieval Architects: a Biographical Dictionary down to 1550* (1954), p. 13.

John Harvey has written: "probably Gloucester Abbey owes much of its stylistic reputation to the complete destruction of its rivals at Evesham, Winchcombe and Cirencester".[1] This is not strictly true, for at Evesham Abbot Lichfield's early sixteenth-century tower survives as well as his work in the two churches, fanvaulting and other features similar to contemporary work on the Cotswolds. Further into Worcestershire, at Kidderminister, there was an arcade similar to those at Northleach and Campden. Harvey himself points out that all the great religious houses possessed widespread manors and churches: "works of importance at these would be carried out by monastic craftsmen, so that careful investigation should provide a sufficient body of material for critical purposes. By such studies the greater part of our architectural history should ultimately be recovered, and the superstitions of anonymous 'folk' architecture be finally laid to rest."

In other words, Harvey is optimistic that we may discover the architectural styles of Winchcombe or Cirencester abbeys from the parish churches on the Cotswolds. Success in this direction is, alas, beyond the scope of this essay, though it is hoped it may go a little towards paving the way by discussing some of the connections that can be demonstrated between various Cotswold churches. The very early Perpendicular of Gloucester Choir did not have much influence in the Cotswolds where there is a recognisably different type of Perpendicular, which is much more akin and nearer in date to the fifteenth-century Perpendicular at the west end of the nave at Gloucester, than to the fourteenth-century work in the choir.

One must however exercise caution in tracing architectural relationships. Professor Geoffrey Webb pointed to an apparent connection "between the monumental stonework of the Gloucester tower and . . . the tower of Chipping Campden, which has the same quality of displayed virtuosity." But he adds the warning that the medieval builder was often required to model his work on some well-known local example and in consequence features, or whole churches, which appear to have a family resemblance are not necessarily built by the same masons.[2]

The fashion for fine clerestories was presumably spread by a

[1] *Ibid*, p. 218.
[2] Geoffrey Webb, *Architecture in Britain: the Middle Ages*, Pelican History of Art (1956).

process of prescribed imitation in the Cotswolds, where the clerestories are distinguished not only for the size of their windows—single, many-lighted windows, not pairs, as in the east of England—but also by their being raised well above the chancel arch, with a window even larger and structurally more daring than those above the main arcades. The result is to produce a lantern-like quality which is very distinctive. It is as though some great College Chapel had been dropped into the middle of the parish church.

Northleach and Chipping Campden are both good examples of this clerestory treatment; but the handling of the piers and arcades is just as remarkable. In both churches, which are very similar, the piers are octagonal in plan, with exaggeratedly concave sides and moulded capitals adapted to this form. The arcades above these piers have notably broad and low four-centred arches. This is a form of arch which is definitely characteristic of the Cotswold area and is usually considered one of the determining motifs, sometimes called "Tudor", of the final development of Perpendicular in the first half of the sixteenth century. In contrast to the normal medieval pointed arch, the four-centred arch, especially when combined with an almost flat ceiling, introduces an entirely different type of space composition of which the Cotswold churches appear to be "early examples".[1] But are they all that early? It would seem from a careful study of the documentary evidence that they are not.

Dr. Joan Evans in describing Chipping Campden, besides saying that the "arches of the nave arcade are struck from four centres thus renouncing the true pointed arch which was the basis of Gothic construction", informs us that this was just before 1401, and that the whole scheme was followed at Northleach, and must surely have been by the same master mason.[2] The date 1401 is selected because it is the year William Grevel died, who is described on his brass as the "flower of the wool-merchants of all England", and it has been supposed he built Chipping Campden church. But of course he did not build it all.

Grevel's will of 1401 shows that he desired to buried in the church and he left 100 marks (£66) for building. It is true that this sum would buy a large quantity of stone and labour, and it

---

[1] *Ibid.*, pp. 180 and 183.

[2] Joan Evans, *The Oxford History of English Art, 1307–1461* (1949), p. 211.

is suggested that his money provided for work in the north aisle and north chancel chapel. Rudder records a legend in the window over the door of the north aisle asking for prayers for the souls of William Grevel and his wife, and the many mullets, part of his arms, which were dispersed over the windows of the north aisle support this view.[1] The brass of William Grevel and his wife has been moved, and it was probably situated on top of a tomb-chest—like the Tames' one at Fairford—and would have been placed where he was buried in that part of the church which owed its existence to him, "perhaps the north aisle or chapel temporarily monopolized for performance of the rites directed under his will, whereby four chaplains were to celebrate daily for ten years".[2]

The transformation of the fifteenth century at Campden started *c.* 1450 and finished with the nave arcades, clerestory and tower at the end of the century.[3] Grevel's money may have provided a building fund after expenditure on his tomb and chapel; but for the main expense later in the century we must look at the will of William Bradway, dated 6 June and proved July 1488.[4] The abstracts include, "To the building of the nave and body of the church 100 marks." This is as much as Grevel gave, and it clearly states that it is for work in the nave. Other wool merchants in the fifteenth century have left brasses like William Welley, who died in 1450 but whose will is not known. Two of the three main forms of tracery in the church are dateable to before 1488. The date of 1460 for work on the south is based on the sculptured label stop of a woman's headdress similar to that in the Prelatte brass at Cirencester, *c.* 1462. The problem for the builders in 1488 was that of inserting a new nave with arcades between two existing aisles, an existing chancel, and to allow for the tower on a restricted site to the west. This was exactly the same problem as there had been at Northleach.

John Fortey died in 1458, and his will desired that he should be buried in Northleach church in the "new middle aisle": he gave £300 to carry on and complete work "already begun by

[1] S. Rudder, *A New History of Gloucestershire* (1779).

[2] P. Rushen, *History and Antiquities of Chipping Campden* (1911).

[3] David Verey, *The Buildings of England: Gloucestershire, the Cotswolds* (1970), p. 153.   [4] P. Rushen, *op. cit.* p. 25.

me". Fortey was paying to have the nave finished. Could this
nave and the one at Campden be by the same master mason?
The Northleach nave would antedate Campden by thirty years
according to this, though work could have been in progress at
Campden when Bradway died. Is it likely that a master mason
would use a plan thirty years after he first used it? Something
like this must have happened. The nave arcade mouldings,
bases, capitals and soffits are similar. Elevationally too, they are
the same with five tall arcades resting on octagonal piers with
exaggeratedly concave sides, producing the distinctive capital.
Above the arches are recessed clerestory windows with strip
pilasters rising from the capitals to surround the windows.
Although the clerestory tracery of the two churches is rather
different, there are not enough differences generally to suggest
that a new master mason was involved, and thirty years is not
after all an unreasonable working-life span for a mason. There
is nothing quite like these two naves anywhere near, except at
Kidderminster, and Rock, at Church Hanborough in Oxfordshire on a smaller scale, and at St. Helen's church, Abingdon.
At Abingdon there are not only the nave arcades, north and
south, with the same concave moulding carried up into the
capitals, and four-centred arches, but also there are additional
arcades either side treated in exactly the same way. In the
Cotswolds, however, there is also the arcade at Rendcomb,
which is presumably copied from Northleach.

The builders of the church at Winchcombe were more
economical than they were at Northleach and Campden; for
instance, the piers are octagonal but they did not go to the
expense of fluting them. Henry VI was somewhat precariously
on the throne when Abbot William of Winchcombe began to
build a parish church. The abbot, of course, made the chancel,
and the rest was built by the parishioners, helped by Sir Ralph
Boteler of nearby Sudeley Castle, before his disgrace in 1469. In
this case there is no structural division between nave and chancel. The abbot's dates are 1454–74. Some of the tracery in the
aisles can possibly be related to Northleach (a possession of
Gloucester Abbey), and some to the west front of Gloucester,
which dates from 1421–37. There are diagonal buttresses on
the tower and east end, free use of crocketed and ogeed pinnacles, and continuous battlements with mitred mouldings, all

found in other places on the Cotswolds. The Winchcombe clerestory however, is set in the plain wall, not divided by vertical mouldings as it is at Northleach and Campden, and the tracery is square-headed causing strain on the central mullion. Building their church cost the lay parishioners of Winchcombe £200.

Fairford also can be classed as a complete rebuild except that the position of the central tower was retained. It was paid for by the merchant John Tame, and was built during the last quarter of the fifteenth century. The feeling of unity is enhanced by the complete set of contemporary stained-glass windows, now famous throughout the world. Most of the architectural detail shows great refinement, particularly the bowtell mouldings. The bowtell is a small round moulding, or bead; also the word is used for the shafts of clustered pillars, window and door jambs, and on mullions.

At Cirencester, the story is more like Northleach and Campden with another inserted nave; but there is also a far greater degree of lateral expansion, and the tower came before the nave. It was begun, in fact, soon after 1400, directly after the rebellion of the Hollands, half-brothers of Richard II, against Henry Bolingbroke, when Thomas Holland, Earl of Kent, and the Earl of Salisbury, were taken by the townspeople of Cirencester and beheaded. Henry IV was obviously pleased with the Cirencester folk and his arms (France ancient changed to France modern, *c.* 1406), once appeared, according to Bigland, on the west front of the tower.[1] The west window tracery is like the south-west window at Gloucester (1421–37). The Trinity Chapel at Cirencester must be *c.* 1430 because of the use of the Duke of York's badge, the falcon and fetterlock, and Richard Dixton's will, 1438. Dixton and Prelatte were members of the weavers' guild of the Holy Trinity. Almost at the same time the Garstang family chapel was formed on the south, and the tracery of the windows on the south are similar to the four in the Trinity Chapel on the north. The Lady Chapel cannot be much after 1458. However, the really big Perpendicular alteration was the insertion of the nave and that was altogether later, and financed by the tradesmen of the town. The will of a butcher called John

[1] R. Bigland, *Historical . . . collections relative to the county of Gloucestershire* (1791), i, 347.

Pratt in 1513 left £40 for work to begin within one year on the middle aisle. Leland, who visited Cirencester between 1535 and 1543, describes the church as ". . . very fair. The body of the chirch is al new work, to the which Ruthal, Bisshop of Duresme, borne and brought up in Cirencestre, promisid much, but preventid with deth gave nothing. One Alice Aveling, aunt to Bisshop Ruthal by the mother side, gave an hundreth markes to the building of the right goodly porche of the paroch chirch."[1]

The nave, which has a pierced parapet with sculptures on the stringcourse resembling St. George's Chapel, Windsor, rises many feet above its thirteenth-century predecessor with an almost continuous clerestory row of four-light windows including a great window over the chancel arch. The arcade piers are very tall, compound, with eight thin shafts. The arch below the clerestory is panelled. On each side of every pier are shields born by demiangels, carrying the arms or merchants' marks of the contributors. As late as 1532 a merchant left £20 for the completion of the rood screen.

This is getting very near the end of Cirencester Abbey, which was dissolved in 1539. The last abbot's monogram, which must be 1522 or after, appears on the external keystone of the east window of the nave of the parish church, whilst his predecessor Abbot Hakebourne's is over a pier capital, showing the progress in building. Hakebourne's mitre and initials also appear in the fanvault of St. Catherine's Chapel, with the date 1508. This may by similar to destroyed cloisters in the abbey; but it seems impossible to think that it is part of them, reset at the time of the Dissolution, as has been suggested by some writers, though not by Bigland, who says Bishop Ruthal paid for it. Henry VIII's injunction that the abbey should be totally destroyed would, in any case, preclude such a work of conservation.

I have now described what happened to the four or five most splendid Perpendicular or "wool" churches in the Cotswolds during the fifteenth century; but similar alterations took place to a lesser degree in almost all the smaller parish churches.

At Bibury the nave was heightened and given an almost flat ceiling and clerestory with two-light straight-headed windows under an embattled parapet. It appears also that Oseney Abbey

[1] J. Leland, *Itinerary*, ed. Lucy Toulmin Smith (1907), vol. i, part ii, 129.

must have provided the chancel with a Perpendicular roof, destroyed in the nineteenth-century restoration. One window, that on the west end of the south clerestory, has ogee lights with many cusps, and the great west window of the nave is not unlike the west window of the Trinity Chapel at Cirencester. If then, these alterations are mid-fifteenth century, the lay donors' names are unknown. The late fifteenth-century wills at Bibury do not appear to give moneys for church building other than for chantries.

At Chedworth, the south wall of the nave was rebuilt with a magnificent series of very typically Cotswold Perpendicular windows by one, Richard Sely, who was either a wool merchant or the Nevilles' bailiff, about the time of the Battle of Bosworth, 1485.

At Withington the tracery of the big east and west windows resembles the work of Abbot Morwent's time at St. Peter's Abbey, Gloucester, full-blown Perpendicular with the horizontal transom element in the central top light. The upper stage of the tower is extremely elegant with its large bell opening having four trefoil-headed compartments surmounted by six small traceried lights under an ogee-shaped and crocketed hoodmould. The buttresses are not diagonal as is usual in the Cotswolds, but straight and panelled. The battlements have tall panelled pinnacles with pretty finials rising from winged gargoyles at the corners. The lord of the manor was the Bishop of Worcester.

The majority of churches were given Perpendicular towers; but Withington is specially elegant, as is the tower at Hawling, which belonged to Winchcombe Abbey.[1] It does not have diagonal buttresses, but they are at right angles over-run by a continuous stringcourse. Ogee-headed bell openings, battlements, pinnacles and gargoyles are all on an elegant small scale, the work of an exceptional master mason. The tower at Coates appears also to be fifteenth century, with the more usual diagonal buttresses, but all refined and delicate.

Nowhere in the Gloucestershire Cotswolds are there comparably ambitious Perpendicular alterations as the naves of Northleach, Chipping Campden and Cirencester. There is however Chipping Norton, which could by a stretch be considered to be a Cotswold place in Oxfordshire, and its circumstances

[1] Gordon Haigh, *The history of Winchcombe Abbey* (1947).

are similar, in that it underwent a complete remodelling from the profits of the wool trade. The nave of Chipping Norton, *c.* 1485, must therefore rank with the other Cotswold churches which had naves inserted into existing buildings. It has piers with clustered shafts which continue upwards unbroken by capitals to support the now modern roof. They are the only division between the windows of the continuous straight-headed clerestory. The wall below has a panelled grid with cusped arches that continue the pattern of the tracery, and large quatrefoils in the spandrels of the pointed arches of the arcade. There is the familiar east window over the chancel arch. This is said to have been paid for by a wool merchant called Asshefylde, and it certainly achieved the desired lantern-like effect.

If we followed the river Evenlode on its course from the Cotswolds, just before it joins the Thames near Oxford, we should find the most beautiful and unspoiled church of St. Peter and St. Paul, Church Hanborough. The advowson belonged to Reading Abbey and the manor was part of the royal manor of Woodstock. In the fifteenth century there was considerable building activity at two or more periods. The tower and spire must be quite early in the century and were evidently inserted in the west end of the nave.[1] The arcades and clerestory must be later as there is visual evidence of an earlier roof line over the east tower arch. It has been suggested that the alterations were possibly of 1399, when a Papal indulgence was granted to contributors to the church fabric;[2] but this ought not to be regarded as putting the nave so early in view of the fact that the tower came first. Therefore, for the nave we have an unknown date in the fifteenth century. The extraordinary thing is that these arcades so closely resemble those at Northleach and Campden, except that the arches are more pointed. Here are the same elegant octagonal piers with exaggerated concave mouldings which are repeated and emphasised by the capitals. Miss Sherwood says this is a type common in the Cotswolds;[3] but I know of no others except at Northleach, Campden and Rendcomb. Can this be the work of the Northleach master mason? The ashlar came from Taynton, near Burford.

[1] E. T. Long, *The story of the Parish Church of Hanborough* (1972).
[2] J. Sherwood, *The Buildings of England: Oxfordshire* (1974), p. 544.
[3] *Ibid.*, p. 360.

The neighbouring church at Eynsham is almost in the same case, but there are other possible prototypes in the Oxford Colleges, in the antechapels at New College, All Souls and Magdalen. Eynsham received a new nave *c.* 1450, or later,[1] with octagonal piers with concave mouldings having extra concave pilasters either side, so that the whole pier is usually described as oval or oblong in section, and this is similar to the Oxford Colleges. The capitals follow the concave mouldings, and are strikingly like those at Northleach and Campden in spirit.

This treatment of capitals is a usual Perpendicular mannerism but generally on the bowtells of an even more composite pier, and therefore smaller in size and clustered together. Indeed this is what the mason of the Oxford Divinity School, Richard Winchcombe, did there and elsewhere, notably in the Wilcote Chapel at North Leigh, another border-line Cotswold place in Oxfordshire. Communication between the Cotswold quarries at Barrington, Taynton and Burford, and these Oxfordshire places was provided by the river Windrush. Once the stone had reached the Thames, it could, of course, be sent on to Windsor and London.

In trying to assess by eye the influence of the Perpendicular architecture of St. Peter's Abbey, Gloucester, on the Cotswold churches, we are driven to the conclusion that there is little trace before *c.* 1400. The first Perpendicular window at Gloucester is dated 1335, and there followed the transformation of the choir which has pointed Gothic windows in the clerestory, with Perpendicular tracery. The panelled walls have arches divided in the middle and this feature does occur in some Cotswold churches, usually with less success; but the later four-centred arches are not to be found here. The Cloister, *c.* 1377, also has pointed two-centred arches and panelled walls, and of course, the first fanvaults.

The alterations of Abbot Morwent, who had it in mind to re-build the nave and started at the west end some time between 1421 and 1437, are, however, very much copied in the Cotswolds, particularly the windows on the south-west corner with their four-centred arched heads, vertical mullions running through the sub-arches (this occurred in the windows of New College Chapel, Oxford in 1379), and bowtells on the jambs

[1] *Ibid.*, p. 600.

with little bases and capitals, though in this case they are never concave. The great west window has a four-centred arched head, tracery which seems familiar on the Cotswolds, and flying buttresses (c.f. Chipping Campden). The west doorway has a neat bowtell frame, hollow moulding, and carved spandrels, the prototype of many. The south porch which is of this date or earlier, seems very like the early fifteenth-century porch at Northleach, with its vault and bosses, and panelled walls having only the central lights glazed and therefore treated differently on the exterior. The Gloucester porch is much restored, but the south doorway has its original concave mouldings, and bow-tells with bases and caps. Northleach was a possession of Gloucester Abbey, and the interiors of these two porches create much the same artistic feeling.

The great tower was built in the 1450s and is covered in canopy work with arches flatter than most in the cathedral, but hardly to be called four-centred. There is a great transom band of quatrefoils, and the splendid open-work parapet and pinnacles are, of course, far more elaborate and expensive than most things attempted on the hills. The Lady Chapel was built *c.* 1450–99, and the windows have pointed arches and come into the grid category, which is not a usual feature of the great Cotswold churches, although there are sub-arches in the tracery pierced by verticals as in the first Perpendicular window a century before. They are very tall windows with no less than four layers of transoms all with varying tracery.

The finest small-scale Perpendicular work is in the little Chapel of the Salutation of Mary, and this is refined in almost the same kind of way that Richard Winchcombe's work was refined.

The Bristol or Berkeley influence on Gloucester in the flat many cusped arches of the ambulatory screen is not often found in the Cotswolds, though there are exceptions in the south door-ways at Coberley and Newington Bagpath.

The problem of dating, which we have been discussing with reference to documentary and architectural evidence, may be further illuminated by a study of masons' marks. R. H. C. Davis's report on "banker" marks in Oxfordshire throws an interesting light on the development of the local style of Perpendicular architecture in the Cotswolds.[1]

[1] *Oxford Archaeological Society Report, 1938*, no. 84.

Royal Ontario Museum: Altar, height 1.067 m., from Dorn near
Blockley.

By courtesy of Royal Ontario Museum, Toronto

Royal Ontario Museum: Altar, height 1.144 m., from Dorn near
Blockley.

By courtesy of Royal Ontario Museum, Toronto

Northleach from the east looks as though some great college chapel has been dropped into the middle of the parish church.

Photograph by P. D. Turner

The late Perpendicular west doorway at Fairford, elegantly detailed with bowtell mouldings.

Photograph by P. D. Turner

Grotesque human head on the Perpendicular parapet of Chedworth Parish Church.

Late fifteenth-century gargoyle at Chedworth.

Above: Detail from the south porch of Cirencester Parish Church.

Below: Fanvault in the south porch at Cirencester.

Above: Late fifteenth-century tracery, pinnacles and parapets of Fairford Parish Church.

Photograph by P. D. Turner

Below: Nave arcade in Northleach Parish Church showing the exaggerated concave mouldings.

Photograph by P. D. Turner

The marks emphasise that, although most of the greater Perpendicular churches far from being finished in one generation may not have been completed within a century, the concentrated period of building in Oxfordshire and the Cotswolds was *c.* 1440–80. At Cirencester, for example, the tower is *c.* 1402, though the nave arcades are as late as *c.* 1514–36. Winchcombe alone was built almost at once. The amount of church building in the period 1440–80 is a reminder not to exaggerate the disruption caused by the Wars of the Roses. R. H. C. Davis comments: "not only is it clear that while the land was not sufficiently disordered to make church-building impossible, the political uncertainties of the age prompted such safe investments as the Church and stone and mortar." It also appears that throughout the century the uncertainties of the wool trade may have encouraged building.[1]

The great Perpendicular churches were built by first-class masons, whose marks are elaborate; many of them have "pedigrees" or "parent marks". They were the personal trade marks of individual masons. It seems that they were usually used when many masons were being employed on a building as a check against faulty workmanship. When a mason wanted to perpetuate the mark of his father or master, he adopted it with a "difference", usually adding an extra line or curve. For instance, a mason's mark at Kempsford is found at South Leigh and at Northleach with added differences, another at Chipping Norton appears the same, and with a difference in Northleach nave. This suggests that the same mason (and his son or pupil) worked at Chipping Norton and on Northleach nave.[2] The same relationships can be deduced between Church Hanborough nave and Northleach porch.

Gargoyles and grotesques were as popular with the masons in the fifteenth century as they had been in the twelfth. Unlettered masons probably had a system of symbolism in their carvings which slyly mocked their employers.

Once finished, these great new churches were the marvel of the neighbourhood and small details were copied by the village

[1] *Ibid.*
[2] There are other theories, however, which hold that differences denote qualifications or proficiency. Freemasons read many secret meanings into lines and numbers.

craftsmen in their own churches. Such eccentricities of design as the crown of the tracery of the east window of Northleach chancel are found repeated in the neighbouring churches of Turkdean, Aston Blank and Coln Rogers. Similar masons' marks are not found here; it was just a case of copying.

The more skilled masons moved around, and it is obviously important for the purpose of dating to know the average working life of a fifteenth-century mason. One cannot expect it to have been more than thirty years, so that if a mark can be dated by documentary or other evidence, the same masons' mark elsewhere provides a most useful date bracket.

The heyday of the Cotswold churches did not last long. By the beginning of the sixteenth century the number of new works was decreasing and the supply of masons falling. The marks show that the "Cotswolds school" was just as closely connected with Oxford as with Gloucester. None of the marks in the Lady Chapel of Gloucester Cathedral, finished *c.* 1500, have been found elsewhere, nor does it resemble the Cotswold churches. The earlier west end of the Cathedral, as I have already indicated, is a different matter.

A mason working in 1383 on New College Chapel, Oxford (founded by William of Wykeham in 1379), also made his mark on Northleach porch for which there is no documentary evidence but the costume portrayed in the carvings is very early fifteenth century. The ante-chapels of New College, Magdalen and All Souls have apparently stylistic influence in the Cotswolds. Another mason whose mark appears on the Northleach porch, made it again at the Wilcote Chapel, North Leigh, begun in 1438 to the designs of the master mason Richard Winchcombe, who died about that time. The Northleach porch as we have already observed, resembles in style the great south porch of Gloucester Cathedral, dated *c.* 1420. The panelled walls have certain lights glazed but not all, and some arch forms are very pointed.

Another mason, whose mark looks like a simple loop, flourished in the last half of the fifteenth century. His mark appeared on the south nave aisle wall at Northleach before 1489, on the Burford nave arcades in the mid-late fifteenth century, at Minster Lovell before 1485, at St. George's Chapel, Windsor, on the north wall of the nave, 1475–83, and at Oxford

Cathedral Cloister a year or two before 1499. The occurrence
of his mark at Windsor is not surprising, since masons were
impressed from all parts of the country to work there, and
because much Taynton stone was used in the building of the
Chapel.

There is a legend that John of Gaunt, who died in 1399, built
the tower at Kempsford; but this is documentarily groundless
and chronologically improbable. A more interesting tradition is
held by the family of Couling, that its ancestor was a mason
brought from Oxford to build the tower. This tradition cor-
roborates the mason's mark at Magdalen College, Oxford
(founded in 1458), which may, according to the Magdalen
Register, have belonged to one, John Colas, who worked on the
chapel. This was between 1474 and 1479; but before this, the
mark appears at Burford, on the south porch and north chancel
aisle, at Stanton Harcourt in the exquisite Harcourt aisle
c. 1471, and in Pope's Tower, and in the marvellously beautiful
church at South Leigh. The Bear and Ragged Staff in the
porch at Burford suggests that it was built by the Nevilles who
held the manor 1439–99. A similarity between the design of the
work at Stanton Harcourt and Kempsford has been observed.
The use of single-light rectangular windows in Pope's Tower is
reminiscent of the lower stages of the tower at Kempsford.

The next mark to be noticed by R. H. C. Davis is a cross +
on top of a W, $\overset{+}{W}$ found between 1430 and 1461. It appears on
the Trinity Chapel at Cirencester *c.* 1430–38, at Sudeley Castle
c. 1450, on the church tower at Kempsford and at Winchcombe
church 1454–61.

We now come to the most interesting connection of all as it is
the one most obviously expected from stylistic grounds, that
between Northleach and Chipping Campden. It is a St.
Andrew's cross, joined on three sides but open at the top $\boxtimes$.
This mark has not been found elsewhere except at Chipping
Norton. The dating of the two similar naves has already been
discussed, and the connection with Chipping Norton is cor-
roborated by another mason's mark; however, the nave arcades
at the latter are quite different and have composite piers, and
the clerestory looks almost like a wall of glass, the windows
having straight heads and grid tracery with only narrow divisions between them.

Another mark on the Northleach nave arcades *c*. 1458, appears at Winchcombe, at Fairford, and on the lower portion of Cricklade church tower. At Fairford we must, therefore, presume a date prior to *c*. 1488. All the churches in this group belong to the Cotswold type of Perpendicular. The work is characterised by its four-centred arches, deeply hollow casement mouldings, neat detail and elaborate and varied tracery, in contrast to the broad details and gridiron tracery of much Perpendicular elsewhere.

At Northleach on the south-east column of the nave arcade there is the graffito of Henrie Winchcombe, and on the other side the words "God grant us his grace" and "Edmunde". It has been supposed that Henrie Winchcombe could have been the master mason or quarryman; but this is making an unconfirmed supposition about its date, given there were Winchcombes in the district for many years subsequently. Merton College in 1448–50 bought Taynton stone from one John Wynchecombe of Windrush.[1] Richard Winchcombe died about 1440. He was the master mason employed at the building of the chancel of Adderbury between 1408 and 1418, for New College, Oxford. In 1413–14 he visited Taynton to obtain stone, his travelling expenses being charged in the accounts. The whole family might have originated in the Windrush/Taynton quarrying area.

Masons' marks do not provide any direct evidence for the identity of the master mason of a building. The master mason, *lathamus*, was both the medieval architect and the chief of the working masons. He supplied such designs as were used and supervised the actual work of building. There is little to be found in medieval archives about plans or drawings. The master mason supplied patterns for mouldings and other details; but much work must have been done by eye alone, without plan or elevation.

The master mason, however, does appear to have attained almost professional status. He is frequently called "Magister", not in the academic sense, but as a title of honour. He had special privileges such as a gown of livery, a house or lodging, various special allowances and above all, he took and trained

[1] *Oxford City Documents*, ed. J. E. Thorold Rogers, Oxford Historical Society, xviii, 323.

apprentices. His importance will be realised when it is remembered that practically every problem of building was a masonry problem, and that in the absence of text books all necessary knowledge was acquired by practical work at the bench. Powerful and brilliant men like William of Wykeham were no doubt great builders in that they originated and financed great works of building, but they were not architects.[1]

We know quite a lot about the master mason Richard Winchcombe because of the survival of the detailed accounts of the building of the chancel of Adderbury, Oxfordshire, 1408–18. He was there in each of these years except in 1411, and was in fact the "architect". It may well be that the authorities of New College, satisfied with the work done for them at Adderbury, recommended him to the notice of the University. By 1430 he was in complete charge of the building of the Divinity School, which he had designed. There are the most striking likenesses between Adderbury and the Divinity School. Both works are remarkable for the subtlety and delicacy of their mouldings. The bowtells are especially slender, and in both buildings they are provided with little bases of a most refined section. At Adderbury these bowtells do not have capitals. The great east window has five ogee-headed lights and fitting tracery under a four-centred arch with hollow moulding, and a castellated transom. The doorways have quatrefoils in the spandrels and hood-moulds with deep stops. There are buttresses with pinnacles below the parapet level, and triangular shaped, with little ogee gables, winged gargoyles on the parapet, and in several places sculptured heads of William of Wykeham, who was actually dead before the building began. On the north of the chancel is a vestry with an oriel window, all part of Winchcombe's design, which has a neat bowtell surround, tracery over the ogee-headed lights, and battlements on the parapet. This distinctive Perpendicular style of Richard Winchcombe found just on the Oxfordshire side of the Cotswolds, occurs also at Deddington, Broughton, Bloxham, and of course, in the Wilcote Chapel at North Leigh. We can in this case, associate a series of medieval buildings with a master mason whose name we know. He not only designed his buildings, but he also built them, as a

[1] "Richardus Wynchecombe, Lathamus" in *Oxfordshire Record Society Series*, viii.

true architect should, and as apparently it was the custom to do until the architects of the Renaissance decided to leave the actual construction to others. He preferred the four-centred arch to the two-centred usual at the time, and this, and his trick of treating the top and bottom of tracery lights with a similar pointed and trefoiled arch, fitting neatly into the cinque-foiled ogee arches of the main lights is found in many Cotswold windows. Winchcombe's style is generally more delicate and refined than, for instance, the Perpendicular to be found at Canterbury or even the Winchester School of the period, which is marked by boldness of scale and largeness of detail.

In the work of this known master mason and in default of any other, we can see at least one influence spanning right across the Cotswolds, in the early part of the century, just before the great Cotswold Perpendicular churches were built, an influence which may well have affected the anonymous master masons of many subsequent buildings in between Gloucester and Oxford, as they pressed their daring innovations to the very brink of structural failure, and to a perfection both ascetic and elegant, breathing an intellectual Gothic confidence which denied the need for any Renaissance.

This confidence was exemplified best by the Court style at Windsor where Edward IV, returning fresh from exile, was determined to live splendidly. The last fling, however, owed something to foreigners. Such things as polygonal turret from Spain were so skilfully integrated into the Tudor style that the stair turret at Campden looks no more out of place than the sibyls in the stained glass at Rendcomb. The Renaissance had begun.

VII

Projects for Gentlemen, Jobs for the Poor: Mutual Aid in the Vale of Tewkesbury, 1600—1630

By Joan Thirsk

A FIERCE political controversy raged in Parliament between 1586 and 1624 around the granting of monopoly privileges by the Crown. These privileges were accorded to individuals who promised to set up new industrial and agricultural enterprises or to engage in new branches of overseas trade. The abuse of these privileges by some holders aroused deep anger in the country at large, and gave rise to monopolies debates in the Commons which developed into trials of strength between Crown and Parliament. They raised serious constitutional issues, and it is in this light that historians have generally discussed them. But considered from the economic standpoint, the monopolies scandal was a small shadow lying across an impressively large and constructive effort to introduce new occupations to the English economic scene. New crops and new industries created employment for the labouring poor; when they succeeded and their full potential came to be more widely understood, enthusiasm developed for setting up similar enterprises in colonial territories, first of all in Ireland, and then in America. The economic consequences were far-reaching.

In this paper I propose to explore the impact of these agricultural and industrial innovations in one district of Gloucestershire, the eastern half of the Vale of Tewkesbury.[1] First, it will reveal the relative unimportance in the provinces of the

[1] The same theme in a national setting was explored in my Ford lectures, given at Oxford in Hilary term, 1975. These are to be published. I wish to thank Mr. C. R. Elrington and the Rev. Canon J. E. Gethyn-Jones for their comments on this paper.

monopolies scandal—monopolists were a bane in London and
some provincial cities but they made only rare appearances in
rural areas. Secondly, it will illustrate the pronounced and
beneficial impact that new economic projects made in one
country district far from London, where the social circumstances were favourable. So many projectors thronged the
streets of London and the corridors of power in royal palaces
that the very term "projector" became an insult carrying with
it overtones of malpractice. But the ideas of projectors were
nevertheless carried to country areas with remarkable speed,
and in a purer air were translated into practical realities which
had nothing but healthy economic consequences.

The eastern half of the Vale of Tewkesbury in the sixteenth
century was a region peculiarly receptive to new economic
ventures. It had been the centre of four religious houses—
Tewkesbury Abbey, Winchcombe Abbey, Deerhurst Priory, and
Hailes Abbey, all dissolved in 1539.[1] It is unfashionable to
believe that abbeys and priories had given much charity to the
poor. Nevertheless, they had employed labour and stimulated
local trade, and their dissolution helps to explain the extreme
poverty which characterised the population in this area in the
later sixteenth century.

In the early seventeenth century, poverty in the eastern half
of the vale was a byword. Thomas Dekker claimed that a
beggars' fair was held at Deerhurst near Tewkesbury every year
on the two Holy Rood Days, at which "you shall see more
rogues than ever were whipped at a cart's arse through London,
and more beggars than ever came dropping out of Ireland".[2] A
satirical pamphlet, claiming to be the work of Harry the
Hangman, and published in 1655, described how the author
had been accustomed regularly to visit Deerhurst Fair, "a place
in Gloucestershire famous for three things, old clothes, lice, and
shitten stiles".[3] The old clothes were abundant at the fair because "the comers thereunto wanted money to buy new", the

---

[1] See the *Map of Monastic Britain, South Sheet*, Ordnance Survey (1950).

[2] A. L. Beier, 'Vagrants and the Social Order in Elizabethan England',
Past and Present, vol. 64, p. 24, quoting *Thomas Dekker*, ed. E. D. Pendry
(1967), p. 287.

[3] *Harry Hangman's Honour: or Gloucestershire Hangman's Request to the
Smokers or Tobacconists in London*, British Library, E 842 (13).

lice were so "goodly, fat, and tall that a louse from that fair . . . hath carried as much tallow as an ox that comes within Smithfield bars". The shitten stiles were "done out of state policy to preserve the place from any infection or contagion that might be left there by means of clothes coming from diseased parts and places". Harry the Hangman used to look forward to attending Deerhurst fair because he collected so many customers there. "Then 'twas a merry world with me", he sighed nostalgically, referring to former days when there was no work to employ idle hands in the Vale. "Before tobacco was planted, there being no kind of trade to employ men and very small tillage, necessity compelled poor men to stand my friends by stealing of sheep and other cattle, breaking of hedges, robbing of orchards, and what not; insomuch that the place became famous for rogues, as 'twas taken up in a proverb by many that stood on the top of Breedon Hill viewing the country would say, "Yonder is rich Worcester, brave Gloucester, proud Tewkesbury, beggarly Evesham, drunken Pershore and roguish Winchcombe. And Bridewell was erected there to be a terror to idle persons."

The Vale of Tewkesbury's economic difficulties stemmed, as Harry the Hangman explained, from its small tillage and absence of industry. It was a pastoral region with an excess of unused or under-used labour. Its towns suffered the same poverty as the countryside around. Winchcombe was a very poor town in Elizabeth's reign, when the grant of a fair and market recited that the borough was "fallen into so great ruin and decay that its inhabitants were not able to support and repair it for the great poverty that reigned amongst them".[1] When a list of Gloucestershire's male inhabitants was drawn up in 1608, it was plain that Winchcombe had not yet discovered a new economic role. Some were glovers and clothmakers but no other occupations seemed to command the labours of many.[2]

The geographical handicaps which left the Vale of Tewkesbury in this forlorn state were not irreparable. It is true that many rivers and streams that wend their way through the Vale made its lower-lying land wet and unsuitable for crop cultivation. Its abundant pasture was frequently of poor quality and its spacious commons were not attractive to fine gentlemen,

[1] S. Rudder, *A New History of Gloucestershire* (1779), p. 825.
[2] John Smith, *Men and Armour for Gloucestershire in 1608* (1902), pp. 77–8.

though they were ideal for supporting a poor population. But a new attitude to poor pastoral country began to take hold in the early seventeenth century as campaigns to improve fens, forests and chases got under way and improvers began to look upon run-down pastoral areas with fresh eyes. Elizabeth encouraged a start on the fens and James's ministers began to improve the forests. This concern for their royal estates reflected a general interest in the possibilities of improving pastoral country. Whether this was a consideration influencing Londoners to take an interest in land in the Tewkesbury Vale at this time is not definitely established. But it is noticeable that when dissolved monastic estates came onto the market in James's reign, together with other Crown lands earlier acquired by Elizabeth from the Bishop of Worcester (in exchange for the rents of impropriated rectories), some notably vigorous and able London merchants appeared as purchasers. Baptist Hicks, London mercer and moneylender, bought the site of Tewkesbury Abbey, and although this property was settled on his daughter, and he went to live in Chipping Campden (whence he took his later title of Viscount Campden), he retained a strong interest in Tewkesbury's affairs. He was M.P. for Tewkesbury in 1624, 1626 and 1628 and, at his death, left money for Tewkesbury's poor as well as funds for the support of a preaching ministry.[1] Two of the estates of Deerhurst Priory, namely Uckington and Staverton manors, along with other properties in Bishops Cleeve parish, passed *c.* 1608 to Paul Bayning, later Viscount Bayning, a London merchant trading to the Levant, who was worth £20,000 in goods at his death.[2] Finally, Winchcombe manor was bought by the two brothers, Sir George and Thomas Whitmore, sons of William Whitmore who had been a London haberdasher, Merchant Adventurer, and charter member of the Spanish and Portuguese Company. Sir George Whitmore was master of the Haberdashers' Company, a member of the Virginia Company, and later Lord Mayor of London. His eldest brother, William, who later took over sole possession of the manor from George and Thomas, was also a freeman of the

[1] *DNB, sub nomine; VCH. Glos.*, viii, 136, 153, 155, 168, 239.

[2] *VCH, Glos.*, viii, 52, 91; R. G. Lang, "Social Origins and Social Aspirations of Jacobean London Merchants", *Economic History Review*, xxvii, 46; *Cal. S.P.D., 1591–4*, p. 400.

Haberdashers' Company, lent money to the Crown and bought its land, but did not become deeply involved in City affairs.[1]

There is no evidence to show that these London merchants set about improving their estates in the conventional manner of new brooms sweeping dusty corners clean. At Winchcombe, indeed, the reverse occurred: until the mid-1630s the new land-lord let sleeping dogs lie. Nevertheless, industrial and agri-cultural schemes which were being hotly canvassed in London and which employed the poor, were imported into the Tewkes-bury Vale at the same time that the Londoners became land-owners there. It is unlikely that this was simply a coincidence.

The merchants-turned-landowners did not achieve this result single-handed, however. Many of the indigenous gentry at this time were far from munificently endowed, and they consorted readily with the new arrivals in their midst. Moreover, being markedly modest parish gentry, they were disinclined to develop a self-conscious pride that separated them from the lower orders. For one thing, they lacked the means to set themselves apart; for another, the geography of settlement was a discouragement. In parishes like Winchcombe and Cleeve, numerous hamlets dispersed the gentry in many different centres; their neighbours were few but for that very reason, they met at close quarters. At Farmcote, George Stratford, esquire, lived with 10 servants and only 2 husbandmen. At Postlip, Giles Broadway was lord, employing 11 servants but having no other neighbours.[2] In such an environment, a gentleman had no opportunity to cut a fine figure and overawe those around him. On the contrary, he might well develop a strong paternal concern for servants and the one or two tenant farmers who depended on him and on whom he in turn depended.[3]

Many complex factors explain the varied relationships be-tween the social classes in different regions of England, and in this paper no general discussion is appropriate. But facts drawn from some parishes in the eastern half of the Vale of Tewkesbury suggest that a single stereotyped image of the gentry irons out

---

[1] *DNB, sub nomine*; Lang, *op. cit.* p. 32.   [2] John Smith, *op. cit.* p. 88.

[3] This argument is developed at greater length in Joan Thirsk, "New Crops and their Diffusion: Tobacco-growing in Seventeenth-century England", *Rural Change and Urban Growth, 1500–1800*, ed. C. W. Chalklin and M. Havinden (1974), pp. 88–93.

interesting and important differences. It is an image drawn from examples in southern and eastern England where the village was the principal, and sometimes the only, centre of population, and where the manor house and parish church stood as twin symbols of authority in the community. In the west and north of England, people distributed themselves in a different geographical pattern, and while authority and deference were elements in the relationship of gentlemen with their humbler neighbours, they obtruded less sharply, since men held permanently in mind another fact of life, that in small communities survival depends on mutual aid. Mutual aid, indeed, was the most conspicuous common factor underlying all the employment schemes introduced into the Vale of Tewkesbury in the early seventeenth century. The new occupations gave work to the poor *and* yielded an income to their gentlemen-undertakers. The partnership benefited both sides, and both parties acknowledged their mutual advantage.

Some clues to the economic standing of the gentry who engaged in new projects explain their interest in the partnership. They were often the younger brethren of gentle families, who could only maintain their father's rank in society by their own efforts. This is revealed in an analysis of the six families who were involved in the project of tobacco-growing, when it was first introduced into the Vale in 1619. They were parish gentry with little land outside their home parish, claiming gentility, but lacking the generous means to support it. One was Giles Broadway, esquire, of Postlip, who was among the first to lease his land for tobacco-growing. At the Heralds' Visitation in 1623 he traced his pedigree no further back than his grandfather and claimed no grand connections. He had bought the manor of Bishops Cleeve in 1606 from Peter Vanlore, and with this land (newly on the market at the beginning of the seventeenth century after centuries in the dead hand of the church) Giles Broadway was raising the status of his family.[1]

The second owner of land for tobacco-growing was the wife of Timothy Gates, the parson. She owned land in Bishops Cleeve. Timothy's forebears were established gentry in East

---

[1] H. Chitty and John Phillipot, *The Visitation of the County of Gloucester, 1623*, Harleian Soc., xxi (1885), *sub* Bradway; subsequently referred to as *1623 Visitation*: *VCH, Glos.*, viii, 8.

Anglia, of whom one son in an earlier generation had married Francis Walsingham's sister. The main branch of the family remained in the eastern counties, but Timothy's father was a younger son who moved off into the Midlands, and there Timothy too remained, marrying a Herefordshire woman and becoming the parson of Cleeve.[1]

A third local landowner who allowed some of his land to be sown with tobacco was Thomas Loreng, gentleman, of Haymes in Bishops Cleeve parish. He was the owner of a modest estate and the heir of a family that had lived in the same place since before 1500.[2] He had a firm attachment to the local community but kept out of the limelight.

The fourth family was that of John Ligon, esquire, who leased twelve acres of his land at Arle Court, Cheltenham for tobacco. He was the younger son of Sir William Ligon, head of a Worcestershire gentry family, living at Beauchamp Court, Madresfield. The Worcestershire property had been inherited by the family as a result of a marriage alliance in the early sixteenth century between Richard Ligon and the second daughter of Lord Beauchamp of Powick. The main estate, in due course, passed to the elder son of Sir William, who also inherited the precious heirlooms of the family, its armour, weapons, books, and manuscripts. John Ligon, however, the younger son, was given a start in life by receiving from his father before his death a detached piece of family property in Cheltenham. It was from this land that he selected twelve acres to let to the tobacco-growers.[3]

The fifth and most illustrious family was the Tracys. The main branch lived at Toddington, the parish next to Winchcombe, and in the sixteenth century counted four generations living in the same place.[4] They were successful at rearing many sons, and more than one of these established himself on his own estate in a neighbouring parish, for they were a closely-knit family. The eldest son, Sir John Tracy, became the tobacco-grower, and his higher status in local society may explain the

[1] *1623 Visitation, sub* Gates.
[2] *VCH, Glos.*, viii, 13; Gloucestershire Record Office: D 127/46/48–54.
[3] *VCH, Glos.*, viii, 91; *VCH, Worcs.*, iv, 187, 120; Worcestershire Record Office: Will of Sir William Ligon of Madresfield, 6 November 1618. I wish to thank Mr. Peter Large for this reference. [4] *1623 Visitation, sub nomine.*

more advantageous terms he was given when the lease of his
land for tobacco was negotiated. But his willingness to enter
upon the project may in part be explained by the friendship
subsisting between the Tracys and the Stratfords who pioneered
the crop. Paul Tracy (later Sir Paul) of Stanway was executor
of the will of George Stratford, the senior representative of the
Stratford family, and Tracys and Stratfords more than once
sold land to one another.[1]

This catalogue of tobacco growers ends with John Stratford,
the principal undertaker. The Stratford family as a whole
claimed a long ancestry in the Midland counties. The family
pedigree in the seventeenth century was traced back to John
Stratford, member of Edward II's Parliament in 1319–20, at
which time the family's marriage alliances were being forged
with Nottinghamshire and Staffordshire families. The association with Gloucestershire seems to have started later with a
John Stratford who described himself as a gentleman of Farmcote, in Winchcombe parish, and whose children thereafter
married into Gloucestershire families. Like the Tracys, they
were a healthy stock and produced many sons. Thus John
Stratford, who married Mary Throckmorton, had five sons. Of
these George, the eldest, inherited his father's seat at Farmcote
along with the title of gentleman. Robert, the second son, went
on an expedition with Sir Francis Drake, during which he died.
Anthony went to live in Ireland and married there. (Was he
perhaps the Lieutenant Anthony Stratford who was deputy
governor of Duncannon fort in Ireland in 1614?[2]) Finally,
there was John, the tobacco-grower, the son who is described
in the pedigree as of Prestbury. He was apprenticed in London
to a salter and duly became a member of the London Salters'
Company. No further details concerning the careers of John's
brothers are vouchsafed to us. But even on this meagre evidence,
it is not altogether surprising to find this family in the forefront
of the tobacco-growing enterprise in Winchcombe and the

---

[1] *1623 Visitation, sub* Tracy; *PRO*: Prob. 11/148, will of Sir Paul Tracy
of Stanway.

[2] *1623 Visitation, sub* Stratford; *Cal. S. P. Ireland*, 1611–14, p. 434. Anthony
Stratford started life as a salter in London. See *PRO*: Stac 8, Bdle 266, no. 24.
For further references to John Stratford's career, see also Joan Thirsk, "New
Crops and their Diffusion", *op. cit.*, p. 81ff.

neighbourhood. Its sons were all of an adventurous spirit, not one of them being inclined to live at home "like a mome" knowing "the sound of no other bell but his own".[1]

The three Stratford brothers who chose such different walks of life in which to make their careers reached their late teens in the 1580s or 1590s. In London this was the age of daring projects, which inspired many young men with hopes of easy fortune. Their impact may be gauged from the career of John Stratford whose life story is comparatively well documented. John arrived in London in the 1580s when a war with Spain was brewing, and the preliminary skirmishes were already interfering with the supply of some essential imports from Spain such as oil, wine, woad and soap. The flow of other goods that came from France, including woad and salt, was also being disrupted by that country's internal struggle against the Huguenots. For these reasons projects were being energetically set on foot to produce these essential commodities in England. Oil, wine, woad, salt, and soap provide, as it were, the orchestral accompaniment to the projects which emerge as dominant themes in the Vale of Tewkesbury in the next forty or fifty years.[2]

Salt was one project high on the projectors' list and was, we must suppose, a prime concern of the salters, in whose company John Stratford found himself on his arrival in London. Already in 1549 the author of the *Discourse of the Commonweal* had expressed apprehension at the insufficiency of salt produced at home, and had deplored England's dependence on overseas supplies. Threatened shortages were accompanied by threats of steeply rising prices because the French kings were also increasing the salt tax. The search for ways of evaporating sea salt had therefore started in England and in Scotland in the 1550s and 1560s, and though energy flagged when French supplies resumed at the peacemaking, anxiety revived again *c.* 1575. French saltpans were then in decay as a result of the civil war in France, troubles in the Netherlands had destroyed Dutch saltpans, salt arrived in England in uncertain quantity, and was high in price. The government was forced to the conclusion that

[1] Joan Thirsk and J. P. Cooper, *Seventeenth-Century Economic Documents* (1972), p. 756.
[2] See my Ford lectures, 1975, to be published.

foreign supplies could no longer be relied upon to furnish English needs.[1]

The parish of Winchcombe is traversed by a salters' route and has a Salters Hill. Indeed, saltways criss-cross the area, and it is tempting to think that they had some bearing on the Stratford family's close association with the Salters' Company.[2] However, John Stratford does not, himself, appear to have taken an active interest in the salt trade, though he undertook business in other related commodities. His first experience of independent trade, on completing his apprenticeship, was gained from dealings in Cheshire cheese and woollen stockings, which chapmen collected in the provinces and brought for him to sell in London. At first sight this statement, coming from Stratford himself, suggests that he bought his stockings in Cheshire along with the cheese, but since confirmatory evidence of a stocking industry in that county is lacking, we may speculate whether, even in his early days in business, Stratford turned to his native parish for some of the wares he sold in London. Stocking knitting was certainly carried on in Winchcombe after the Restoration.[3] Was it introduced fifty years earlier?

Stratford next turned his hand to the Eastland trade to the Baltic. *Circa* 1601 he began to sell English broadcloth in northern Europe and to import undressed flax. This enterprise was markedly successful, and, having started with a capital of £200 he built up a fortune of £1,200 in two years. He then agreed to hand over the broadcloth trade to his partners and concentrate on flax, which he put out to be spun in and around London. But the flax trade did not last. The Netherlanders were even more adept than the English at developing labour-intensive occupations to employ their poor, and they began to send to England flax that was ready dressed, rather than the undressed, raw flax. They outpriced the English flax dressers and Stratford's business fell away.[4]

[1] *A Discourse of the Commonweal of this Realm of England*, ed. E. Lamond, pp. 42, 44, 61; E. Hughes, "The English Monopoly of Salt in the Years, 1563–71", *English Historical Review*, xl, *passim*, but esp. pp. 334–5, 348–9; British Library: Lansdowne MSS. 21/23; 86/72; 52/53.

[2] A. H. Smith, *The Place-names of Gloucestershire*, i, 19–20, English Place-Name Society, xxxviii.

[3] For John and George Stratford's dealings in stockings and cheese, see *PRO*: Stac 8, Bdle 266, no. 24.   [4] *PRO*: C2, Jas. I, S3/11.

At the same time, however, John Stratford had other irons in the fire. He conducted a trade in miscellaneous goods that were traditionally salters' business—tallow, potash, soap ashes, and oil.[1] By 1616 he was in partnership with his half-brother Ralph who was also a salter[2] and they set up a soap boiling house. New ways of making soap greatly interested projectors when the high cost of imported oil began to make soap expensive. A search for substitutes in the 1570s had already produced an answer in "specle soap", made of tallow instead of oil. This proved to be sufficiently cheap to win favour among the "common people".[3] By 1616, however, yet another solution was in sight as Benedict Webb's experiments with growing rape and pressing the seeds for oil began to show promising results both in the making of soap and the fulling of cloth. At a later date, *c.* 1624, Stratford compiled a document showing his familiarity with Webb's work[4] (it was, after all, being conducted in Gloucestershire) but whether Stratford was himself experimenting with the use of rape oil in 1616 is not clear. He certainly used both tallow and oil in his business, but did not explain the source of either.[5] Nor did he explain the source of his soap ashes: were they imported from Danzig or were they soap ashes produced experimentally at home? Suffice it to say that he had a soap boiling business in London at a time when soap manufacture was passing through a highly experimental phase.[6]

Soap boiling, however, was not sufficiently remunerative to compensate Stratford for the shrinking flax trade from the Baltic. The latter struck a heavy blow at his livelihood and his fertile brain turned to other schemes. He was buying land avidly in the Winchcombe area, and his partners in business watched his extended financial dealings with some misgivings. "He charged himself with too many trades and occupations"

[1] *PRO*: Req. 2, Bdle 308, no. 45.   [2] *PRO*: Stac 8, Bdle 266, no. 24.
[3] British Library: Lansdowne MS. 18, no. 63. Dated (in pencil) 1574.
[4] *PRO*: SP14/180/79.   [5] *PRO*: Req. 2, Bdle 308, no. 45.
[6] The description of three kinds of soap made in England in 1574 specified Danzig soap ashes as one ingredient in every case—British Library: Lansdowne MS. 18, no. 63. By 1624 "new soap" and "soap with home materials" and "work with home ashes" were being discussed, suggesting that the ashes were being produced at home (from bracken and weeds perhaps, as they were in the eighteenth century?), in addition to the oil. See, for example, *Cal. S.P.D., 1623–25*, pp. 127, 272, 330.

said one of them later.[1] They urged him to reduce the number
of his enterprises by handing over the flax trade to them. No
doubt the reasons that persuaded John Stratford to accept their
advice were more complex than he described, but the upshot
was that Stratford decided to try his hand at tobacco-growing.[2]
Where else more suitable as the scene for his experiments than
his native heath, the Vale of Tewkesbury, which offered the
right sort of land (old pasture long unploughed) *and* plentiful
labour?

Tobacco-growing, then, appears as the first firm project
offering new employment in the Vale of Tewkesbury. But was it
really the first? A possible forerunner of tobacco-growing as an
employer of labour was woad-growing.

Woad-growing was a project that spread rapidly in southern
England in the early 1580s when woad supplies from the Azores
were interrupted. It was quickly taken up in many southern
counties, including neighbouring Oxfordshire and Wiltshire.
Unfortunately, the careful census taken of this crop in 1586 does
not enumerate the acreage so employed in Gloucestershire.[3]
But at Painswick, in the more specialised clothmaking area
around Stroud, tithes were being paid on woad in 1615; at Over
Guiting, close to Winchcombe, a woad mill was at work in
1634; and later still in 1656 a woad mill was working in
Slaughter Hundred.[4] The Vale of Tewkesbury had plenty of
suitable land for woad, and woad-growing was highly com-
mended as a means of employing many poor. Against this background, one small piece of evidence—that land let out by
Thomas Loreng for tobacco-growing in 1619 in Cleeve had been
used to grow woad shortly before—takes on a larger significance.[5] This clue, set in the wider context, gives some ground for
suspecting that an experiment with woad had already been
undertaken, before the growing of tobacco was introduced. We
can only speculate on its scale, however, and must regard
tobacco-growing as the first fully identified project in the Vale
of Tewkesbury.

The first season of tobacco-growing in 1619 in Winchcombe,

---

[1] *PRO*: Req. 2, Bdle 308, no. 45.   [2] *PRO*: C2 Jas. I, S3/11.
[3] The Ford Lectures contain fuller details on woad-growing.
[4] *VCH, Glos.*, ii, 159; *PRO*: E134, 10 Car. I, Mich. 9; *VCH, Glos.*, vi, 75.
[5] *PRO*: Req. 2, 308/44.

Cleeve and Cheltenham, started with a crop of 100 acres. John Stratford leased fragmented pieces of land from different owners to make up this acreage and paid out £1,400 in labour costs in the first year. At 8d. a day this represented the labour of 42,000 man days, and if we roughly estimate daily toil on the crop for 7 months from 1 May to 30 November (214 days) it must be reckoned that about 196 men were at work in the tobacco fields each day, or, at the rate of 6d. a day, 262 women. These figures give a rough indication of the work afforded by the tobacco-growing enterprise in its first year. As John Stratford later described his venture, he took himself to Gloucestershire "where poor people do much abound" and thereby relieved them.[1] Winchcombe's total population was 340 families in 1650, and that of Cleeve at the same date 200. If we estimate that one third of the population was in need of such employment, then work in the summer for 200 labourers could have engaged a member of every single poor family in Winchcombe and Cleeve, thus making a substantial contribution to their relief.[2]

Tobacco-growing undertaken by merchants and gentry, however, was a short-lived affair. At the end of 1619 the government banned tobacco-growing in England in order to improve the chances of the growers in Virginia. John Stratford promptly ceased his operations. But his year's work had been enough to teach many poor men in the Vale of Tewkesbury how to cultivate tobacco and it continued as a poor man's crop in the region for another 70 years as well as spreading to twenty-two other counties. A seemingly brief experiment had created a new kind of work for the poor that was to last for many decades.[3]

Meanwhile, however, John Stratford had to find himself another occupation. The government's ban on tobacco had left him in deep financial trouble since he had pledged himself to pay high rents for four years ahead for tobacco. It was known as

[1] *PRO*: C2 Jas. I, S3/11; SP 14/180/79.

[2] C. R. Elrington, "The Survey of Church Livings in Gloucestershire, 1650", *TBGAS*, lxxxiii, 89, 90. In 1609 Winchcombe manor was said to have 80–100 tenements, but two and three families occupied one tenement in the later 1630s. In 1650 it was said to have 340 families. In the 1620s even a population of 340 families may be on the low side: Winchcombe was much damaged in the Civil War. David Royce, *Landboc sive Registrum Monasterii . . . de Winchcumba* (1892), pp. lxii, lxvii.

[3] Joan Thirsk, "New Crops and their Diffusion", *op. cit.*

a profitable but exhausting crop, and landlords expected to be compensated. Though tobacco could no longer be grown, the courts of law insisted that he continue to pay the same high rents. He had to find another project and turned to flax-growing. His earlier business ventures had given him experience of the trade in flax from the Baltic and of flax dressing around London. He became convinced that England could produce a better quality flax than that imported; again he could count on a good supply of labour and suitable land in the Vale of Tewkesbury.[1]

Thus began John Stratford's next venture, growing flax on 40 acres of land in Winchcombe and Cockbury. For growing and dressing the flax, he employed a labour force of 200 people. Needless to say, he made himself unpopular with his former partners in London who were still counting on imported flax to give them their living.[2] However, he held to his conviction that it was desirable to employ Englishmen "for their better relief and the good of this commonwealth, seeing an inconceivable distress and misery increasing amongst the multitude of poor people that live in cities and towns where no clothing or help of other work is". With the same flax, he also tried making a small quantity of linen cloth, though "only for trial".[3]

Stratford was not unique at this time in arguing the case for labour-intensive crops and providing careful estimates, based on personal experience, of the numbers employed. Forty acres of flax, grown and made into linen cloth, employed 800 people in one year, he maintained.[4] It was his belief that oil from flax seed was capable of being used to make sweet soap, just as Benedict Webb had used rape oil. Had he, one wonders, attempted to crush the flax seed which he stored in his barns for this purpose?[5] Or did he, perhaps, send it on to Benedict Webb? The tangled connections between projectors engaged in various enterprises makes it a tempting guess that Benedict Webb and John Stratford had more than a passing acquaintance with each other.

Benedict Webb was a contemporary of Stratford and a man of the same stamp, energetic and enterprising. Webb had high hopes for the future use of rape oil both for soap and in the

[1] *PRO*: SP14/180/79; SP16/57/28.   [2] *PRO*: C2 Jas. I, S3/11.
[3] *PRO*: SP14/180/79.   [4] *Ibid.*   [5] *PRO*: C2, Jas. I, S3/11.

cloth industry, and had been conducting experiments with an oil mill at Kingswood since 1605. He even grew his own crop of rape on land in the Forest of Dean, leased to him by Sir William Throckmorton, and by 1618 he had successfully persuaded clothiers to use rape oil in cloth manufacture. He had other high achievements to his credit. He had perfected the manufacture of a multi-coloured cloth, known as medley or Webb's cloth. All this had followed from his early training with a linen draper in London, followed by travels in France. From these beginnings he had built up a trade with France, principally in cloth but also in salt.[1] Stratford, for his part, could claim to have started tobacco-growing in Gloucestershire, now flourishing as an illicit crop, and was looking ahead to a great future for the linen industry. "The more flax we sow, the greater quantity of tillage it will beget, as the sowing of woad does prepare the land better for corn afterwards", he wrote. In other words, flax, like woad-growing, paved the way in some places for a more general improvement of agriculture on poor pasture. They offered the chance to put to better use "mean land such as the uplands of remote forests, chases, and other commons which doth now increase and nourish idle people and is the breed [breeding ground?] of weak and unserviceable horse and the bane of sheep".[2] Surely, as Stratford wrote, he was thinking especially of the Vale of Tewksbury, which had so much common and waste and offered such scope to improvers? Surely he was thinking of Winchcombe's poor when he wrote of the work afforded by such crops. "If our idle poor had flax raised here, as they might have, and [were] compelled to work, if they will not willingly otherwise, whereas now they are an intolerable burden to the abler sort by begging and stealing, they would contrariwise become profitable to the commonwealth, paying for food and clothing and live according to God's ordinance by the sweat of their face in a more religious order."[3] Stratford's aspirations were not distant dreams, but drew their strength from his own experience.

The flax-growing enterprise in Winchcombe which started in

---

[1] Esther Moir, "Benedict Webb, clothier", *Economic History Review*, x, 256–64.   [2] *PRO*: SP14/180/79.

[3] *Ibid.* See also similar words in another of John Stratford's appeals for the growing of hemp and flax. *PRO*: SP16/57/28.

1623 was still under way in 1627 when Stratford claimed that it had enabled him to pay off £8,000 of the debts he had incurred in tobacco-growing. A lawsuit in 1634 adds supporting evidence for this claim, by revealing that Giles Broadway, who had leased his land for tobacco in 1619, had received 300 sheep (worth £10 a score) in 1622–3 in payment of the rent that Stratford owed him; while on another occasion in 1623–4, he had taken payment in 20 cwts. of flax. Broadway had thereupon engaged flax-dressers in Winchcombe. At one time he had three dressers, dressing 33 lbs. apiece each week for three weeks; in the following 9–10 weeks, he had seven dressers.[1]

Giles Broadway, it will be recalled, lived at Postlip and owned Cleeve manor. He had a local surname, but no grand pedigree. He had once spent three months in France, and although we are not told what business took him there, it may be significant that the information was given to the court of Exchequer by Humphrey Kirkham, a labourer, from the woad mill at Over Guiting, who had been his servant in France.[2] Was Broadway perhaps in France to learn skills that might serve to improve the Englishman's dyeing of flax? It may seem over-speculative to put such questions, but the proven interconnections of projects and projectors show that these were possibilities.

In this case we cannot proceed beyond guesswork. But a chain of friendship and mutual support linked projectors who had various different schemes afoot, to grow new crops, start new industries, improve old skills, and, above all else, provide more work for the poor. The circle of Winchcombe tobacco- and flax-growers has introduced us to one such group of projectors and friends. The activities of that same group invite us to look still further afield to colonising schemes overseas. Members of the same families were interested in the settlement of Virginia, and depended on Winchcombe and its neighbourhood to produce colonists to assist that venture. In short, they were involved in yet another scheme offering work and a new future for the local population.

The Virginia plantation first aroused the enthusiasm of Gloucestershire gentry from another part of the county before

[1] *PRO*: SP16/57/14; E134, 10 Car. I, Mich. 9.
[2] *PRO*: E134, 10 Car I, Mich. 9.

those in the Winchcombe district took any serious interest. Richard Berkeley of Stoke Gifford, John Smith of North Nibley, Sir William Throckmorton of Clearwell,[1] and George Thorpe of Wanswell Court in Berkeley had been responsible for sending a ship *The Margaret* with 36 men to Virginia in September 1619.[2] The vessel sailed in the autumn of the year in which the first tobacco crop was being harvested at Winchcombe. The intention was to build in Virginia a new town, to be called Berkeley, its name indicating clearly that the gentry from the Vale of Berkeley were the principal promoters. However, it is doubtful if all the four original partners ever intended to go personally to Virginia. In March 1620 one of them, George Thorpe of Wanswell, had certainly set sail to direct affairs on the spot, but in May Sir William Throckmorton withdrew from the partnership, and William Tracy, esquire, was brought in.[3] The Tracys and the Throckmortons were related by marriage, but in addition to this, William Tracy's father, Sir Thomas Tracy, was a member of the Virginia Company, and in May 1620 attended a Quarter Court of the Company.[4] The gentry of the Winchcombe area were now firmly involved in the scheme for colonisation.

We have already met the Tracys as a large and ramified family in the Vale of Tewkesbury. Sir John Tracy of Toddington leased some of his land for tobacco-growing. Other members lived in close proximity, at Stanway, and at Hailes. William Tracy was living at Hailes when he entered upon the agreement to take his wife and two children to Virginia, and his letters to John Smith make clear his eagerness to start a new life

[1] Sir William Throckmorton had leased some land in the forest of Dean for growing rape to Benedict Webb (see p. 161). The Throckmortons held one manor in Deerhurst, formerly belonging to Deerhurst Priory, until 1604, and another in Apperley hamlet, belonging to Westminster Abbey, until 1613. *VCH, Glos.*, viii, 34ff. Sir John Tracy of Toddington was married to Anne, daughter of Thomas Throckmorton of Coscourt. *1623 Visitation, sub* Tracy.

[2] *Records of the Virginia Company of London*, iii, *1607–22.* ed. Susan Kingsbury, p. 379. This venture was the subject of the Rev. Canon J. E. Gethyn-Jones's presidential address to the Society in 1975.

[3] Kingsbury, *op. cit.* 271–4, 379–81.

[4] See above, n. 2; Conway Robinson and R. A. Brock, *Abstract of the Proceedings of the Virginia Company of London, 1619–24*, Virginia Historical Society (1888), i, 60.

overseas. With his own household of 16–30 people, he planned to take others, making a party of about 65 settlers, of which he would be governor and captain.[1]

A circle of influential friends in London and in Gloucestershire rallied to Tracy's aid. Sir Edwin Sandys, Treasurer and Governor of the Virginia Company, promised to lend cows when the party arrived overseas, and Lady Delaware, whose land lay next to the proposed plantation, promised goats and silkworms.[2] The colonists were recruited in Gloucestershire. A gardener, a glover, and a husbandman came from Wotton-under Edge,[3] much nearer Berkeley than Winchcombe. But the passage of another 20 men and women was paid "from the parts of Hailes to Bristol", from which we may perhaps reasonably infer that they were recruited locally. Certainly Giles and Alexander Broadway came from the same neighbourhood (the Broadways lived at Postlip). The surnames of others who arrived safely in Virginia include familiar Winchcombe families like the Halls and the Pages.[4]

Organising the supplies for the voyage caused Tracy endless trouble and anxiety, but his problems shed more light on his circle of Gloucestershire friends. Thirteen broadcloths were delivered to him at Bristol by Benedict Webb.[5] When money to pay the bills was hard to find, Tracy gave up all hope of help from "his cousin", Richard Berkeley of Stoke Gifford, and sent urgent letters to John Smith at North Nibley.[6] But on the eve of Tracy's departure, when he was thrown into gaol for debt, one of his most effective helpers was Timothy Gates, the parson of Cleeve, whose wife had leased her land to John Stratford for tobacco-growing. Timothy Gates addressed William Tracy as his good cousin and referred similarly to his "cousin Bridges".[7] Cousin Bridges was John Brydges, a member of the family of

---

[1] Kingsbury, *op. cit.* 368–70.

[2] Kingsbury, *op. cit.* 293, 290, 291. In December 1621, the Deputy Governor of the Virginia Company ordered a translation of a treatise on silkworms and silkmaking, written by a Frenchman who was master of James I's silkworms at Oatlands. The book was to be sent to Virginia by the next ship. This is another example of a project being simultaneously pursued in England and America. See E. D. Neill, *History of the Virginia Company of London* (New York, 1869), 250, 258.

[3] Kingsbury, *op. cit.* 393–4.   [4] *Ibid.*, 392, 426.   [5] *Ibid.*, 390, 391.

[6] *Ibid.*, 373–4, 266.   [7] *Ibid.*, 409.

Grey Brydges, fifth lord Chandos of Sudeley Castle. Grey Brydges was renowned for his hospitality ("twice a week his house was open to his neighbours") and for his generosity to the poor.[1] When Tracy was released from gaol and the good news was passed on by John Brydges, he likewise referred to Tracy as his 'cousin".[2]

The many threads that linked these adventurers and projectors linked their numerous projects. Tracy's contract with the gardener from Wotton under Edge promised him houses and land in Virginia for orchards, gardens, grain and grass, and also for vineyards, tobacco-growing, woad, silk, flax, and hemp-growing.[3] In short, the new crops that were the subject of experiments at home were also to be grown in Virginia. Meanwhile in London, the governing court of the Virginia Company entertained grander and more official schemes to promote the same crops and industries that were occupying the energies of the Gloucestershire projectors. John Stratford's partner in tobacco-growing at Winchcombe had been Henry Somerscales; his brother, Robert Somerscales, engaged the Court in discussions about a plan for "the curing and ordering of tobacco"—evidently in Virginia, since the plan was approved in July 1620, after tobacco-growing in England had been banned. Other projectors urged upon the Company plans for making in Virginia soap ashes, and potash, and for establishing improved methods of sowing and managing flax and hemp.[4]

William Tracy's party for Virginia patiently endured their trials and tribulations before they could leave England. Their ship lay becalmed for several days at Bristol, and as Tracy surveyed the cargo being stowed on board and the passengers installing themselves, he wrote, on 24 September 1620, a melancholy description of the prospect before them. The middle and upper decks were so overcrowded that no one could lie down comfortably. "The best is purgatory that we shall live in till landing and long after." More people had offered themselves for the voyage than Tracy could accommodate, and at least ten

---

[1] *DNB*: *sub* Grey Brydges, fifth Lord Chandos.

[2] Kingsbury, *op. cit.* 410.   [3] *Ibid.*, 393–4.

[4] *Records of the Virginia Company of London*, i. *1619–24*, ed. S. Kingsbury, 364–5, 403. Another contract was made with Thomas Peirse, who professed skill with hops and woad, but travelled on a different ship. Kingsbury, iii, 197.

had been turned off the ship and had to stay for the next boat. As the ship waited for a favourable wind, Tracy's money worries loomed again. His party could not live on air, and " 'tis not a little fifty persons at least will spend," he observed wistfully.[1] When the ship did sail, it sprang a leak in the Irish Channel and had to put into Kingfall [Kinsale?] in Ireland for repairs. The party finally arrived safely in Virginia in January 1621, and in July 1621 the master of the vessel was back in England with a cargo of tobacco from Virginia, some sassafras, some "pieces of walnut tree" (perhaps cuttings?), and members of the crew claiming the remainder of their wages for transporting Tracy and his company to their journey's end.[2]

Meanwhile in Gloucestershire, John Smith and Richard Berkeley settled up the account and kept in close touch with the new planters in Virginia. Smith ordered tobacco seed from Virginia, and in October 1621 sold his crop, presumably grown from the same seed, to John Stratford. Stratford, being now prevented by statute from growing tobacco, continued in England to trade in the commodity.[3]

What was the net result of all this economic effort in the Vale of Tewkesbury? William Tracy's party of colonists settled in Virginia. William Tracy himself died there in April 1621; his daughter lived there long enough to marry, but died in the massacre of March 1622. However, William Tracy had taken his wife Mary and his son Thomas, and the Tracys who appear in Virginian land grants in the 1650s and 1660s may well be descended from Thomas. Mary Tracy, who appears in 1654, may even have been the widow of William.[4]

Giles Broadway, who travelled with the same party to Virginia (his family came from Postlip), was reported slain soon after his arrival, but other members of the family must have followed him thither, for a number of Broadways were involved in land grants in the 1640s, 1650s and 1660s.[5] Two members of the Stratford family participated in land grants in 1657; and

[1] Kingsbury, iii, 410–12.	[2] *Ibid.*, 403–5, 426–7.

[3] *Ibid.*, 402–4, 195, 509–10; i, 150.

[4] *Ibid.*, i, 520, 535; E. D. Neill, *op. cit.*, 189; Kingsbury, *op. cit.*, iii, 405; N. M. Nugent, *Cavaliers and Pioneers. Abstracts of Virginia Land Patents and Grants, 1623–66* (Baltimore, 1969), i, pp. 227, 250, 279, 293, 300, 307, 512.

[5] Kingsbury, *op. cit.*, iii, 397; Nugent, *op. cit.*, 146, 296, 356, 458, 450.

a Robert Loreng (the Lorengs lived at Haymes in Cleeve parish and had leased some of their land for tobacco in 1619) was in Virginia in 1664.[1]

The dispersal of the Ligon family overseas carries us into yet another area of colonial enterprise. John Ligon of Arle Court, Cheltenham, had leased some of his land for tobacco to John Stratford in 1619. He was alleged to have promised Stratford that, if tobacco-growing was prohibited, he would engage his influential friends to procure an exemption for Stratford from such tiresome legislation.[2] He proved not to be as influential as he thought. But the Ligons, like the Stratfords, were vigorous adventurers. At least one member of the Ligon family, Thomas, was buying land in Virginia in the 1660s.[3] Yet another representative of the family, Richard Ligon, having lost his property in what he termed "a barbarous riot" in England in 1647, set sail from England, he cared not whither, in a vessel that was bound for the Caribbean. He stayed in Barbados from 1647–50, and on his return wrote his remarkable history of the Island of Barbados, published in 1657, to inform and persuade other Englishmen to settle there.[4]

In these fragmented scraps of information, we see the offspring of the Gloucestershire gentry dispersing themselves overseas and encouraging others to make a new life there. Other members of the same group of gentry families created more work at home. We have traced the beginnings of a successful new occupation—tobacco-growing—that became so firmly entrenched that it could not be rooted out—illegal though it was—until 1690. We have found evidence of at least ten years of flax-growing, and have suggested reasons for adding the occupation of woad-growing. None of this enterprise completely solved the problem of poverty. The structure of these communities militated against such a possibility. Winchcombe, Cleeve, and Deerhurst were open villages; Tewkesbury was an open town. As soon as a project was successfully launched and labour was

[1] Nugent, *op. cit.*, pp. 357, 452.
[2] *PRO*: Req. 2, Bdle 399, no. 68.
[3] Nugent, *op. cit.*, pp. 440, 516.
[4] Richard Ligon, *A True and Exact History of the Island of Barbados* (1657), Dedication, 1–2.

recruited to it, it attracted a throng of poor people from elsewhere. The large number of subdivided tenements in Winchcombe in 1638, housing two and three families in place of the single families for which they were built, bore witness not only to the success of projects in creating work, but to the fresh problems created by the influx of more people.[1] A visitor to Winchcombe from Oxford in 1641 dubbed it "a poor beggarly town".[2] But Harry Hangman's testimony in 1655 was not altogether frivolous when he claimed that tobacco-growing had put him out of business. This and other labour-intensive occupations had brought work into an area where there had been almost none in 1600.

Similar successes in providing work for the poor, not only in Gloucestershire but elsewhere, taught the political economists new lessons about the value of occupations requiring small capital resources but many willing hands. After the Restoration they wrote in new and more appreciative terms about the role of labour in an expanding economy. Carew Reynel in 1674 even urged a relaxation of the government's prohibition on the growing of tobacco because of its beneficial effect in employing the poor.[3] The consequences of projects thus went far beyond the expectations of their founders.

The most impressive efforts in starting new agricultural and industrial occupations were made by a generation of men at work in the period 1580–1630. In the Vale of Tewkesbury they worked to most effect in the period 1610–20, though the consequences of their labours were felt throughout the seventeenth century. In how many other poor towns and villages in England did the same generation of men try to work the same miracles? Benedict Webb's labourers in Kingswood and in the Forest of Dean have impinged upon this story at several points. Dr. Paul Slack has recently described the efforts of the town officials of Salisbury, who in the 1620s, embarked on ambitious schemes for providing work and food for the poor—organising jobs in lacemaking, pinmaking, stocking knitting, cloth weaving, hemp and flax spinning, and also establishing a brewhouse and store-

[1] *PRO*: E134, 14 Chas. I, Mich. 31.

[2] John Allibond of Magdalen College to Dr. Peter Heylyn, cited in Eleanor Adlard, *Winchcombe Cavalcade* (1939), p. 28.

[3] Carew Reynel, *The True English Interest* (1674), p. 19.

house of cheap food.[1] It is unlikely that these are the only examples of business enterprises mixed with philanthropy, of projects devised by gentlemen that created jobs for the poor. Parliamentary history in the years 1600–30 sheds a harsh light on many speculations that went awry and created scandals. In the provinces, however, some men experienced the more constructive consequences of these projects. How many more are waiting to be uncovered?

[1] Paul Slack, 'Poverty and Politics in Salisbury, 1597–1666', *Crisis and Order in English Towns, 1500–1700: essays in urban history*, ed. P. A. Clark and P. A. Slack (1972), p. 181ff.

VIII

The Gloucestershire Spas: an eighteenth-century parallel

By Bryan Little

THE eighteenth century saw the beginnings of England's spa mania, with a proliferation, in many counties, of mineral water resorts of varying fame and frequentation. But few counties had, within their borders, two spas of major note. Gloucestershire, however, in the Hotwells in Clifton parish and in Cheltenham, did have two such resorts, to some extent overshadowed, within the West of England, by Bath but both in the front rank of such places of healing and social diversion. One reached its peak during the eighteenth century. The other, of a rising importance, got its greatest single encouragement late in the 1780s but saw its main expansion in the first few decades after the fall of Napoleon. Both of them were summer spas with architectural achievements not to be despised, but modest compared to those of Bath. They were frequented at a time of the year when outdoor amusement was as important as the indoor enjoyment of balls, the theatre, or assemblies.

The "Bristol" Hotwell was not officially within the City of Bristol till its boundaries were extended in 1835 to include Clifton. It was a geological curio, for its water, milky white and of a temperature of about seventy-six degrees fahrenheit (some fifty degrees less than the more sulphur-laden waters of Bath) gushed up through the mud of the tidal Avon, between the normal levels of high and low water, but closer to the latter. The spring was, in its natural state and before its main period of popularity, in a remote, somewhat inaccessible position, at a point in the Avon Gorge where it was closed in by steep rock faces and where it could not be approached by road or even by a decent path. It was not so much ignorance of the spring's qualities, but poor access that delayed its intensive exploitation.

The warm spring's existence, and its unusual qualities, were known as far back as the fifteenth century. William Worcestre refers, in his account of the Clifton gorge and St. Vincent's Rocks, to the spring *circa bowshott apud le blak Rok . . . in fundo aque*; he goes on, inaccurately so far as Bath was concerned, to equate its warmth with that of milk or *aqua Badonis*;[1] he does not enlarge on its curative qualities. In the seventeenth century the well became better known. In June of 1630 John Bruckshaw obtained a forty years' licence from the Crown not only to dig in the rock of the gorge for gold, silver, and crystal but also to "take in" the Hotwell water and to make baths for the use of those who frequented the spring.[2] Its popularity seems, from then onwards, to have increased, for in 1634 the three cavaliers from Norwich, who stayed in Bristol on their tour of England, reported a "good store of company" at the Hotwell.[3] At about the same time Dr. Samuel Ward, who was Master of Sidney Sussex College at Cambridge from 1610 to 1643, anticipated the later practice and had Hotwell water sent to him to drink away from its source.[4]

Queen Catherine of Braganza's visit in 1677 gave the Clifton Hotwell the respectability of royal patronage, while in a few more years its reputation grew when it came to be recommended for a complaint other than the "hot livers, feeble brains, and red pimply faces"[5] for which its water had previously been drunk. It was found helpful to those suffering from diabetes; Sir Robert Atkyns and Daniel Defoe both mention it in this connection.[6] By the time, early in the eighteenth century, that these writers noted the Hotwell water, its exploitation, by local commercial enterprise, was well under way.

[1] Mrs. Frances Neale, who is preparing a new edition of William Worcestre's Itinery of Bristol, has kindly given me this reference to MS. 210, p. 101, among the manuscripts of Corpus Christi College, Cambridge.

[2] *Cal. S.P.D. 1629–1631*, pp. 222, 276.

[3] *A Relation of a Short Survey of 26 Counties . . . by a Captain, a Lieutenant, and an Ancient . . . of Norwich*, ed. L. G. Wickham Legg (1904), pp. 96–7.

[4] Vincent Waite, *The Bristol Hotwell* (Bristol Branch of the Historical Association, 1960), p. 5.

[5] Waite, *op. cit.* p. 5.

[6] Sir Robert Atkyns, *Ancient and Present State of Gloucestershire* (1712, reprinted 1974), p. 360; Daniel Defoe, *A Tour Through England and Wales*, Everyman's Library; ii, 38.

In 1676 the Bristol Society of Merchant Venturers bought the moiety of the manor of Clifton which included the Hotwell. They could have been interested both in the commercial and navigational importance of this riverside section of the parish and in the exploitation of the warm spring whose popularity seemed likely to increase. In 1687 they leased the well to two tenants for no more than £2 a year;[1] in 1695 a more ambitious arrangement was made. The Merchant Venturers negotiated with some prominent Bristol citizens, headed by Sir Thomas Day, then Mayor of the city and soon to be one of its Members of Parliament, and by Robert Yate, Day's predecessor in the mayoralty and his colleague in Parliament. In April of the same year the well was leased, for ninety years and at an annual rent of £5, to Charles Jones, a Bristol soapboiler, and Thomas Callowhill, a draper. These partners were to build a Pump Room and lodging houses and to lay out walks giving better access to the well.[2] As this was all to be done for £500 it was no surprise that the Pump Room, which served its purpose all through the eighteenth century, was an unimpressive, barnlike building, projecting from the river bank over the steep tidal mud, so as to enclose the spring and screen it from the influx of the drastically tidal Avon. By the end of the seventeenth century the scene was set for the peak period of Hotwell history.

A satirical sketch of 1723 suggests that the Bristol Hotwell was already attracting fashionable company.[3] The Duchesses of Kent and Marlborough were there, and the author, whose politics seem to have been somewhat libellously Whig, also refers to Lord R-mn-y (Romney), and to Sir D-w-y B-lkl-y (Bulkeley) who is said to have begotten children at the age of fourteen and to have been a valetudinarian by forty. Nothing is said on the lodgings available for the company at the Hotwell; from other sources it can be guessed that facilities close to the spring were still primitive, with several patrons staying on the edge of the main city in houses round College Green. As at Bath there was a time lag between the spa's early social popularity and its major architectural expansion. By the end of 1727 work

---

[1] John Latimer, *Annals of Bristol in the Seventeenth Century* (Bristol, 1900), p. 471.

[2] Latimer, *op. cit.* p. 472.

[3] *Characters at the Hot-Well, Bristol in September, 1723* (1724).

had started on the terraced sequence of houses which lie along the upper side of the charming three-sided enclosure of Dowry Square. Though Palladianism was now fashionable in country mansions, and in some urban settings, these houses, with two doorways having segmental broken pediments, and with the early eighteenth-century fenestration and segmental pediments displayed by numbers 10 and 11, still reflected the "vernacular Baroque" of Bristol's earliest Georgian years; so too do the grotesque masks on the keystones of some window heads, below the three-sided enclosure of the square, as one continues along Hotwell Road. Like Queen Square and St. James' Square in the middle of Bristol this beginning of formal development in the Hotwells was a little earlier than equivalent housing work in Bath. Eighteenth-century urbanism started in Bristol a few years before it took root in the spa city a few miles up the Avon, the supply of window glass and softwood timber in particular being easier to obtain in the industrial and seaport city.

Worship in the parish church of Clifton meant a journey of some two miles from the Hotwell, with a stiff climb up to the church, while Bristol Cathedral (though used for the burial of some visitors to the spa who found no relief) and the churches of central Bristol were also inconveniently distant. So a chapel within Clifton parish was built, by subscription, amid the houses just below Dowry Square. Known as the Dowry Chapel, it was finished by the end of 1746. It was a simple building, of moderate size and with a porch in the middle of its southern side.[1] William Cole, who stayed at the Hotwells while the chapel was being built and who combined his quest for health with antiquarian visits to Bristol's old churches, says that the total cost was to be £320.[2] Mrs. Strangways Horner of Dorset, who gave £50, was the top subscriber, while the Marquis of Granby, whose family owned property in the parish (hence Granby Hill) contented himself with a modest two guineas. Later in the century a grimmer note was evident in the provision, halfway up the hill to Clifton church, of a special "strangers' burial ground" which could accommodate those who had failed in their health-seeking visits either to the Hotwell or to an increasingly favoured upper Clifton.

[1] For a photograph, see Reece Winstone, *Bristol as it was, 1866–60*, pl. 65.   [2] British Library: Add. MSS. 5811, f. x, under May 1746.

As the popularity of the Hotwell continued to increase, the provision of more lodging houses continued in the middle decades of the century. Dowry Parade, across the wide road from the new chapel, was built, behind a broad pavement edged with pollarded limes, as a row of houses, with features typical of Bristol's brick-faced mid-Georgian domestic architecture. A little way uphill, Albemarle Row, dated 1763 in its central pediment, showed, as also did some steeply rising terrace ranges in Bath, how a terrace composition could still be "stepped" to fit onto a sloping site. A second "Long Room", or Assembly Room, supplementing the first one, which stood across the road from it, was built about this time. It survived as a school, with some fireplaces and ceilings of about 1760, till the recent demolitions to clear the site for the flyways which take traffic above the lock into the Cumberland Basin of the Floating Harbour.

The peak period of the popularity of the Hotwell, and of its social importance was between about 1760 and the year 1785 when the Merchant Venturers were faced by the problem of a new lease. These years included, in 1771 and 1778, the publication of the two literary works[1] in which the Hotwell lives as does Bath in the pages of Sheridan and Jane Austen. There was also the subtle influence which the regime and the scenery of such a resort could exercise on English taste.

The water itself, milky in colour, was naturally warm but differed much from that of Bath and was prescribed for different complaints. As *Sketchley's Bristol Directory* put it in 1775[2] it was, by that time, taken for various internal complaints which included diabetes, dropsy, scorbutic maladies, dysentry, cancer, and venereal disease; ailments of the lungs, kidneys, and bladder are specially mentioned. By now, moreover, and in the end more controversially, it was recommended for consumptives. The water was drunk twice a day, early in the morning and at some time in the afternoon, total daily consumption being six glasses.[3] Bathing in the Hotwell water was of little importance, but an aspect of the business, to which Bath provided no parallel, was the bottling of the water for sale (and presumably for reheating) not only in other parts of England and on the

---

[1] See p. 177.
[2] Reprinted with Introduction by Bryan Little, 1971.
[3] William Matthews, *Bristol Directory, 1794*, p. 103.

Continent but in the West Indian colonies. The bottles used for this particular trade must have been a considerable item in the output of the Bristol glass works.

For a full understanding of the Hotwells in the eighteenth century one must remember that this was a summer spa. The season lasted from late in April till about the end of September. Except at the beginning, there was little overlapping with Bath, and the two spas, at all events in their social aspects, were complementary rather than competitive. The Bristol newspapers, which report the arrivals at both places, have no note during most of the Hotwell season of new visitors to Bath, while their record of those coming to the Hotwell stops abruptly in the early autumn, once they begin to list those arriving for the winter in Bath. Tradesmen who did business in Bath during the winter could thus switch, in the summer, to the Bristol Hotwell,[1] while many leisured patrons could transfer their attentions from one spa to the other. The clientele of both resorts was thus to some extent the same, though the lists of Bath's arrivals suggests that aristocratic patronage of the winter spa considerably exceeded that of the Hotwell. Yet the Hotwell was not without visitors of distinction. Exactly two centuries ago, in 1776, eight peers (one of them on two occasions), several baronets and knights, a judge, and many clergymen made their journeys to the Clifton Gorge.[2] For most weeks the list in *Felix Farley* adds "etc", at the end of the specific names, so that one cannot get a total of the season's visitors. But well over seven hundred are named between 30 April and 5 October. The strain on lodging accommodation must have been considerable, and some at least of the Hotwell's "company" found it more agreeable to stay in the better air of upper Clifton. Several unmarried young ladies are listed along with their parents, the real-life counterparts of Fanny Burney's Evelina.

Advertisements in the paper reveal other aspects of life at the Hotwell. The managers of both Long Rooms—Mrs. Shirley at the Old Room and Joseph Norman at Loggon's New Rooms—drew attention, through most of the season, to their respective establishments; their addresses are given by Sketchley as 3 and 4 Paradise Row. Public breakfasts, with cotillions and country

---

[1] See Bryan Little, *The City and County of Bristol* (1954), pp. 231–2.
[2] See weekly lists in *FFBJ*, April–October 1776.

dances, were held by Mrs. Shirley on Mondays and by Norman
on Thursday mornings at ten. Mrs. Shirley's charge was 1s. 6d.
a head, and Norman, one imagines, charged much the same.
Both Rooms had stabling as well as their other facilities, while
Mrs. Shirley let bedrooms. Joseph Norman had a tavern and a
coffee house, and made the point that turtles were "dressed
during season". Mrs. Shirley emphasised that she employed a
"good man cook". The Rooms could also be used for auctions,
for Mrs. Shirley's were to be the scene, in June, for the sale of
an organ, suitable either for a church or a public room.[1] A
somewhat whimsical note is struck by the advertisements, first
printed on 20 July of Mr. and Mrs. Levis, describing themselves, respectively, as a Surgeon Dentist and a Ladies' Dentist,
previously at Bath but now in Hotwells across the way from the
General Draper inn. During the summer season they planned
to divide their time, for alternate weeks, between the Hotwell
and Bath. All dental activities were to be carried out, including
the making of artificial teeth, and the couple assured their
patrons that they would "keep the strictest honour and pro-
foundest secrecy if required". The teeth of the poor were to be
pulled out "gratis, as usual".

Diversions more agreeable than visits to the dentist were of
the essence of a summer stay at the Hotwell. As the scenery was
superb and a novelty to many of those who came there, outdoor
enjoyment was at least as important as forgathering in the Pump
Room or balls and assemblies. The architectural setting remained modest, with no effort, before later developments in
upper Clifton, to exploit the splendour of the scene.

For those who wanted only a gentle saunter down at river
level, the Pump Room was approached from the lodging area
by a pleasant avenue of pollarded limes. The Avon, at high
tide, was itself an element of scenic charm. Ships passing the
spa on their way to or from the port of Bristol provided an item
of interest such as one might expect at a seaside resort. River
picnics, sometimes with musical accompaniment, and trips
downstream as far as the site of present-day Avonmouth, or
even out into the Severn estuary as far as Portishead, were
another favoured pastime. Alternatively, and in the absence of
a bridge so low down the Avon, Hotwells visitors could cross by

[1] *FFBJ*, 1 June 1776.

the long-established Rownham Ferry, repairing thence to the village of Long Ashton where fruit gardens abounded, and where the summer season made it possible to enjoy sumptuous repasts of strawberries or raspberries and cream.[1] For those who liked more energetic pursuits the Downs above the gorge were available for walks, rides, or drives. Many who had gone to the Hotwell to get relief from consumption may well have had more benefit from the good air of the Downs than they obtained from the tepid, all too often polluted, water which came up through the mud of an increasingly dirty river. There may also have been some effect on an aspect of English taste of growing importance as the eighteenth century progressed—the impact on many members of the upper and middle classes of scenery more dramatic and "romantic" than that of most districts of fashionable England. One has also to remember that excursions to Clifton, or lower down the Avon to see the view across to the hills of South Wales from such vantage points as Kingsweston or the Gothick tower of Blaise Castle, were much favoured by the numerous and fashionable visitors to Bath.

We know that Chatterton, who was certainly a pioneer of romantic neo-medievalism, was influenced by the scenery of the Avon gorge as well as by the late Gothic architecture of St. Mary Redcliffe.[2] By the end of the eighteenth century, and in the opening decades of the nineteenth—in which an important local school of landscape painters flourished in Bristol—the scenery near the Hotwell was a subject much favoured by artists. Less easily traceable, but not on that account to be ignored, was the effect of the scenery at the Hotwells on those who came, from all parts of the country, and stayed a few weeks or months. All, one may assume, were from the trend-setting aristocracy or upper middle classes. For many of them, particularly the ladies who seldom travelled and did not make the Grand Tour, the Avon gorge, pent in by precipitous rocks, and with the river narrower and the channel more rocky than it is today, must have been the most "romantic" scenery they had ever seen. It was too early, in the peak decades of the Hotwell, for many travellers to reach the later haunts, in the Lake District or amid the mountains of North Wales, of the amateurs of "the Picturesque". Even the comparatively adjacent Wye

[1] Waite, *op. cit.* pp. 10–11.   [2] See, for example, his poem *Clifton.*

Valley, in the continued absence of a good coaching road up from Chepstow past Tintern Abbey, to Monmouth, was seldom visited except by those who were, like Wordsworth in 1798, prepared to rough it on foot. But thousands of Georgian fashionables, whether they stayed at the Hotwell or came over from Bath, knew the Avon gorge.

The Hotwell had, in addition, its more definite literary associations. Smollett's *Humphrey Clinker*, with its satirical passages on the visit for a mere fortnight by Matthew Bramble and his party, came out in 1771. Fanny Burney's *Evelina*, with a much fuller narration of Miss Anville's eventful visit of a month and a half, was published in 1778. They gave Hotwells something of the literary fame which Sheridan in the same decade and Jane Austen considerably later bestowed on Bath. From Fanny Burney, if not from the coarser satire of Smollett, one can assume that many of those who came to the Hotwell were people of a refined, if at times affected and artificial culture. As in London and in Bath, they enjoyed music and delighted, more than many Bristol residents, in the theatre. The Hotwell thus became important for the blossoming of the Bristol stage.

The first permanent theatre built to serve the Bristol public, along with visitors to the Hotwell, was opened in 1729.[1] It was carefully sited, on the western side of Woodwell (now Jacob's Well) Road, a few yards on the Clifton, and thus on the Gloucestershire side of the City and County boundary of Bristol. Its activities were thus immune from the attentions, much feared at that time, of the Bristol magistrates. Being half way between the city centre and Hotwells, and not too far from the lodging area of College Green, it was convenient both for Bristol residents and for visitors to the spa. Access from the Hotwell, or upper Clifton, was less easy when, thirty-seven years later, the new theatre off King Street, large by the standards of its time and modelled on the London theatre of Drury Lane, was opened to succeed the earlier playhouse.[2] The ample capacity of this Bristol theatre must largely have been determined by its owners' expectation of bookings from visitors to the Hotwell, and it was no accident in the early years that the theatrical

[1] Kathleen Barker, *The Theatre Royal, Bristol, 1766–1966* (1974), p. 4.
[2] Barker, *op. cit.* pp. 5–15.

season and that of the Hotwell coincided in the summer months. When, in 1778, a royal licence, under which it could be called the Theatre *Royal*, was obtained, the patronage of Bristol "by Persons of Rank and Fortune on account of medicinal waters" was mentioned to Parliament as a reason for the concession.[1] Though the Hotwell spa has ceased to function, Bristol's Theatre Royal still serves as a reminder of the social entertainment which went with the cure.

In 1784, when the ninety year lease of the well was soon to expire, the Merchant Venturers advertised for a new tenant.[2] The financial conditions which they wished to impose deterred applicants. For five years, till a new tenant came in 1790, the Merchants had to maintain the spa themselves. In 1785 William Pennington was appointed, in the Bath manner, as Master of Ceremonies; he was still there, with an address in Dowry Square, in 1794.[3] A physical improvement was also made close to the Pump Room. For in 1785 a site for a colonnade was offered in four lots.[4] By the end of 1786 some improvements had been made in the Pump Room itself, and the colonnade, with its row of elegant little shops, had been finished, curving gracefully towards the Pump Room and closing the tree-lined vista which led up to it. The shops were for the sale of such things as millinery and stationery, and in one of them Ann Yearsley, Clifton's literary milkwoman, kept her circulating library.[5] Support for the spa continued, and in the summer of 1788, while George III was at Cheltenham, those who arrived were numerous and often well connected.[6]

Soon, however, an irreversible decline overtook the fortunes of the Hotwell. The new tenant of 1790 had to pay a higher rent, and the increased charges which followed deterred visitors.[7] There was also by now more opposition, on medical grounds, to the Hotwell cure. The effectiveness of the water as a specific for consumption was strongly challenged, most notably by the famous local physician Dr. Beddoes, who set up his "Pneumatic Institution" down in Dowry Square, but who lived

[1] *House of Commons Journals*, xxxvi, 638–9.   [2] Waite, *op. cit.* p. 12.

[3] *Matthews' Directory*, alphabetical list, p. 65.

[4] Records of the Society of Merchant Venturers of Bristol.

[5] *Matthews' Directory*, alphabetical list, p. 85 (under 4 Hotwell Crescent).

[6] *FFBJ*, July–August 1788.   [7] Waite, *op. cit.* p. 12.

in upper Clifton, much preferring the fresh air of the Downs to Hotwell water. Consumptives still, however, came to Hotwells, but as many were already past cure frequent deaths lowered the reputation of the spa. Though Matthews' *Directory* of 1794 still gives a glowing account, the Hotwell was then well on the way to decline. But it still had its consumptive patients to whom, in 1797, the American Quaker Joshua Gilpin referred, with the curt note that the Pump Room and the wells were "not on the elegant style they are in Bath".[1] Ten years later the scene was even gloomier. The Bristol-born author Robert Southey, writing as "Don Manuel Alvarez Espriella", held the Hotwell water to be of no use whatsoever for consumption. He refers, in a pathetic passage, to "several unhappy patients who had been sent there to die at a distance from home", crawling out on the parade "as if to take their last gasp of sunshine."[2]

For Cheltenham one may start with Joshua Gilpin's notes on his visit. Gilpin was at Cheltenham in the summer of 1796,[3] finding the spa not in decline like the Hotwell but near the start of its most spectacular development as a Greek Revival counterpart to Palladian and neo-classical Bath. He found it, as others had done, "a neat town consisting of one main street". The "company" at the single well, on the walks, and in the public rooms was considerable. Lords, ladies, and other members of the upper class were often to be encountered. The spa was clearly prosperous but still laboured under a severe disadvantage. Gilpin was only there for a week, but this was enough for him to find that Cheltenham was, of all English spas, "the most extravagant place with the worst accommodation". Though something had been done, by now, to give Cheltenham the social appurtenances of an important spa, poor transport and the distance from a good navigable waterway, still hindered a massive growth in the town's dwellings and lodging houses.

Cheltenham's history, before its rise as a spa, had not, as at Leamington, been that of an almost insignificant village. It had enjoyed a respectable existence, of some economic importance, as a small country town. Most of its houses were strung out, not

---

[1] A. P. Woolrich, 'An American in Gloucestershire and Bristol",' *TBGAS*, xcii, 187.

[2] *Letters from England* (1814 ed.), iii, 344.   [3] *TBGAS*, xcii, 174–7.

far to the north of the little river Chelt which gave the place its name. The parish church, a few yards south of the street, was, and is, of some pretence and architectural importance. With eloquent traces of its cruciform, transitional-Norman ground plan, and with outstanding work of the Decorated period and of the transition from Decorated to Perpendicular, it had reached structural maturity before the great outburst of building activity which, elsewhere in Gloucestershire, gave the county its wealth of woolmen's and clothiers' churches. The town had a market. Its endowed Grammar School, the successor to a chantry school, raised it above the educational level of surrounding places. Cheltenham had, in the previous century, been a leading centre of England's trade in home-grown tobacco. It was, in the eighteenth century, of more than local importance as a malting centre. Sir Robert Atkyns, in 1712, mentions 321 houses and a population of about 1,500. Though the "original" mineral spring had long been known to the local countryfolk,[1] he gives no hint of Cheltenham's coming fame as a nationally known spa.

The story that the unusual qualities of the spring near the Chelt were first noticed in 1716, when pigeons were seen pecking at the salty deposit, seems more in tune with the rustic background of the Cheltenham waters than with their more sophisticated exploitation. But it was certainly in the period about 1716–18 that the "original" well attracted medical attention, was analysed, and declared to have curative properties. The Cheltenham waters, with their saline, purgative nature, are unlike the hot springs of central Bath in that they occur beneath a wide area of the parish and can be pumped at several widely scattered places. Cheltenham thus came, in time, to have not one single well but several spas, each with its own pump room and its own lodging or residential area. But nothing was done, before 1800, to sink wells in spots other than that of the "original" spring. For the rest of the eighteenth century the curative and social activities of Cheltenham as a spa town were confined between the High Street and the spring a little to the south of the Chelt. The Well's earliest accompaniments were of the simplest. The land, which was part of the Bayshill estate, belonged to William Mason, a local Quaker

[1] Gwen Hart, *A History of Cheltenham* (1965), p. 124.

who had been in business as a hosier.[1] Mason himself, averse perhaps to the social dissipations which could, as at Bath under Beau Nash, occur in a watering place, did little to popularise the spa. It was left to his son-in-law, with Bristol connections and perhaps with Bristol advice, to establish Cheltenham's first spa régime.

Not long after his simple exploitation of the well at Cheltenham, William Mason moved, for family reasons, to Bristol.[2] He took his place, as a Quaker would naturally do, amid the commercial and trading circles of England's leading provincial port. But by the early months of 1725 he was dead.[3] His daughter Elizabeth, who became the heiress of the Bayshill property, married, as his second wife, a man whose energy was truly decisive for the early growth of Cheltenham as an important spa.

Captain Henry Skillicorne, by birth a Manxman, took service as a master mariner with the Elton family who were important in the trading and industrial community of Bristol.[4] On his activities as a seaman, and on other aspects of his career, the best authority is not on paper but on his simple memorial tablet, in the parish church of Cheltenham. He had a full and varied life, trading to many Continental and North American ports but not, so far as one can tell, in the slave trade or on direct runs to the plantation colonies. As one who had avoided the slave trade and whose habits were, so his monument says, of unusual sobriety, he would have been the more acceptable to the daughter of a Quaker who, though herself remaining within the Society of Friends, committed what was considered the misdemeanour of marrying outside the Society.

Henry Skillicorne and Elizabeth Mason were married, probably in Bristol, in 1731.[5] In another seven years Captain Skillicorne, by now a man of sixty and, to quote his epitaph, "a strict valetudinarian", came to live in Cheltenham. He now

---

[1] Hart, *op. cit.* p. 121.   [2] Hart, *op. cit.* p. 124.

[3] Minutes of the Men's Monthly Meeting (Bristol) of the Society of Friends, 5th of 2nd month, 1725, Bristol Record Office. The reference is to William Mason, late of Cheltenham, *deceased*.

[4] For more of his connection with the Eltons, see Bryan Little, *Cheltenham* (1952), pp. 32–3.

[5] See J. Sawyer, *Cheltenham Parish Church* (1903), pp. 22–3, quoting Skillicorne's memorial tablet in St. Mary's, Cheltenham.

turned, in an enterprising spirit and perhaps with the Bristol Hotwell in mind, to the development and extension of the spa. Having found the original well "open and exposed", he improved and covered the spring. He built no pump room of the Bath or Hotwell type, but contented himself with a simple, four-arched canopy of brick.[1] To one side of the well he put up a building which contained both a ballroom and a billiard room. More important, for the diversion of those who came to Cheltenham and who lodged in the inns and houses of the High Street, were the scenic accompaniments of the spa régime.

The present town of Cheltenham, its comparatively level site allowing a more spacious layout than was possible at Bath, is notable for its broad, tree-lined streets; the specially famous thoroughfare of the Promenade is but one among many. The origin of these streets of terraces or villas lay in the comparatively simple yet formal "walks", lined with trees as in the avenues of early Georgian parks and making attractive vistas to or from the focal points of spa activity. They were thus an analogy, in the gentle scenery of Cheltenham, to the avenue of trees which led the Hotwell Pump Room in the romantic Avon Gorge.

The first of Cheltenham's "walks", created by Skillicorne soon after he came to live in the parish, was Well Walk, with its two rows of trees running both north and south from the central point of the original well and, in its longer, more northerly section, carefully aligned on to the "romantic" feature presented by the medieval tower and spire of the parish church. In his Journal, Skillicorne recorded the number of trees (mostly elms, many of which soon died and had to be replaced) planted in each of the years from 1739.[2] He was advised over the layout of his formal walk by a Gloucestershire gentleman, who soon figured large in the county's affairs, whose home was not far from the Hotwell, and who took a close interest in the more recent of Gloucestershire's two spas. This was Norborne Berkeley, the last, as things turned out, of the male line of the Berkeleys of Stoke Gifford near Bristol, aged twenty-two by the end of 1739, soon to be allied, by the marriage of his sister to Lord Charles Noel Somerset, to the Beauforts at Badminton,

[1] See Bryan Little, *Cheltenham in Pictures* (1967), illustration on p. 20.
[2] John Goding, *History of Cheltenham* (1863 ed.), pp. 249–50.

and in 1741 elected as one of the county's Knights of the Shire.[1]
He is best known, under his eventual title of Baron Botetourt,
as the last but one of the colonial governors of Virginia. He was
wealthy, deriving most of his income from the coal pits in
Stapleton parish of which he was also the manorial lord, and a
man of taste who had travelled in France and elsewhere on the
Continent.[2] The laying out of formal walks, in his own grounds
or as the adornment of a semi-rural spa, would have been a
congenial pastime for such a gentleman in the 1740s.

The Cheltenham waters are pronouncedly saline and came to
be recommended, not for gout or rheumatism or, as eventually
at the Bristol Hotwell, for consumption, but for digestive and
other internal troubles, and in particular for liver complaints.
Hence, in due course though mostly in the nineteenth century,
the popularity of Cheltenham as a residential town among
those who had served in India and had there acquired the
peppery livers which one associates with Anglo-Indian colonels.

The situation and surroundings of the original well were very
different from what habitués of the Hotwell found at the foot of
St. Vincent's Rocks. Though the spring came up not far from
the edge of a stream, the Chelt is a petty waterway beside the
tidal Avon. But the régime of the spa and the pursuits followed
by many of its patrons, were not unlike those at the Hotwell.
The influence of that spa, as transmitted by Skillicorne who
must have known it well, could have been important for
Cheltenham's early career as a watering place. Another practice, which was common at the Hotwell but not at Bath, and
which was followed at Cheltenham and a few other spas, was
the sale, in bottles, of the mineral water for consumption elsewhere. The destinations of Cheltenham water included Chester,
Oxford, London, and Bristol.[3]

Like the Hotwell, Cheltenham was at first a summer spa,
with a rural setting for its original well, a town of mainly rural
character and with the scenery of the Cotswolds and the Severn

[1] See Bryan Little's account of Norborne Berkeley's career in Gloucestershire in *Virginia Magazine of History and Biography*, October 1955, pp. 379–
409.

[2] There is further material on Norborne Berkeley's travels and finances
among uncatalogued manuscripts in the Muniment Room at Badminton
(seen by kind permission of His Grace the Duke of Beaufort).

[3] Goding, *op. cit.* p. 255.

Vale for rides, walks, and other excursions. What was surprising, in view of the new spa's quick acceptance, was its extreme architectural modesty. No fully covered pump room was built for many years, while before Skillicorne's death in 1763 the spa's patrons, though numerous and aristocratic, had to content themselves with the retired seaman's modest building for dancing and billiards. A stay at Cheltenham must, in such conditions, have been something of a therapeutic *fête champêtre*. A simple theatre was, however, fitted out in a building in a stable yard,[1] while lodgings were still confined to the buildings along the High Street. Skillicorne's early energies seem more to have been directed towards the advertising of his Cheltenham waters and the building up of patronage.

In these aims, however, Skillicorne seems to have been quickly and remarkably successful. As early as the summer of 1739, as he noted in his Journal, he had 414 subscribers, with 674 in the following year;[2] the figures did not, from what we know of Hotwells in 1776, fall far short of those who came to the spa in Clifton. Though it was depressed by an unaccountably lean season in 1747, the yearly average was 571 for the seven years between 1742 and 1747. It is as well that we have details from this source, for there was still no Cheltenham newspaper to record the weekly arrivals, and the *Gloucester Journal*, though it had Cheltenham within its circulating area, did not, as early as the 1740s, record this particular detail. Nor did Skillicorne have to worry about the social standing of his visitors. A London paper, appearing on 11 August 1743,[3] speaks highly of Cheltenham spa, adding (inaccurately if we may believe Skillicorne's statistics) that the "company" had been larger in that year than in any previous season, and listing some of the "persons of great fortune and gentility" who were there at the time of writing. The Duke and Duchess of Argyll, the Earl of Chesterfield, Lady Suffolk, Lord and Lady Westmorland, Lord and Lady Tracy, Lord Chedworth, Lord Gage, Lord Saye and Sele, some knights and baronets, and Judge Fortescue were among those mentioned; so too was Norborne Berkeley, as a Gloucestershire Member of Parliament giving attention to what was clearly an

---

[1] For the theatrical history of Cheltenham, see T. Hannam Clark, *Drama in Gloucestershire* (1928).

[2] Goding, *op. cit.* p. 250.   [3] Quoted by Goding, p. 256.

important new element in his county's life. Handel was there in 1751,[1] Dr. Johnson had already paid a visit and the spa, with its fashionable company, drew evangelising attention from Whitefield and the Countess of Huntingdon.[2]

Captain Skillicorne's energies may have declined towards the time of his death at the age of eighty-four in 1763, and there may, about that time, have been a temporary fall in Cheltenham's fortunes.[3] Poor access by road, much worse than to Bath or the Hotwell, may also, along with the scarce and expensive lodging of which Gilpin could still, at the very end of the century, complain, have contributed to a slackening in progress. Yet the lists of arrivals in the 1760s, reported in the *Gloucester Journal*[4] suggest that Cheltenham could still attract a good clientele with a sprinkling of the aristocracy. In 1763 William Skillicorne, son of the Captain, took over what was still Cheltenham's only well. In a few more years there started a sequence of events which reversed the spa's fortunes and in a little more than ten years made it a more suitable place for the reception of its sovereign. In 1774, when John Wesley came, not for the first time, during what he styled "the high season for drinking the waters", he found the town "full of gentry",[5] some of whom may have been among the open-air hearers who made up the largest congregation ever seen in the place. Arrival lists, for that month of August, in the *Gloucester Journal*, bear out what Wesley noticed.[6]

William Miller, a Londoner, came to Cheltenham as William Skillicorne's lessee of the Original Well. He saw that a recreational and social building, better than that put up soon after 1738, was needed. In 1775–6 he therefore built the first of Cheltenham's "Long", or Assembly, Rooms, a comparatively simple building, but with a doorway in the Adam style. It seems probable, from the rows of blank upper windows which could have indicated a lofty ceiling inside, that the interior was of some dignity and sophistication. The building must have been complete by the end of July in 1776, for on the 29 July the *Gloucester Journal* carried an advertisement for a concert and

[1] Hart, *op. cit.* p. 127.   [2] Hart, *op. cit.* p. 127.   [3] Hart, *op. cit.* p. 128.
[4] *GJ*, 18 August 1761; 8 and 22 July 1765.
[5] *John Wesley's Journal*, ed. Curnock (Standard ed.), vi, 34.
[6] *GJ*, 1 and 8 August 1774.

ball, with tickets at 3s. each, in the "New Long Room at the Well".[1] Cheltenham, by now, was a serious summer competitor with the Hotwell, so in September of 1776 the *Gloucester Journal* featured a satirically humorous "Poem to the NAI(A)D of the Hotwell", by a scribbler styling himself TWEEDLE-DUM, whose first stanza ran:

> Shall the fair nymphs of Cheltenham's healthy stream,
> Though round their forms a thousand beauties beam
> Bear sovereign sway, and be unrivall'd sung;
> Thy lyre, Avonia, silent and unstrung?"[2]

Five years later, Lord Fauconberg, who had been at Cheltenham in 1776,[3] thought it worth his while, on a site higher up in the Bayshill estate, to build a free-standing mansion of moderate size. By now, moreover, there had established itself in the little spa a family whose activities rivalled those of Skillicorne and Miller, and were to give a salutary stimulus to Cheltenham's physical and social improvement.

Miller's rival was Thomas Hughes, a lawyer from a family well-placed in Monmouthshire, who had first come to Cheltenham as the apprentice to a local solicitor and who later became his partner.[4] His marriage to Elizabeth, the twin daughter and joint heiress of Harry Brydges of Keynsham, brought him considerable wealth. In 1776, about the time of Miller's completion of his Long Room, Hughes set up on his own, both in legal practice and as a developer of local property. His family had been Parliament supporters in the Civil War, and he himself was a strong Whig; political antagonism may have sharpened his rivalry with the Skillicorne-Miller camp.

What Hughes did, from about four years after the start of his own legal practice, was to set in train a sequence of events which included the appointment of Cheltenham's first Master of Ceremonies, the building of a fine Assembly Room, the first serious effort, with Parliamentary sanction, to improve road access to Cheltenham, and the passing of the town's first Paving and Cleansing Act. The first years of the 1780s were a vital prelude to the crowning events of 1788.

---

[1] *GJ*, 29 July 1776.   [2] *GJ*, 16 September 1776.   [3] *GJ*, 10 June 1776.
[4] Hart, *op. cit.* p. 134.

Cheltenham's first Master of Ceremonies, presiding in a converted room in the High Street and later in more palatial quarters, came to work in 1780. Though described as "self appointed", and though the simple circumstances of Cheltenham needed none of the formal election procedure which prevailed at Bath, some arrangement with Hughes may well have been necessary. The newcomer was Simeon Moreau who had, for some years, been socially active in Bath and did not wholly sever his links with the older spa. The son of a Lieutenant Colonel in the 13th Regiment of Foot he may have been of Huguenot origin. In 1777, when Captain William Wade had resigned as Bath's Master of Ceremonies, Moreau was one of seven candidates who stood for the post. When he advertised his candidacy he emphasised his perfect knowledge of French, German, Italian, and Spanish, and that he had always, in England and abroad, moved "in the circle of polite company".[1] He added that he was encouraged by "some very respectable friends", ending that he would, if elected, give a third of the profits of his office to the General Hospital in Bath.[2] But despite his solicitations Moreau was not elected; his failure turned out to be of considerable advantage to Cheltenham. For Moreau, who held his post till his death in 1810, was one of the best of what was, in those day, of spa mania, a rising profession.

The first Guide Book to Cheltenham had come out in 1781, but in 1783 Moreau got to work and published one of his own which he called a *Tour* of the town. It reappeared, with suitable changes, almost to the end of his life. Moreau maintained his connection with Bath, and must have spent some of the winter months there, for the introductions to later editions of his *Tour* were written there, and the book was printed by Crutwell's, the Bath printers who published the *Bath Chronicle*. No less important than Moreau's literary endeavours was the building, as a replacement of the "Town Rooms" in which Moreau first presided, of new and handsome Assembly Rooms in the High Street The project, actively encouraged by Thomas Holland, described as "an eminent architect from London", surveyed the site in the High Street and got out plans either for the enlargement of the existing ballroom or for a wholly new

---

[1] *Bath Chronicle*, 4 September 1777.   [2] *Bath Chronicle*, 16 October 1777.

Dowry Square, Hotwells: houses on the north side, c. 1725.

These houses mark the beginning of the architectural development of the Hotwells area and are somewhat earlier than equivalent work at Bath.

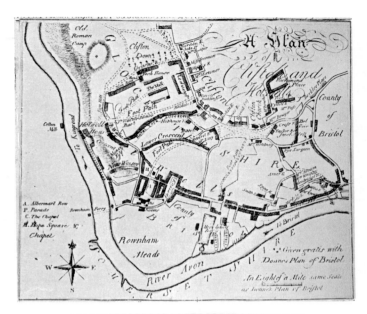

Above: A map of Clifton and the Hotwell, by M. P. Hill, 1787. The two sets of Rooms are above the words "Rownham Meads".

Below: George III at Cheltenham under the first canopy of the original well, 1788.

Clifton Suspension Bridge

Completed in 1864 as a memorial to Brunel, the bridge still carries a heavy
flow of traffic across the Avon Gorge. This view gives a good impression of
the double sets of three chains, each composed of wrought iron bars 25 feet
long and bolted together in groups of ten to make the links.

Photograph by John Cornwell

Old Temple Meads Station

Photograph by John Mosse

The train shed of the oldest surviving railway terminus station in the world to remain in anything like its original condition has now been converted into a car park. But Brunel's mock hammer-beam roof is still clearly visible.

building.[1] Holland, the Whig architect par excellence, was the ideal designer for so staunch a Whig as Hughes. In 1783–4 the new Assembly Rooms were completed; they were the result of what was probably the first incursion into Cheltenham of an architect of national standing. Little is known of their external appearance, but an engraving of the Grand Ball Room suggests an interior, with its curved end wall, Corinthian pilasters, and a small side gallery for musicians, of considerable size and elegance.

But if Cheltenham was to expand as a really important spa two things were needed. Access to the town by road, and roads and paving within Cheltenham itself, needed massive improvement. New houses, in terraces or other formal compositions, were required to provide more lodgings and, as in Bath after the elder John Wood had got to work, to bring their prices down.[2] The former task was soon taken in hand but building expansion had, for the most part, to wait till after the fall of Napoleon.

The first of Cheltenham's long-distance roads to be improved was that from the direction of Oxford and London, an important approach as this was the route which many of the spa's more fashionable visitors had to use. The old turnpike road, from Cheltenham to Andoversford and so towards Northleach and Oxford, was rugged and tortuous. So in 1785 an Act of Parliament was passed;[3] its prelude made the point that Cheltenham had "on account of its mineral waters, become a place of great resort", and that it would be "more frequented" if its road communications, particularly the London road, were "more commodious". The Act authorised amendments to the road from Cheltenham to Kilkenny, but the new highway, with its gentle gradient up the Chelt valley and so between Whittington and Sandywell Park, followed an easier and more direct course to Andoversford. Thomas Hughes and Simeon Moreau were both among the Commissioners appointed to carry out the Act.

The next important step, by an Act of 1786,[4] was the "improvement" and paving of the actual town. The Act, whose Commissioners came both from the Skillicorne and the Hughes

---

[1] Bryan Little, *Cheltenham*, p. 37.
[2] See John Wood, *An Essay Towards the Description of Bath* (1749 ed.), preface to Vol. ii.
[3] 25 George III cap. cxxv.   [4] 26 George III cap. cxvi.

camps, provided for the proper paving of such footways as did not already have smooth surfaces, for better cleansing and lighting, for the taking down of some old buildings, and for the removal of such country town "nuisances" as projecting sign irons and gutters. The emphasis was largely on greater ease for vehicular traffic, and no one was to use the pavements for such things as wheeled vehicles, wheelbarrows, sledges, carriages, casks, horses, or cattle. The streets, still, in the main, the High Street, were not to be the scene of football, cockthrowing, bull-baiting, or firework displays. Sophistication, in a town where spa and social activities were to become predominant, was to replace crude rusticity.

The visit to Cheltenham, in July and August of 1788, of George III, Queen Charlotte, and three of their daughters was decisively valuable for the fortunes of the spa, was of less obvious value for the king's health, but was of no small importance for the standing and development of the English monarchy.

The royal party, with Lord Courtown as Comptroller of the Household and Lady Weymouth in charge of the Ladies in Waiting, including Fanny Burney whose *Evelina* had described the Hotwell, travelled to Cheltenham from Windsor. They arrived on Saturday 12 July. It was the first time, since the beginning of the century, that a king of England had been so far from the London area or so deep into the provinces. The only place in Cheltenham large enough to accommodate visitors of such standing was Fauconberg House, so it was there (with the owner staying on his Yorkshire estates) that the king and his entourage resided. Even so, the mansion was cramped and, according to Fanny Burney, somewhat unsuitable for its purpose.[1] The lack of space indoors imposed on "the royals" an informality of régime and behaviour which was not, in any case, displeasing to a king whose habits and morals were those of a bourgeois rather than a Baroque monarch. "Farmer George" was more at home with simple, unaffected provincials than with the aristocratic artificialities of most courts of his time.

Half an hour after he had arrived the king appeared on the steps outside the hall door and acknowledged the large crowd

---

[1] *Diary and Letters of Mme D'Arblay*, ed. Barrett, notes by Austin Dobson (1904), iv, 5–7, 13–14.

which had gathered outside Fauconberg House. He bowed to the people and was soon out on Well Walk for the first of his many public promenades.[1] The king's strolls on the walks at Cheltenham were a counterpart, as Fanny Burney noticed, to his walks on the terraces at Windsor.[2] They were, however, in a more rustic and provincial setting, and though the king's closest companions were gentry and aristocrats whom he already knew, most of those who crowded to see him, on one occasion "in ranks ten deep with their hats off",[3] were local folk from Cheltenham and the surrounding villages. As at Windsor the king constantly saluted the crowds; we also hear, as with the farmer to whom the king spoke and gave a welcome *pourboire*,[4] of more personal and individual encounters. The impression created was immense and was the greater, among the thousands of Gloucestershire people to whom the monarchy had long been remote and little understood, for being quite unexpected. A letter, printed in a Bristol newspaper, said that the poor rustics had been surprised, on seeing the king, to find him "only a man"; they could scarcely believe, the writer added, that a gentleman in a blue coat and a bob wig was really their sovereign.[5] George III, in his turn, went out of his way to be approachable. When he was asked whether he would have with him a detachment of Guards he said that he could, on such an occasion, have no better Guards than his people.[6] In time, the frequency of the king's strolls on the Walks diminished their novelty and "divested them of the inconvenience of an attendant crowd": the "idea of royalty" gave way to "the contemplation of pre-eminence of those virtues that constitute the happiness of private life".[7]

The king's visit was not, however, without its more formal and official aspects. Not long after George III's arrival, Moreau, who deserved the honour, was formally presented to the king and queen and gave them copies of his *Tour* of the spa town.[8] On 30 July Mayor, Sheriff, and Recorder of Bristol waited on the king and presented an address. They asked him to honour Bristol with his presence, being told by the king (without any eventual result) that he would "eagerly embrace the next

[1] *FFBJ*, 19 July 1788.   [2] *Diary*, iv, p. 23.   [3] *FFBJ*, 26 July 1788.
[4] *FFBJ*, 26 July 1788.   [5] *FFBJ*, 9 August 1788.
[6] *FFBJ*, 26 July 1788·   [7] *FFBJ*, 26 July 1788.   [8] *GJ*. 14 July 1788.

opportunity".[1] Later in the royal stay there was a similar encounter with the Mayor of Bath, while the Mayor of Hereford came over to Worcester when the royal family was there for the Three Choirs' Festival.[2] Religious observance, by a monarch who was genuinely pious, was duly maintained, and the king gave orders that the Cheltenham waters should not be pumped on Sundays.[3] On the day after their arrival the royal family attended service in the parish church of Cheltenham, with a sermon by Bishop Hallifax of Gloucester; after church the king walked through the town with Lord Courtown and Col. Digby.[4] In July he was again at the parish church, with the rector preaching; the choir, who seem to have been mute on the first occasion, "mustered up courage" and "performed two psalms".[5]

The papers noticed that one of the king's evening walks in the fields saw him accompanied by a "vast concourse of well dressed persons".[6] Royal patronage inevitably drew attention to Cheltenham as never before and the number of fashionable visitors in 1788 must have reached a peak. The *Gloucester Journal* made no effort that year to list the Cheltenham arrivals. This may have been because they were too numerous to record; many of them, in any case, had to lodge away from the spa, in such places as Prestbury and Tewkesbury.[7] The inanities of fashion also cashed in on the upsurge of Cheltenham's popularity. In London the *Morning Post* spoke of Cheltenham bonnets, Cheltenham buckles, and Cheltenham buttons as being "quite the go", with the whole country's fashions "completely Cheltenhamised".[8] The popularity of Cheltenham turned out to be more lasting than the benefit which the *Gloucester Journal* reported as having come to the king's health from his quaffing of the waters.

The king's activities were by no means confined to Cheltenham itself. A leading feature of his stay was the frequency of his visits to country houses and other places of interest; the knowledge of the country round Cheltenham which George III thus obtained gave rise to his remark, at Weymouth in the following year, that the Vale of Gloucester was the finest part of his

---

[1] *FFBJ*, 2 August 1788.   [2] *FFBJ*, 16 August 1788.
[3] *FFBJ*, 2 August 1788.   [4] *FFBJ*, 19 July 1788.   [5] *FFBJ*, 26 July 1788.
[6] *FFBJ*, 26 July 1788.   [7] Goding, *op. cit.* p. 289.
[8] Goding, *op. cit.* p. 289.

kingdom that he had beheld.[1] A visit to Prestbury to see the grotto there could have caused no trouble, but other trips involved much longer journeys.

One of George III's first expeditions away from Cheltenham was not in the Vale but across the Cotswolds to see Lord Bathurst at Cirencester Park. Significantly, for a monarch whose interests included the growing practice of inland navigation, the excursion included a visit to the imposing eastern entrance of the Sapperton tunnel on the Thames and Severn canal which opened in the following year.[2] Sudely Castle was also on the programme but not, to the disappointment of its people, the town of Winchcombe.[3] Tewkesbury was an obvious attraction. George III's first visit, with the king riding and the queen and princesses in a carriage, was at somewhat short notice, so that the gathering of loyal people was less that it might have been.[4] The royal party went into the abbey and fairly soon returned to Cheltenham. But a second visit, on the way to call on Lord Coventry at Croome, was better publicised. The party drove under a triumphal arch, and as they passed over King John's bridge the king warned some of the crowd against the danger of standing on the parapet to get a better view of him.[5] At the top of the Mythe Hill, the king stopped for a time to admire the view, and Mr. Wakeman, the Catholic owner of the patch of ground on which the king had stood, made a bonfire that night and illuminated his house.[6]

The county town and its cathedral naturally got their share of royal attention. The first, more informal occasion was on 24 July.[7] The initial rendezvous was at the Palace, where six of Bishop Hallifax's children cast flowers on the path, and where the Mayor and Town Clerk were introduced. The royal party visited the cathedral, and from there went on to some important buildings of varied interest. The king saw the new County Gaol which was then being built to incorporate Howard's reforming ideas, under the supervision of that most assiduous of magistrates, Sir George Onesiphorus Paul. Thomas Cooke, the

---

[1] S. Y. Griffith, *New Historical Description of Cheltenham* (1826), p. 20.
[2] Humphrey Household, *The Thames and Severn Canal* (1969), p. 61.
[3] *GJ*, 28 July 1788.   [4] *GJ*, 21 July 1788.   [5] *FFBJ*. 26 July 1788.
[6] *GJ*, 28 July 1788.
[7] For this first visit, see *GJ*, 28 July 1788 and *FFBJ*, 26 July 1788.

building contractor, showed the king what was being done, and the *Gloucester Journal* made the point that the walls were manned by the building workers. The next stopping point was the Infirmary, a building some thirty years old at the time and typical of the hospitals erected, in many English county towns, in the eighteenth century. The king left a donation of £50. He also saw something of Gloucester's industries. He did not go to Rudhall's famous bell foundry, but he paid a visit to the pin manufactory of Weaver and Jefferis where he left a "handsome present" for the workmen.

George III's next trip to Gloucester was on Sunday 27 July when he and his family came over to morning service in the cathedral.[1] Handel's *Coronation Anthem* was one of the items rendered by the choir. Two days later he drove through the city before calling on George Augustus Selwyn at Matson. He and his host walked up the slopes of Robin's Wood Hill through groves which Selwyn had "improved" and at the house the king partook of a cold collation.[2] The king's final visit to Gloucester was quick and unceremonious, for on the day before he left Cheltenham he rode over, with his equerries, for an hour's private conversation with the bishop.[3]

In addition to walks and rides, the royal diversions at Cheltenham included two visits to the theatre. The loft in which, in 1774, the young Mrs. Siddons had appeared had now been replaced by a small purpose-built playhouse, which Fanny Burney found to be a "very pretty little theatre".[4] The first occasion was on Friday 1 August, by which time the Duke of York had joined the royal party at the spa. The playhouse, as was normal in Georgian theatres on special occasions, was lit with wax rather than by the smellier tallow candles, and the whole town was brightly illuminated.[5] The two items on the playbill were *She Would and She Would Not* and *The Sultan*. The young star comedienne Mrs. Jordan, not yet out of the king's favour as the mistress of Prince William Henry and the mother of ten Fitzclarence bastards, played Hippolyta and Roxolana,[6] and the newswriter assured his readers that the king was pleased with the whole performance. "The Royals" as Fanny Burney

---

[1] *GJ*, 28 July 1788.   [2] *GJ*, 4 August 1788; *FFBJ*. 2 August 1788.
[3] *GJ*, 18 August 1788; *FFBJ*, 23 August 1788.   [4] *Diary*, iv, 47.
[5] *FFBJ*, 9 August 1788.   [6] *FFBJ*, 9 August 1788.

called them, went again on 15 August,[1] the night before they left Cheltenham; before the play Queen Charlotte had held court, with music, in the Long Room by the Original Well.[2]

The other major entertainment item in George III's expedition to the lower Severn valley was his visit to the Three Choirs Festival at Worcester. The trip meant that the king and queen slept a few nights away from the spa; one wonders if a suitable supply of bottled Cheltenham water was taken to keep up the proper sequence of doses.

The king and queen came to Worcester on Tuesday 5 August in the evening and stayed at the Palace; they were greeted by illuminations and by what a news writer called "emblematical transparencies".[3] Early next morning the king walked through the city with a vast crowd accompanying him. He was pleased both with the situation of the buildings and with the cleanliness of the main streets. Later he went to the cathedral for one of the season's concerts. Proceedings started with a sermon, the Three Choirs bishops of Gloucester, Hereford, and Worcester all being present. The musical programme included the overture to Handel's *Esther*, the Dettingen *Te Deum*, two Coronation anthems and two other items. In the evening of the same day the king went to the carpet works of Michael and Watkins, and to Flight's porcelain factory. At the latter place members of the royal party placed orders, and it was remarked that "as usual" the king showed a great knowledge of trade and manufactures.

The days at Worcester were clearly among the most successful of this royal foray into provincial England; one unhappy side of the visit was the rich harvest reaped, among the close-packed crowds, by the local pickpockets.[4] The magnificent Guildhall was the scene of a formal call on the Mayor and Corporation, and the king drank to the "Prosperity of the City and Corporation of Worcester." A more Trollopean touch came when the royal party had tea with the Dean. The crowds coming in were extraordinary for a city of such a size; it was reckoned that not less than 50,000 people were in Worcester on the morning of Saturday 9 August. On the previous morning the king, with nearly three thousand in the cathedral audience, had been to

---

[1] *FFBJ*, 23 August 1788.   [2] *FFBJ*, 23 August 1788.
[3] For the Worcester visit, see *FFBJ*, 9 and 16 August 1788; *GJ*, 11 August 1788.   [4] *FFBJ*, 16 August 1788; *GJ*, 4 August 1788.

what was described as the "sublime mental repast" of *The Messiah*,[1] and in the evening he was in the one-time monastic refectory for a "grand miscellaneous concert". By the evening of the 9 August he was back in Cheltenham.

The last of George III's trips from Cheltenham was, for a bourgeois monarch who was as much interested in trade and economics as in high politics, among the most significant. As Queen Charlotte was unwell the royal visit to the "clothing country" of Gloucestershire was put off for a day; it occurred on 14 August.[2] As usual the royal party started early, were through Painswick at half past eight, and between nine and ten stopped at Stroud where, at Wallbridge, they watched boats passing through locks on the Stroudwater Canal.[3] They also saw Richard Hawker's mill at Dudbridge, but the highlight of their industrial inspection, predictably in view of Sir George Paul's position in the county, was his Woodchester Mill, where clothmaking was then carried on, as a lessee, by Sir George's cousin Obadiah Paul. As at other places the throng was enormous, and a letter from Minchinhampton makes the point that some three thousand people from that clothing town went over "to Paul's" and that hardly anyone but cripples were left in the parish. The royal party spent an hour at the mill, where Paul had arranged, presumably by the temporary transfer of some looms from weavers' cottages, for the king to see, "in regular gradation", the whole process of clothmaking. A déjeuner followed at Sir George's residence, Hill House at Rodborough, and the party then moved on to a cold collation with Lord Ducie at Spring Park—now the site of the derelict, bat-ridden Victorian Gothic mansion of Woodchester Park. At five in the afternoon the royal party started on the return journey of a long and busy day. They had been pleased, so a newswriter of Gloucester remarked, to "survey most picturesque country" and to have had a "nearer inspection" of so important an industry.[4]

The king and his party left Cheltenham for Windsor on Saturday 16 August. They went when they did, so that they

[1] *GJ*, 11 August 1788.
[2] For this visit, see *FFBJ*, 27 August 1788; *GJ*, 18 August 1788.
[3] Household, *op. cit.* p. 61 (quoting *Gentleman's Magazine*).
[4] *FFBJ*, 23 August 1788.

could be at the castle, late in August, for the simultaneous
celebration of four royal birthdays. The king was then due to
return to the semi-rural spa whose informality he had obviously
enjoyed. But the first serious onset of what was taken to be
insanity spoilt the plan and it was at Weymouth, almost
annually from 1789, that the king continued to make the
provinces personally familiar with the monarch's presence.
George III's long sojourn from the London area had, in terms
of the diffusion of his popularity among simple people, been a
pronounced success. A letter from Cheltenham, dated two days
after the king had left, said that "never did a Monarch gain the
hearts of his people more than our gracious king has of this
country, who regret his having left us",[1] while a Gloucester
correspondent made the point that the royal family's departure
seemed to be regretted "more like the loss of private friends than
a party so exalted and august".[2] Moreau, in the meantime, had
gained great credit for his "laudable exertions" in keeping
down the price of provisions in Cheltenham during the hectic
weeks of the royal stay; the writer stressed that similar action
would be essential on any future occasion.[3] By the end of
August, Moreau had arranged for a medal to be struck to
honour the royal visit.[4] It was commissioned from the Birmingham medallists John Gregory Hancock and William Phipson;
the design which they worked out makes an attractive composition. On one side, the medal shows the Original Well with
its simple brick canopy; beneath it, with the date 1788, the
inscription records that it was Simeon Moreau, as ARBITER

---

[1] *FFBJ*, 23 August 1788.   [2] *FFBJ*, 23 August 1788.

[3] *FFBJ*, 23 August 1788.

[4] *FFBJ*, 22 August 1788. For more particulars of the medal, see pp. 8–10 of
the 9th ed. (1797) of Moreau's *Tour of Cheltenham* (details kindly communi-
cated by Miss Pringle of the Central Library, Cheltenham). Phipson was
probably William Phipson (1770–1845), who in 1792 became Master of the
Birmingham Assay Office; see the catalogue of the exhibition "Birmingham
Gold and Silver, 1773–1973" held in the City Museum and Art Gallery,
Birmingham, 1973. The senior of the two medallists was John Gregory
Hancock (fl. 1775–1815) who worked in his early days for Matthew Boulton
at Soho and who became a prominent and prolific producer of medals and
tokens. The *Birmingham Directory of 1788* refers to him as an "Artist".
(Information kindly sent from L. Farrer, *Biographical Dictionary of Medallists*
(1904), and other sources, by Miss Dorothy McCulla of the Local Studies
Dept., Birmingham Public Libraries).

ELEGANTIARUM, who had the medal made. On the other side, the symbolic figure of Hygeia holds the serpent of Aesculapius, a symbol of longevity, which drinks from a shallow dish resting on a column. From that column there hangs a portrait medallion of George III, while the column is also shrouded by the branches of a sapling oak, another symbol of long life. But here the date, in a reference to the year of the medal's actual appearance, is 1789. For there were production difficulties in Hancock's workshop. Two dies got broken, and by the time that the medal was issued in April 1789, the king had recovered from the serious illness which had followed his return from Cheltenham. Hancock therefore suggested that the medal could fitly commemorate the two episodes, so that the words OB SALUTEM RESTAURATAM refer to the later of the two events. When the work was done, Lord Courtown handed copies to the king and queen, also to the Prince of Wales, the dukes of York and Gloucester, and to the three princesses who had been on the trip to Cheltenham. It had been hoped, when Moreau ordered the medal, that the visit to Cheltenham would soon be repeated. But the king's major illness which did not, in 1789, stop the first of his numerous journeys to Weymouth, prevented the king's further appearance at Cheltenham.

From 1788, and for several decades to come, Cheltenham's future as spa, and later as a residential town, was assured. But its physical expansion was slow in coming. Within less than five years of George III's stay the country was deep in the French Revolutionary War, and in the collapse of financial confidence and of building activity, which soon followed its outbreak. But before the war started, a move had been made to provide easier access, not all the way to Cheltenham, but to a point nearer to the town than the quay at Gloucester, for the bulk transport of coal and of such building materials as glass and softwood timber. An Act of Parliament,[1] given the royal Assent in June 1792, authorised the construction, from the Severn at a point near the mouth of the Chelt to the foot of Coombe Hill between Gloucester and Tewkesbury, of a short canal which would facilitate communications with various collieries and give cheaper and better access to Cheltenham. William Miller was

[1] 32 George III cap. lxxxiii.

one of those who was to pay for its construction.[1] What is surprising, in an age which could achieve such a feat of canal engineering as the Sapperton tunnel, is that no tunnel was proposed, under the relatively minor obstacle of Coombe Hill, so that the canal could reach Cheltenham itself. The canal might, however, have been of some help to Cheltenham, more for its effect on the cost of coal than for any immediate use in the carriage of materials for building development.

In 1797 the population of Cheltenham stood at the still modest figure of about 2,700,[2] while in 1801 the first Census made it only 3,076. By 1811 it was 8,325, but the real growth of the town had to wait till after the Napoleonic War. In 1816 the centenary of the Original Well's discovery was marked by the opening of the new Assembly Rooms by the victor of Waterloo who, as Major General Wellesley,[3] had been at Cheltenham in 1805 on the way to his wedding in Dublin.

[1] Joseph Priestley, *Navigable Rivers and Canals* (1831, reprinted 1969), p. 164.

[2] Griffith, *op. cit.* p. 24.

[3] *GJ*, 7 October 1805.

IX

A Refuge from Revolution: the American Loyalists' residence in Bristol

By Peter Marshall

DURING the period of the War of Independence the presence of Americans in Bristol was not, in itself, unusual: the links between the city and the New World were far too venerable and important for arrivals from that quarter to excite comment. Trade in time of peace no doubt suggested refuge in time of war as those who preferred exile to rebellion sought a place of shelter, but the lot of the Loyalist was all too often marked by poverty and lack of purpose, a contrast with previous conditions that many found to be deeply dispiriting and unacceptable. Education, former wealth, official responsibilities proved handicaps rather than helps to a life of exile passed in conditions which underlined the price of loyalty: time hung heavily upon unemployed hands, but the correspondence and diaries, for which ample opportunity existed, rarely proved to be more than records of dispossession and complaint. The colony of Americans that formed in Bristol during the Revolution was distinguished by its past, rather than by its present, significance: its members had, more completely than they knew, excluded themselves from the life and future of their native land.

In Massachusetts the outbreak of hostilities had brought to a head a political conflict which had drawn attention to the colony throughout the previous decade: during its course, prominence had been accorded not only to leaders of American resistance but also to those who demonstrated, at considerable hazard and discomfort to themselves, their continued loyalty to the Crown. There were few Loyalists who had not experienced threats to their persons and their property. Some had found the strain of conflict unbearable even before it culminated in outright violence. James Boutineau, a Bostonian who, like his wife

Susannah Faneuil, was of Huguenot stock, had accepted office as councillor under the Massachusetts Government Act of 1774, which had replaced election of the Governor's council by the House of Representatives with the more customary method of appointment by the Crown—part of the process of exacting retribution for the vandalism of the East India Company's tea. His service as a "mandamus councillor", a species declared by New England patriots to comprise "monsters more hideous than Hydra", had made him a target for mob harrassment. By August 1775 he could endure no more and left, with his family, for Bristol. Arriving there late in September he made it his home until his death in May 1778.[1]

Henry Barnes, merchant and justice of the peace in Marlborough, Massachusetts, had long been distinguished—or notorious—for fidelity to the Crown and hostility to patriot protests. His refusal to abide by non-importation agreements involved him in controversy. At the end of June 1770 Lieutenant-Governor Hutchinson issued a Proclamation offering a reward of £50 for information against those who had threatened Barnes for importing goods, and two months later had written a private letter to Hillsborough, the secretary of state, specifically commending his refusal to comply with the ban on trade. The situation grew so ugly that Barnes fled to England in November and did not return home until the following year. A period of relative quiet was terminated by a clash of the kind that paved the way to open conflict. In February 1775 military parties twice visited Marlborough: on the first occasion Barnes, as magistrate, issued orders for the billeting of a detachment which was searching the area for deserters, while shortly afterwards he provided hospitality to two imperfectly disguised officers engaged in a survey of the local roads as preparation for troop movements in the spring. Their presence and purpose having been immediately detected, the officers left Marlborough in great haste, on foot, and despite a violent snow storm. Meeting them later in Boston, Barnes

> told us that immediately after our quitting town, the Committee of Correspondence came to his house, and demanded

[1] John C. Miller, *Origins of the American Revolution* (1945), pp. 262–3; E. Alfred Jones, *The Loyalists of Massachusetts* (1930), pp. 44–5. Hereafter cited as *Jones*.

us; he told them we were gone; they then searched his house
from top to bottom, looking under the beds and in the cellar,
and when they found we were gone, they told him, if they
had caught us in his house, they would have pulled it down
about his ears. They sent horsemen after us on every road,
but we had the start of them, and the weather being so very
bad, they did not overtake us, or missed us. Barnes told them
we were not officers, but relatives of his wife's from Penobscot,
and were going to Lancaster; that perhaps deceived them.[1]

Having won a respite, Barnes determined to evade further
inquiries and withdrew to the greater safety of Boston. Here he
remained until news that the death of his uncle in Hampstead
had brought him a modest inheritance permitted his departure
with his wife and niece for England in February 1776. By the
following year he was settled in Bristol, where he remained for
the rest of the war.[2]

Although the disturbed condition of Massachusetts had led a
number of its Loyalists, more perhaps than from other centres of
disaffection, to seek refuge in England in the course of 1775, it
was the evacuation of Boston by the British army in March 1776
that caused the first substantial exodus of native Americans:
some 1,100 Tories, a little under one third of a population
drastically reduced from its pre-war figure by military occupation and rebel encirclement, preferred to depart rather than
face retribution. A calculation of arrival dates in England of
Loyalist heads of families indicates that Massachusetts easily
provided the greatest numbers until the end of 1776. Connected by family relationships, political office, economic
interests and administrative posts, as well as by aversion to
Revolution, many of these early victims of upheaval found their
way to Bristol.[3]

Boutineau was only the first of five mandamus councillors to
take up residence in the city. Thomas Oliver, of West Indian
stock but a graduate of Harvard College, had, as Lieutenant-

---

[1] James H. Stark, *The Loyalists of Massachusetts* . . . (Boston, 1910), p. 402.
Hereafter cited as *Stark*; *Documents of the American Revolution 1770–1783* ed.
K. G. Davies (Shannon, 1972), i, 129, 389.

[2] *Jones*, pp. 19–22.

[3] Wallace Brown, *The King's Friends* (Providence, R.I., 1966), p. 36; Mary
Beth Norton, *The British Americans* (Boston, 1972), p. 37.

Governor and President of the Council, become the particular object of the general outcry against supporters of British authority: in September 1774, he reported, his house in Cambridge "was surrounded by three or four thousand people, and one quarter part in arms. I went to the front door, where I was met by five persons, who acquainted me they were a Committee from the people to demand a resignation of my seat at the Board." This, after an unsuccessful attempt to evade the issue, he was compelled to do. He then withdrew to Boston, where he remained as Lieutenant-Governor until the evacuation when he left with the army for Halifax. He did not stay there for long but made his way, with his wife and six daughters, to Bristol. Although loyalty had incurred him considerable financial loss— he claimed it amounted to over £5,000—the family interests in Antigua enabled him to escape serious impoverishment and ensured a comfortable life in exile.[1] Here he was joined by others whose experiences and commitments had followed a similar course. Richard Lechmere, also a mandamus councillor, had accompanied the army to Halifax and then removed, with his family, to England in May 1776. A Boston merchant and son of a Customs official, Lechmere had ample experience of the discomforts of collaboration with authority, as he explained in September 1774 in a letter to his English commercial correspondents. He had been so imprudent as to let the army occupy his distillery, which would provide accommodation for a regiment, and had sold some 4,000 feet of plank for building additional barracks.

By this step, selling the plank to them, accepting the office of a Councillor, my connection with the navy and army, together with my being an Addresser, Protestor against the Committee of Correspondence, and a variety of other incidents, has render'd me one of the most obnoxious of all the friends of government . . . when these matters are terminated, if I find I cannot sit down quietly and enjoy uninterruptedly the liberty of acting and thinking for myself, without being subjected to insults and abuses, I must be oblig'd to take refuge in a country where a man is sure of protection and freedom; to this end therefore in the mean time, let me ask

[1] *Stark*, p. 180; *Jones*, pp. 225–6.

the favor of you, my friends, to be thinking for me against this evil day (which I fear will come) by laying some plan for me, whereby I may make an addition of three or four hundred pounds sterling a year, either by some office or business in or near London, such an addition, with what income I have, wou'd most certainly determine me to quit this distracted country with all my family . . .

Lechmere claimed that this proposal was not an "effect either of fear or sudden resentment", but "the result of mature deliberation".[1] Less than two years later his fears had become facts, as departure, though not cushioned by any promise of additional income, became essential. In Bristol, Lechmere was joined by other members of his family who, in turn, formed links in a chain of connections that held together the Loyalist community there. His brother, Nicholas Lechmere, formerly a Customs officer at Newport, Rhode Island, where he had long been in conflict with the radicals, and his brother-in-law, the older Jonathan Simpson, a Boston merchant who had been appointed a mandamus councillor but had declined to take the oath of office, settled in the neighbourhood; Simpson's nephew, the younger Jonathan, was married to the daughter of Mrs. Anna Borland, another Loyalist resident of Bristol who had arrived from Boston after her husband's death there during the months of military occupation. Mrs. Borland's maiden name of Vassall suggests a family connection with yet another former councillor who had exchanged life in Cambridge, Massachusetts for residence in Clifton: John Vassall's exile, although he claimed that his losses amounted almost to £12,000, was rendered less uncomfortable by the income from his large Jamaican estates. The parallel between his situation and that of Thomas Oliver was underlined by Vassall's marriage to Oliver's sister. Whatever the degree of Vassall's sufferings in exile, it is evident that their basis was not financial.[2]

Notoriety gained in the course of employment in the Customs service served to distinguish another Loyalist in Bristol. The Hallowell family had long experienced the profits and miseries

[1] Richard Lechmere to Lane, Son & Fraser, 28 September 1774, "Letters of Richard Lechmere", *Massachusetts Historical Society Proceedings*, 2nd Series xvi, 289.

[2] *Jones*, pp. 189–91, 261–2, 41–3, 283–5; *Stark*, pp. 413–14, 287.

of regulating the trade of Boston: Benjamin Hallowell, Comptroller of the port during the Stamp Act crisis, had suffered at the hands of rioters, but despite this example, his brother, Robert, had accepted the same appointment in 1770. He persisted in performing his duties during years of turbulence, was transferred to Plymouth as a consequence of the Boston Port Act, and fled to Boston in April 1775. Evacuated to Halifax with the army, Robert Hallowell eventually made his way with his family to Bristol. In residence there in September 1779, he was of opinion, the following May, that unless his financial prospects improved he would be forced to quit Bristol and live in less expensive Wales. That this did not become necessary was perhaps due to assistance from his father-in-law, Dr. Sylvester Gardiner, formerly a prominent and wealthy Boston doctor. Identified with the British cause by his treatment of casualties after the battle of Bunker Hill, Gardiner had also left with the army in 1776 and on arriving in England had settled at Poole. Gardiner and his family were, however, resident in Bristol for several months in the winter of 1779–80 and at the end of the war, before he returned to Rhode Island, Gardiner took as his third wife, Catherine Goldthwait, niece and adopted daughter of Henry Barnes, a resident of Bristol throughout these years.[1]

Nathaniel Coffin was another exile notorious for his long service to the Crown. His post as Receiver General and Cashier of the Customs in Boston had made the proximity of his house to the Liberty Tree erected by Ebenezer Mackintosh, the mob leader, a natural incitement to conflict and hostility. Coffin's date of departure from Boston is uncertain, but Samuel Curwen dined with him in London at the beginning of February 1776. He was subsequently resident with his family in Princes Street, Bristol, until May 1780 when he left, by himself, to return to Boston on account of his health. He failed to survive the voyage and died before the ship reached New York. His widow stayed on in Bristol and saw one of their five sons enter upon a military career in which he reached the rank of General

---

[1] *Jones*, pp. 158–60, 140–2, 148; *Stark*, pp. 281, 313–15; Robert Hallowell to Edward Winslow, 9 May 1780, *Winslow Papers 1776–1826*, ed. W. O. Raymond (St. John, N.B., 1901), p. 62; *The Journal of Samuel Curwen, Loyalist*, ed. Andrew Oliver (Cambridge, Mass., 1972), ii, 565, 588. Hereafter cited as *Curwen*.

while another became an Admiral. Mrs. Coffin no doubt remained in Bristol to stay in the company of her brother, Henry Barnes.[1]

Although he did not settle in Bristol until April 1778, when expense led him to quit London for lodgings in Orchard Street, Jonathan Sewall—or Sewell as he became convinced his name was spelt, insisting after 1783 on the use of this form—could thereafter be considered the best-known and most talented member of the Bristol Loyalist community. His legal career in Massachusetts bore comparison with that of his close friend John Adams. Their political divergences, emphasised by a swift series of advancements that brought Sewall to the office of Attorney General of Massachusetts in the tumultuous 1760s and in October 1768 to Chief Justice of the newly-established Vice-Admiralty court at Halifax, Nova Scotia, did not terminate their personal friendship until the eve of the Revolution. A cousin, Samuel Sewall, wealthier than his relative and like him a Harvard graduate, took up residence in Clifton during the later years of the war. Jonathan, who remained in Bristol until his departure for New Brunswick in 1788, revealed more clearly than most, in his lively correspondence, the ambivalence of Loyalist feelings towards England. Expressions of admiration and awe alternated with a sense of loss, providing a curiously uneven set of responses to a society that appeared both familiar and strange to the exiles.[2]

These were the principal figures in the known community of refugees, mainly of Massachusetts origin, which, together with their families, added between fifty and sixty Americans to the population of Bristol. Indications can be found of the presence in the city of Pennsylvanians and Carolinians, but there is no reason to believe that, either in number or in eminence, they ever threatened to obscure the Bostonians. Exiles from one colony were reluctant to become intimate with those from another. In London, the various Loyalist groups kept to their own distinct coffee houses, rarely visited those of another colony, and preferred to live in different parts of town. As a

[1] *Stark*, pp. 234–5, 399; *Curwen*, i, 112; ii, 605.
[2] Carol Berkin, *Jonathan Sewall* . . . (New York, 1974), pp. 10–105; Clifford K. Shipton, *New England Life in the Eighteenth Century* (Cambridge, Mass., 1963), pp. 565–83; *Jones*, pp. 258–9.

result, "there was little sustained intercolonial mingling among the refugees, either in residential neighbourhoods or at communal meeting places".[1] In the case of the smaller community established in Bristol it might appear that its Massachusetts character acted as an attraction to those from that colony and as a deterrent to other Americans.

Life in a foreign land was not rendered more pleasant for the Loyalists by financial embarrassments, even though these varied considerably in degree and origin. Refugees whose fortunes extended to possessions in still loyal colonies, such as John Vassall and Thomas Oliver, or officials such as Sewall, who continued to receive his pay as Chief Justice, bar the cost of maintaining a deputy in residence throughout his years in Bristol, suffered less financial loss than those whose capital and income derived exclusively from their former homes. A government policy of assistance was slow to develop, and until the beginning of 1777 only occasional and inadequate payments were made to the refugees. A change in method seems largely to have been secured by the petitions of Massachusetts Loyalists, the first sizable body of exiles to reach Britain. Twenty-nine of their number petitioned for relief in October 1776, and the mandamus councillors did likewise towards the end of the year. In response, the Treasury established a pension list, originally containing about a hundred names, to which others were subsequently added. Payments began at £40, were normally £100, but amounted to £200 a year for mandamus councillors and could be even higher for other civil officers. The pensions proved large enough to maintain a decent existence and sufficiently small to arouse anger. A sense of betrayal, rather than gratitude, derived from support which was initially considered but trifling, and seemed none the less so with the passage of time. Brooding upon the question in 1784, Dr. Peter Oliver concluded, "Blessed are ye who expecteth nothing, for ye then shall not be disappointed."[2]

A tendency to brood upon misfortune was encouraged by a determination to seek each other's company: in the process,

---

[1] Norton, *op. cit.* pp. 68, 102; Wilbur H. Siebert, "The Colony of Massachusetts Loyalists at Bristol, England", *Massachusetts Historical Society Proceedings*, xlv, 409–14.

[2] Norton, *op. cit.* pp. 52–61.

comments upon and relations with British society were subordinate to concern with their own plight, and were coloured by
their habit of judging their surroundings in terms of native
sights and sounds. Thomas Hutchinson was perhaps the most
distinguished Loyalist visitor to Bristol. A brief sight, shortly
after his arrival in England, had left him unimpressed by its
size or appearance. In March 1777, returning for a longer stay
at the Hotwell in fruitless search of a cure for his daughter
Peggy's illness, he was willing to conclude that the city was not
without merit. On 8 May, before taking his departure, he
recorded in his diary that he "took a full view of Bristol from
Brandon hill where they say Cromwell erected his batteries and
beat down their houses. I think take in all circumstances & I
should prefer living there to any place in England. The manners
& customs of the people are very like those of the people of New
England and you might pick out a set of Boston selectmen from
any of their churches . . ." Concern for his daughter, whom he
could not judge helped or hurt by taking the waters, had
"marred the pleasure of so agreeable a city and the country
round it".[1] While at the Hotwell Hutchinson seems to have
enjoyed little social life, but diary comments during a later
visit indicate that the acquaintance with Americans resident in
the city was all that could counter the bitter memories left by
his previous, unavailing stay. "We received visits", he noted on
19 July 1778, "from Mr Barnes, Willard, Waldo, Thomas,
Americans, & a note from Mr Faneuil to desire us to dine with
him and we spent the day among them, the only inducement to
our going to Bristol. . ."[2]

Although family distress distorted Hutchinson's view of
Bristol, his opinions and actions in many ways resembled those
of other, less unfortunate, Loyalist residents. When Samuel
Curwen first arrived in the city in August 1776, he called upon
Joseph Waldo, a Bostonian and Harvard graduate settled there
since 1770, and was invited to dinner with two other New
Englanders. Next day he travelled north to Gloucester "through

---

[1] "Diary of Governor Hutchinson", 8 May 1777, British Library;
Egerton MSS. 2663, f. 161.

[2] *Ibid.*, Egerton MSS. 2664. f. 96. Willard and Thomas had also accepted
appointment as mandamus councillors but were, apparently, only visitors
to Bristol.

fertile country more like the face of New England than any spot of the same extent I have yet seen".[1] On his return in the following month, Curwen was delighted, while viewing the grotto at Goldney Lodge, to encounter Harrison Gray Jr., the son of the treasurer of Massachusetts, who had temporarily quit London to stay in Clifton.[2] In June 1777 Curwen established himself in Bristol for a longer stay: his *Journal* indicates that the majority of his friends there were of New England stock and sufficiently numerous to permit him, in late September of that year, to spend an "evening at quadrille with 13 Americans".[3] If Bristol could never be confused with home, its appearance and facilities rendered it not totally unfamiliar: a refugee with more time than employment could while away the hours at the American Coffee House in Broad Street, attend services at the church or meeting house of his denominational preference, and even renew acquaintances by chance encounters in the street. Curwen, on his way one Sunday afternoon to All Saints, having attended morning service at Lewin's Mead,

> overtook a female who accosting me by name caused me to turn and look at her recollecting a face I had [seen]; enquired her name, it proved to be Molly Church, a maid servant in the family of my late father in law Mr Russell of Charleston, who came over a servant with a Mrs Borland . . .[4]

Such meetings underlined rather than assuaged the pains of exile and did no more than define a condition in which not only friends, but familiar pleasures, were greatly missed. So Jonathan Sewall urged his fellow Loyalist, Edward Winslow, to see to it that their friend, Ward Chipman, in distant Nova Scotia, should "send me by the return Bristol ships, a few Newtown pippins, Shagbarks and Cranberrys—do spur him up. You can't conceive what a regale Newtown pippins, Shagbarks &

---

[1] *Curwen*, 23–24 August 1776, i, 210–11. A later visitor, the New Yorker Peter Van Schaack, echoed this opinion. Of the country round Stroud, he noted in his diary for 17 June 1779: "The country is hilly, and not unlike some parts of America, and the people are of a plain cast and hospitable. Many of their manners remind me of New England." Henry C. Van Schaack, *The Life of Peter Van Schaack* (New York, 1842), p. 145.

[2] *Curwen*, 19 Sept. 1776, i, 225–6.

[3] *Ibid.*, 29 Sept. 1777, i. 405.

[4] *Ibid.*, 26 Oct. 1777, i, 409.

Cranberrys would be to us Refugees. . ."[1] The comforts afforded
by residence in Bristol were never complete.

The needs and fortunes of war brought change to the Loyalist
society of Bristol, adding to the established group of exiles those
whom duty or inclination brought to the city. George Inman
arrived there in April 1780 on a recruiting mission for his
regiment, the 26th Foot. A young graduate of Harvard, whose
father had celebrated his son's receipt of a degree in 1772 by
entertaining 347 ladies and gentlemen to dinner and a ball, he
had persisted, in defiance of paternal wishes, in enlisting in
British service at the close of 1775. After four years in the field,
which had included participation in the battles of Princeton and
Brandywine, he was transferred with his regiment to England
and took up residence in and around Bristol. Here he quickly
resumed old connections and was introduced into the Loyalist
circle, though seemingly any friendships did not prove endur-
ing. Inman later recalled that:

> We met with many American families that were settled there,
> some of the most intimate were: Thomas Oliver, John
> Vassals, Lechmere, Sewal, Bob Holbrook [?Hallowell] Nat.
> Coffin, who died after, Mrs Borland, Mrs Simpson, Mr
> Fennel, Mr Barnes, Mr Coulson, and Mrs Merchant, our
> friend Betsy Davis who resided with her aunt Mrs Vassall.
> But (with) some of these, by some means or other, a coolness
> took place, after which my visits to them were more out of
> form than friendship. . .

Inman's manuscript journal does not, unfortunately, cast light
on the causes for this waning of intimacy: it records only daily
walks and visits to the coffee house in search of news. In these
respects its author only too faithfully reflected the emptiness of
a Loyalist existence.[2]

Circumstances ensured that much of the group's correspondence should assume a depressed tone. Relief at recent
escapes from personal danger and persecution could not make
attractive a life that, though placid, had to be passed among

[1] Jonathan Sewall to Edward Winslow, 7 May 1780, *Winslow Papers*, p. 61.
[2] "George Inman's Narrative of the American Revolution", *Pennsylvania
Magazine of History and Biography*, vii, 246; *Jones*, p. 177; Journal of George
Inman, Cambridge Historical Society MSS., Harvard University Library.

strangers. Henry Barnes did not enjoy his first summer in
Bristol. Admitting his good fortune, he agreed with a friend that

> as you observe we were very well off to come away at our
> Leisure and not be oblidged to scamper, but after all we are
> like indulged Children hardly know what we want tho we
> are in a land of plenty yet we are not contented there is want-
> ing here that cordial Friendship that serves to sweeten the
> cares of Life. the many Repulses we have met with since we
> arrived has made me more anxious for the Fate of America,
> as I long to get back to my own Habitation to spend the
> remainder of my days in tranquillity & Independence. . .

How much more preferable this would be than to remain con-
demned to receive unconfirmed reports of British defeats while
living in a distant city where "I am sorry to say there are many
Malignants here that would rejoice to have it so" and who had
caused the refugees to be "met with such a cold reception".
Barnes himself would by then have been destitute if he had not
been able to draw upon his uncle's bequest, and even this he
looked upon as a mixed blessing: "as it is, I am apt to think I for
my part would have enjoyed more real content in suffering with
my Friends than enjoying the Flesh potts here, which is a very
triffling satisfaction in competition with the cordial friendships
we have left behind".[1] Time did not sustain these brave pro-
testations, for two years later Barnes expressed a very different
view: "While there was any Prospect of returning home I kept
up my Spirits in hopes the Time would not be long but now I
give up all thoughts of returning and shall in earnest ask for a
settlement in England", he confessed to Jonathan Sewall as he
offered advice on the education locally of the later comer's two
sons.[2] In consequence of this resolve, Barnes took steps to secure
a more permanent residence in Bristol. "I have at length", he
wrote at the close of 1779, "so far given up the Idea of returning
to America, that I have hired a Small House in Colledge street
in this City, to try if I can't feel more at Home than I have
hitherto done at Lodgings . . ." Financial problems continued

[1] Henry Barnes to James Murray, August 1776, Massachusetts Historical
Society MSS.

[2] Henry Barnes to Jonathan Sewall, 16 May 1778, Massachusetts
Historical Society MSS.

to ensure an uncertain existence, but there was some consolation to be derived from the fact that "we have a Number of Americans in this City that we are at no loss for agreeable Company".[1]

In the course of time Sewall was likewise compelled to face the problem of whether a temporary exile must be acknowledged to have become permanent residence abroad. He expressed the dilemma, with a degree of wit that distinguished him from his fellows, in a letter written from Bristol in February 1780 to his cousin and life-long friend, Thomas Robie. His initial enthusiasm for life in England vanished, he now declared that

> were it not for my children I should long ago have removed to Halifax & received the whole of my salary [as Chief Justice of the Vice-Admiralty Court] to my own use, upon which I think I could live better there than upon 3/4ths here, but for their sakes I must tarry here yet a little longer. I grew so tired of living with a family at lodgings that I am now again a householder in *Trinity* Street, Bristol. I was formerly in *Unity* Street, from whence I removed hither. Whether this is a change from *heresy* to *orthodoxy* or *vice versa*, or whether, according to St Athanasius, they are *both* the *same*, & so I remain in *statu quo*, or in *quomino*, as our country pedagogue expressed it, I leave you to determine. . .[2]

If the terms of Sewall's correspondence could frequently seek to lighten the gloom which encircled his friends, his own spirits periodically descended to depths of depression more profound than those to which his less cheerful companions were reduced: the worst and most continuous onset of despair would confine him to the bedroom of his house in Bristol throughout the whole of 1786.[3] He had discovered, like many others, that self-exile had not resolved, but rather complicated, personal problems: having chosen to remain in Bristol for the sake of ensuring that his sons received a good education, success in this endeavour only gave rise to a further difficulty. Sewall grew alarmed lest his son's schooling had rendered them unable to live outside

[1] Henry Barnes to James Murray, 7 December 1779, Massachusetts Historical Society MSS.

[2] Jonathan Sewall to Thomas Robie, 11 February 1780, *Massachusetts Historical Society Proceedings*, 2nd Series, xi, 421.

[3] Berkin, *op. cit.* p. 140.

England and was certain that his own slender financial resources would prove insufficient for their maintenance in a
manner appropriate to their upbringing. In 1785 he despatched
his elder son to Canada, though it cost him dear to do so, and
prepared to follow him to Halifax next spring. It seemed the
only escape from his difficulties for, as he wrote to Robie,

> I assure you I am tired of England, & earnestly long once
> more to see you & others of my old American friends &
> acquaintance. I mean in Nov. Sco. & N. Brun; for as for
> those in the 13 States, 2 or 3 excepted, I have not a wish to
> see a devil of them in this world or the next. I wish them no
> harm. God bless them, I say, but as either world is wide
> enough for us all, without jostling, I wish to keep clear of
> them to all eternity. . .

This endeavour to avoid conflict and rationalise his decision
would lead only to that total retreat from the world which
marked the next year of Sewall's life in Bristol.[1]

Sewall's case was not exceptional in nature, only in expression. For many Loyalists the end of the war did not resolve the
difficulties of their existence but, if anything, intensified their
problems. Years had passed since the majority had quit their
native land: where did they now call home? Mrs. Barnes was
deeply disturbed by this dilemma and unhappy at the choices
presented her. Her opinions, she declared, were shared by many
of her acquaintance. "You will", she wrote an old friend,

> find many of them in a very unsettled state, not knowing
> where, or how, to dispose of themselves, few of them wish
> (even were they allowed that libberty) to return to Boston,
> and after enjoying the sweets of Old England for Eight
> Years, they shudder at the thoughts, of repairing to the Wilds
> of Nova Scotia, tho many of them (who have a rising
> generation to provide for) may look upon it as an elligible
> situation. . .[2]

While the refugees pondered their future, they continued to

[1] Jonathan Sewall to Thomas Robie, 8 September 1785, *Massachusetts
Historical Society Proceedings*, 2nd Series, xi, 472; Berkin, *op. cit.* pp. 135–40.
[2] Mrs. Barnes to Miss Murray, 28 February 1874, Barnes MSS, Library
of Congress.

maintain a closely-knit social grouping in Bristol. There is a
note of expatriate penury to be detected in Mrs. Barnes'
description of relations between the Loyalists still to be found in
the city in the spring of 1786.

> We have seventeen American familys in Bristol, very Genteel
> well bred People, all of one heart, and one mind. In this circle
> we are treeted with Cordiality and respect, being quite upon
> a footing with them in the stiles of Vissiting which is no more
> than Tea and cards—a little parade (to be sure) is nessisary
> upon these ocations in order to keep up the Ball, but as it is
> not attended with much Expence we readily consent to
> follow the Lead.[1]

Should one of their number determine to abandon this
separate existence, a choice had to be made between three very
different but equally uncertain courses of action. The erstwhile
Loyalist could settle permanently in the British Isles and prefer
allegiance to upbringing; he might return to North America
and submit to pioneer conditions which he had previously
escaped; he could admit defeat and seek acceptance in the new
Republic, despite, or sometimes on account of, the material losses
he had suffered during the Revolution. Bristol Loyalists followed each of these solutions. Samuel Curwen went home to
Salem in an impartial spirit of general malevolence. His home-
coming was unaccompanied by any sense of relief as on
25 September 1784

> at 20 minutes after 3 o'clock set my foot on the end of Long
> Wharff in Boston in Massachusetts State, America, after an
> absence of 9 and little more than 5/12ths of a year occasioned
> by an execrable and never enough to be lamented civil war,
> excited by ambitious selfish wicked men here and in England
> . . . By plunder and rapine, some few have accumulated
> wealth, but many more in numbers are greatly injured in
> their circumstances; some have to lament over the wrecks of
> their departed wealth and estates; among which pitiable
> numbers is the writer of this, whose affairs by folly, vice,
> wickedness are sunk into irretrievable ruin. . .[2]

[1] Mrs. Barnes to Misses Barker, 1 April 1786, *Letters of James Murray,
Loyalist*, ed. Nina Moore Tiffany (Boston, 1972), p. 259n.

[2] *Curwen*, ii, 1026–7.

If Curwen made his disillusioned way home, Sewall finally opted for the uncertainties of New Brunswick, but despite their differing decisions both had appeared victims rather than warriors of the Revolution. The Loyalist community in England was notable for its lack of belligerency: a British victory would have been welcomed as a means of making a return home possible and only secondarily greeted as a political triumph. Both Curwen and Sewall appeared certain of the superiority of British power, bitterly Francophobe, and persistently homesick in their attitudes, rather than virulently antagonistic to their American adversaries. Sewall expressed a total lack of enthusiasm for "the Rebel Arnold's return to his allegiance—I don't think much of the latter, taken abstractly . . ." but spoke quite differently of his reunion with John Adams, now minister in London of the United States, which took place in 1787, twelve years after they had last met: "our conversation was just as might be expected at the meeting of two old sincere friends after a long separation".[1] Wanting in ideological fervour, not distinguished from British society by evident differences of custom, language or religion, the Loyalists possessed few defences against their third possible fate: absorption by their place of refuge.

Bristol Loyalists were no exceptions to this rule, preferring to spend the rest of their days in the city of their adoption. Benjamin Faneuil, brother-in-law of James Boutineau, formerly a Boston consignee of East Inda Company tea and for which activity he had been threatened with assassination, remained there until his death in February 1787.[2] Others enjoyed a longer life and left descendants who made good marriages or displayed a preference for careers in the Services. Thomas Oliver, the last Lieutenant-Governor of Massachusetts under the Crown, received an official pension until his death in Bristol in November 1815: he had married his daughters into prominent local families.[3] Richard Lechmere had died shortly before him, in December 1813 at the age of 87, and was buried in Bristol

---

[1] Jonathan Sewall to Elisha Hutchinson, 25 November 1780, Massachusetts Historical Society MSS.; to Judge Joseph Lee, 21 September 1787, cited Berkin, *op. cit.* p. 142.

[2] *Jones*, p. 134; Benjamin Woods Labaree, *The Boston Tea Party* (New York, 1968), p. 111.   [3] *Jones*, pp. 225–6.

Cathedral.[1] By the time of their deaths few would have known, and even fewer would have been concerned, that they had come to Bristol from America and by way of a Revolution.

The tragedy of the Loyalists was also their limitation upon sufferings: painful, tumultuous, and threatening though the events had been which had driven them to Bristol, and unsympathetic as their place of exile had appeared in many respects to have been to them, their distinguishing characteristics did not constitute an evident presence in the city as would prove the case in the new settlements of British North America. A number of families knew, perhaps only too well, one another's origins and peculiarities: to the outside world they were no more than elements in the mercantile and professional society of a great seaport. It was the external view that prevailed and in consequence the Loyalists became, in Bristol as in the country as a whole, not a persisting and ultimately vanishing minority group, but a number of family names known only to genealogists, antiquarians and, in recent years, to historians seeking to rescue the refugees from the obscurity to which acceptance had consigned them.

[1] *Ibid.*, p. 190.

X

Brunel in Bristol

By R. A. Buchanan

JOHN LATIMER, the celebrated Bristol chronicler, describing the circumstances of the construction of the Great Western Railway in his *Annals of Bristol in the Nineteenth Century*, first published in 1887, wrote:

> The time has long passed away since there was any difference of opinion as to the deplorable error of the original board in neglecting the sober-minded, practical, and economical engineers of the North, already deservedly famous, and in preferring to them an inexperienced theorist, enamoured of novelty, prone to seek for difficulties rather than to evade them, and utterly indifferent as to the outlay which his reck- lessness entailed upon his employers.[1]

Such asperity about I. K. Brunel, the young engineer of the new railway and arguably the greatest British engineer of the century, sounds strange to modern ears. Now that Brunel has been virtually adopted as one of the favourite sons of Bristol, the tension and animosity which accompanied so many of his engineering enterprises and which is reflected in almost every comment Latimer makes about him has been forgotten. There is an anomaly here: a problem of historical interpretation which requires elucidation. It is the purpose of this paper to explore the relationship between Brunel and Bristol. Many of Brunel's achievements in Bristol, in the shape of bridges, harbour works, railways, and ships, have already been amply recorded, but they have not previously been examined from the point of view of the engineer's attachment to Bristol. Moreover, a close study of the Private Letter Books of I. K. Brunel deposited in the University of Bristol Library, has made it possible to add some

[1] J. Latimer: *Annals of Bristol in the Nineteenth Century*, (Bristol 1887), p. 191.

significant details to these achievements, and to give a reasonably coherent account of the development in the relationship between Brunel and the prominent citizens of Bristol in his time.[1]

Apart from a brief sojourn in his early twenties, Brunel never lived in Bristol. He was born in Portsea on 9 April 1806, while his father was engaged on the block-making machinery commissioned for the Admiralty at Portsmouth Dockyard. Much of his education was in France, and when he set up a home of his own it was over his office at 18 Duke Street, overlooking St. James's Park and convenient for Parliament and Whitehall. When he acquired a country house it was at Marychurch in Devon, and although he did not live long enough to settle there he devoted a lot of attention over many years to preparing the house and its gardens. From 1835, when the Great Western Railway Company was established, until his death in 1859 at the age of 53, Brunel spent little time in Bristol. Most of his visits to attend Board meetings and to inspect his various works seem to have been hurried affairs of one or two nights. There are few details in the records about where he stayed, but there are some suggestions that it might have been at the G.W.R. office on Temple Meads Station, and it is clear from the frequent complaints of shareholders and others in Bristol who thought that he was neglecting their interests that he could not have spent long in the city during these years. Yet despite his lack of any residential qualification, Brunel acquired a special affection for Bristol. He referred on one occasion in 1845 to "our revered parent the City of Bristol"[2] and later in the same year protested to a Bristol colleague that "I have no wish in the matter whatever except the old and strong wish of being considered a Bristol man and one who can always be relied on as sticking to his friends thru' thick and thin."[3] A decade later he wrote warmly of "the spirited merchants of Bristol"[4] who had led the world in steam navigation. It is probable that the close attachment

[1] I am grateful to Mr. N. Higham, University Librarian, and to Mr. G. Maby, the University Archivist, for the unfailing courtesy and patience with which they have dealt with my research on the Brunel papers over several years. Of these papers, the most important for the purpose of this essay are the Private Letter Books (hereafter referred to as *PLB*.) which cover the years 1836 to 1859.   [2] *PLB*, Brunel to J. N. Miles, 28 April 1845.

[3] *PLB*, Brunel to Osborne, 3 June 1845.

[4] *PLB*, Brunel to John Yates, 16 November 1854.

Brunel formed with the circle of Bristol industrialists and businessmen was responsible for his continuing loyalty to the city even at times when official relations had become strained and less than cordial. These personal friendships were crucial to Brunel's links with Bristol. In them, he found men who appreciated his dynamism and who shared his visions. Through them, he was invited to undertake his many enterprises in Bristol.

Brunel was 22 when he first arrived in Bristol in 1828. Until January of that year, he had been working in the Thames Tunnel as Resident Engineer for his father who had designed it, but the young Brunel had narrowly escaped with his life when the Thames broke in and flooded the workings. He sustained such serious internal injuries that he was compelled to spend several months recuperating. With this purpose he went first to Brighton but soon moved to Clifton, the elegant suburb which was then developing on the edge of open downland to the north-west of Bristol. There is a problem about the timing of Brunel's first visit to the Bristol region. His father, Marc Brunel, kept a diary which was both more meticulous and more legible than anything written by his son, and in the year following the disastrous "accident at the Tunnel" which was recorded on Saturday 12 January 1828 there are frequent references to Isambard's state of health.[1] But the only occasion in the course of that year when he mentions Isambard leaving town was on the 12 July, when the entry reads "Isambard has set off for Plymouth in the steam boat", and the first mention of Bristol is in the entry for 23 January 1830: "Isambard set off for Bristol." Nevertheless, Brunel's biographers, with sources at their disposal which are not at present available, are clear about Isambard's visit to Bristol in 1828, even though they give no particulars about its date, its length, where it was spent, or whether or not he went with any introductions which would have put him in touch with the mercantile elite of Bristol.[2] The entries in Marc Brunel's diaries suggest that, in any event, the

[1] The diaries and other papers of Sir Marc Brunel are in the Library of the Institution of Civil Engineers. I am grateful to the Librarian, Mr. H. C. Richardson, for permission to consult them.

[2] The standard biographies are I. Brunel, *The Life of Isambard Kingdom Brunel* (1870); Celia Brunel Noble, *The Brunels, Father and Son* (1938); and L. T. C. Rolt, *Isambard Kingdom Brunel* (1957). The son's biography of 1870

visit was not a protracted one. But Isambard was certainly back
in Clifton the following year, because it was then that he heard
of the announcement by the Bristol Society of Merchant
Venturers of the decision to build a bridge over the Avon Gorge
linking Clifton with Leigh Woods. A competition for designs
was held in 1829, and on the closing day, 19 November, Brunel
submitted four schemes of possible bridges within the terms of
the competition, illustrated with beautiful sepia sketches. By
becoming involved in this competition, Brunel came into
contact with a group of influential Bristolians, many of whom
became his life-long friends, and as the city was poised on the
threshold of a period of vigorous commercial and industrial
activity it was natural that, despite his tender years, Brunel's
great talents should have been called upon when harbour
works, railway projects, and pioneering ship-building enterprises were being mooted in the city.

The Bristol circle with whom Brunel became involved included Tory merchants like Nicholas Roch, Liberal industrialists like T. R. Guppy, shipbuilders like William Patterson, and
Captain Christopher Claxton, a retired naval officer employed
as Quay Warden in the Bristol Docks. He also got to know men
such as Osborne, Secretary to the Bristol Docks Company and a
prominent legal adviser to the Society of Merchant Venturers
and all manner of industrial enterprises. It appears to have been
Roch who introduced Brunel to the Board of the Bristol Docks
Company, and also to the promoters of the Great Western Railway. Although Roch seems shortly afterwards to have retired
to Pembrokeshire, Brunel was anxious in later years not to cause
any offence to his old friend when the South Wales Railway was
being built. We find him in 1844 promising to call on Roch "to
renew a much valued and *now* I may call it an old friendship";[1]
and later in the year he instructed his assistant Brodie, surveying
the line near Pembroke, to "try and keep the line a little further
from Mr. Roches".[2] His warning does not seem to have been

does not mention a visit to Clifton before the bridge competition of 1829, but
both Lady Noble and Mr. Rolt refer to a period of recuperation in Clifton,
presumably in 1828. Both the latter refer to manuscript diaries of Isambard
Kingdom Brunel which I have not had the good fortune to see.

[1] *PLB*, Brunel to Roch, 10 May 1844.

[2] *PLB*, Brunel to Brodie, 28 October 1844.

heeded because a few days later he wrote apologetically to Roch: "a singular chance or fatality has carried my levels almost thru' your house . . .".[1] Brunel never forgot that Roch and the other Bristol men had given him his big opportunities as an engineer. These were "the spirited merchants of Bristol" who chose him as their agent to accomplish the great designs which matured in the city in the 1830s.

The reputation of Bristol had declined since the early eighteenth century, when it had been second only to London amongst the sea-ports and cities of the realm. The vigorous growth of rivals, particularly Liverpool, had combined with a certain complacency among Bristolians to produce comparative stagnation in the trade of the city. Not even the dock improvements undertaken belatedly by the Bristol Docks Company between 1804 and 1809 succeeded in overcoming this lethargy, partly because the improvements were much more expensive than envisaged by William Jessop, the engineer who designed them, and partly because the Docks Company imposed high harbour dues in order to recoup their losses. There was a mounting sense of frustration in Bristol in the years following the Napoleonic Wars, as its more able citizens tried in vain to revive the drooping fortunes of the city. This frustration became directed against the commercial oligarchy of the corporation and the unreformed parliamentary representation, culminating explosively in the Bristol Riots of 1831. The three days of chaos at the end of October, 1831, have been described as "the worst outbreak of urban rioting since the Gordon Riots in London over fifty years earlier",[2] and there has been nothing like them in Britain since. At least twelve rioters died, in addition to those who were later hanged, and large parts of the city centre were laid waste. The Bristol Riots have posed a problem for historians because of the strange detachment from the turmoil shown by the well-to-do middle classes in Bristol, at least for the first two days, and because of the ambivalent attitude of the troops brought in to restore order. The conclusion of one recent study is that:

There can be no doubt that it was the fate of the city Corporation,

[1] *PLB*, Brunel to Roch, 8 November 1844.
[2] Susan Thomas, *The Bristol Riots* (Bristol Branch of the Historical Association, 1974), p. 1.

and not that of the Reform Bill, which was really at issue in Bristol in 1831.[1]

The riots demonstrated the intensity of local feeling against the self-appointed oligarchy of wealthy merchants who kept a tight control over Bristol through the unreformed Corporation and the Society of Merchant Venturers. There was widespread relief when the power of this clique was modified if not entirely broken by the Municipal Corporations Act which became law at the end of 1835 and which established in Bristol an elected council with effective powers to organise a police force and to perform other vital functions.[2] These reforms had become an essential prerequisite of the sort of industrial expansion envisaged by Brunel and his friends.

Brunel was present in Bristol at the end of the riots, and gave evidence at the subsequent trial of the Mayor, Charles Pinney. But although it is intriguing to speculate about Brunel's part in the affray, this cannot be done with any certainty.[3] While it is inconceivable that he could have favoured mob violence, and he seems to have spent part of the time with his friends Alderman Hillhouse and Nicholas Roch, it seems likely that he would have shared the popular antipathy towards the closed Corporation. The next year he was out on the hustings in Lambeth supporting his brother-in-law Benjamin Hawes, who successfully contested the seat in the new reformed House of Commons in the Radical interest. Generally, however, Brunel was reserved about declaring any partisan political interest, and it is probably because he was so much the professional engineer shunning political involvements that he managed to retain the friendship of men with a variety of different political points of view.

The initial impact of the reform agitation, and especially the havoc wrought by the Riots in 1831, was not conducive to commercial vigour in Bristol: even the Clifton Bridge scheme was allowed to languish until confidence began to revive. In the autumn of 1832, Brunel was in a mood of deep despondency

[1] *Ibid.*, p. 26.

[2] See Latimer, *op. cit.* pp. 206–18 for an account of municipal reform in Bristol.

[3] See Rolt, *op. cit.* pp. 59–63 for a reconstruction of Brunel's possible involvement in the Bristol Riots.

about his career, as none of the projects in which he was involved were making any progress. But when plans for a railway link between Bristol and London began to stir again at the end of that year, they initiated a general revival of activity which quickened in the following years. Between 1833 and 1848 Bristol was the scene of a remarkable burst of political and commercial enterprise. The municipal government was reformed, giving the new industrial middling classes the same sort of enlarged scope in local affairs that the reform of parliament had given them at national level. The national agitation for free trade, in which these social classes took the lead, was represented in Bristol by a movement to liberalise trade in the docks by reducing dues and, if necessary to achieve this, acquiring the Docks Company for the Corporation, which was done by 1848. On the commercial and industrial front, the G.W.R. was established with a capital of £2,500,000, increasing to over £8 million by 1844. It was followed by other railway companies, the most important of which were the Bristol & Exeter (established with a capital of £2 million in 1836), the Bristol & Gloucester (built in stages and opened in 1844), and the Bristol & South Wales Junction Railway (promoted in 1845 with a capital of £200,000, but not completed to New Passage ferry until 1863 after further injections of capital). Brunel was involved to some degree in all these railway enterprises, and played a dominant role in most of them.

This railway boom stimulated other activities, many of which also called on Brunel's engineering skills. The prospectus for the Great Western Steamship Company appeared in January 1836 with a capital of £250,000, and its first vessel, the S.S. *Great Western* was launched on 19 July 1837. The S.S. *Great Britain* followed in 1843. With the need for an oceanic terminal in mind, the Portbury Pier and Railway Company was floated in 1846 with a capital of £200,000 to carry out a scheme devised by Brunel. Even the impecunious Dock Company was inspired to put in hand much needed improvements, culminating in the new South Entrance Lock to Cumberland Basin, which became known as "Brunel's Lock" after its designer. A brand new enterprise in Bristol was the Great Western Cotton Company, with a capital of £200,000 and a large factory in Barton Hill, the foundation stone of which was laid in April

1837. Conrad Finzel set up his sugar refinery, destined to become one of the largest in the country, on the Counterslip in 1836. Fry's chocolate, Christopher Thomas's soap enterprise, and Wills tobacco all underwent substantial growth in this period. E. S. Robinson set up his paper bag business in Baldwin Street in 1844, a year after William Butler became manager of the tar distillery which was later to take his name, and which owed its prosperity in part to Brunel's use of one of its products —creosote—for preserving railway timber.

These activities indicate the vigour of commercial and industrial activity associated with Bristol at the time when Brunel was most active in the city. Unprecedented sums of capital were being raised for new enterprises, many of them promoted by friends of Brunel and all of them by people who knew him and who turned to him for engineering advice. By 1848, however, some of these relationships had started to turn sour. The G.W.R. had serious internal difficulties, and was having trouble with subsidiary companies and with rivals. In 1846 it had lost the "gauge war" when the government had ruled that all future railways must be constructed on the standard gauge. The reverberations of the failure of Brunel's "atmospheric principle" on the South Devon Railway harmed his reputation in 1848. In the same year the Bristol Docks Company was acquired by the Corporation of Bristol, and the new Docks Committee began to harry Brunel over his delays in completing the South Entrance Lock. Perhaps the biggest blow of all to Brunel, however, was the accident which befell the S.S. *Great Britain* in November 1846, when the ship ran aground in Dundrum Bay, for although the measures taken to protect the ship from the winter storms and to refloat her the following summer were successful, and although her endurance of this ordeal justified confidence in her construction, the accident brought about the collapse of the Great Western Steamship Company and helped to disperse the precious group of Bristol friends on whom Brunel had relied for good relations with his Bristol clients. So the quality of the relationship changed, formality replacing intimacy, and a chiding tone of anxiety replacing the previous sense of confidence in Brunel's judgement.

Ironically, the Bristol enterprise of Brunel which was least affected by this boom in commercial activity and by the subsequent set-backs was the one from which all the others stemmed: the Clifton Bridge. While capital flowed readily into the railway and steamship undertakings, the Bridge remained permanently short of money. It had been promoted as the result of a legacy of £1,000 left in 1753 by William Vick, a Bristol merchant, with the instruction that when it accumulated to £10,000 it should be used to build a bridge over the Clifton Gorge. By 1829, the sum had reached £8,000, and inspired by the recent completion of Telford's Menai Suspension Bridge the Society of Merchant Venturers held the competition which fired Brunel's imagination. Of the twenty-two designs received by the Merchant Venturers in November, those of Brunel and four others were short-listed. Thomas Telford, the elderly President of the Institution of Civil Engineers and the outstanding engineer of his day, was called in to judge the competition and faulted all the schemes submitted. Experience at the Menai Suspension Bridge with lateral wind resistance had convinced him that 600 ft. was the maximum possible span for a suspension structure. As Brunel's designs varied from 870 ft. to 916 ft. for their main span, Telford dismissed them as impracticable despite Brunel's careful engineering calculations to show their feasibility. The result was that Telford was invited to submit a design of his own, which he did, but as this involved the construction of massive piers from the foot of the Gorge it was rejected by the Merchant Venturers on account of its estimated cost. So a fresh competition was held in October 1830, and Brunel submitted a new design in which he compromised with the caution of the Merchant Venturers by reducing the projected span to 630 ft. with a massive abutment on the Leigh Woods side. It was this design which was, after some uncertainty on the part of the new judges, accepted in March 1831. Brunel wrote to Benjamin Hawes:

> . . . I have to say that of all the wonderful feats I have performed since I have been in this part of the world, I think yesterday I performed the most wonderful. I produced unanimity amongst fifteen men who were all quarrelling about the most ticklish subject—taste.

The Egyptian thing I brought down was quite extravagantly admired by all and unanimously adopted; and I am directed to make such drawings, lithographs, etc. as I, in my supreme judgment, may deem fit; indeed, they were not only very liberal with their money, but inclined to save themselves much trouble by placing very complete reliance on me . . .[1]

The reference to the "Egyptian thing" shows that Brunel had converted the "Gothic" style which had been adopted for most of his earlier designs and that the conception of the bridge had reached a form recognisable as the familiar shape which survives today, even though it underwent much further modification, mainly in order to effect economies.

Having at last agreed on the plan, the Bridge Committee of the Merchant Venturers was anxious to begin work quickly. The first sod was turned on 21 July 1831, to the accompaniment of a ceremony at which Sir Abraham Elton and Lady Elton of Clevedon Court played a leading part. The recorded account of Sir Abraham's address closed on a prophetic note, as he drew the attention of the assembly to the young engineer:

The time will come when, as that gentleman walks along the streets or as he passes from city to city, the cry would be raised: "There goes the man who reared that stupendous work, the ornament of Bristol and the wonder of the age".[2]

Little immediate progress was made, however, as there were legal difficulties about the approaches on the Leigh Woods side of the Gorge, and it was clear that barely half the estimated cost of £52,000 had been subscribed. So the project faltered, and when it was overtaken by the riots in October it was shelved for five years. A new start was made in 1836, the Marquis of Northampton laying the foundation stone of the southern abutment on 27 August during the proceedings of the British Association, which was being held that year in Bristol. The piers were completed in 1840, and a contract made for the iron work, but in February 1843 it was announced that the sum of £40,000, including the original Vick legacy, had been spent and that another £30,000 would be needed to finish the project. This sum was not forthcoming until after Brunel's death, so that

[1] Brunel to Hawes, 27 March 1831, quoted Noble, *op. cit.* p. 109 and Rolt, *op. cit.* p. 56.   [2] Quoted Rolt, *op. cit.* p. 58.

the bridge remained for twenty years as merely "two unsightly piers which deformed the landscape".[1]

Apart from a few trivial items, the first reference to the Clifton Bridge in the Private Letter Books in Bristol University Library is in 1839, when Brunel asked the Trustees for payment for his services beyond the £4,200 paid in 1831 on the assumption that the work would be finished in four years.[2] The next year, in the course of a letter to Guppy on other business, he reported on the Bridge:

> between the two gothic parties we settled amicably into the Egyptian.[3]

which indicates the continuing debate amongst the Trustees about the style. There are then some technical letters on the iron work, and some concerned with raising money, but otherwise a long gap until 1848, when Brunel was being pressed by the Trustees to sell off the iron work as scrap.[4] He was reluctant to do so as it would mean admitting complete failure on the project. In the spring of 1849 he wrote to Ward, the Secretary to the Trustees:

> Now a sudden light has come upon me—only I fear to show however our utter darkness—I mean that I really believe that I could get the bridge finished—but what is to be done with the Ferry? If you can devise and procure relief from this I think I will manage the bridge. What can be done—is it hopeless.[5]

From this it is clear that the Trustees were encountering formidable opposition from the proprietors of the Rownham Ferry, who operated a flourishing business across the Avon from Hotwells to Rownham Hill. This problem persisted later in the year:

> My Dear Ward,
>   Pray do not let anything be done if you can possibly prevent it which can in any degree be a stop towards the

[1] Latimer, *op. cit.* p. 133.

[2] *PLB*, Brunel to Trustees of Clifton Bridge, 22 March 1839.

[3] *PLB*, Brunel to Guppy, 15 January 1840.

[4] *PLB*, Letters of 6 December 1848, 11 December 1848, and 13 December 1848.   [5] *PLB*, Brunel to Ward, 10 May 1849.

abandonment of the bridge—out of evil sometimes comes good, and the very badness of the times in all mechanical manufacturing engineering (Engineering properly speaking is not *bad* but *dead*) will be the cause of our finishing the bridge. If I can limit the capital required to manufacturer's capital that is materials and work 1 can get parties to undertake it, and I think I can manage all (with some little personal sacrifice) except the Ferry.

If you will get that burden or bug-bear—for it is more alarming than it ever ought to be—removed I think I see my way set to work now manfully, and you will succeed and then I shall be bound to also.

Yours very truly—
I. K. Brunel[1]

Two years passed, and Brunel tried to present further proposals to finish the bridge in order to stay execution:

I cannot think that the Trustees are wise—I am ordered to sell the iron and thus destroy for ever all hopes of its completion at the moment when this is at last rendered practicable.[2]

But despite further prevarications, the Trustees firmly resolved to sell the iron in order partially to recoup their losses[3] and Brunel commented in the course of a letter describing his terms for continuing the work: "the whole must be closed as I am sick of it".[4] The delaying tactics continued, however, and Brunel was still negotiating the sale of the iron work in a desultory manner at the beginning of 1853.[5] Brunel was keenly disappointed at this collapse of his first engineering commission, and it may be regarded as symbolic of his relationship with Bristol affairs that the gradual winding-up of the Bridge project coincided both with the dispersal of his group of personal friends in Bristol and with an increasing estrangement from other

---

[1] *PLB*, Brunel to Ward, 19 October 1849. The sense of this letter is clear enough, but the expression is convoluted and there seems to be a missing negative in the first sentence.   [2] *PLB*, Brunel to R. Palmer, 16 July 1851.

[3] *PLB*, Brunel to Knapp, 13 November 1851.

[4] *PLB*, Brunel to G. Hennet, 6 December 1851.

[5] *PLB*, Letters of 4 January 1853 and 7 January 1853.

Bristol clients. Yet the Bridge was completed, but only after Brunel's death and specifically as a memorial to him. A new company was formed in 1861, raising a capital of £35,000 and acquiring the property of the original undertaking. Sir John Hawkshaw and W. H. Barlow were given the engineering responsibility, and made several modifications in Brunel's design. They were able to use the double chains from Brunel's Hungerford Bridge, then being dismantled to make way for Charing Cross Railway Bridge, and added a third chain on each side of the bridge platform. Brunel's intended embellishment of the two piers with ornamental cast-iron plates was abandoned. The work was completed in 1864 and the Bridge was formally opened on 8 December.[1]

If the story of the Clifton Bridge was the least satisfactory part of Brunel's relationship with Bristol, in so far as it led to no achievement in his lifetime, his contribution to the city docks became the most acrimonious. All began well, in 1832, when Brunel was introduced to the Board of the Bristol Docks Company by Nicholas Roch, who was one of its members, and invited to report on the problems of the docks. These were complex, and have been the subject of previous papers.[2] Briefly, the trouble was that although William Jessop had greatly improved the dock facilities in 1804–9 by providing permanent high water in the "Floating Harbour", he had not allowed for a sufficient supply of water to the harbour so that it was prone to silt up and to act as a stagnant sewer for the city. The latter problem had been alleviated by the construction of a culvert in 1828, which redirected the foul water of the River Frome and discharged it directly into the tidal waters of the New Cut. But the problem of an inadequate water supply persisted, and in his report of August 1832 Brunel suggested means of improving the flow and of removing the banks of mud which were threatening to make the Harbour unusable. Not all Brunel's ideas were

---

[1] There is an extensive literature, mainly of a pamphlet nature, on the Clifton Bridge. For a recent discussion of its technical features, see R. F. D. Porter Goff, "Brunel and the design of the Clifton Suspension Bridge' *Proceedings institution of civil engineers*, Part I, August 1974.

[2] See R. A. Buchanan, "The Construction of the Floating Harbour in Bristol, 1804–1809" in the *TBGAS*, lxxxviii, 184–204; and *Nineteenth Century Engineers in the Port of Bristol* (Bristol Branch of the Historical Association, 1971).

immediately adopted, but over the next fifteen years he was frequently consulted by the Bristol Docks Company and commissioned to undertake specific improvements such as the construction of the "trunk" under the dam at the lower end of the Harbour, which converted it from an "overfall" to an "underfall" dam and made it possible to scour large quantities of silt into the New Cut. The Company also adopted his device for a novel form of self-propelled scraper-dredger, one of which was completed in 1844 and remained in active service for over a hundred years.[1]

There were occasional complaints by the board of the Bristol Docks Company that insufficient attention was being given to their business, but matters only began to go seriously wrong with his last major commission: the reconstruction of the South Entrance Lock. He had frequently had cause to warn the Board of the decay of the entrance locks and when asked to give his opinion on the southern lock in 1844 he observed that "the repair of that Lock is a most serious business and will probably involve a *very heavy* expense".[2] At the same time he wrote to his friend Captain Claxton, who had been closely associated with him in his earlier work on the docks, "I think of recommending a thoroughly good lock."[3] The directors quailed at Brunel's estimated cost of £22,000, but the need for action was pressing and so it was agreed to adopt his plan for a completely new lock 54 ft. wide and 245 ft. long. In February 1845 the tender of Mr. Rennie, a building contractor, to do the bulk of the masonry work, was accepted.

Brunel's design for the lock was ingenious, overcoming the limitations of a cramped site and the need to keep traffic moving through the North Lock. The operating length of the lock was maximised by using single-leaf gates of a novel wrought-iron caisson construction so that they became partially buoyant at high water, which made them more manoeuvrable than conventional gates. But after a brisk start, the work seemed to slow down so that in April 1846 the Board expressed its "extreme

---

[1] See R. A. Buchanan, "I. K. Brunel and the Port of Bristol", *Transactions of the Newcomen Society*, vol. 42; and "Cumberland Basin, Bristol", *Industrial Archaeology*, vol. 6, no. 4, November 1969.

[2] Letter of 3 June 1844 in Port of Bristol Authority archives.

[3] *PLB*, Brunel to Claxton, 3 June 1844.

disappointment" at the rate of progress[1] Brunel responded promptly and somewhat emotionally in a private letter to "My Dear Osborne", objecting to criticisms of his work:

> My feeling is that I have taken great pains and given great attention as a friend much more than as a professional man to the interests of the Dock Co. as a body and without reference to the contending interests and have amongst other things devised and taken upon myself the responsibility of directing a work which when done will cost about one third what any such work ever did cost—or what any other Engineer would have taken the trouble and responsibility and anxiety of doing for them and have watched their work as I have before watched and carefully directed everything for Bristol and especially for the Dock Co. as amongst my first Bristol clients —and yet I hear nothing but the most contemptible lying reports always in circulation—the most childish impediments thrown in one's way—all by an officer of the Dock Company who by his own weak rather than mischievous character is so entirely beneath my notice as are the reports propogated, that I cannot stoop to wipe him or them out of my way—yet the result is annoying and in any other case I should find some excuse for dropping the business and if the Dock directors really were to ask me any question founded on these reports I believe I should get angry and cut the concern.[2]

A pencilled note against the personal comments reads "Hillhouse", who was the Bristol Docks Company Dock Master. Brunel went on to assert his complete confidence in the contractor and in the work so far completed.

This outburst does not appear to have achieved either a curtailment of the criticism or a discernible increase in the rate of work. In fact, there was a serious set-back a few months later when a retaining dam collapsed in the lock, causing further long delays.[3] Brunel had his Chief Assistant J. W. Hammond on the Bristol Docks' work, and there is evidence of some vexation with his subordinate, although not directly connected with the new lock:

[1] Minutes of the Bristol Docks Company, 27. April 1846
[2] *PLB*, Brunel to Osborne, 1 May 1846.
[3] Report in PBA archives, 14 August 1846.

When I referred to our "angry discussions" I meant simply and truly that I was angry, and if I failed to make you sensible that I was angry I must be a much milder and gentler being than I thought.[1]

Hammond complicated matters shortly after this by dying, and there is little doubt that this was a serious blow to Brunel. When the Docks Committee assumed responsibility from the Dock Company in September 1848, the work was still unfinished and one of the first resolutions of the Committee called on Brunel "to adopt every means in his power to place the Lock in working order as early as possible".[2] But there were more delays before the lock gates were in working order (probably about April 1849), and the swing bridge over the lock was not completed until the following autumn.[3]

Meanwhile, Brunel wrote another prickly letter to Osborne on a related matter:

I have heard accidentally perhaps incorrectly that at the last Dock meeting instead of replying to my inquiries some question arose as to them consulting me *at all* on the subject of the steam boat landing places. Now if any such question was asked I must beg of you to put the matter quite clear. It was no wish of *mine* but I was specifically asked by the Directors or I suppose more correctly by the members of the Committee to consider the subject and give them some plan. . . . I only require to be told what is expected I can then choose for myself.[4]

Mutual dissatisfaction between Brunel and the Dock authorities now seemed well established, and it appears to have been a relief to both parties when the end of the relationship came in sight. But it was not to come smoothly, because there were first some accounts to be settled. Apart from the size of the amount (Brunel estimated that Rennie had done £20,740 worth of work by 21 April 1849, and Hennet's price for the gates was

[1] *PLB*, Brunel to Hammond, 27 November 1846.

[2] Minutes of the Bristol Docks Committee, 4 September 1848.

[3] See R. A. Buchanan "I. K. Brunel and the Port of Bristol" *loc. cit.* and *PLB*, Brunel to Bell, 6 October 1848 and 27 December 1849.

[4] *PLB*, Brunel to Osborne, 25 October 1848. The writing is particularly difficult to decipher.

another £675) there was a long wrangle whether Rennie was entitled to additional payments for sums incurred as a result of Hammond's verbal instructions, which had not been ratified on paper. Bell, who appears to have assumed responsibility for Bristol works after Hammond's death, was summoned to Duke Street urgently early in 1850 . . . "to settle the Bristol Dock a/c. Please bring all papers that can possibly be required."[1] Some weeks later Brunel wrote to Rennie, and the letter is worth quoting at length as an insight into Brunel's treatment of contractors:

Mr. James Rennie.
Bristol Dock Co.
My Dear Sir,
    You are quite right in consulting your partners.
    You must not consider that I am calling upon you to make a sacrifice to the Dock Company.
    The circumstances are very peculiar—the Dock Company entered upon a certain work because they believed they could ensure it being done for a specific sum—you having undertaken to do it for that sum. The work turned out much more difficult than was expected and many expenses were incurred which had not been contemplated, the question of whether any of these were extra or not ought to have been settled at the time—Unfortunately the only man who can explain these circumstances and who could admit on the part of the Company that orders were given if they were given verbally and settle that point is now dead—and no traces remain of letters on the subject. I am therefore compelled to look mainly to the Contract.
    That you will be a loser I admit and regret it—I wish that it were in my power to deny it—I have a great respect for the integrity and straight forwardness always shown by you in the business you have conducted with me and am very sorry to see you a loser—perhaps from the very circumstances of your confidence in Mr. Hammond as my representative—but I am helpless—and such misfortunes will sometimes happen . . .[2]

[1] *PLB*, Bennett (Brunel's Chief Clerk) to Bell, 1 February 1850.
[2] *PLB*, Brunel to James Rennie, 15 April 1850.

Almost two years later, the business was still not settled, and Brunel again wrote to Rennie:

> After again examining the Bristol Docks accounts with you I am prepared to agree with you that I should certify to the final or total amount of £21058.6.7 from which has to be deducted all previous payments on account: and that I recommend strongly to the Directors of the Dock Company the payment of the further sum of £2000 in respect of your claim of £2759.8.0[1]

Incredibly, Brunel's clerk was writing to Mr. Bell later that year asking for basic information about the contract:

> Will you please write Mr. Brunel a short statement of the reasons for the excess in the contract . . . for the work done at the Bristol Docks by Rennie . . . there was Ashlar work in the invert on account of the bad nature of the ground—walls (?) of masonry for reception of the machinery of the gates—general increase in thickness of the masonry on account of insecure nature of ground—I merely mention these as being likely to be reasons—but you can state whatever you think proper as the cause for the increased items which were allowed by Mr. Brunel. . . .[2]

More months elapsed before Brunel wrote to the Docks Committee stating his case for paying Rennie £2,000:

> The principal portion of the excess is not an increase in the price of any contract work but an actual extension or enlargement of the contract.[3]

The Committee made an offer of £1,000 which Brunel con-

---

[1] *PLB*, Brunel to Rennie, 16 January 1852: a letter of the following day stated this recommendation to the Docks Committee. On 5 November 1851 Brunel had given a warm reference for Rennie to his namesake Sir John Rennie—they do not appear to have been related—who was seeking a contractor for Cardiff Docks.

[2] *PLB*, Brunel to Bell, 24 June 1852. Bell appears to have been about to depart for employment elsewhere.

[3] *PLB*, Brunel to Richard Poole King, 21 October 1852. Brunel also points out that the lapse of over four years since completion of the contract has meant that the Committee has gained 20 per cent in interest on the sum due.

veyed to Rennie who refused it,[1] but agreement was finally reached by the end of the year.[2]

This settlement was the effective termination of Brunel's active involvement in Bristol Docks, although there are a few references in the Private Letter Books to advice on various points of detail.[3] But there is a rather moving swan-song to report. When Bristol was once more considering major port improvements in 1858, Brunel was approached about undertaking them. He was out of the country at the time, recuperating partially from a prolonged illness, but on his return his clerk wrote to L. Bruton of the Bristol Docks Committee:

> Mr. Brunel has returned to England and I have communicated to him the movement that is being made at Bristol towards improving the Port. . . . I am writing this note to you as a *private* one by Mr. Brunel's desire to say how much gratified he would be if the Bristol people were to put the matter into his hands, so many of them being his friends, the Miles', Brights' and others, and the circumstance that it was at Bristol that he commenced his professional life. At the same time Mr. Brunel would wish it to be clearly understood that he would not on any account wish that the promoters of the intended projects should on his account be prevented from consulting and employing any other Engineer, rather than himself, if by so doing all interests in the work would be more benefitted, and in any other case, Mr. Brunel would feel much disappointed if he had not the offer made to him to become the Engineer of so interesting and important a work.[4]

Nothing came of the approach, and a little over a year later

---

[1] *PLB*, Brunel to Rennie, 8 November 1852 and 20 November 1852.

[2] *PLB*, Letters of 26 January 1852, 31 October 1852, 20 December 1852, and 27 December 1852. The sum paid in settlement of the account is given as £6,000, but it is not possible to tell what proportion of this represented the excess being claimed. The Docks Committee were rather tart in their letters to Brunel at this time.

[3] See, for instance, letter of 8 May 1852, when he advised the Resident Engineer T. E. Blackwell on some technical points. There is sufficient evidence to cause me to modify my earlier judgement that he lost all interest in the Docks after completion of the South Lock, but nothing as yet to indicate that he made any charge for his services after 1848.

[4] *PLB*, Bennett to L. Bruton, 17 August 1858.

Brunel was dead. Bristol had to wait another decade for the improvements, and then on a much more modest scale than those which had been projected. The fact was that the traditional port of Bristol, in the heart of the city several miles from the mouth of the Avon, the fierce tidal flow of which made it an increasing hazard as the size of ships grew, was no longer suitable for ocean traffic. Brunel had realised this as early as 1844, when submitting his proposals for the reconstruction of the South Lock:

> I have recommended these dimensions because I believe they would be sufficient to accommodate all ordinary Steam Boats built for the Irish Trade—and this I now think is sufficient for the Port of Bristol.[1]

The future for the port lay nearer the mouth of the Avon, and, as we will see, Brunel had views on this also. But the fact that the Floating Harbour survives today is in part a monument to Brunel, for it incorporates his improvements in water flow and scouring technique which have prevented it from silting up. And his South Lock, although long disused and deprived of its spectacular gates, is still an impressive piece of masonry when viewed at low tide, with the swing bridge which he designed to cross it now disused but intact nearby.

Although his life-span was so short, Brunel was one of those rare men to become a legend in his own time, and the outstanding reasons for his prominent place in the public imagination were his identification with the visionary Great Western Railway and the three great ships which in a sense stemmed from it. Latimer, of course, was right to see the adoption of Brunel's schemes such as the broad gauge as economic mistakes, and if the counsels of caution and economy had prevailed over vision and imagination Brunel's services would have been anathema to all railway companies. Latimer quotes with approval a remark by George Stephenson that all the railway lines in the kingdom would eventually be linked together as an overwhelming argument for the narrow gauge.[2] But Brunel's objective was to provide a radically new system of comfortable high-speed travel, and if the detailed fulfilment of this aim could have matched its imaginative conception it is more than likely that

[1] Brunel's Report to the BDC, June 1844.   [2] Latimer, *op. cit.* p. 247.

all main lines would have adopted his broad gauge. The remarkable thing, after all, is not that Brunel failed but that he came so close to success. The broad gauge system was established first between London and Bristol, but pushed on into Devon and Cornwall and fanned out into South Wales and the Midlands. From his appointment as Engineer to what was shortly to become the G.W.R. in 1833 until his death Brunel master-minded one of the largest railway empires in the country, and the only one which attempted to apply rational and systematic principles to developing a new pattern of high-speed transport.

The new railway was promoted by a group of the same enterprising Bristol merchants and businessmen who supported the Clifton Bridge project, harbour improvements, and other innovations. They included Robert Bright, John Cave, Henry Bush, C. P. Fripp, Peter Maze, George Gibbs, John Harford, and T. R. Guppy, to most of whom Brunel was already an admired acquaintance, and in the case of Guppy at least he was shortly to become a close personal friend. It is hardly surprising, therefore, that when Nicholas Roch suggested him as their engineer they were ready to accept him, even though he refused to agree with their proposal to adopt the lowest estimate for the route: "You are holding out," he warned them, "a premium to the man who will make you the most flattering promises, and it is quite obvious that he who has the least reputation at stake, or the most to gain by temporary success, and least to lose by the consequence of a disappointment, must be the winner in such a race."[1] The committee accepted the admonition from the 26 year-old engineer. Both these Bristol men and the London men who shortly joined them—George Henry Gibbs, Charles Russell, C. A. Saunders, and others—were charmed and impressed by Brunel's abilities, and remained strikingly loyal to him throughout the early vicissitudes of the G.W.R. It is perhaps significant, however, that the original preponderance of Bristol men dwindled over the years, as the G.W.R. system expanded.

The Great Western Railway Act was approved, on the second attempt, in August 1835. Five years later the stretch from Bristol to Bath was opened to public traffic, and by June 1841

[1] Quoted Celia Noble, *op. cit.* p. 116.

through rail communication between Bristol and London was completed. In the same month, the Bristol & Exeter railway opened its first stretch from Bristol to Bridgwater. Exeter was reached by 1844 and Plymouth by 1848. Meanwhile, the Bristol & Gloucester Railway, authorised in 1839, was opened as a broad gauge railway in 1844, although it was subsequently acquired by the Midland Railway and converted to standard gauge. The Wilts, Somerset & Weymouth Railway was authorised in 1845 and many other important local links put in hand under Brunel's auspices, one of the last and most important being the South Wales Junction project which was still incomplete at the time of his death. At the centre of this Bristol network was the G.W.R. terminus at Temple Meads, designed by Brunel and opened in 1841, and the Bristol and Exeter terminus built at rightangles to it—an arrangement which drew further caustic comment from Latimer.

The main features of the G.W.R. and its associated railways have been very adequately chronicled, and it is not necessary to review any of the details here.[1] For our purposes it is enough to observe that the establishment of this great railway empire was one of I. K. Brunel's outstanding achievements, and that it was built largely on the base of Bristol enterprise and Bristol capital. Other interests, and particularly those of the London promoters of the G.W.R., were represented in the managerial direction (although great care was taken to exclude the dissident voices of Liverpool and other northern investors), but Bristol remained the natural hub of the broad gauge system. Many of the relevant company meetings were held there, and much of the business in the early years was administered from Temple Meads. The directors confronted an especially difficult meeting of proprietors at the station in August 1849 when they proposed reducing the dividend from 4 per cent to 2 per cent. The circumstances of the half-yearly meeting were not propitious, with the railway boom clearly running itself out, with the collapse of

---

[1] The standard account is still E. T. MacDermot, *History of the Great Western Railway* (1927. Revised edition by C. R. Clinker, 1964). See also Jack Simmons (ed.) *The Birth of the Great Western Railway—Extracts from the Diary and Correspondence of George Henry Gibbs* (Bath, 1971). Much early documentary material on the GWR survives in the archives of the British Transport Commission

George Hudson's Midland Railway empire, with the recent engineering problems on the South Devon Railway, where Brunel had been obliged to recommend the abandonment of the atmospheric experiment, and in addition a serious cholera epidemic was then raging in the city of Bristol. But the oratory of Charles Russell and C. A. Saunders, the Chairman and Secretary of the G.W.R. respectively, succeeded in mollifying the critics. The local newspaper noted that:

> little Isidore (sic) Brunel, creeping into a corner, laughed securely over Lord Barrington's shoulder.[1]

But the same newspaper recalled this incident twenty-two years later in less disparaging terms, when giving a notice to the publication of the biography of Brunel by his son. Under the heading "Isambard Kingdom Brunel and the Old Railway Days" it commented:

> Though the "little giant", as some one called him has been "gone from our gaze" about thirteen or fourteen years, we can still see him with our mind's eye sitting "calm as the halcyon" behind the row of Directors at the stormy half-yearly meetings in Temple-meads. . . . He contemplated the hurly-burly before him with the composure of a philosopher and the quiet enjoyment of a humourist, even though his own "extravagance" was the subject under discussion.[2]

Brunel's presence was certainly regarded as essential to the smooth running of any G.W.R. meeting in those formative years.

The Private Letter Books contain a few interesting references to Bristol railway material, although not to the G.W.R. Much of it relates to the Bristol and Gloucester Railway, perhaps because its development was more tortuous than the other local lines, but most of it is of a purely routine nature. In April 1843 there is a draft paper on relations between the Bristol and Gloucester and the G.W.R., with pencil annotations by Brunel.[3] A year later Brunel wrote to the Bristol and Gloucester Directors advising caution on the construction of a new goods station:

[1] *Bristol Times and Bath Advocate*, 18 August 1849.
[2] *Bristol Times and Mirror*, 28 January 1871.
[3] *PLB* (no date) Vol. 2C, pp. 163–71.

Bristol is not Liverpool and if you carried for nothing you would not make a larger *regular Trade*—than even at moderate prices. . . . Railway people at the present moment are all mad —and excuse my saying it the B. & G. amongst the number but when Nov comes—and shares drop and the public begin to learn that you and the rest have been carrying on an enormous trade at a loss like the cheap linen Drapers there will be a dreadful reaction.[1]

Similar caution had been shown in Brunel's instructions to the locomotive engineers a year earlier:

I shd. wish also the engines to be altogether rather lighter and to omit the ornamental brass work—cover to the dome etc.[2]

On the southern branches from Bristol, Brunel responded to an invitation in May 1844 to become engineer for the Weymouth line, but expressed reservations about the proposed route:

I observe you speak of a *Bath* and Weymouth line—now I think the practicability of a direct line from Bath itself is more than questionable. The Gt. Westn. Rly Compy are now projecting a line to Frome. . . . On the other hand it is quite necessary to consider whether the Bristol & Exeter Ry does not really offer the most advantageous line of communication[3]

In the last year of his life, Brunel was engaged on the Bristol & South Wales Junction Railway, projecting a line north from the city through Ashley Down and Patchway to the proposed New Passage Ferry. He was concerned to obtain the services of a competent Resident Engineer to do the preliminary work and wrote to a former Assistant, C. Richardson:

I want a man acquainted with tunnelling and who will with a moderate amount of inspecting assistance look after the Tunnel with his own eyes—for I am beginning to be sick of Inspectors who see nothing—and resident engineers who

[1] *PLB*, Brunel to G. Jones, 18 April 1844.

[2] *PLB*, Brunel to R. Jackson of Fenton, Murray & Jackson of Leeds, 28 August 1843. The firm was building locomotives for the B & G. The comparison is with "those made by you for the GWR Co."

[3] *PLB*, Brunel to A. Jamieson, 6 and 9 May 1844.

reside at home and he must be one to whom salary is not the principal object.

Brunel was only able to offer £300 p.a. rising to £450 when the full works commenced, but as a compensation he pointed out:

> the country immediately north of Bristol I should think a delightful one to live in—beautiful country—good society near Bristol & Clifton etc.—I can't vouch for any cricketing but should think it highly probable . . .[1]

Richardson clearly did not find the salary very attractive, but as he was not then in employment Brunel was able to press him:

> If you desire on the other hand to go to work again . . . I think this an excellent opportunity and again offer it you provided you assure me that you enter upon it with pleasure and that a resumption of active life is an object to you.[2]

Richardson accepted and Brunel soon found a pretext for increasing his salary to £400,[3] but the project languished with his death, and was not completed in 1863.

The extension of the broad gauge network of railway lines from Bristol was a matter of great concern to Brunel, and until the Midland Railway acquired the Bristol and Gloucester and pushed the narrow gauge through to Temple Meads in 1854 he had a virtual monopoly on railway engineering in the region. Many physical monuments remain to this activity, from the railway routes themselves to many points of detailed design such as the decorative entrances to the tunnels between Bristol and Bath. The most important of these monuments, however, is the original Temple Meads terminus, still substantially intact although converted into a car park and in a poor state of repair. Brunel designed the station with the wide wooden-beamed roof as it exists today except for the introduction of a channel for light and ventilation along the ridge. This gives an unimpeded space 72 ft. wide between the two rows of iron

---

[1] *PLB*, Brunel to C. Richardson, 14 September 1858. The tunnel mentioned would have been that at Patchway. The reference to cricket is interesting because Brunel had earlier had cause to reprimand Richardson for over-indulgence in such relaxation—14 September 1853.

[2] *PLB*, Brunel to C. Richardson, 17 September 1858.

[3] *PLB*, Brunel to C. Richardson, 22 July 1859.

columns which carry the beams in cantilever fashion, with their outermost extremities anchored in the masonry walls. The elegant "hammer beams" were added for decorative effect and have no constructional significance. The other important part of Brunel's station is the neo-Tudor facade on Temple Gate, intact except for one wing which was removed to make way for the approach to the enlarged Temple Meads station in 1878. The whole structure survives as the oldest railway terminus in the world to preserve most of its original shape, and as such it is a national monument of outstanding importance. Various projects have been discussed for the re-use of this important building, but as yet nothing has been decided about its future.[1]

The story has frequently been told of how members of the G.W.R. board of directors took the decisive step towards extending their railway from Bristol to New York by way of a steam ship, although it is not certain whether the initial conception of the idea was Brunel's or Guppy's.[2] Suffice it to say that the decision gave Brunel the opportunity to reveal his genius as a marine engineer. There is a saga associated with all three of Brunel's great ships. The first two were built in Bristol and their stories have become part of the history of the city. Unfortunately, the Private Letter Books have little to add to this story, and most of the documents associated with the Great Western Steamship Company, the business formed to build the two Bristol ships, seem to have disappeared without trace. After the collapse of the Company in 1848, and when he was already engaged on preliminary work for an even more gigantic ship, Brunel tried to obtain a copy of one of his own reports. His clerk wrote to one of the men who had been involved in the company:

> Mr. Brunel will be much obliged if you can obtain for him a complete set of the Half Yearly reports of the Steam Ship Comp. Mr. Brunel thinks that he wrote a report to the Directors recommending the use of iron in building the Gt. Britain. If so could you send a copy of it and at the same time

[1] For a general account, see R. A. Buchanan and Neil Cossons, *Industrial Archaeology of the Bristol Region* (Newton Abbot, 1969). There are more specialised treatments in: J. W. Totterdill, "A peculiar form of construction", *Journal Of The Bristol & Somerset Society of Architects*, vol. 5, pp. 111–12; and J. Mosse, "Bristol Temple Meads", *BIAS Journal 4*, 1971.

[2] Rolt, *op. cit.* p. 191, contrast Latimer *op. cit.* 218.

can you inform Mr. Brunel of the date of his long report to
the Directors upon the screw . . .[1]

There is no clue to the answer received to this enquiry, but it is
possible that the reports had already disappeared together with
other papers of the Steamship Company.

The Great Western Steamship Company was set up in 1835
with Peter Maze, a Bristol merchant with interests in railways
and the cotton industry, as its chairman, and with Claxton as
managing director. The first ship, the *Great Western*, was a
timber-hulled paddle steamer designed by Brunel and built by
William Patterson in his yard at Prince's Wharf. Maudslays'
provided the power unit with a pair of side-lever steam engines.
The ship was launched on 19 July 1837 and made its maiden
voyage to New York in April 1838, being narrowly beaten for
the honour to be the first westward steam-powered crossing of
the Atlantic by the hastily adapted *Sirius*. By July 1839, work
had begun on the construction of a much larger vessel, to be
built in iron—the *Great Britain*—and within a year the original
design for paddle wheels had been abandoned in favour of screw
propulsion. Brunel had the major responsibility not only for the
hull, which was—and is—a brilliant work of technical perfection, but also for the engine and the screw. All of this required
detailed experiments, consultation, and reports, but as we have
seen only fragments of the latter survive, where they are incorporated in the Private Letter Books. Thus in 1840 there is a
20-page report on the experiments conducted on screw propulsion concluding:

> From all that I have said it must be evident to you Gentle-
> men that my opinion is strong and decided in favour of the
> advantage of employing the screw in the new ship.[2]

And about the time of the launching ceremony in July 1843 two
long letters to Guppy are included in the series on the design of
the screw[3] and the construction of the hull.[4] For the next

---

[1] *PLB*, Bennett to W. H. Bennet, 18 February 1852.
[2] *PLB*, Report by Brunel, 1 October 1840.
[3] *PLB*, Brunel to Guppy, 11 July 1843.
[4] *PLB*, Brunel to Guppy, no date, vol. 2C, pp. 189–93: the subject matter
suggests that it was a much earlier letter than the former one. Both letters
include some interesting line-drawings.

eighteen months the great ship was trapped in the Floating Harbour until modifications could be made in the two locks through which it had to pass. This involved delicate negotiations with the Docks Company, and compounded the unhelpful attitude of the Company towards the *Great Western*, which had been denied a decrease in dues on account of its inability to use the main harbour facilities regularly. This contributed to the increasing stiffness between Brunel and the dock authorities.[1] With great difficulty the *Great Britain* eventually left the harbour on 11 December 1844, and late that night Brunel wrote to the directors of the South Wales Railway apologising for his inability to attend their meeting the next day:

> We have had an unexpected difficulty with the Gt. Britain this morning—she stuck in the Lock—we *did* get her back—I have been hard at work all day altering the masonry of the lock—tonight our last tide we have succeeded in getting her through but being dark we have been obliged to ground her outside—and I confess I cannot leave her till I see her afloat again and all clear of our difficulty here—I have as you will admit much at stake here and I am too anxious to leave her.[2]

Once she was away from the harbour, the link between Bristol and the *Great Britain* was effectively broken until her triumphant return in July 1970. The *Great Western* also had started to use Liverpool regularly from 1843, and with the collapse of the Company she was sold at an auction in 1847 and spent the next nine years until being broken up operating from Southampton. Thus ended the association of Brunel as a ship-builder with the City of Bristol.

We have now reviewed the major areas of Brunel's activities in the Bristol region, but there were a number of minor activities—or at least less significant activities in terms of their achievement—which deserve a mention. First among these, and deriving from his involvement with big ships and dock

---

[1] *PLB*, Brunel to BDC 6 July? 1844, setting out his request for modifications to the locks in order to release the ship. See also the account in Grahame Farr, *The Steamship Great Britain* (Bristol Branch of the Historical Association, 1965).

[2] *PLB*, Brunel to Hunt, 11 December 1844. Like many of the "prime" passages in the Letter Books, this is quoted in Rolt, p. 207.

improvements, was Brunel's part in plans to provide deep-water docking facilities in positions more accessible than the Floating Harbour. A scheme had been canvassed for a "floating pier" in the early 1830s, and W. S. Mylne carried out an engineering survey for this (the beautifully finished drawings survive in the Port of Bristol Authority archives). The scheme was revived and modified at the end of the decade, when Brunel submitted a long report to a committee investigating port improvements, in which he strongly recommended the project for a pier at Portishead in a bid to capture the leadership of trans-oceanic trade. He concluded:

> . . . it is now for you to determine whether, by a compara-tively easy, if prompt, effort you will place Bristol in that position, while there is yet time to command a decided preference in the establishment of such a trade, which can afterwards be easily maintained, and which must lead to an immense extension: but which, if now lost, and if the present opportunity be allowed to escape, may never be regained.[1]

Shortly afterwards Brunel was offended by the committee and complained that it had consulted another engineer:

> I need hardly say that it is with great pain that I feel obliged in justice to myself to address this letter to a committee of gentlemen of Bristol, with the prosperity of which place I had flattered myself I had already and was about still more to associate my name, but I think no professional man, having the slightest regard to his reputation could do otherwise.[2]

In a letter of the same day to a personal friend on the com-mittee he was more specific:

> . . . the person preferred to me was my Surveyor Assistant, a short time back, on the Plymouth Railway, a man unknown . . . a stranger (and) in every respect my acknowledged inferior.[3]

The subject of this disparaging comparison was J. M. Rendel, a

[1] Report by Brunel, printed by order the Committee, 26 December 1839. Latimer, p. 397, curiously attributed the scheme to John Macneil.

[2] *PLB*. Brunel to Protheroe, Chairman of the Portishead Pier Com-mittee, 27 January 1840.

[3] *PLB*, Brunel to Robert Bright, 27 January 1840.

fellow civil engineer with whom Brunel had several clashes during his career. But in this case the trouble was cleared up, because five years later Brunel put forward another scheme which led to the establishment of the Portbury Pier and Railway Company with a capital of £200,000.[1] This caused some anxiety among the trustees of the Clifton Bridge:

> I have heard from Osborne of the difficulty arisen as to what I may call my *scheme*—however altho *paternal* affection made me determined to do everything I could for Clifton Bridge which must and shall be finished *filial* affection for my parent shall not fail me—Bristol interests must be first thought of—and if one can't have a Portishead line that will benefit the bridge—we must have some other—for I quite agree with you that all hands must pull together for our revered parent the City of Bristol—and I am always ready to help.[2]

The resources of this venture appear soon to have been exhausted, as Brunel submitted an account in February 1849 for £674.13.1 "up to the time of the suspension of the works",[3] and Latimer records that the project was formally abandoned in 1852.[4] Brunel's final comment was one of exasperation:

> Sir—I must beg of you not to address me letters on the subject of your affairs with the Portishead Ry. Co. I never had anything to do with the matter. I know nothing about it and cannot be bothered with it . . .[5]

A new attempt to establish a railway to Portishead with a deep-water pier was made in the following decade. The railway was opened in 1867 and the pier in 1868, but the latter was subsequently made redundant by the construction of Portishead Dock.

Another Bristol project in which Brunel was involved was the provision of water works. The decades of the 1840s and 1850s were distinguished by a new civic consciousness in Britain, born out of cholera epidemics and other scourges, which showed itself amongst other ways in the establishment of pure water supplies.

[1] Report in PBA archives. See also the account in Latimer, *op. cit.* pp. 396–7. [2] *PLB*, Brunel to J. N. Miles, 28 April 1845.
[3] *PLB*, Bennett to F. R. Ward, 22 February 1849.
[4] Latimer, *op. cit.* p. 397. [5] *PLB*, Brunel to W. Clarke, 6 July 1853.

Brunel was consulted on several such schemes, including Glasgow and Manchester, and it was appropriate therefore that he should make a contribution to the health of Bristol in this way. The first mention of his involvement in "Clifton Water Works" is in a letter of 1841,[1] and a year later he reported to a Committee of the Society of Merchant Venturers that the estimated cost of establishing water works in Clifton would be £1,364.[2] Brunel was optimistic about the amount of water which the spring, discovered in 1836, could provide. Latimer alluded to:

> Mr. Brunel having, characteristically, asserted that the Society's springs would furnish an "ample" supply for the whole population[3]

The next development was in 1845 when Brunel wrote to his Chief Assistant in Bristol:

> I am very much surprised at the determination of the Society of Merchnts. not to employ Guppy who would certainly have given us the best engines—did you tell them so?[4]

The Society of Merchant Venturers' pumping station at Black Rock in the Clifton Gorge was built in this year, the "somewhat fantastic design" winning a sneer from Latimer.[5] Surviving photographs of the building show a structural similarity with the Italianate engine houses designed by Brunel for the atmospheric section of the South Devon Railway. In 1846 Brunel was called in to consult with representatives of a rival undertaking, Bristol Water Works Company, which was endeavouring to supply the whole city rather than Clifton:

> The promoters of the Clifton Water Works Bill will be very happy to meet any parties representing the promoters of your water works Bill to endeavour to see if a more satisfactory

[1] *PLB*, Brunel to J. Marmont?, 7 October 1841.

[2] *PLB*, Brunel to Society of Merchant Venturers, 20 September 1842 and 4 October 1842.

[3] J. Latimer, *The History of the Society of Merchant Venturers of the City of Bristol* (Bristol, 1903), p. 264.

[4] *PLB*, Brunel to J. W. Hammond, 7 June 1845. I am inferring that this is a reference to the water works engines, although it is not completely certain.

[5] Latimer, *Annals*, p. 281 and *History of the Society of Merchant Venturers*, p. 264, although he does not attribute it in either work to Brunel.

plan can be suggested by which the public objects they have in view can be attained, and which at the same time shall be satisfactory to your company—It appears to them that a fair Division of district will be the most rational principle on which to go, but this may be a matter of discussion.[1]

But Parliament preferred the more comprehensive scheme, and this eventually absorbed the Society's water works, the Merchant Venturers receiving £18,000 for its plant. It was presumably in the course of negotiating a satisfactory purchase price that Brunel wrote again:

I have not been able to reduce any of the expenses and liabilities of the Society of Merchants by counterordering any works or orders for materials or machinery.[2]

The only other reference to this enterprise is a cryptic note to James Simpson in 1848:

I was very much disgusted to hear the other day that an assistant of mine J. Yockney (?) had been making a fool of himself in some arbitration case against your W. Works Cy . . .[3]

Brunel's cordial relations with Simpson are illustrated by another letter enquiring about the availability of water for his work on the site of the South Entrance Lock:

"My Dear Sir—I would very much like to use some water power at Bristol at two different places—Temple Meads and near the Locks at Cumberland Basin. Will you tell me whether you have now or are likely soon to have and *when* water laid on with a high pressure and *what pressure* at either of these places? Some plans of mine are entirely dependant on your answer, and I shall therefore be glad to hear at your earliest convenience.[4]

[1] *PLB*. Brunel to C. Savery, 23 March 1846. There is another reference in the middle of Brunel's aggrieved correspondence with Osborne about his treatment at the hands of the BDC (Brunel to Osborne 8 May 1846: see above, and letter to Osborne of 1 May 1846.)

[2] *PLB*, Brunel to Savery, 5 November 1846.

[3] *PLB*, Brunel to Jas. Simpson, 30 March 1848: a copy of his Assistant's letter of apology is appended, from which it is clear that the company in question is Bristol Water Works Company.

[4] *PLB*, Brunel to Jas. Simpson, 30 November 1848.

Brunel was experimenting with hydraulic machinery at Temple Meads for operating lifts in order to connect the goods shed with the main line, 12 ft. above it.[1] Such apparatus was still in its infancy and it was not used at the entrance locks until the improvements of 1871.[2] James Simpson was an engineer with extensive experience of water works, who became President of the Civil Engineers in 1854, and Brunel treated him with genuine respect.[3] The Black Rock pumping station was demolished in 1864 to make way for the railway to Avonmouth. Latimer says that it was "a puzzle to strangers owing to its bizarre architecture" and reports that it was at one point considered converting it into a church for sailors and bargemen.[4]

Among the more unexpected of Brunel's Bristol projects was the work he did on the Cathedral. The Dean invited him to examine some defects in the fabric of the Cathedral, so that Brunel wrote in June 1850 proposing:

> to give a couple of hours for a cursory inspection to form some opinion of the subject. . . . I can be at the Cathedral at 5 o'clock on Tuesday morning next, having to leave Bristol by train to Exeter at 7.50 . . .[5]

This early appointment must have been kept, as three weeks later Brunel submitted his report to the Dean. He referred favourably to a previous survey by J. F. Welsh, but differed from this in thinking that the defects were those to be expected in any old building and presented no immediate threat.

> Mr. Welsh no doubt would feel little anxiety as to the building standing 24 hours—I feel little as to its standing 24 years —we both feel that repairs are required. . . . The next or the following generation will probably be called upon for more extensive repairs and restoration.[6]

[1] Brunel, *Life*, p. 84.

[2] See R. A. Buchanan, *Nineteenth century Engineers in the Port of Bristol* (Bristol Branch of the Historical Association, 1971).

[3] See *PLB*, letter of 30 November 1848, where Brunel went on to say: "I like your aqueducts very much" and to make some suggestions, with marginal illustrations, for the cross-section of the aqueducts.

[4] Latimer, *Annals*, p. 281n.

[5] *PLB*, Brunel to the Revd. E. Banks, 1 June 1850. The Dean at this time was G. E. May, who had just begun a term of office which was to last for 41 years.   [6] *PLB*, Brunel to the Revd. Dean of Bristol, 24 June 1850.

Despite this reassurance, the Dean decided to commission a thorough survey of the Cathedral, and Brunel was again invited to give his advice.[1] Shortly afterwards he consulted Welsh about the costs of repairs:

> have you any instance of work at all similar being latterly executed in Bristol to compare it with—what is doing at St. Mary Redcliffe?[2]

Whatever the repairs involved, they do not appear to have required any subsequent correspondence, although the exchange throws an interesting light on Brunel's method of work.

There are many other Bristol regional references, of an even less substantial nature. These include a qualified approval of Stephen Moulton's india rubber springs, then being manufactured at Bradford-on-Avon;[3] many references to the use of creosote as a timber preservative, possibly in connection with the Crews Hole firm;[4] and an interesting and prophetic reference to the possibility of a Severn Bridge at the site of the Old Passage:

> I believe firmly that before 50 years are over there will be one (or a tunnel).[5]

The bridge took rather more than a hundred years to materialise, but the tunnel was operating in just over thirty years so on balance the forecast was accurate.[6]

It is probably not exaggerating to say that I. K. Brunel made a greater contribution to the landscape of the Bristol region than any other single individual before or since, with his splendid bridge over the Clifton Gorge, the railway network

[1] *PLB*, Brunel to the Dean, 25 September 1850. Brunel advised including an architect in the survey team.

[2] *PLB*, Brunel to J. F. Welsh, 24 October 1850.

[3] *PLB*, Brunel to Stephen Moulton, 20 January 1852.

[4] *PLB*, see letters of 24 December 1839, 30 June 1843, 30 January 1846, 23 September 1846, and 18 June 1847—the last of these being an enquiry about the effect of creosote to Michael Faraday.

[5] *PLB*, Brunel to J. Hooper, 30 May 1854.

[6] The Severn Tunnel was open to traffic in 1886, and the Severn Bridge in 1966. But of course the Sharpness Bridge further up the Severn, was open in 1879: this was demolished after a barge struck one of the piers and put it out of action in the 1960s.

radiating from the original Temple Meads Station, the improved harbour, and now the great ship which occupies the dry dock from which she was launched in 1843. Most of this work was done by 1848, although at that time the piers of the bridge stood gaunt and unfinished. The twenty years 1828–48 were certainly the most creative in the relationship between Brunel and Bristol. By 1848, the group of intimate friends on whom the success of the relationship depended had begun to disperse. Roch had already gone into retirement in Pembroke, Guppy removed to Italy in 1849 after the collapse of the Great Western Steamship Company, and established an engineering business in Naples.[1] Claxton remained involved in Brunel's enterprises, but left Bristol. So were loosened the bonds of personal affection which had tied Brunel closely to Bristol and which made him proud to regard himself as "a Bristol man", and other preoccupations removed him still further from the affairs of the city. To the end, however, he retained his interest in Bristol and, as we have seen, proclaimed his readiness to assist "the spirited merchants of Bristol" in any worth-while enterprise. If Latimer's views accurately reflect the feeling of late nineteenth-century Bristolians about Brunel, counting the cost of the broad gauge, it is little credit to their powers of discernment. With the advantage of greater hindsight it is possible to perceive the wisdom of Daniel Gooch's valedictory remarks on Brunel:

> By his death the greatest of England's engineers was lost, the man with the greatest originality of thought and power of execution, bold in his plans but right. The commercial world thought him extravagant; but although he was so, great things are not done by those who sit down and count the cost of every thought and act.[2]

Posterity has decided in favour of the judgement of Gooch rather than that of Latimer, and however much his projects might have cost their ancestors, Bristolians are generally happy now to acknowledge I. K. Brunel as an adopted citizen. He is certainly one of the handful of masterminds whose imagination helped to mould the city and one of those in whose works the city can still take pride.

[1] Rolt, *op. cit.* p. 98.   [2] Gooch, *Diary*, quoted Rolt, *op. cit.* p. 289

XI

The economic development of Bristol in the nineteenth century: an enigma?

By B. W. E. Alford

I T is an oft-repeated fact that until the early nineteenth century Bristol was the second city in England after London in terms of population, wealth and general standing. It is, of course, a convenient way of underlining Bristol's prominence in the eighteenth century; yet it also reflects a certain proclivity among historians and other local commentators to devote close attention to various aspects of Bristol's economic, social, and political life in the eighteenth century and to eschew corresponding interest in the century that followed. Whatever the reasons for this omission, it is certainly true that the economic development of Bristol over the nineteenth century remains something of an unknown. Perhaps, it is more of an enigma than an unknown, since although it is generally accepted that the basis of Bristol's eighteenth-century prosperity had crumbled by the 1840s, over the nineteenth century as a whole its population continued to expand; while the bay windows, carved freestone, and terracotta of Cotham, Redland and late Victorian Clifton are apparent monuments to the existence of a reasonably prosperous and fecund middle class during this period. The purpose of this very general and wide-ranging essay is to attempt to suggest some answers to this puzzle and, at least, to indicate some avenues of enquiry which might prove profitable to others.

It is necessary to begin with a brief summary of the position of Bristol in the national economy at the end of the eighteenth century. Although past its height Bristol was still the commercial and industrial capital of a large region. Through the Avon, the Bristol Channel, the Severn and the Wye, Bristol possessed, by eighteenth-century standards, good communications with Cornwall, South Wales, the south Midlands, and the West Country. The city was the centre of a network of roads which ran to the east as far as London, and to the north-east as far as Leeds. The population of the urban area at the turn of the century was of the order of 60,000, and the region of which it could claim to be the centre accounted for over one-quarter of the total population of Great Britain.[1] In the industrial field, in the metal trades, in particular, Bristol was noted for the production of brass of exceptional quality, for its large iron foundries which cast "all kinds of utensils and cutlery including large cannon", and for its near monopoly of lead shot.[2] As the direct consequence of the port's West Indian trade there were twenty sugar refineries in Bristol and the local boast was that "loaf sugar is made here and sold on better terms than it can be anywhere else";[3] and closely allied to this industry was that of distilling. Twelve glass houses, producing every conceivable type of glass for domestic and overseas markets, made Bristol one of the leading centres of the industry in the country.[4] Among other less important industries were those of soap, leather, wool, porter brewing, tobacco, chocolate, and a variety of finishing trades, which linked the industries of the port and its hinterland to its own large urban and regional market and to its major trading areas of the Atlantic Triangle, Ireland and North-West Europe. Furthermore, as a leading port it contained a whole range of trades and services associated with ships and ship-building.[5]

In the nineteenth century all this changed. The story is

---

[1] For a good survey of the evidence relating to this period see W. E. Minchinton, "Bristol—metropolis of the West in the eighteenth century", *Transactions of the Royal Historical Society*, 5th ser., vol. 4, 69–89.

[2] See John Latimer, *Annals of Bristol in the Eighteenth Century* (Bristol, 1893), pp. 453–4.

[3] *Mathews's Bristol Directory* (Bristol, 1794), pp. 40–1, and generally; I. V. Hall, "The Sugar Trade of Bristol", (unpublished M.A. thesis, University of Bristol, 1925); and by the same author, "The Garlicks, two generations of a Bristol family", *TBGAS*, lxxx–lxxxi, 132–59.

[4] B. W. E. Alford, "The flint and bottle glass industry in the early nineteenth century: a case study of a Bristol firm", *Business History*, x, 12–21; A. C. Powell, "Glassmaking in Bristol", *TBGAS*, xlvii, 211–57.

[5] See Grahame Farr, *Bristol Shipbuilding in the Nineteenth Century* (Bristol Branch of the Historical Association, 1971).

usually told as follows:[1] up to the 1840s the Bristol economy remained fairly buoyant, though the war and post-war years from 1810–20 had proved a difficult time; from the 1840s to the early 1860s Bristol went through a period of stagnation—as the forces of general industrial development undermined the basis of Bristol's economy—and, it is claimed, the most unpleasant symptoms of Bristol's relative national economic decline were festering houses in the centre of the city, the stench of effluent which saturated the banks of the Avon, and mortality rates surpassed only by Liverpool and Manchester; in the 1860s and the 1870s economic revival based on the boot and shoe, cocoa, tobacco, printing and stationery, and soap industries, combined with a "forward" dock policy and better provisions for sanitation, changed the face of the city; economic growth, bolstered by a new sense of civic awareness, then continued to the end of the century, although a little haltingly at the very end of the period because of growing competition from the South Wales ports.

Unquestionably, this picture of phoenix-like economic recovery in the latter part of the nineteenth century is inspired by the accepted pattern of population change in Bristol, and it is appropriately coloured by a selection of largely impressionistic evidence of economic and social developments. Shannon and Grebenik, and Hewitt, have analysed the population of Bristol between 1801 and 1901 in some detail.[2]

[1] See A. J. Pugsley, "Some Contributions towards the Study of the Economic Development of Bristol in the Eighteenth and Nineteenth Centuries", (unpublished M.A. thesis, University of Bristol, 1921), which contains a fairly comprehensive survey of the literature to that date, and the general line of approach adopted by Pugsley has been followed by subsequent writers. In particular see F. Hewitt, "Population and Urban Growth in East Bristol, 1800–1914", (unpublished Ph.D. thesis, University of Bristol, 1965); Donald John Webb, "The Changing Industrial Geography of the Port and City of Bristol since 1861: A Study in Port Function", (unpublished M.A. thesis, University of London, 1967); Helen E. Meller, "The Organized Provisions for Cultural Activities and their Impact on the Community 1870–1910: With Special Reference to the City of Bristol", (unpublished Ph.D. thesis, University of Bristol, 1968). These works together provide detailed references to more ephemeral accounts of Bristol's economic development over the nineteenth century.

[2] H. A. Shannon and E. Grebenik, *The Population of Bristol* (Cambridge 1943); also see F. Hewitt, *op. cit.*

On the face of it Table 1 does support the account of the general rhythm of Bristol's development outlined above. Hewitt certainly interpreted his evidence in this manner and in doing so followed closely the analysis put forward some years earlier by Pugsley, which dealt more specifically with economic development; in turn, both of them have been followed by

TABLE 1   Intercensal Rates of Population Change

Decade	Bristol Cluster* %	England and Wales %
1801–11	21.6	14.0
1811–21	18.3	18.1
1821–31	21.8	15.8
1831–41	19.1	14.3
1841–51	10.0	12.7
1851–61	11.5	11.9
1861–71	22.3	13.2
1871–81	20.6	14.4
1881–91	13.6	11.7
1891–1901	14.0	12.2

* The total population of the Bristol Cluster rose from 73,860 in 1801 to 360,984 in 1901.

[Source: F. Hewitt, "Population and Urban Growth in East Bristol, 1800–1914", (unpublished Ph.D. thesis, University of Bristol, 1965), p. 56.)

others writers. Yet their broad conclusions are, at the very least, open to serious question. For a start, there are well-known problems in using overall population figures as indicators of economic change, whether at the level of country, region or town. By themselves such data tell us nothing about occupational structure, the degree of unemployment, or the extent of underemployment. In the case of a town or city they tell us nothing about the nature of the surrounding region or how this affects patterns of migration between town and country. They tell us nothing about age structure, fertility, or mortality; for example, it has all too frequently been shown in the mid-twentieth century how, in some of the less developed parts of the world, improved medical provision of a fairly basic preventative type can cause prodigious upsurges of population leading to a falling level of economic well-being. Who is to say, therefore, that if there was an upsurge of population in Bristol in the mid-decades of the nineteenth century, it was not the consequence of the general national extension of basic measures of disease prevention, and thus by no means necessarily represented a corresponding improvement in economic well-being? In short, living longer should never automatically be associated with an easing of economic misery.

Quite apart from these general points, which amount to saying that the "accepted" interpretation of Bristol's population growth between 1801 and 1901 is not proven, there are more specific criticisms which it is necessary to bring out. Hewitt measures the growth of Bristol's population on the basis of the Bristol Cluster, which is defined as the geographical extent of the conurbation as it had developed by 1914. As a measure for Bristol alone it is very good since it does get over the problem of changes in boundaries between different census years, and it concentrates attention on the growth of the urban area as a whole, which is important when one is attempting to assess economic or social consequences of the expansion of population. But it is quite unsatisfactory, in the broader context, to compare population change between Bristol and the country as a *whole*. The growth in Bristol's population was, in effect, composed of two main elements: it was part of the general growth in the country's population, and it resulted, also, from the growing degree of urbanisation; indeed the whole point of defining a cluster area is in order to catch the full impact of suburban growth, which was such a major feature of the expansion of towns and cities towards the end of the nineteenth century. The latter development is not just simply a matter of net additional immigration within a given period (which Hewitt does take into consideration) but also one of the effects of this immigration in subsequent generations on birth and death rates, *combined* with age patterns and fertility and mortality rates, which tended to vary significantly between urban and rural areas. Therefore, to compare Bristol with England and Wales, as against comparing it with other urban cluster areas, is a comparison of extremely limited value. Furthermore, it is clear from Hewitt's figures that in the 1860s and 1870s a significant proportion of the expansion of Bristol's population was accounted for by immigration, and even though this might have been a response to the relative economic attractiveness of Bristol, by itself it tells us nothing about the absolute level of the urban economy at that time. Moreover, it is argued below that the figures for immigration are, in themselves, suspect.

At the comparative level, therefore, one needs to look at Bristol's growth against that of other leading towns and cities. Unfortunately there is no completely satisfactory way of doing this without an enormous investigation far beyond the bounds of this essay. The figures which are available for the main towns in the United Kingdom are calculated on the basis of administrative boundaries at the time of each census and not on the basis of cluster areas in 1914. Table 2, therefore, has been

TABLE 2   Intercensal Rates of Population Change*

Decade	Bristol Administrative Area %	72 Principal Towns in the U.K. %
1801–11	16	23
1811–21	20	30
1821–31	22	32
1831–41	19	26
1841–51	10	25
1851–61	12	18
1861–71	19	20
1871–81	13	21
1881–91	7	17
1891–1901	14	15

* Up to 1851 town populations are based on the areas of towns in 1851, as nearly as is possible. For 1851 onwards the figures used for decadal comparisons are based on town areas at the second of the two dates.

[Source: B. R. Mitchell with Phyllis Deane, *Abstract of British Historical Statistics* (Cambridge, 1962), pp. 24–7.]

produced by comparing the growth of Bristol with the largest towns in the United Kingdom (excluding London) on the basis of census boundaries. Now, although this has the unavoidable disadvantage of allowing some degree of randomness of comparison between towns in terms of when and how often boundary changes were made, this is, at least, counterbalanced by the fact that such changes tended to be made in the same census year—1891 being a prime example of this. Moreover, the

decadal growth rates which are shown in the table are calculated for consistent areas: as defined by the area of a town at
the subsequent census. Even so, this comparison is still open
to discrepancy but, significantly, the likelihood is that this
occurs in such a way as to *strengthen* the deductions which we
shall draw from Table 2. For, as an old established city, Bristol
possessed less "spare capacity" within its boundaries than a
young rapidly growing town and, thus, over the early decades
its apparent rate of growth would be lower because it would not
take account of expansion outside existing boundaries; con-
versely, boundary changes in the late nineteenth century have
the effect of exaggerating Bristol's growth in comparison with
towns generally. At any event, in the broad picture such dis-
tortions would appear to be minimal, and this assumption will
be borne out a little later by evidence of a different kind.

The picture given by Table 2 contrasts quite markedly with
that shown by Table 1. Throughout the whole period Bristol's
growth, by decade, was always below that of the large towns,
at certain times very much below. Moreover, the somewhat
special significance which some previous writers have claimed
for the 1860s and 1870s is not borne out by our figures. And
even if over the earlier decades this method of calculation works
to Bristol's disadvantage, it is clear from the table that the
margin of difference between Bristol and other towns is so wide
that the disadvantage would have to be extraordinarily large
before Bristol's growth could match the national rate, which
seems quite improbable. Further evidence along these lines can
be provided by simply ranking large towns: this shows Bristol to
have fallen from second to tenth position between 1801 and
1901, even after allowing for the enlargement of Bristol's
boundaries at the end of the period. More significant is the fact
that in 1901 there were seven other towns which were within
two-thirds the size of Bristol, whereas as late as 1841 only
Sheffield came within that category.[1]

To sum up: a careful balancing of the evidence of population
change does not support the view that there was a marked break
in Bristol's growth from 1861 onwards; indeed, the real break
is in the 1840s and 1850s when the rate of expansion drops

[1] See B. R. Mitchell with Phyllis Deane, *Abstract of British Historical
Statistics* (Cambridge, 1962), pp. 24–7.

significantly below the very moderate rate for the previous period. Even more strongly, population figures provide no support for the contention that such growth was "above the national average" over the latter part of the nineteenth century. With the exception of the 1861–71 period, the rate never again reached the levels of the first four decades and in the 1880s it was the lowest for the whole century. Of course, in the light of our earlier strictures on the relation between population change and economic development, it would be incorrect to dismiss completely the thesis of a return to economic buoyancy in Bristol in the late nineteenth century, but at least it encourages us to look harder at the evidence which has been brought forward to support such a thesis.

In some ways the first signs of Bristol's relative, if not absolute, economic decline were to be seen in the fortunes of the port.[1] Towards the end of the eighteenth century dock facilities had begun to prove inadequate—in particular there was need for a new floating harbour so that cargo handling could be more independent of the abnormally wide tidal range of the Avon-Severn confluence. A new harbour was eventually opened in 1810, but during the six years it had taken to construct it an acrimonious debate between various groups in the city had exposed many weaknesses in the organisation of the Dock Company. Theoretically the docks were financed through a series of dues levied on different services provided by the port authorities, but the multiplication of these dues and the corrupt and inefficient manner in which they were administered by the Corporation and by the Society of Merchant Venturers were contributing to the general and gradual strangulation of the port's commercial life. Then in 1807, as is well-known, the Society of Merchant Venturers secured the passage of the Bristol

---

[1] Subsequent details are drawn from Charles Wells, *A Short History of the Port of Bristol* (Bristol, 1909); A. J. Pugsley, *op cit.*; H. A. Cronne, T. W. Moody and D. B. Quinn (eds), *Essays in British and Irish History* ... (1949), pp. 200–17; B. W. E. Alford, *W. D. & H. O. Wills and the Development of the U.K. Tobacco Industry, 1786–1965* (1973), pp. 39–41. Pugsley, in particular, provides a full bibliography of the considerable amount of contemporary pamphleteering and propaganda on this issue. A major, and largely un-tapped series of records which contain a great deal on the development of the port over the early nineteenth century is the Treasury Letter Book series held at the Customs and Excise Library, London.

Wharfage Act which gave legal force to the dubious titles of various dues which they had collected, and secured those dues to the Society on a lease from the Corporation for £10 per annum: the dues in question were worth £4,000 per annum and very little of this money found its way back into the port in the form of improved facilities. This act has been described, almost certainly justifiably, as "an elaborate piece of legal chicanery" since it diverted resources which should have been for public benefit to private gain. However, the interlocking connection between the Corporation and the Society effectively removed any threat that the public interest would be served. Not surprisingly, venality was compounded with inefficiency. On average, taxes payable on ships and goods coming into the port of Bristol were inordinately more than corresponding taxes levied in London or Liverpool; for example, although many years earlier preferential charges had been applied to tobacco, Bristol merchants still had to pay taxes totalling three shillings per hogshead as compared with fivepence in Liverpool.

Apathy, inefficiency, vested interests, technical problems of land levels, exceptional tidal range, the declining national importance of industries located in the hinterland, and what proved to be the over-dependence of the port on West Indian and Irish trade, were forces too powerful to be surmounted. Evidence of the port's decline down to the late 1840s is plentiful. There were attempts to revive its fortunes, and one of the more important of these was the foundation of the Bristol Chamber of Commerce in 1823 by certain individuals who had been active in seeking reform of port administration. It published a number of reports on the docks, issued various legal challenges to the Corporation and Society of Merchant Venturers, and achieved very little—which is not surprising.[1] What is interesting, however, is that running through the records of years of protest, from individuals and organised groups such as the Chamber of Commerce, is a common feature: a general misunderstanding of the factors affecting the prosperity of Bristol and its region. Even the fiercest critics of port administration saw the problems affecting the economic fortunes of the city through a haze of mercantile glory which distorted their vision. For them, the

---

[1] See *Incorporated Chamber of Commerce and Shipping—Annual Reports* (1823–1830) in the Bristol Central Reference Library.

major issue was the port's declining trade and the relationship between this and the organisation of the Docks Company. Less understandable is the manner in which later commentators have tended to view the economic development of Bristol in the same light—though very recent arguments over Bristol's suitability as a national port tend to illustrate the almost mythological importance which many attach to its fortunes. As for the nineteenth century, however, it will be argued that the affairs of the port were of minor economic importance and, moreover, that there is no reason to think that during that period it missed its true role.

To place this judgement in clearer perspective it is necessary to look at the development of local industries over the period. Unfortunately, little is known of their detailed business operations. Indeed, only one of the leading industries of these earlier years has been examined in this way, namely, glass.[1] Even this has been done on the records of only one firm, the Phoenix Glass Works, covering a relatively short period. However, there is sufficient evidence to suggest that the firm was fairly representative of the industry at the time and the period concerned was critical for Bristol glass-making. Thus, it can be seen that the industry was doing well up to 1820, indeed the years immediately after the end of the Napoleonic wars in 1815 were particularly prosperous ones, the main reason for this being a buoyant demand for Bristol glass from the U.S.A., the West Indies, Ireland and Europe. Then in 1820 there was a slump. General economic conditions in the U.S.A. showed a marked downturn and the situation was even worse in the West Indies with a sharp fall in sugar prices, which in turn stemmed from a big drop in United Kingdom demand. Ireland and Europe also fell into economic depression; and, undoubtedly, the depression in the United Kingdom economy, which came after a somewhat speculative post-war boom, was a major factor causing more widespread international economic difficulties. The effect on the Bristol glass industry was serious and, gradually, from this time onwards one firm after another was forced to close its doors. The Phoenix Works was seriously weakened by heavy bad debts—particularly on its American and

[1] B. W. E. Alford, "The Flint and Bottle Glass. . .", *op. cit.*; see also A. C. Powell, *op. cit.*

West Indian trades—and quite apart from general trade conditions it lost a steady, lucrative market for bottles as a result of large porter brewers gaining control over the export of porter (particularly to Ireland) and in the process substituting casks for bottles.

Quite apart from these immediate problems, local glass manufacturers were suffering increasingly from longer-term disadvantages associated with the growth of the industry in Lancashire, which was well-placed in terms of fuel, raw materials and rapidly expanding markets.[1] Nevertheless, on the available evidence, it would be incorrect to suggest that because of these factors the decline of the local industry was inevitable, since Bristol was by no means being left at a complete disadvantage as an industrial centre; and in so far as transport developments were of increasing importance, Bristol was adequately supplied with water communications and was in the vanguard of railway promotions. However, industrial location is not simply a question of geography: it involves, also, the whole economic ethos of an area. An important part of this is the nature of local business enterprise.

Again, it is illuminating to begin with the Phoenix Glass Works.[2] The partners in the firm between 1814 and 1824 were John Cave, David Evans, Jacob Wilcox Ricketts and Henry Ricketts. John Cave was a leading figure in the City being Master of the Merchant Venturers in 1807–8, member of the Corporation from 1822–35, Sheriff in 1822–3, and Mayor in 1828–9. David Evans had a similar civic career: he was a member of the Corporation from 1795–1816, Sheriff in 1795–6, Mayor in 1803–4, and Alderman from 1807–16. The Ricketts family also played a part in municipal affairs, though Jacob Wilcox Ricketts concentrated his energies more on building up a local financial and industrial empire. First he became the senior partner in a tobacco business in Mary-le-Port Street, as well as having at least a family connection with one in Castle Street. In 1788, as senior partner, he joined Philip George to found the Bristol Porter Brewery, soon to become the largest

---

[1] For a full discussion of the development of the national industry over this period see T. C. Barker, *Pilkington Brothers and the Glass Industry* (1961).

[2] See B. W. E. Alford, "The Flint and Bottle Glass. . .", *op. cit.* for more detailed references.

brewery in the city. The following year he became senior partner in the Phoenix Glass Works. Later on in 1810 he helped to found the Castle Bank, and as its senior partner he was responsible for its expansion until 1826, when it was taken over by Stuckey's Bank—the year in which its most celebrated manager, Walter Bagehot, was born. Moreover, there can be little doubt that Jacob Wilcox had his finger in many more pies. A staunch Whig in politics, he lived at Vincent Lodge, Redland, a small estate on the outskirts of the city. He died in 1839 at the age of 86, having outlived 39 partners. He left a fortune of about £250,000. The fourth partner, Jacob's son Henry, was associated with his father in a number of ventures and died in 1859 worth £70,000.

These individuals were leading examples of a coterie of local businessmen linked together by a variety of interlocking business interests involving those industries already cited and others such as sugar, brass, shipping, and iron founding.[1] Perhaps even more important was that they controlled the local banking and financial network which was probably the most developed in the country outside London.[2] Indeed, the business activities of this group would repay detailed investigation, though sufficient evidence is available to give us an insight into their operations. What is particularly interesting is that these men were strongly representative of families which had, for successive generations, been heavily involved in commercial-cum-mercantile activities; moreover, the nature of their involvements in local industry would appear to have been strongly influenced by their mercantile experience. They took shares in industrial enterprises, which were often largely bound up with foreign trade, but they did not engage directly in management. The limited evidence available at least gives the strong impression that when these enterprises began to experience difficulties leading to the point of actual decline, these men were to a degree unable and to a degree unwilling to promote the necessary kinds of change and adaptation to meet such difficulties. Their response seems to have been much more typical of the

---

[1] Cf. I. V. Hall, *op. cit.*; also, "The Daubenys: . . . Part II", *TBGAS*, lxxxv, 175–201; Joan Day, *Bristol Brass: A History of the Industry* (Newton Abbot, 1973); Grahame Farr, *op. cit.*; A. J. Pugsley, *op. cit.*

[2] See Charles Henry Cave, *A History of Banking in Bristol* (Bristol, 1899).

merchant concerned with short-term trading operations than that of the industrialist concerned to maintain the viability of his long-term capital commitments: willingness to write off, to run down and abandon tended to prove stronger than determination to innovate, reorganise and seek new markets.

It would be foolish to suggest that the nature of local entrepreneurship was of overriding importance because, as has been pointed out, there were other powerful factors at work; but it was a continuing element and, it will be argued, one that probably became increasingly significant. More generally, it is interesting to reflect on a much broader theme in British economic history of the nineteenth century, namely, the alleged decline in entrepreneurial ability after 1870: the so-called "third generation thesis" which was first advanced by the celebrated economist Alfred Marshall in the 1880s.[1] As a number of writers have pointed out, however, it is not too difficult to find businesses run by a fourth generation at any time during the nineteenth century, or earlier for that matter; though of course, the pattern of British industrial development resulted in more examples of this after 1870 than before. Nevertheless, in so far as one should view this general thesis somewhat sceptically perhaps one should also consider it somewhat more specifically in terms of industries and areas. Might it not have been the case that the "third generation" was particularly strong in the industrial and commercial life of Bristol after 1820? Writing in the 1850s Richard Ricketts commented, somewhat ruefully: "Grandfather J. W. Ricketts [Jacob Wilcox] left about £250,000 behind him but this [is] nearly all gone. The Ricketts were too grand and lived in too fine places ever to be rich."[2]

The substantial wealth accumulated by Bristol's mercantile oligarchy by the early nineteenth century is well-documented and well-testified to by some splendid examples of eighteenth-century architecture which still remain.[3] Moreover, as detailed

[1] Alfred Marshall, *Industry and Trade* (1919 ed.), pp. 91–2. There is a large subsequent literature on this subject and much of it is critically surveyed in S. B. Saul, *The Myth of the Great Depression 1873–1896* (1969).

[2] Bristol Archives Office, MS. 12143 (41), p. 52.

[3] See G. W. A. Bush, "The Old and the New: The Corporation of Bristol 1820–51", (unpublished Ph.D. thesis, University of Bristol, 1965, 2 vols.), esp. (vol. 1) pp. 238–83 (vol. 2) pp. 539–96, for more detailed information on Bristol merchant families.

business histories have shown, once an individual businessman has achieved a solid level of prosperity, profit maximisation usually becomes an "inferior good". Both glass and tobacco provide examples of later generations of established families withdrawing altogether from business during the 1820s and 1830s in order to follow more gentlemanly pursuits and, from what is known of others of their kind, they appear quite typical.[1] Yet this commercial oligarchy still retained a firm grip over important institutions in the city, and the manner in which they exercised their control provides further testimony to their particular business outlook. Dr. Bush's detailed researches into the history of the Corporation between 1820 and 1835 reveal a group of men who were not alive to the economic problems of the city at the time. And throughout the years up to 1851, the Council was composed mainly of a merchant body with a leavening of manufacturers and professional men. Recruitment was restricted to a few families among whom the Ames's, Caves, Daniels, Pinneys, Ricketts's and Vaughans figured prominently; and these social and political ties were frequently strengthened by bonds of marriage. To complete the system there was a strong interlocking membership between the Corporation and the Merchant Venturers. The Mayoralty and the Mastership thus became interchangeable chief offices of this largely self-appointed oligarchy.[2]

Not surprisingly the predominant attitude of the Corporation to economic and social affairs was intensely obscurantist. Attention has already been drawn to the venal activities of the Corporation and the Society of Merchant Venturers over the administration of the port, and Dr. Bush provides detailed evidence of similar activities in other fields. For example, the Corporation was quite opposed to any form of municipal trading and, as a consequence, Bristol did not enjoy the benefits of an extensive muncipal gas service.[3] And the power of the Merchant Venturers, operating through the Corporation, is revealed by its success in blocking the development of a central

[1] B. W. E. Alford, "The Flint and Bottle Glass. . .", *op. cit.*; B. W. E. Alford, *W. D. & H. O. Wills . . .*, *op. cit.*, pp. 21, 70, 73, 89, 90; I. V. Hall, "The Daubenys . . .", *op. cit.* pp. 195–200; G. W. A. Bush, *op. cit.*

[2] G. W. A. Bush, *op. cit.* and (vol. 2) pp. 608–11.

[3] *Ibid.* (vol. 2) pp. 632–7.

water supply.[1] Indeed, it is interesting to speculate to what extent the effects of this on the health and mortality of the city's inhabitants counterbalanced the benefits of the Society's more publicised charitable acts on their behalf. Apparently, such reactionary attitudes were so engrained that Bristol merchants sometimes failed to serve their own longer-term best interests. In listing a number of reasons for the decline of the West of England cloth industry in the nineteenth century, Miss Mann describes how, in the 1830s, cloth manufacturers ". . . complained that for bulky goods such as oil they were confined to Bristol merchants who took advantage of the lack of competition to charge higher prices, and freight charges were extremely heavy . . . in 1839 freight charges on heavy goods by trow from Bristol was ten shillings to twelve shillings per ton, and insurance seven shillings per cent."[2]

Allowing for the fact that some of those who sat on the Common Council of the City and on the Court of the Merchant Venturers also sat in the banking parlours of the city, it appears reasonable to assume that the accumulated wealth of Bristol was not made readily available to more enterprising spirits. Significantly, two firms which did survive and which subsequently achieved outstanding success—Wills and Frys— developed largely outside the city's existing commercial freemasonry.[3] More generally, it seems reasonable to suggest that the whole commercial ethos of the city was, by the 1830s, unfavourable to the kind of change and adaptation in Bristol's commercial and industrial life which was necessary to rescue it from economic stagnation.

As early as 1828 a local guide, which annually extolled the excellence of all aspects of the city's life, commented:

> Bristol for centuries ranked as the second city in England in respect of riches, trade and population; but the present extent of its foreign commerce will bear no comparison with that of

[1] Helen E. Meller, *op. cit.* pp. 18–19. Dr. Meller's claims are somewhat stronger than indicated above but more recent research suggests that after the 1840s the Merchant Venturers lost interest in the subject. See P. V. McGrath, *The Merchant Venturers of Bristol* (1975), pp. 413–426.

[2] J. De L. Mann, *The Cloth Industry in the West of England from 1640 to 1800* (Oxford, 1971), p. 192 and n. 4.

[3] B. W. E. Alford, *W. D. & H. O. Wills.* . . .

the port of Liverpool; and it appears to be exceeded in population by the manufacturing town of Manchester . . .[1]

It hastened to add that Bristol was still a much more desirable place in which to live than either Liverpool or, "the extensive manufacturing village [sic] of Manchester": in truth, a somewhat hollow claim since the sanitary condition of Bristol was appalling, even by contemporary standards, and according to reports in the 1840s and 1850s the rate of mortality in Bristol was only marginally lower than the rates for Liverpool and Manchester.[2]

Some industries did survive and retained a measure of regional importance, in particular tobacco, chocolate, boots and shoes, and printing. But such industries were in no sense large enough to counterbalance those in decline. All of them survived because they had yet to experience technologcial changes of a kind to transform them into truly national industries. As consumer goods industries they continued to produce for local and regional markets; and, quite apart from changes in manufacturing techniques, to varying degrees they had to wait upon changes in consumer demand, which in turn were determined by levels of income and education and patterns of leisure. If tobacco is anything to judge by, then inertia and accidental factors determined its continued existence in Bristol.[3]

The early 1860s are commonly taken as the turning point of Bristol's fortunes in the nineteenth century. We have already cast doubt on this thesis in so far as it rests upon figures of population growth. Moreover, these doubts are strengthened considerably if population change in Bristol between 1861 and 1881 is examined a little more closely. Tables 3 and 4 shows the relative contributions of natural increase and immigration to population growth over the period.

From these data Hewitt concludes that expansion was mainly caused by natural increase, except for 1861–81 when it was significantly boosted by a net increase of nearly 23,000 immigrants. In other words, if migration is discounted, the

[1] *Mathews's Bristol Directory* (1828), p. 196.
[2] Sir Henry T. de la Beche, *Health of Towns Commission: Report of the State of Bristol and Other Large Towns* (London, 1845).
[3] See below for fuller analysis.

TABLE 3 Bristol as a Whole: Migration* and Natural Change 1841–91

Decade	Census Enumerators' Population	Total Intercensal Change		Natural Increase		Net Migration	
		Actual	%	Actual	%	Actual	%
1841 to 1851	172,798 188,329	15,531	9.0	13,535	7.8	1,996	1.2
1851 to 1861	188,329 208,300	19,971	10.6	19,916	10.6	55	0
1861 to 1871	208,300 249,753	41,453	19.9	26,067	12.5	15,386	7.4
1871 to 1881	249,753 298,186	48,433	19.4	41,220	16.5	7,213	2.9
1881 to 1891	298,186 336,975	38,789	13.0	44,520	14.9	—5,663	—1.9

* Net migration is calculated simply by accumulating the net addition through births and deaths for each year of the decade and subtracting this amount from the total change in population between the censuses. Therefore, the figure for net migration is a residual stock amount as at the second census year and it gives no direct indication of the annual flows of migration over the decade.

[Source: F. Hewitt, *op. cit.*, p. 90—the enumerators' population figures necessarily differ in magnitude from those for the cluster area as used in Table 1.]

TABLE 4 Bristol: Migration and Natural Growth 1861–1931

	1861–71 %	1871–81 %	1881–91 %	1891–1901 %
Natural Increase	12.3	16.5	14.8	13.3
Net Migration	10.0	3.8	—1.1	1.1
Total:	22.3	20.3	13.7	14.4

[Source: H. A. Shannon and E. Grebenik, *The Population of Bristol* (Cambridge, 1943), p. 11.]

increase in population over the two decades to which some writers attribute so much importance, is far less remarkable. The question is, therefore, why did such a volume of immigration occur over this period?

To some extent, if not entirely, the increase in immigration could be a statistical illusion, for the manner in which the numbers are calculated for a given decade can mean that the final figure represents either an annual accumulation of people, or an increase in turnover of immigrants passing through Bristol, which peaked around the early 1870s and the early 1880s.[1] The relative scale of the figures for 1861–71 and 1871–81 does not suggest that this latter was entirely the case, but the apparent net outflow from 1881 onwards indicates that it might have been an important element; furthermore, if all the 23,000 immigrants had remained in Bristol, then one would have expected a significantly higher natural increase in the following decades than in fact occurred, particularly bearing in mind that natural increase was almost certainly very substantially boosted by a rapidly falling death rate—indeed, on the figures cited above this could well account for all the increase in the natural rate.[2] If this was the case, then Bristol was acting primarily as a clearing centre for migrants, who subsequently moved overseas, or to other centres within the United Kingdom on a permanent basis or preparatory to moving overseas.[3]

To the extent that migrants were drawn to Bristol itself, the problem remains why they were so attracted. To allow that Bristol was becoming economically attractive to people in the surrounding area by no means implies a rising level of prosperity in the city: insofar as migration is determined by economic considerations, it is a question of relatives. There is

[1] See note to Table 3.

[2] For details on death rates see *Report of the Committee to Inquire into the Condition of the Bristol Poor* (London and Bristol, 1885), p. 26; T. A. Welton, *England's Recent Progress: an Investigation of the Statistics of Migrations, Mortality etc. in the Twenty Years from 1881–1901 as Indicating Tendencies Towards the Growth and Decay of Particular Communities* (London, 1911), pp. 598–9, 606–7. 614–15, 622–3.

[3] For a masterly discussion of the range of possibilities in this connection see H. J. Habakkuk, "Fluctuations in House-Building in Britain and the United States in the Nineteenth Century", *Journal of Economic History*, xxii, 198–230.

certainly evidence of economic difficulty in agriculture in the
region as one of the assistant commissioners working in Somerset for the *Royal Commission on Agriculture* reported in 1882: "I
believe that, except in the extreme West of the county, very
severe depression prevails."[1] Some years ago, however, Cairncross warned against assuming that flows of migrants from
country to town were determined by the level of prosperity of
local agriculture—he laid stress on the positive attractiveness of
towns, which drew surplus population from the countryside
without causing rural depopulation.[2] Yet while this might have
been the general, longer-term pattern it does not necessarily
apply in specific local areas, or at particular times. There is
nothing inconsistent between Cairncross's analysis and the
possibility of Bristol having become an urban centre to which
migrants from Somerset and Gloucestershire were first attracted
before moving to towns elsewhere, either immediately or after
a relatively short period. Moreover, Cairncross's analysis does
not appear to explain adequately peaks in migration, and in
this respect the depression in agriculture in the early 1870s
would seem to have been of special importance. In short, the
figures for immigration into Bristol, as they stand, are by no
means sufficiently refined to provide convincing evidence for a
sharp rise in the city's prosperity.

In support of the recovery thesis, attention is often drawn to
the upsurge of house-building in Bristol between the late 1860s
and the 1880s. It was during this period that Redland, Cotham
and parts of Clifton were built up as new, middle-class suburbs.
On the face of it this is solid, tangible evidence of economic
buoyancy. But before this can be accepted as evidence of
economic recovery, it is necessary to answer a number of
questions which are thrown up when one begins to probe the
nature of the "boom" a little more deeply. It is certainly clear
that much of this building was very speculative. Both the *Royal
Commission on Working Class Housing* and a local enquiry into the
state of the Bristol poor made pointed references to the number
of unoccupied houses in Bristol available for the better-off

[1] *Royal Commission on Agriculture: Reports of the Assistant Commissioners
(Southern District)* (1882), c. 3375 I, p. 38.

[2] A. K. Cairncross, *Home and Foreign Investment 1870–1913* (Cambridge,
1953), pp. 74–5.

sections of the community. Moreover, rents were correspondingly low.[1] Such conditions were fostered by the manner in which land was developed for building. A common practice—with variations—was for an owner of land considered ripe for city development to commission an agent to divide it up into small parcels and then to sell it or convey it to developers (usually small builders) subject to a perennial rent charge, which would be enforced by a form of lease often specifying the type, or standard, of house which had to be erected on the land in question. In Bristol such rent charges commonly worked out at £50 per acre which was ten, or more, times the corresponding rent for agricultural land and, in turn, this meant that from rent charges alone the original owner could recoup the capital value of the land within three years. At the same time, this method of disposal encouraged speculative building, since it enabled developers to acquire land for little, or no, capital outlay and then to build houses in anticipation of demand; and it was usual to pass on the rent charge to the eventual purchaser of the house.

It must be stressed, however, that evidence on this aspect of Bristol's development is extremely sparse and much detailed research into this field needs to be done before any firm conclusions can be drawn.

No doubt partly related to housing developments was the improvement in the general health of the city during the 1870s and 1880s. There was, without question, ample room for such amelioration, and although there had been a steady fall in the death rate from 22.6 per thousand in 1876 to 17.9 per thousand by 1883, there was still room for much more.[2] Nevertheless, Bristol now compared favourably with other large towns and cities in Great Britain.[3] This improvement resulted from the extension of preventative measures which was a general feature of urban development during this period; and, more particularly, from the dedicated work of a small group of medical

[1] *Report of the Committee to Inquire into the Condition of the Bristol Poor*, p. 39; *Royal Commission on the Housing of the Working Classes* (1885), c. 4402 I, paras 6773, 6900, 6901, 6992, 7039, 7118. Para. 6778 of this report indicates that building wages in the city were low and this might have meant that homes were relatively cheap to build thus encouraging speculative building.

[2] *Report of the Committee to Inquire into the Condition of the Bristol Poor*.

[3] T. A. Welton, *op. cit.*

practitioners in the City.[1] At the same time, however, statistics of mortality such as these can be somewhat misleading at their face value since they refer to the city as a whole and, therefore, the registered improvement to some extent reflects the expansion of the city into newer middle-class suburbs. Accordingly, it is by no means clear that there was a corresponding improvement in health and sanitary conditions in the central areas; indeed, reports of 1885 and 1907 describes a picture of extremely insanitary conditions among the working-class population.[2] And there is no reason to suppose that matters of health and sanitation provide an exception to the rule that the middle classes are usually first to benefit from social improvements. Moreover, at the general level Bristol's consistently favourable bill of health, in comparison with other large towns and cities over the latter part of the nineteenth century, could be taken as supporting the view that the city did not experience rapid economic expansion with its attendant problems of overcrowding.

Port reform is another primary example used to support the recovery thesis. Undoubtedly, the evidence of improvement in the administration of the port after 1848, the opening of Avonmouth dock in 1877 and of Portishead dock in 1879, and the amalgamation of all the city's docks in 1884 to form a new port of Bristol, is clear enough.[3] But in terms of the general economic development of the city this does not amount to very much. With the new deep-water facilities the port could certainly cope with bigger ships and it became more important in the handling of certain bulk commodities, in particular grain. Yet although, as one writer has pointed out, by 1897 676,345 tons of grain came in through Bristol, it should be added that this represented only 8 per cent of total United Kingdom

[1] See David Large and Frances Round, *Public Health in Mid-Victorian Bristol* (Bristol Branch of the Historical Association, 1974).

[2] *Report of the Committee to Inquire into the Condition of the Bristol Poor*, p. 39; A. Cooke (General Secretary), *Bristol Hovels; The Report of the Bristol Housing Reform Committee* (Bristol, 1907)—among other things Bristol is compared unfavourably with Glasgow and Liverpool, and attention is drawn to the unsatisfactory manner in which the Bristol Waterworks Company operated, through its inadequate supply of water at unduly high prices (see pp. 19–21).

[3] Charles Wells, *op. cit.*; A. J. Pugsley, *op. cit.*

imports of grain.[1] And against this rise there was a decline in old import trades, in particular that of sugar. Much more important, in this context, was the failure of the port to attract export trade either from Bristol or from the broader hinterland. For example, Midlands industries preferred other ports and it was claimed that Birmingham sent only 6 per cent of its export trade through Bristol at the turn of the century.[2] Indeed, it would be interesting to know a great deal more about the economics of the port operation over these years, since, although its facilities were enlarged and its administration made more efficient, it is difficult to see how it could have provided very good returns to the city either directly or indirectly. And it is quite clear that it was of no significance to the so-called "newer" industries which were expanding in Bristol at this time.

Boots and shoes, tobacco, printing and stationery, and chocolate were the "new industries" of late nineteenth-century Bristol; and through their success the names of W. D. and H. O. Wills, J. S. Fry, and E. A. & O. Robinson became nationally, even internationally known. All were industries involved with the growth of mass consumer markets, and their rise to prominence was the result of inter-relationships between growing demand based on rising real incomes and technological changes which replaced traditional and labour-intensive methods with highly productive machines. The development of these industries was all the more striking since their growth was closely associated with revolutionary methods of mass advertising and the sales techniques of universal providers such as chain and department stores. For this reason it is understandably easy to lose perspective when assessing the economic significance of these firms at the local level. For example, by 1907, W. D. & H. O. Wills was by far the largest producer of tobacco goods in the United Kingdom accounting for 55 per cent of United Kingdom sales of cigarettes. The financial

[1] Donald John Webb, *op. cit.*, p. 28—and see generally for a somewhat enthusiastic account of the port's importance, which appears unconvincing to the present author. The comparison for grain is based on Webb's figures for Bristol and U.K. returns taken from B. R. Mitchell with Phyllis Deane, *op. cit.*, p. 99.

[2] Donald John Webb, *op. cit.*, pp. 39, 43, 74.

success of the firm was prodigious, considerably exceeding that of any other enterprise in Bristol; and members of the Wills family emerged as a new breed of merchant princes, far out-doing their eighteenth- and earlier nineteenth-century counter-parts in terms of sheer wealth. Yet, against all this, total employment at the Wills factories at this date was only just over 3,000, of whom two-thirds were women and girls; or, in other terms, under 3 per cent of the local labour force.[1]

Moreover, Wills was the exception: the importance of the other well-known firms in the local economy was somewhat less. The local printing industry accounted for no more than 2 per cent of the total labour force employed in the United Kingdom industry in 1901.[2] And despite the many references to the importance of Bristol as a centre of boot and shoe manufacture, employment in the industry in the entire south-west—including the major firm of C. & J. Clark at Street—was only 7 per cent of the total United Kingdom employment in the industry in 1881, and this figure had fallen to 3 per cent by 1901.[3] Furthermore, the Bristol section of the industry was slow in making certain fundamental technical innovations and this was a major cause of its sharp relative decline in national terms over the 1890s.[4] And, lastly, Frys employed 1,000 work-people in 1901—of whom two-thirds were women—which, again, amounted to a very small proportion of the local labour force.[5]

In 1883 the *Bristol Times and Mirror* published a series of articles on the leading Bristol firms, extolling their enterprise,

[1] See B. W. E. Alford, *W. D. & H. O. Wills* . . ., p. 233 n. 12 and generally for a full account of the development of this firm.

[2] Census Returns.

[3] P. Head, "Boots and Shoes", in *The Development of British Industry and Foreign Competition, 1875–1914*, ed. Derek H. Aldcroft (1968), p. 173.

[4] In this connection Donald John Webb, *op. cit.*, cites *Royal Commission on Labour*, Minutes of Evidence, Group C, *B.P.P.* 1892, xxxvi, ii, p. 652; and for much fuller evidence see R. A. Church, "Labour Supply and Innovation 1800–1860: The Boot and Shoe Industry", *Business History*, xii, no. 1, 25–45; and by the same author, "The Effect of the American Export Invasion on the British Boot and Shoe Industry 1885–1914", *Journal of Economic History*, xxviii, no. 2, 223–54.

[5] "Work in Bristol" (*Bristol Times and Mirror*, Bristol, 1883), p. 35.

efficiency and general importance.¹ However, an over-developed sense of local pride—and maybe the need to sell newspapers—was allowed to bias objective reporting. Almost entirely, the firms featured were relatively small, not infrequently family affairs, which, even on the evidence provided, could in no sense lay claim to being in the vanguard of industrial development. There were coachmakers, furniture makers, brewers, soap makers, sanitary-ware makers, builders, engravers, and others of a similar nature, which were making goods mainly for local markets. Among the whole lot only Wills, Frys, and Robinsons were firms of some national importance.²

Attention has already been drawn to the high proportion of female labour in certain expanding industries; and, more generally, it seems likely that employment opportunities for unskilled women and girls in Bristol were somewhat better than for unskilled men.³ For example, although towards the end of the century W. D. & H. O. Wills experienced more difficulty than earlier in recruiting female labour there was never any problem with men.⁴ In general, wages for men in Bristol were low by comparison with other towns;⁵ and maybe this was an important cause of Bristol experiencing a net loss of migrants between 1891 and 1901.⁶

Table 5 shows an analysis of the changing occupational structure of Bristol over the period 1861–1901. It is important to stress, however, that it provides only a very rough picture, though adequate for our purpose and all that is possible within

¹ *Ibid.*; see also a series of articles published in the *Bristol Times and Mirror* under the general title "Bristol's Many Industries" in 1923. These are collected into one volume which is available at the Bristol Central Reference Library.

² Cf. *Royal Commission on the Housing of the Working Classes*, para. 6845.

³ *Report of the Committee to Inquire in to the Condition of the Bristol Poor*, pp. 28–30.

⁴ B. W. E. Alford, *W. D. & H. O. Wills . . .*, p. 128 citing *Royal Commission on the Factory and Workshops Acts*, c. 1443 (1876), paras, 13284–303.

⁵ *Report of the Committee to Inquire into the Condition of the Bristol Poor*, p. 28; *Royal Commission on the Housing of the Working Classes*, paras, 6778, 6993, 7030–3, 7098–7107; E. H. Hunt, *Regional Wage Variations in Britain 1850–1914* (Oxford, 1973), p. 112. Tobacco was an exception in that it paid very good wages. For details and an explanation of this see B. W. E. Alford, *W. D. & H. O. Wills . . .*, pp. 128, 130, 235, 284–7, 292–3.

⁶ See tables 3 and 4 above.

the present context. The nature of the information available makes it an extremely difficult exercise to reconstruct accurately occupational structure for any area of Great Britain, even if it were attempted as a full-scale research enterprise. A major problem is changes in occupational classification from one census to another: 1861 and 1871 are reasonably comparable in this regard but there were major changes in 1881 and again in 1891, with further alterations being made to the 1891 system in 1901. And even if classifications were completely consistent, they would still not be sufficiently closely defined as to provide a basis for making detailed comparisons between one area and another for either a given year or over time. Nevertheless, so long as these difficulties are clearly understood some useful insight into economic change can be gained by looking at occupational returns.

TABLE 5   Incidence of Occupations of Males in Bristol as Compared with Great Britain, 1861–91*

(In each case the first figure is the incidence of the occupation—i.e. Bristol employment/G.B. employment—followed by the % of total males in Bristol in brackets)

Class	1861 %	1871 %	1891 %	1901 %
Civil Service		1.5 (0.6)		1.7 (0.6)
Customs	2.5 (0.3)			
Police	1.8 (0.8)	1.5 (0.7)		
Solicitor	1.8 (0.4)	1.7 (0.4)		
Surgeon/Apothecary	1.5 (0.3)			
Chemist, Druggist	1.8 (0.4)			
Chemist, Druggist and others in chemicals, oil, grease, soap, resin				1.6 (1.3)
Maltster	1.7 (0.3)			
Brewer		1.6 (0.6)		
Publican	1.5 (0.9)			
Beerseller	2.0 (0.4)	1.8 (0.4)		
Wine Merchant	2.5 (0.3)	2.5 (0.4)		
Student (over 15 years)			2.0 (1.5)	
Musician, Music Master		1.7 (0.3)	1.5 (0.3)	
Merchant	1.8 (0.4)			
Accountant	7.2 (0.8)	6.6 (1.0)	3.0 (0.3)	
Merchant, Agents, Accountants				1.7 (2.0)

Class	1861 %	1871 %	1891 %	1901 %
Life, House, Ship etc. Insurance Service			1.6 (0.5)	
Commercial Clerk	1.5 (1.1)		1.6 (3.5)	1.5 (3.8)
Commercial Traveller	2.8 (0.6)	2.7 (0.8)	2.6 (1.1)	
Shopkeeper (Undefined) General Dealer		1.5 (0.5)		
Railway Engine Driver	2.4 (0.4)			
Coachman (not domestic)	1.9 (0.6)			
Coachman, Cabman, Flyman		1.7 (1.1)		
Carman, Carrier, Haulier, Carter, Wagoner (not farm)			1.5 (2.5)	
Others on roads in conveyancing				3.3 (0.9)
Seaman (Merchant Service)	2.4 (3.6)	2.3 (3.1)	1.9 (2.0)	
Harbour, Dock Service, Labourer		1.8 (0.8)	3.0 (1.6)	2.4 (2.0)
Others in Shipping	4.3 (0.5)			
Warehouseman	2.3 (0.6)	1.9 (0.9)	2.2 (0.5)	
Messenger, Porter, Errand Boy	2.2 (1.4)	2.0 (1.2)	1.8 (3.0)	
Land Proprietor	1.6 (0.5)			
Printer	1.5 (0.6)	1.7 (0.9)	1.5 (1.2)	
Lithographer, Copper and Steel Plate Printer			3.6 (0.3)	
Printer and Lithographer				1.9 (1.7)
Stationer, Law Stationer			2.4 (0.3)	
Stationer, Print and Books				2.4 (0.6)
Engine and Machine Maker	1.5 (1.4)			
Coachmaker	2.1 (0.6)	2.0 (0.7)		
Ship builder, Shipwright	1.9 (0.9)	2.3 (1.3)		
House Proprietor	1.7 (0.4)			
Mason, Paviour	2.5 (3.4)	2.6 (3.6)	2.3 (1.9)	
Mason, Mason's Labourer				2.8 (2.2)
Plasterer	2.0 (0.6)	2.2 (0.8)		
Plumber, Painter, Glazier	1.9 (2.2)	1.8 (2.6)		
Cabinet Maker, Upholsterer	2.2 (1.2)	2.1 (1.4)		

Class	1861 %	1871 %	1891 %	1901 %
Cabinet Maker, Upholst., Furniture Dealer, French Polisher			2.0 (1.5)	
French Polisher		2.8 (0.3)		
French Polisher, others in Furniture and Fittings				1.7 (1.9)
Sawyer		1.7 (0.7)	2.0 (0.4)	
Workers in Wood and Bark				1.7 (1.4)
Timber, Wood, Merchant/Dealer		1.9 (0.3)	2.3 (0.3)	
Cooper	3.1 (0.9)			
Cooper, Hoop-Maker/ Bender		2.9 (0.8)	2.2 (0.4)	
Basket Maker	2.4 (0.3)	2.3 (0.3)		
Draper, Mercer	1.6 (1.0)			
Hatter, Hat-maker	4.9 (0.9)	2.7 (0.5)	1.9 (0.3)	
Tailor			1.6 (1.8)	1.5 (1.5)
Shoemaker, Boot-maker	1.5 (5.1)	1.8 (5.1)	2.4 (4.7)	3.2 (5.2)
Corn, Flour, Seed- Merchant		2.6 (0.5)		
Cowkeeper, Milkseller	1.7 (0.4)			
Baker	1.7 (1.3)	1.7 (1.2)		
Confectioner, Pastry- cook	2.1 (0.3)	2.8 (0.4)	2.5 (0.4)	
Sugar Refiner	12.6 (0.6)	18.3 (0.7)		
Grocer, Tea-dealer	1.5 (1.7)			
Tobacco-, Cigar-, Snuff- Maker, Tobacconist		2.3 (0.3)	2.2 (0.4)	13.0 (0.8)
Currier	2.4 (0.5)	2.0 (0.4)	1.7 (0.4)	
Tanner		5.5 (0.7)	46.0 (0.5)	
Brush-, Broom-Maker	3.0 (0.4)	4.0 (0.5)		
Gas Works Service	2.5 (0.4)	2.1 (0.5)	1.7 (0.5)	
Gas, Water, Electricity				1.6 (0.8)
Sanitary Service				3.5 (0.5)
Earthenware Manu- facture	1.7 (0.6)	1.8 (0.6)		
Brick-maker, Dealer		2.1 (0.5)		
Brass Founder, Manu- facturer	1.9 (0.4)	1.7 (0.4)		
Dealer in Metals, Machines, Imple- ments, etc.				2.0 (0.4)
Others in Engines				1.7 (0.7)
Ironmonger	2.1 (0.3)	1.7 (0.4)	1.9 (0.4)	

Class	1861 %	1871 %	1891 %	1901 %
Others in Precious Metals, Jewels, Watches, Instruments, and Games				2.4 (0.7)
Labourer	2.0 (9.0)			
Annuitant	1.6 (0.3)			
TOTAL MALES	38,357 (Bristol and Clifton)	43,777 (Bristol and Clifton)	75,767 (All Bristol)	115,472 (All Bristol)
0.25% of males equals	96	109	189	288

* (a) For 1861 and 1871 the totals are for males 20 years and upwards and for 1891 and 1901 10 years and upwards. Only occupations accounting for 0.25% ,or more, of males are included. (b) No attempt has been made to order occupations in precise terms of social categories. (c) 1881 is omitted since it is not easily comparable with either 1861/71 or 1891/1901; correspondingly the years compare most directly in these pairs.
[Source: *Census Returns for England and Wales*—Tables of Occupations.]

We have analysed only male workers and only those occupations which account for 0.25 per cent, or more, of the total male population above a certain age. To a degree this has the effect of under-weighting the importance of industries in which female labour accounts for the bulk of employment, but the distortion is not great since male and female employment in an industry is usually quite closely correlated over the country as a whole and, therefore, comparisons between Bristol and Great Britain are not likely to be seriously affected. The problem of classification certainly reduces the value of comparisons over time, but the wider the comparison the more significant it becomes.

We have simply listed those occupations which are 1.5 times, or more, incident in Bristol than in Great Britain as a whole. The pattern in 1861 is much as one would expect with certain of Bristol's traditional occupations still showing up strongly— for example, seaman, hatters, and sugar refiners—and some measure of concentration in a fairly wide range of trades and services. However, many of these latter show measures of concentration which cluster around 1.5 and as such are probably not exceptional for towns of even moderate size: the degree of concentration reflecting the fact that we are taking Great Britain as a whole (that is, including rural areas) as the basis of comparison. Bristol was obviously still a regional commercial and financial centre but, again, the extent of this was not exceptional since the numbers of merchants, accountants, commercial clerks and commercial travellers, while large in proportion, were absolutely quite small.

More revealing of the nature of changing economic structure are broad comparisons over the whole period, notwithstanding the difficulties which have already been alluded to. All the industries represented by those occupations listed in Table 5 are absolutely quite small. This simply bears out a point already made; and tobacco manufacture is the most conclusive example of it. It shows a concentration of 13.1 for 1901 but the total number of males employed in the industry in Bristol was still only 924, and yet it was the industry where Bristol's national importance was of most significance.[1]

Another fact which emerges from the analysis is that over the period 1861–1901 Bristol became more "average" in its occupational structure. Moreover, this view has been borne out by other investigators who have examined the economic and social structure of the city.[2] It is somewhat more problematical, however, to know quite what to deduce from this kind of evidence. It has been suggested that Bristol was, therefore, a highly diversified economy, broadly (and soundly?) based. But in these terms of analysis, from an economic viewpoint "highly diversified" is little less than pure abstraction, since a simple occupational classification totally ignores qualitative differences within a given occupation. For example, it is evident that the "average worker" in one of the so-called new industries in Bristol in 1901—boots and shoes—was a different animal from his counterpart in Leicester or Northampton: there was an even chance that he (or she) was an outworker, whereas the latter was almost certainly a semi-skilled factory machine-operator.[3] Indeed, the "diversified" pattern of Bristol occupations

---

[1] This remains true if the high level of female employment is taken into account.

[2] F. Hewitt, *op. cit.*, especially pp. 185–99, lays considerable stress on this point.

[3] See notes 3 and 4, p. 274 above for references on the technical development of this industry.

emphasises the generally small-scale nature of the industries concerned and, for the greater part, this implies crucial differences in terms of techniques, organisation and economic importance, from heavier concentrations of such industries elsewhere. In short, by the turn of the century, Bristol was a location for many industries and trades but a national centre for almost none.

Finally, as some small contrast to the foregoing analysis it is worth suggesting that it is possible that one field in which Bristol was developing quite rapidly at the end of the nineteenth century was in the provision of commercial, retail, and distribution services for the City and its surrounding regions. The service sector is notoriously the most difficult of all sectors of the economy to analyse and, once again, definitions of occupations are by no means specific enough when dealing with the wide range of jobs it embraces. Nevertheless, in the light of the importance which this aspect of the Bristol economy has assumed in the present century there are good *a priori* grounds for suspecting that the city's advantages in this field were beginning to come into play in the 1880s and 1890s, particularly with the growth of markets for more standardised and mass-produced consumer goods. But without more detailed investigation this must remain no more than a strong suspicion.

This essay opened by posing the question of whether the economic development of Bristol over the nineteenth century presents an enigma to the economic historian. In attempting to unravel the puzzle we began by presenting a survey of what we termed the accepted view, and from this the following picture emerged: after a period of uneven but somewhat sluggish growth over the early nineteenth century, in the 1840s the local economy moved into a period of stagnation which lasted until the 1860s, and which might even have included a shorter period of absolute decline; in the 1860s, however, there was a sharp recovery which lasted through to the 1880s, and even though the tempo slackened from then until the end of the century the trend remained upwards, so that over the whole period from the 1860s to the turn of the century Bristol compared very favourably with the economy as a whole. We described how this picture has been appropriately coloured by a selection of evidence relating to local industries, the fortunes of the port, and the physical expansion of the City; and in the last respect, in particular, it was shown how considerable weight has been placed on the available figures for Bristol's population growth. But against this picture we set another, contrasting one. It was shown how, on closer examination, available population figures are open to a number of interpretations, and how it is far from certain that they can be taken to support the accepted view. Furthermore, as soon as we began to probe more deeply into other areas of evidence, doubts concerning the accuracy of the traditional view were strengthened. Indeed, even in interpreting their own evidence previous commentators on the economic development of Bristol in the nineteenth century have often been uncritical and unduly impressionistic, and this is particularly so in relation to industrial development. Of course, when evidence is so flimsy the opposite to the "traditional view" does not become true through default; but at least there would appear to be good grounds for suggesting that a more pessimistic account of Bristol's economic development over the nineteenth century is worthy of more serious consideration.

Thus, the safest answer to the question posed by the title of this essay is that the enigma remains. Yet this is perhaps unduly cautious and does not match the tone of the preceding analysis. Indeed, the general thrust of our argument is that over the last century the Bristol economy muddled through and that, although there were highlights and bright spots, its performance was generally mediocre. And if, for a moment, a purely impressionistic approach is permitted, it would seem to confirm this pessimistic appraisal: nineteenth-century Bristol has left us with few monuments to civic pride and local enthusiasm such as are characteristic of other rapidly expanding towns and cities of the period; such amenities which are enjoyed by Bristolians today are usually either remnants of the city's eighteenth-century glory or outcrops of early twentieth-century munificence. Brunel's magnificent Clifton Suspension Bridge is something of an exception, though the enterprise which promoted the project did not match its technological achievement: after decades of being mooted, it was not until 1829 that the scheme was finally got under way and then it took another 35 years to complete.[1]

[1] J. Latimer, *Annals of Bristol in the Nineteenth Century* (Bristol, 1887), pp. 131, 229, 375, 377.

It is true, of course, that in the nineteenth century, as in the mid-twentieth century, Bristol has been the home of some spectacular and extravagant transport technology. Some years earlier than the opening of the Suspension Bridge, in 1844, the S.S. *Great Britain* passed through the same gorge *en route* for her sea trials. The building of this ship had been stimulated by the record performance of the S.S. *Great Western*, whose success on the round trip to New York amounted to a serious threat to Liverpool shipping lines. However, the Cunard Company of Liverpool soon had four steamships in operation and two more nearly ready, while in 1846 a few hours after leaving Liverpool on her second voyage the S.S. *Great Britain* became stranded off the Irish coast. It was subsequently rescued and in 1850 was bought for a fraction of its original cost and, with the S.S. *Great Western*, sent to ply in the trades of rival ports.[1] This project, not based on sound commercial enterprise, is perhaps strikingly symptomatic of much of Bristol's industrial and commercial life of the nineteenth century.

[1] *Ibid.*, pp. 218, 219, 221, 271

Index

Abingdon 134
Abona(e) *see under* Bristol, Sea Mills
Abundantia 83
Adams, John 206, 215
Adderbury 144, 145
Adlam, William 5
agriculture 107, **147-69**, 269-70
Alfred, *Bishop of Worcester* 109 n. 6, 115, 116-17, 118, 119, 120
allées couvertes *see* gallery graves
Amberley 28
America 147, 159, 162-7, 184, **200-216**, 261
Ames family 265
An Analysis of the Domesday of Gloucestershire (Taylor) 19
Ancient Bristol Exploration Fund 30
Anderson, *Sir* Alan 28
Andoversford 189
Andrew of St. Victor, *Abbot of Wigmore* 114
Anglesey 51
Antigua 203
L'Antiquité expliquée et representée en figures (Montfaucon) 53
Apperley 163 n. 1
Apsley, *Lady* Viola 46-7
Argyll, John Campbell, *2nd Duke* 185
Arle Court, Cheltenham 153, 167
Arlington 129
Arnold, Benedict 215
Arrowsmiths, J. W., Ltd. 16
Art in Britain under the Romans (Toynbee) 62
Ashburnham Library 15
Asshefylde, — 138
Aston Blank 142
Atkinson, Richard 57, 59
Atkyns, *Sir* Robert 16, 171, 181
atmospheric railway 224, 239, 247

Attis 67, 75-6
Aubrey, John 51
Augustine, *Saint*, of Canterbury 119, 122, 123, 124-6
Augustine, *Saint*, of Hippo 124
Augustinians 105, 111, 112, 116, 118, 123
Aust 125
Austen, Jane 174, 178
Austin, Roland 4, 10, 11, 12, 17, 20, 39, 45, 48
Avebury 51, 60
Aveling, Alice 136
Avening 21
Avon Archaeological Council 31
Avon Gorge 170, 177, 178, 183, 220, 225, 226, 250, 283
Avon Gorge National Nature Reserve 32
Avonmouth 176, 236, 249, 272
Aylesford 73
Azores 158

Bacchus 79-80
Baddeley, William St. Clair 17, 22, 23, 25, 36, 44
Badgeworth 129
Badminton 183
Bagehot, Walter 263
Bagendon 25
Bagendon: a Belgic Oppidum (Clifford) 25
Bagnall-Oakley, E. M. 12, 15
Bagot, Richard 129
Bailey, Dulcie 47
Baltic 156, 157
Banbury 46
'banker' marks 140-1
Barbados 167
Barkly, *Sir* Henry 8, 15

Barlow, W. H. 229
Barnes, *Mrs.* 213, 214
Barnes, Henry 201–2, 205, 206, 208, 210, 211–12
Barnwood 26
Barrington 139
Barrington, *Lord* 239
barrows 21, 22, 25, 26, 28–9, 30, 50, 56–7, 58–9, 93
Bartholemew, *Bishop of Exeter* 109 n. 6, 115 n. 2
Barton Regis 102
Barton-under-Needwood 46
Bath 2, 70, 103, 170, 173, 174, 175, 177, 178, 182, 188, 192, 240
General Hospital 188
Bathurst, Allen Alexander, *6th Earl Bathurst* 8, 13
Bathurst, Henry, *2nd Earl Bathurst* 193
Bathurst, William Lennox, *5th Earl Bathurst* 41
Bayeux 102
Baylis, Thomas Henry 43–4
Bayning, Paul, *1st Viscount Bayning* 150
Bayshill 181–2, 187
Bazeley, William 7, 8, 9, 15, 20, 22, 24, 44
beaker folk 30
Beauchamp, Richard, *Baron Beauchamp of Powick* 153
Beauchamp, William, *7th Earl Beauchamp* 44–5
Beaufort, Henry Charles Fitzroy Somerset, *8th Dvke* 3
Beaufort, Henry Hugh Arthur FitzRoy Somerset, *10th Duke* 31
Beaulieu Abbey 23
Beddoe, John 1, 2, 5, 6, 15
Beddoes, Thomas 179–80
Bede 124
Before civilization (Renfrew) 55, 58
Belas Knap long barrow 26
bell founding 194
Bellows, John 6, 14, 15, 17, 22, 38, 40
Benedictines 105
Berkeley 18, 33, 41, 104, 105, 109, 111, 113, 140, 163, 164
Berkeley, Norborne, *4th Baron Botetourt* 183–4, 185
Berkeley, Richard 163, 164, 166
Berkeley Castle steamboat 43
Berry, *Sir* James 26

biblical links sought in antiquarian investigations 51
The Bibliographer's Manual of Gloucestershire Literature (Hyett and Bazeley) 20
Bibury, Arlington Row 2, 35, 36, 129
Biddulph, Michael 43
Bigland, Ralph 17, 135, 136
Birdlip viii, 22, 41–2
Bishops Cleeve 150, 151, 152, 153, 158, 159, 162, 164, 167
Bisley 92–3, 97
Black Death 130
Blance, Beatrice 57–8
Bloxham 145
Bolingbroke, Henry *see* Henry IV, *King*
Boniface [sic], *Bishop of Exeter see under* Bartholemew, *Bishop of Exeter*
Bonstetten, Gustav Carl, *Baron* 54
boot and shoe manufacture 254, 267, 273, 274, 278, 280
Bordeaux 107
Borland, *Mrs.* 209, 210
Borland, Anna 204
Boston, Massachusetts 202, 203, 204, 205, 206, 208, 213, 215
Boteler, *Sir* Ralph 134
Botetourt, Norborne Berkeley, *4th Baron* 183–4, 185
bottled spa water 174–5, 184, 195
Bourton-on-the-Water 27
Boutineau, James 200–1, 202, 215
Bradford-on-Avon 95, 250
Bradway, William 133, 134
Brakspear, Harold 22
Brandywine 210
brass 253, 263, 278
Bray, Warwick 58
Breasted, James Henry 55
Breedon Hill 149
brewers 275, 276
Bridges, John 164–5
Bridgwater 238
Bright, Robert 235, 237
Brighton 219
Brimpsfield 42
Bristol 2, 4, 6, 7, 10, 14, 17, 19, 20, 21, 30, 31, 34, 37, 39, 40, 44, 48, 49, **101–8**, 140, 164, 165, 184, 191–2, **200–16**, **217–51**
Albemarle Row 174
All Saints 105, 209

Bristol—*contd.*

American Coffee House 209
Ashley Down 240
Baldwin Street 224
Barton Hill 223
Bedminster 104
Benedictine house 105
Blaise Castle 177
Brandon Hill 208
Broad Street 209
Brunel's Lock 223, 230–5, 236, 248–9
Castle 102–3
Castle Bank 263
Cathedral 32, 105, 173, 249–50
City Library 2
City Museum 3, 7, 15, 31, 38
Clifton 41, 170, 171, 173, 175, 176, 178, 180, 206, 209, 219, 220, 241, 252, 270, 282
College Green 172
Cotham 252, 270
Counterslip 224
Cumberland Basin 223
Downs 177, 180
Dowry Chapel 173
Dowry Parade 174
Dowry Square 173, 179
Dutch House 2, 10
Floating Harbour 229, 236, 244, 245, 259
Goldney Lodge 209
Horfield Common 98
the Hotwell **170–80**, 184, 185, 190, 208
Hotwell Road 173
Jacob's Wells Road 178
Kingsweston 24, 177
Lewin's Mead Chapel 209
Lord Mayor's Chapel 46
Miles Bank 5
Minster House, College Green 32
New Cut 229, 230
Orchard Street 206
Paradise Row 175
Princes Street 205
Prince's Wharf 243
Queen Square 173
Queen's Hotel, Clifton 41
Red Lodge 10, 38, 48
Redcliffe 104
Redland 252, 263, 270
Registrar's House 10, 32

Rownham Ferry 177
St. Augustine the less 117, 119, 122
St. Augustine's Abbey 18, 105, **109–126**
St. James 105
St. James' Square 173
St. Mary le Port 105
St. Mary Redcliffe 177, 250
St. Michael's Hill 105
St. Peter's Hospital 10
St. Werburgh 6, 105
Sea Mills 24, 77–8, 99
South Entrance Lock 223, 230–5, 236, 248–9
Southmead 105
Stuckey's Bank 263
Temple Meads Station 218, 238, 239, 241–2, 248–9, 251
Theatre Royal 2, 178–9
Trinity Street 212
Unity Street 212
Westbury College 32
bridges 217
cholera epidemic 239, 246–7
Clifton Bridge project 220, 222, 225–9, 237, 246, 250–1, 282–3
domestic architecture 34, 172–4, 179, 252, 263, 264
as financial centre 102, 263, 266
first flourished when western Europe was single economic system 106–107, 108
freebooting tendencies of bugesses 103
harbour works 217, 220, 237, 245
housing 252, 254, 270–2
level of economic activity in nine-teenth century 218, 219, 220, 221, 223, 224, 237, 251, **252–83**
links with Ireland 103–4, 107, 236, 253, 260, 261, 262
migration of population 255, 256–7, 267–70, 275
occupations 273–4, 275–81
oligarchy in control at beginning of nineteenth century 221–2, 259–260, 263, 264, 265, 266
police 222
population 107, 252, 255–8, 266–270, 282
as port 102, 106, 107, 108, 176, 216, 221, 236, 253, 254, 259–61, 266, 267, 272–3, 277, 281–2

railways 217, 218, 220, 223, 224, 236–40, 243, 246, 250–1, 262, 277
as regional centre for services 252, 262, 280–1
rent charges 271
Riots 221–2, 226
royal charters 103–4
sanitation 246, 254, 266, 267, 271–272, 278
shipbuilding 217, 220, 253, 277
slave trade 102, 182
water supply 246–9, 265–6, 278
Bristol Archaeological Notes (Pritchard) 10, 17
Bristol Chamber of Commerce 260
Bristol Church Plate (Cole) 20
Bristol Corporation 221, 222, 223, 224, 259, 260, 262, 265–6
Bristol and District Joint Planning Committee 33
Bristol Docks Company 220, 221, 223, 224, 229–36, 244, 259, 261
Bristol and Exeter Railway 223, 238, 240
Bristol Exploration Committee 13
Bristol and Gloucester Railway 223, 238, 239–40, 241
Bristol and Gloucestershire Archaeological Society vi–x, 1–49
  Archaeological Trust 11, 12, 27, 35–6
  conservation 2, 5, 8, 10, 14, 31–5, 36, 49
  Council vii, viii, ix, 3, 4–6, 7–8, 9–10
  Excavation Fund 11, 12–13, 24
  excavations 21–31
  Excavations and Buildings Committee 13, 25, 29, 34
  exchange of publications 6, 37
  Finance and General Purposes Committee 5, 8, 13
  foundation 2–6
  'junketing and picnics' viii, 2, 40, 41, 43, 44, 45, 47, 48
  libraries vii, 5, 6–7, 11, 37–9
  Library Committee 39
  London visit, 1898 43–4, 46
  meetings 39–49
  monograph publications 18–20
  museums 5, 6–7
  organisation into districts 5, 6, 10
  presidential portraits 8–9
Records Section 20, 21
Robinson Bequest Committee 20–1
Royce Memorial Collection 38
rules 5
standing committees 13
Transactions vii, viii, 1, 6, 7–8, 9, 12, 13, 14–17, 19, 22, 23, 28, 30, 31, 37, 38, 42–3, 47–8
West Gloucestershire District 40
women officers ix, 3, 12, 46, 47, 49
Bristol Literary and Philosophic Club 38
Bristol Marriage Licence Bonds, 1637–1700 21
Bristol Porter Brewery 262
Bristol Society of Merchant Venturers 172, 174, 179, 220, 222, 225, 226, 247, 248, 259–60, 262, 265–6
Bristol and South Wales Junction Railway 223, 238, 240
Bristol Times and Mirror 274–5
Bristol University Library 217, 227
Bristol Water Works Company 247–248
Bristol Wharfage Act, 1807 259–60
'Bristow' 122, 126
British Archaeological Association 2
British Association 55, 226
British Museum 29, 73, 92, 93
British Record Society 19
Brittany 54, 56, 58–9, 106
Broadway, Alexander 164
Broadway, Giles 151, 152, 162, 164, 166
Brodie, — 220
Bronze Age 31
Broughton 145
Browne, Barwick 46, 47
Bruckshaw, John 171
Brunel, Isambard Kingdom 217–51, 282–3
Brunel, *Sir* Marc 218, 219
Bruton, Leonard 235
Brydges, Elizabeth 187
Brydges, Grey, *5th Baron Chandos* 164–165
Brydges, Harry 187
Brydges, John 164–5
builders 189, 194, 198, 275, 277
Bulkeley, *Sir* D-w-y 172
Bunker Hill 205
Burford 127, 128, 129, 138, 139, 142, 143

Burney, Fanny 175, 178, 190, 191, 194
Bush, Graham William Arthur 265
Bush, Henry 237
Busshe, Thomas 128
Butler, John, *Bishop of Hereford* 195
Butler, William 224

Caerleon 125
Caesar 51
Cairncross, Alexander Kirkland 270
Calais 128
Calendar of Bristol Wills 1572–1792 and Wills in the Great Orphan Books 1378–1694 (ed. Fry) 19
Callowhill, Thomas 172
Cambridge, Sidney Sussex College 171
Cambridge, Massachusetts 203, 204
Campbell, John, *2nd Duke of Argyll* 185
Campden 33, 45, 127, 131, 132, 133, 134, 135, 137, 138, 139, 140, 143, 150
Campden, Baptist Hicks, *1st Viscount* 150
canals 193, 196, 198–9, 262
Cannon, John 13
Canterbury 146
Carbon–14 dating 50, 56, 58
Carnac 54
Carnuntum 72
Carolina 206
carpet making 195
Catherine of Braganza, *Queen* 171
Cave, John 237, 262, 265
Cernunnos 67
chambered long barrows *see* barrows
Champion, Sara T. 26
Chandos, Grey Brydges, *5th Baron* 164–5
chantries 127, 129, 130, 137
Chapel Haye 25
Charfield 129
Charlotte, *Queen* 190, 195, 196, 198
Chatterton, Thomas 177
Chedworth 22, 25, 80–2, 95, 127, 137
Chedworth, John Thynne Howe, *2nd Baron* 185
Cheltenham 25, 33, 39, 40, 41, 49, 153, 159, 167, 170, 179, **180–99**
  Fauconberg House 190, 191
  High Street 181, 183, 185, 188, 189
  Museum 28
  the Promenade 183
  Well Walk 183, 191

Chepstow 43, 98
Cherington 93
Chester 184
Chesterfield, Philip Dormer Stanhope, *4th Earl* 185
Childe, Vere Gordon 55, 57
Chipman, Ward 209
Chipping Campden 33, 45, 127, 131, 132, 133, 134, 135, 137, 138, 139, 140, 143, 150
Chipping Norton 137–8, 141
chocolate 224, 253, 267, 273, 274
Chronicle of Wigmore Abbey 109, 113, 118, 119
Chubb, Thomas 19
Church Hanborough 134, 138, 141
Church, Molly 209
church building expenditure divided: laity seeing to naves, clergy to chancels 127, 130, 134, 135
church plate 19, 20, 32
Church Plate of Gloucestershire (ed. Evans) 14, 19
Churcham 97–8
Churchdown 25, 96
Churchill, Sarah, *Duchess of Marlborough* 172
Cinderford 94–5
circulating libraries 179
Cirencester 24, 25, 27, 41, 47, 63–71, 87, 91, 92, 99, 127, 128, 129, 131, 133, 135–6, 137, 141, 143
Cirencester Excavations Committee 25
Cirencester Park 193
Cistercians 22, 118
Clapham, *Sir* Arthur 35
Clark, C. & J., Ltd. 274
Clark, F. Hannam 10, 13
Clark, G. T. 15
classical links sought in antiquarian investigations 51, 52
Claxton, Christopher 220, 230, 243, 251
Clearwell 163
Cleeve 150, 151, 152, 153, 158, 159, 162, 164, 167
Clevedon Court 226
Clifford, Elsie M. 11, 12, 13, 23, 24, 25, 26–7, 28, 29, 30, 35, 46, 49
Clifford, *Hon. & Rt. Rev.* William Hugh, *Bishop of Clifton* 3, 4, 9
Clifton *see under* Bristol
Clifton Antiquarian Club 9

Clifton Water Works 247–9
cloth 107, 128, 149, 156, 158, 161, 168, 181, 196, 223, 243, 266
coachmakers 275, 277
coal 184, 198, 199
Coaley 96–7
Coates 137
Coberley 140
Cocherel 52–3
Cockbury 160
cocoa 254
Coffin, Nathaniel 205–6, 210
Colas, John 143
Cole, Marwood Anselm Rauceby Thorold 20
Cole, William 173
Collingwood, Robin George 27
Coln, Rogers 142
colonial enterprises linked to innovations at home 147, 165
The Commission for Ecclesiastical Causes within the Dioceses of Bristol and Gloucester, 1574 (ed. Price) 21
Commissioners of Works *see under* Department of the Environment
Committee for Rescue Archaeology in Avon, Gloucestershire and Somerset (CRAAGS) 31
Compton Grove 82
Compton, Spencer Joshua Alwyne, 2nd *Marquis of Northampton* 226
Congress of Archaeological Societies 8, 29
Cook, Thomas 193–4
Coombe Hill 198, 199
Cooper, John 20
Corbridge 73
Corinium *see under* Circencester
Cork 104
Coronation Anthem (Handel) 194
Coscourt 163 n. 1
Cotswolds 2, 22, 25, 41, 56–7, 59, **127–46**, 184, 193
Cotteswold Naturalists Field Club 2, 25, 38, 41
cotton 223, 243
Couling family 143
Coulson, — 210
Council for British Archaeology 29–30, 34
Council for the Preservation of Rural England 34
court cairns 59

Courtown, James Stopford, *2nd Earl* 190, 192, 198
Coutances, Bishop of 102
Coventry, George William, *6th Earl of Coventry* 193
CRAAGS 31
creosote 224, 250
Crete 57, 58
Creully 102
cricket 241
Cricklade 144
cromlechs *see under* megaliths
Cromwell, Oliver 208
Croome 26, 193
Crutwells, printers, of Bath 188
Cunard Steamship Co. 283
Cupid 65, 79, 83, 84, 99
Curwen, Samuel 205, 208–9, 214–215
Custom Scrubs 93–4
cutlery 253
Cyclades 57, 58
Cyclops Christianus (Herbert) 53

Daglingworth 22, 88–9
Daniel family 265
Daniel, Glyn 29, 47
Danish National Museum 50
Danzig 157
Datini, Francesco di Marco 127–8
Davis, Betsy 210
Davis, H. Stratton 11, 13, 35, 36, 45
Davis, *Sir* John 3
Davis, Ralph Henry Carless 140, 143
The dawn of European civilisation (Childe) 57
Day, *Sir* Thomas 172
Déchelette, Joseph 56
de Clare family 129
Deddington 145
Deerhurst 26, 35, 40, 43, 148, 150, 163 n. 1, 167
Defoe, Daniel 171
Dekker, Thomas 148
Delaware, *Lady* 164
Denmark 50, 52, 56, 58, 59
dentists 176
Department of the Environment 5, 23, 24–5, 26, 27, 28, 29, 30, 31, 32, 34
Derham, Walter 11
Dermot, *King of Leinster* 104

A descriptive Catalogue of the printed maps of Gloucestershire, 1577–1911 (ed. Chubb) 19
Despenser, Hugh le, the elder, *Earl of Winchester* 129
Dettingen Te Deum (Handel) 195
Diana 65, 79
Dicton, *Lord* 44
diffusion theory of prehistoric culture 55–60
Digby, — 192
Discourse of the Commonweal 155
dissolution of the monasteries 22, 129, 136, 148, 156
distilling 253
Dixton, Richard 135
Dobunni 25
dolmens *see under* megaliths
Domesday survey 102
Donovan, Helen (Mrs. H. O'Neil) 27, 29, 30, 31, 37
Dorchester-on-Thames 31
Dorn 95–6
Dorrington, *Sir* John 4, 8, 42, 43
Drake, *Sir* Francis 154
Dreux 52–3
druids 51, 60
Dublin 101, 103
Ducie, Francis Reynolds Moreton, *3rd Baron, of Tortworth* 196
Ducie, Henry John Moreton, *3rd Earl* 3
Dudbridge 196
Dugdale, *Sir* William 15, 40
Durham, Bishop of 136
Dursley 32, 33, 34
Dutton, Edward Lenox, *4th Baron Sherborne* 8, 18–19
Dutton, James Henry Legge, *3rd Baron Sherborne* 3
Dynevor, *Lord* 3

East India Company 201, 215
Edward, the Confessor, *King* 101
Edward II, *King* 127, 129, 130
Edward III, *King* 127, 130
Egypt 56–8
Elizabeth I, *Queen* 150
Elton family 182
Elton, *Sir* Abraham 226
employment 147, 149, 151, 152, 156, 158, 159, 160, 161, 162, 167–8, 169, 255, 274–80

English Place-Name Society 125
engravers 275
entrepreneurship 148, 150, 155, 156–158, 160–1, 168–9, 263–5
Epidaurus 82
Essai sur les dolmens (Bonstetten) 54
Essay towards the description of the north division of Wiltshire (Aubrey) 51
Esther (Handel) 195
Eure 52–3
Eutychides 83
Evans, David 262
Evans, Joan 13, 17, 132
Evans, *Sir* John 1
Evans, John Thomas 19
Evans, Seriol 47
Evelina (Fanny Burney) 175, 178, 190
Evesham 131, 149
Exeter 77
Exeter, Bishop of 109 n. 6, 115 n. 2
Eye 114
Eynsham 139

Fairford 127, 133, 135, 144
fairs 128
Fane, John, *7th Earl of Westmorland* 185
Faneuil, Benjamin 208, 215
Faneuil, Susannah 201
Farmcote 151, 154
Fauconberg, *Lord* 187, 190
Fennel, — 210
fens 150
Fenton, Murray & Jackson, locomotive builders 240 n. 2
Fergusson, James 54
Finzel, Conrad 224
fitz Hamon, Robert 102
Fitz Harding, Maurice 115 n. 2
Fitz Harding, Nicholas 117
Fitz Harding, Robert 104, 105, 109 n. 6, 110, 111–12, 113, 115, 119, 120, 122, 123, 125
Fitzhardinge, Francis William, *2nd Baron Fitzhardinge* 3, 8, 18, 41
five-stage division of prehistory 50, 51, 55
flax 156, 157, 158, 160, 161–2, 165, 167, 168
Fleure, Herbert John 57
Flight's porcelain factory, Gloucester 195
Florence 127, 128

Forde, Cyril Daryll 57
Forest of Dean 42, 43, 161, 163 n. 1,
  168
Fortey, John 133–4
Fortuna 67, 74, 83
Fosbroke, Thomas Dudley 16
Fox, *Sir* Cyril 30
Fox, Francis 6, 48
France 52–3, 54, 56, 58–9, 73, 102–3,
  105–7, 128, 155, 162, 218
Frederick Augustus, *Duke of York* 194,
  198
Fripp, C. P. 237
Frome 240
fruit 177
Fry, Edward Alexander 19
Fry, J. & Co. 224, 266, 273, 274,
  275
Fryer, Alfred 17
Fullbrook-Leggatt, Lawrence Edward
  Wells Outen 36, 37
furniture makers 275, 277–8

gallery graves 53, 57, 58, 59
Gardiner, Sylvester 205
Garstang Chapel, Circencester 129,
  135
gas 265, 278
Gascony 107
Gates, Timothy 152–3, 164
gauge of railways 224, 236–7, 238,
  241, 251
Genii 66, 88, 92, 94, 95, 96
Genii Cucullati 68, 69, 86, 87, 88, 89,
  90–1, 99
gentry 150–69, 186, 191
Geoffrey, *Bishop of Coutances* 102
Geoffrey, *Count of Anjou* 103
George III, *King* 179, 190–8
George IV, *King* 198
George, Philip 262
Germany vii, 59, 106
giants supposed builders of megaliths
  52, 53
Gibbs, George 237
Gibbs, George Henry 237
Gilpin, Joshua 180, 186
Glasgow 247
glass in churches 46, 135, 142, 143
glass manufacture 175, 253, 260–3,
  265
Gloucester (Glevum) 6, 7, 10, 14, 20,
  27, 32, 36–7, 38–9, 40, 45, 48, 49,

64, **71–7**, 87, 96, 99, 131, 149,
  193–4, 198, 208–9, 238
Barbican site 37
Bell hotel 40
Blackfriars 35
Bon Marché site 37
Castle 130
Cathedral 40, 46, 74, 127, 142
City Library 20, 38–9
City Museum 7, 22, 24, 37, 38, 64,
  72, 92, 96, 98
Cross 48
Crypt School site 37
Friar's Orchard 37
King's School garden 37
1–5 King's Square 37
Kingsholm 71–2
New Inn 33
Newmarket Hall 75, 76
Northgate Street 74, 75
St. Michael's Rectory 39
St. Peter's Abbey 129–31, 134, 135,
  137, 139–40
Upper Quay Street site 37
Gloucester, Bishop of 192, 193, 194,
  195
Gloucester and Bristol, Bishop of 2,
  3
Gloucester, William Frederick, *2nd
  Duke* 198
Gloucester and District Archaeological
  Research Group 37
Gloucester Journal 185, 187, 192, 194
Gloucester Panel of Architects 34
Gloucester Roman Research Com-
  mittee 27, 36–7
A Gloucestershire and Bristol Atlas (King
  and Gray) 20
glovemaking 149
Godfrey, *Bishop of St. Asaph* 109 n. 6,
  115 n. 2
Godwine, *Earl of Wessex* 101
Goldthwait, Catherine 205
Gooch, Daniel 251
gothic revival 1
grain 272–3
Granby, John Manners, *Marquis* 173
Gray, Harrison, Jr. 209
Gray, Irvine 20
Great Britain, steamship 223, 224, 242,
  243, 244, 251, 283
Great Western, steamship 223, 242, 243,
  244, 283

Great Western Cotton Company 223
Great Western Railway 217, 218, 220, 223, 224, 236–40
Great Western Steamship Company 223, 224, 242, 243, 251
Grebenik E. 254
Greenaways, printers 17
Gregory VII, *Pope* 107–8
Gregory [sic], *Bishop of St. Asaph see under* Godfrey, *Bishop of St. Asaph*
Grevel, William 132–3
Grimes, William Francis 27
Grundy, George Beardoe 20
guilds 135
Guise, *Sir* William Vernon viii, 2, 3, 4, 6, 7, 8, 9, 18, 40, 42, 50
Guppy, Thomas Richard 220, 227, 237, 242, 243, 247, 251

H.M. Office of Works *see under* Department of the Environment
Haberdashers' Company 150–1
Hadrian's Wall 87
Hailes 148, 163, 164
Hakebourne, *Abbot of Cirencester* 136
Halifax, Nova Scotia 203, 205, 206, 212, 213
Hall family 164
Hallett, Palmer 2, 5, 7
Hallifax, Samuel, *Bishop of Gloucester* 192, 193, 194, 195
Hallowell family 204–5
Hallowell, Benjamin 205
Hallowell, Robert 205, 210
Hammond, J. W. 231–3
Hampnett 27
Hancock, John Gregory 197–8
Handel, George Frederic 186, 194, 196
Harford 130
Harford, John 237
Harold, *King* 101
Harrison, Douglas 47
'Harry the Hangman' 148–9, 168
Harvard College 202, 206, 208, 210
Harvey, John 130–1
Hastings, Selina, *Countess of Huntingdon* 186
hatters 278, 279
Haverfield, Francis John 23, 69
Hawes, Benjamin 222, 225
Hawker, Richard 196
Hawkes, Christopher 57, 60

Hawkshaw, *Sir* John 229
Hawling 137
Hayles Abbey 22, 23
Haymes 153, 167
Hazelwood 93
hemp 165, 168
Hennet, G. 232–3
Henry I, *King* 102, 103, 108
Henry II, *King* 103, 104, 108, 110–11, 112, 113, 119, 120
Henry IV, *King* 135
Henry VI, *King* 134
Henry VIII, *King* 136
Henry, *Prior of Wigmore* 114
Herbert, *Hon.* Algernon 53, 54
Hereford 192
Hereford, Bishops of 113, 195
Hetty Pegler's Tump 21, 59
Hewitt, Frederick 254, 255, 256, 267–269
Hicks, Baptist, *1st Viscount Campden* 150
hill forts 22, 25, 82
Hillhouse, — 231
Hillhouse, Abraham 222
Hills, Wills, *2nd Viscount Hillsborough* 201
History of Gloucestershire (Bigland) 17
Holland, Thomas, *Earl of Kent* 135
Holland, Thomas, architect 188–9
hops 165 n. 4
Horner, *Mrs.* Strangways 173
Hotwell *see under* Bristol
Howard, Frank E. 146
Howard, Henrietta, *Countess of Suffolk* 185
Howard, John 193
Howard, John Thynne, *2nd Baron Chedworth* 185
Hucclecote villa 24
Hudson, George 238–9
Hughes, Thomas 187, 188, 189
Huguenots 155, 188, 201
Human History (Smith) 57
Humphrey Clinker (Smollett) 178
Hundred of Berkeley (Smyth) 18
Hungerford Bridge 229
hunter-gods 81, 93
Huntingdon, Selina Hastings, *Countess* 186
Hurd, Richard, *Bishop of Worcester* 195
Hurry, Arnold Eardley 10
Hutchinson, Thomas 201, 208
Hyett, *Sir* Francis 8, 10, 17, 20

Ile Longue 56, 58
India 184
Inglesham 1
Inman, George 210
Institution of Civil Engineers 225, 249
Ireland 52, 56, 58, 59, 73, 101, 102, 103–4, 107, 147, 166, 236, 253, 260, 261, 262
iron 253, 263
Iron Age 22, 28, 32, 82, 85
Ivy Lodge round barrow 30

Jackson, Arthur 94–5
Jackson, R. 240 n. 2
Jamaica 204
James I, *King* 150
Jeavons, S. A. 20
Jeffries, printers, of Bristol 15
Jessop, William 221, 229
John, *King* 103
John, of Gaunt, *Duke of Lancaster* 143
John, de Sponlee 130
Johnson, Samuel 186
Jones, Charles 172
Jordan, *Saint* 122
Jordan, Dorothea 194
Jupiter 72, 77, 78, 80, 83
Jupiter Dolichenus 67

Kay, *Sir* Brook 3, 8
Keith, *Sir* Arthur 25, 30
Kempsford 141, 143
Kent, Jemima, *Duchess of Kent* 172
Kerne Bridge 43
Kerslake, Thomas 6
Keynsham Abbey 123
Kidderminster 131, 134
Kimball, Elisabeth Guernsey 14, 20
King, W. L. 20
King's Stanley 30, 92, 93
Kingsweston *see under* Bristol
Kingswood 161, 168
Kirkham, Humphrey 162
Knill, *Sir* John Stuart 44
Knowles, William Henry 25, 26, 27, 29, 33, 36, 37, 45

labour-intensive occupations 156, 158, 159, 160, 161, 168
lace 168
lake villages 50
Lancaster, Massachusetts 202

Landboc, sive Registrum Monasterii de Winchelcumba 18–19, 159 n. 2
Lang, Robert 5, 40
Langben Rises Høj 52
Lares 66
laterally chambered barrows *see* barrows
Latimer, John 6, 15, 48, 217, 236, 238, 246, 247, 249, 251
lead shot 253
leather 107, 253, 278
Lechlade 1, 96, 127
Lechmere, Nicholas 204
Lechmere, Richard 203–4, 210, 215–216
Leckhampton Hill 25–6
Ledbury 43
Leeds 240 n. 2, 253
Leigh Woods Trust 32
Leighton, Wilfrid 11–12, 13, 21, 35–36, 48
Leland, John 122, 136
Lemington 95
Levant 150
Levis, *Mr. & Mrs.* 176
Lhwyd, Edward 52
Liberty Tree 205
libraries 179
Lichfield 46
Lichfield, *Abbot of Evesham* 131
Ligon, John 153, 167
Ligon, Richard 153, 167
Ligon, Thomas 167
Ligon, *Sir* William 153
Limerick 104
linen 160, 161
Liverpool 221, 238, 244, 254, 260, 266–7, 283
Lives of the Berkeleys 18
Llandaff, Bishop of 109 n. 6, 115 n. 2
Llanthony Priory 32, 112
Lloyd-Baker, A. B. 9, 11, 13, 22
Local Government in Gloucestershire 1775–1800 (Moir) 21
locomotive building 240 n. 2
locus in placenames 121, 122
London 43–4, 128, 139, 164, 184, 189, 218, 223, 253, 260
    Guildhall 44
    Middle Temple 43–4
    Tower 44
Long Ashton 177
long barrows *see* barrows

long houses 59
long stone cists 56
Loreng, Robert 167
Loreng, Thomas 153, 158
Los Millares 56
Lower Slaughter 89–92
Loyalist refugees in Bristol **200–16**
Lubbock, *Sir* John 50, 53
Lydney 37, 82–5
Lypiatt Park 4, 93
Lysons, Samuel 23, 29, 40

McGrath, Patrick 13, 21
Mackintosh, Ebenezer 205
Maclean, *Sir* John 3, 6, 7–8, 9, 14, 15, 18, 22, 37
Madresfield Court 45, 153
Magnus, Olaus 53
Maiden Castle 66
Malmesbury 22, 45
malt 181, 276
Malta 58, 60
Malvern 44–5
Manchester 247, 254, 266–7
Manching 72
Manners, John, *Marquis of Granby* 173
The Margaret, ship 163
Marlborough, Massachusetts 201–2
Marlborough, Sarah Churchill, *Duchess* 172
Mars 67, 87–8, 91, 92, 93–4, 96, 97
Marsham, Robert, *1st Baron Romney* 172
Marychurch 218
Mason, Elizabeth 182
Mason, William 181–2
masons 140–6
Massachusetts 200–15
Matilda, *Queen of William the Conqueror* 102
Matilda, *wife of Geoffrey Count of Anjou* 103
Matres 68, 69, 86, 88, 89, 91, 97
Matson 194
Matthews's Bristol Directory 180, 267
Maudslays', engineers 243
Maze, Peter 237, 243
medical provision and its long-term effect on economic well-being 255–256
The megalith builders of Western Europe (Daniel) 57
'megalithic people' theory 54–5, 59–60

megaliths **50–61**
Menai Suspension Bridge 225
mercers 150
Merchant Adventurers 150
Merchant, *Mrs.* 210
Mercia 102
Mercury 64, 74, 90, 98, 99
Merton 116, 118
Mesopotamia 58
The Messiah (Handel) 196
Michael and Watkins, carpet factory, Worcester 195
Midland Railway Company 43, 238–239, 241
Miles, Edward Wheeler 235
Miller, William 186, 187, 198–9
Minchinhampton 28, 196
Minerva 65, 83, 90, 91
Mithras 76
Ministry of Housing and Local Government *see under* Department of the Environment
Ministry of Works *see under* Department of the Environment
Minster Lovell 142
Le mirage orientale (Reinach) 58
Mitford, John Thomas Freeman, *1st Earl of Redesdale* 3
Moir, Esther 21
Mona antiqua restaurata (Rowlands) 51
Monasticon Anglicanum (Dugdale) 15
Monmouth and Caerleon Antiquaries Association 37
monopolies 147–69
Montacute, John de, *3rd Earl of Salisbury* 135
Montelius, Oscar 54, 55, 56, 58
Montfaucon, Bernard de 53
Moreau, Simeon 188, 189, 191, 197–8
Moreton, Francis Reynolds, *3rd Baron Ducie of Tortworth* 196
Moreton, Henry John, *3rd Earl of Ducie* 3
Morning Post 192
Mortimer, Hugh de 114
Morwent, *Abbot of Gloucester* 137, 139
motorways and rescue archaeology 31
Moulton, Stephen 250
Municipal Corporations Act 222
municipal trading 265–6
Mycenae 56, 58
Mylne, William Chadwell 245
Mythe Hill 193

Naples 251
Nash, Richard ('Beau') 182, 188
National Coal Board 35
National Trust 23, 25, 32, 36
Naunton 130
neolithic period 21, 53
Netherlands 155, 156
Neville family 137, 143
New Brunswick 206
New Grange 52, 56, 58
New Passage 223, 240
New York 242, 243, 283
Newington Bagpath 97, 98, 140
Newland, John, *Abbot of St. Augustine's Abbey, Bristol* 109, 113, 115, 116
Newport, Rhode Island 204
Nicholas, *Bishop of Llandaff* 109 n. 6, 115 n. 2
Nodens 82–5
Norman, Joseph 175–6
Norman Bros., printers, Cheltenham 17
Norman Conquest **101–8**
North Leigh 139, 142, 145
North Nibley 163, 164
Northampton 46
Northampton, Spencer Joshua Alwyne Compton, *2nd Marquis* 226
Northleach 127, 128, 131, 132, 133–4, 135, 137, 138, 139, 140, 141, 142, 143, 144, 189
Norwich 171
Nostell Priory 112, 121, 123
Notes or Abstracts of the Wills contained in the Great Orphan Book (Wadley) 19
Notgrove 27, 28, 59
Nympsfield 21, 27, 28–9, 59

Office of Works *see under* Department of the Environment
oil 155, 157, 160, 266, 276
Olaus Magnus 53
Oliver, Peter 207
Oliver, Thomas 202–3, 204, 207, 210, 215
Oman, *Sir* Charles 48
O'Neil, *Mrs.* Helen (Miss Helen Donovan) 27, 29, 30, 31, 37
Der Orient und Europa (Montelius) 54, 55
Orkneys 57
Osborne, — 220, 231, 232
Osborne, printers, Gloucester 15–16

Oseney Abbey 129, 136–7
Ostia 79
Oswald, *Saint* 123
Over Guiting 158, 162
Overbury, Thomas 27, 34, 45, 46
Overton Hill 52
Oxford 47, 138, 143, 184, 189
  All Souls College 139, 142
  Ashmolean Museum 65, 96, 97
  Cathedral 142–3
  Divinity School 139, 145, 146
  Magdalen College 139, 142, 143
  Merton College 144
  New College 139, 142, 144, 145

Page family 164
Page, Paul 47
Painswick 23, 158, 196
paper 224, 254, 273, 275, 277
Paris, Abbey of St. Victor 105, 111, 114, 118, 119, 120, 123
Parry, Thomas Gambier 8
passage graves 56, 57, 58–9
Patchway 240
Patterson, William 220, 243
Paul, *Sir* George Onesiphorus 193, 196
Paul, Obadiah 196
pavements *see* Roman pavements
Peake, Harold John Edward 57
Peers, *Sir* Charles 27
Peet, Thomas Eric 54
Peirse, Thomas 165 n. 4
Pennington, William 179
Pennsylvania 206
Penobscot, Massachusetts 202
Perry, William James 57
Pershore 149
Phipson, William 197–8
Phoenix Glass Works 261–3
the picturesque 176–8, 183
Piggott, Stuart 59
Pilgrim Trust 27, 36
pin making 168, 194
Pinney family 265
Pinney, Charles 222
Pitt-Rivers, Augustus Henry Lane Fox 1, 8, 43
Plymouth 205, 219, 238
Plympton 116
Poole 205
pope 107–8, 110, 121, 128, 138
population statistics as indexes of economic change 255–9, 272, 282

porcelain making   195
Portbury Pier and Railway Company
   223, 246
porter brewing   253, 262
Portishead   176, 245, 246, 272
Portsea   218
Portsmouth   218
Portugal   56, 57, 58
Postlip   151, 152, 162, 164, 166
potash   157, 165
Pratt, John   135–6
The Prehistoric foundations of Europe
   (Hawkes)   57
Prehistoric times (Lubbock)   50, 53
Prelatte   133, 135
Prestbury   29, 31, 154, 192, 193
Price, F. D.   21
Princeton   210
printing   254, 267, 273, 274, 277
Pritchard, John E.   10–11, 17, 24, 32,
   38, 48
Psyche   79
Pugsley, Alfred John   255

quarries   138, 139

radiocarbon dating   50, 56, 58
Rahtz, Philip   26
railways   217, 218, 220, 223, 224,
   236–240, 243, 245, 246, 250–1, 262,
   277
Ralph, Elizabeth   vii-viii, xiv-xv, 13,
   49
Ramsay, William de (III)   130
rape oil   157, 160–1, 163 n. 1
Reading Abbey   138
Red Book of St. Augustine's, Bristol
   109, 110, 111, 113, 115–16, 120, 122,
   124
Redesdale, John Thomas Freeman
   Mitford, *1st Earl*   3
Reinach, Saloman   58
Rendcomb   134, 138
Rendel, James Meadows   245–6
Renfrew, Colin   55, 58
Rennie, —   230, 231, 232–5
Rennie, *Sir* John   234 n. 1
Repton   46
rescue archaeology   31
Reynel, Carew   168
Reynolds, John   5, 41
Rhodes, Fairfax   26
Richard II, *King*   135
Richard, of Warwick, *Abbot of St.*

Augustine's Bristol   113, 114, 116,
   118, 120, 123
Richardson, C.   240–1
Richmond, *Sir* Ian   25, 47
Ricketts, Henry   262, 263, 265
Ricketts, Jacob Wilcox   262–3, 264,
   265
Ricketts, Richard   264, 265
river-gods   66
roads   82, 107, 156, 171, 177–8, 180,
   186, 189–90, 253
Robert, of Cherbourg, *Abbot of Wigmore*
   114, 115
Robert, *Earl of Gloucester*   102, 105
Robert, *Bishop of Hereford*   113
Robert [sic], *Bishop of Worcester   see
   under* Roger, *Bishop of Worcester*
Robert fitz Hamon   102
Robie, Thomas   212, 213
Robin's Wood Hill   194
Robinson, E. S. & A. Ltd.   224, 273, 275
Roch, Nicholas   220–1, 222, 229, 237,
   251
Rock   134
Rodborough   28, 30–1, 196
Rodmarton   21, 27, 29
Roger, *Abbot of Wigmore*   114
Roger, *Bishop of Worcester*   109 n. 6,
   115 n. 2
Rolleston, George   5, 15
*Rolls of Gloucestershire Sessions of the Peace
   1361–1398* (Kimball)   14, 20
*Roman Antiquities of Lydney Park, Glouces-
   tershire*   37
Roman Britain   17, 21, 30, 36–7, **62–
   100**
Roman pavements   22, 23, 24, 28, 42,
   62, 78, 81
Roman villas   13, 21, 22, 23, 24, 25,
   27, 30, 36, 78–82
Romney, Robert Marsham, *1st Baron*
   172
Romulus   94
roods   48, 136
Roper, Ida   12
Roskilde   52
Rosmerta   64, 74
Ross, Anne   94
Rough stone monuments and their builders
   (Peet)   54
round barrows   *see* barrows
Rouse, Clive   35
Rowlands, Henry   51

Rownham Ferry 227–8
Royal Archaeological Institute 37, 45
Royal Historical and Archaeological Association of Ireland 37
Royal Society 1, 2
Royce, David 15, 19, 38, 159 n. 2
rubber 250
Rudder, — 16, 133
Rude stone monuments in all countries (Fergusson) 54
Rudge, Thomas 16
Rudhall's bell foundry 194
Rushforth, Gordon McNeil 45–6
Russell, — 209
Russell, Charles 237, 239
Ruthall, Thomas, *Bishop of Durham* 136

S.S. *Great Britain* 223, 224, 242, 243, 244, 251, 283
S.S. *Great Western* 223, 242, 243, 244, 283
S.S. *Sirius* 243
Sabin, Arthur 109
St. Asaph, Bishop of 109 n. 6, 115 n. 2
St. Briavels 42
St. Helens 262
St. Oswald's Priory 32, 35
Salem 214
Salisbury 46, 168
Salisbury, John de Montacute, *3rd Earl* 135
salt 154, 155–6, 161
Salters' Company 154, 155
Sandys, *Sir* Edwin 164
Sandywell Park 189
sanitary-ware makers 275, 278
sassafras 166
Saunders, Charles Alexander 237, 239
Saxon Charters of Gloucestershire (Grundy) 20
Saye and Sele, John Twistleton, *6th Baron* 185
Scandinavia 50, 52, 53, 55, 56, 57
schools 181
Scotland 59
Sea Mills *see under* Bristol
Sedbury Park 43
Selwyn, George Augustus 194
Sely, Richard 137
Severn Wye and Severn Bridge Railway Company 43
Severn Bridge 250

Sewall, Jonathan *see under* Sewell, Jonathan
Sewall, Samuel 206
Sewell, Jonathan 206, 207, 209–10, 211–13, 215
Shannon, Herbert Austin 254
Sharp, Margaret 21
She Would and She Would Not 194
Sheffield 258
Sherborne, Edward Lenox Dutton, *4th Baron* 8, 18–19
Sherborne, James Henry Legge Dutton, *3rd Baron* 3
Sheridan, Richard Brinsley 174, 178
Sherwood, Jennifer 138
Shipley, Arthur 32
shipping 253, 263, 277, 279
Shirley, *Mrs.* 175–6
Shobdon 114, 120
shoe manufacture 254, 267, 273, 274, 278, 280
Sicily 107
Siddons, Sarah 194
silk 164, 165
Silvanus 93
Simpson, *Mrs.* 210
Simpson, James 248, 249
Simpson, Jonathan 204
Sirius, steamship 243
Sketchley's Bristol Directory 174
Skillicorne, Henry 182, 185, 186
Skillicorne, William 186, 187
Slack, Paul 168
Slaughter Hundred 158
slavery 102, 182
Smalley, Beryl 114
Smith, *Sir* G. Elliot 56–7
Smith, John 163, 164, 166
Smollett, Tobias 178
Smyth, John 18
soap 155, 157, 160, 165, 224, 253, 254, 276
Society of Antiquaries 8, 17, 25, 26, 29, 32, 37
Society for the Preservation of Ancient Buildings 1
Somerscales, Henry 165
Somerscales, Robert 165
Somerset, *Lord* Charles Noel 183
Somerset, Henry Charles FitzRoy, *8th Duke of Beaufort* 31
Somerset, Henry Hugh Arthur FitzRoy, *10th Duke of Beaufort* 31

Somerset Archaeological and Natural History Society 3, 9
Song of Dermot 104
South Devon Railway 224, 239, 247
South Leigh 141, 143
South Wales Railway 220–1, 244
Southampton 128, 244
Southern, Richard William 107
Southey, Robert 180
Spain, 56, 57, 58, 155
Spanish and Portugese Company 150
spas **170–99**
specle soap 157
Spoonley 130
Spoonley Wood villa 27, 36, 79–80, 99
Stamp Act 205
Stanhope, Philip Dormer, *4th Earl of Chesterfield* 185
Stanton Harcourt 143
Stanway 154, 163
the staple 128
Stapleton 184
Staverton 150
steam navigation 223
Stephen, *King* 103, 104, 110, 112
Stephenson, George 236
stockings, 156, 168
Stoke Gifford 163, 164, 183
Stoke Orchard 35
Stokeleigh 32
Stonehenge 51, 53, 60
Stopford, James, *2nd Earl Courtown* 190, 192, 198
Stow-on-the-Wold 96
stow in place names 121, 122, 125–6
Stratford family 151, 154, 156, 166
Stratford, Anthony 154
Stratford, George 151, 154
Stratford, John, *of Farmcote* 154
Stratford, John, *member of Edward II's Parliament 1319–20* 154
Stratford, John, *tobacco grower* 154–60, 164, 165, 167
Stratford, Robert 154
Street 274
Strickland, Edward 6
Stroud 34, 42, 93, 158, 196, 209 n. 1
Stroudwater Canal 196
Stukeley, William 40, 51
Sudeley Castle 22, 134, 143, 164, 193
Suffolk, Henrietta Howard, *Countess* 185

sugar 224, 253, 261, 263, 273, 278, 279
The Sultan 194
Sweden 56
Switzerland 50
Symmondsall 97
Symonds Yat 43
Syria 67

tallow 157, 194
Tame, John 133, 135
Tamworth 46
tanning 107, 253, 278
tar 224, 250
Taylor, Charles S. 6, 7, 15, 16, 19
Taylor, Isaac 20
Taylor, John 2, 5, 15, 18
Taynton 138, 139, 143, 144
Telford, Thomas 225
Templars 104
Tetbury 45
Tewkesbury 40, 44, 46, 102, 105, 129, **147–69**, 192, 193, 198
Thames and Severn Canal 193
Thames Tunnel 219
theatre 2, 178–9, 194–5
thermoluminescent dating 58
'third generation thesis' 264
Thomas, — 208
Thomas, Christopher 224
Thompson, Hamilton 121
Thomsen, Christian Jurgensen 50, 55
Thorpe, George 163
three-age system of dividing prehistory 50, 51, 55
Three Choirs Festival 192, 195
Throckmorton, Anne 163 n. 1
Throckmorton, Mary 154
Throckmorton, Thomas 163
Throckmorton, *Sir* William 161, 163
Tintern 42
tobacco 148, 152, 153–5, 158–60, 161, 162, 163, 165, 166, 168, 181, 224, 253, 254, 260, 262, 265, 267, 273–4, 278, 280
Tockington Park 22
Toddington 153
Tormarton 31
Toronto, Royal Ontario Museum 95
Town Planning Act 1919 33, 35
Town and Country Planning Act 1932 33

Town and Country Planning Act 1947 34
Tracy family 153–4, 163–4
Tracy, *Sir* John 153–4, 163
Tracy, Mary 166
Tracy, *Sir* Paul 154
Tracy, Thomas 166
Tracy, *Sir* Thomas 163
Tracy, William 163–6
Triton 83, 84
Trustees of the Croome Estates 26
Turkdean 142
Turner, *Sir* Christopher 44
'Tweedledum' 187
Twistleton, John, *6th Baron Saye and Sele* 185

Uckington 150
urbanisation 255, 256, 270
Usk 129

Valentinian 52
Vanlore, Peter 152
Van Schaack, Peter 209 n. 1
Vassall, *Mrs.* 204, 210
Vassall, Anna 204
Vassall, John 204, 207, 210
Vaughan family 265
Venus 82

Verey, David 13, 33, 34
Vick, William 225, 226
Victorines 105, 111, 114, 119, 120
Virginia 159, 162–7, 184
Virginia Company 150, 163, 164, 165

Wade, William 188
Wadfield 22, 27, 36
Wadley, Thomas Proctor 19
Wagner, *Sir* Anthony 21
Wakeman, — 193
Waldo, Joseph 208
Wales 52, 101, 205
'walks' 172, 183, 184, 191
wall paintings 35, 44
Wallbridge 196
Walsingham, Francis 153
Walter, of Harford 130
Wanswell Court 163
Ward, — 227
Ward, Samuel 171
warrior-gods 67, 91, 92
Wars of the Roses 141
water-nymphs 67

Waterford 104
Way, Lewis Upton 48
Wayland's Smithy 59
Weaver and Jefferis, pin manufactory 194
Webb, Benedict 157, 160–1, 163 n. 1, 164, 168
Webb, Geoffrey 131
Wellesley, Arthur, *1st Duke of Wellington* 199
Welley, William 133
Wellington, Arthur Wellesley, *1st Duke* 199
Wellow Abbey 124 n. 2
Welsh, J. F. 249–50
Were, Francis 17
Wesley, John 186
Wessex 102
West Indies 167, 182, 202, 203, 204, 253, 260, 261–2
Westbury College 32
Westminster, St. Stephen's Chapel 127
Westminster Abbey 163 n. 1
Westmorland, John Fane, *7th Earl* 185
Weymouth 192, 197, 198, 240
Weymouth, *Lady* May 190
Wheeler, *Sir* Mortimer 27
Whitefield, George 186
Whitmore, *Sir* George 150
Whitmore, Thomas 150
Whitmore, William 150
Whitmore, William (II) 150–1
Whittington 13, 30, 189
Wigmore Abbey 109, 109 n. 6, 113–115, 116, 118, 119, 120, 123
Wilcote Chapel, North Leigh 142, 145
Wilcox Chapel, Bibury 129
Willard, — 208
William the Conqueror, *King* 101–2
William, Earl of Gloucester 112, 118 n. 3, 120, 123
William, of Malmesbury 102
William, de Ramsay (III) 130
William, *Abbot of Winchcombe* 134
William, Worcestre 117, 171
William, of Wykeham 142, 145
William Frederick, *2nd Duke of Gloucester* 198
Wills, W. D. & H. O. 224, 266, 273–4, 275
Wilson, Titus, printers, Kendal 16, 17

Wilts, Somerset & Weymouth Railway 238

Wiltshire Natural History and Archaeological Society 3, 43

Winchcombe 18–19, 127, 129, 130, 131, 134–5, 141, 142, 143, 144, 148, 149, 150, 151, 153, 154, 156, 157, 159, 160, 161–2, 167, 168, 193

Winchombe, Henrie 144

Winchcombe (Wynchecombe), John 144

Winchcombe, Richard 139, 140, 144, 145–6

Winchester 146

Windrush 139, 144

Windsor 139, 190, 191, 196–7
  Castle 130
  St. George's Chapel 130, 136, 142, 143

wine 107, 155, 165

Winslow, Edward 210

Witcombe 22, 23, 80

Withington 47, 137

woad 155, 158, 161, 162, 165, 167

women workers 274, 275, 279

Wood, John 189

Wood-Martin, William Gregory 60

Woodchester 22, 30, 42, 78–9, 99, 196

Woodstock 138

wool 127, 128, 136, 138, 181, 253

Worcester 149, 192, 195–6

Worcester, Bishops of 102, 109 n. 6, 115, 116–17, 118, 119, 120, 137, 150, 195

Worsaae, Jens Jacob Asmussen 55

Wotton-under-Edge 34, 164, 165

Wulfstan, *Bishop of Worcester* 102

Wycomb 85

Wynchecombe *see* Winchcombe

Yate, Robert 172

Yearsley, Ann 179

Yold 23

York, Yorkshire Museum 70

York, Frederick Augustus, *Duke* 194, 198